Confessions of a
Second Story Man

PHILADELPHIA P

(officia

ISSUED TO

RANK

DATE

Louis J. Kripplebauer
PP# 304713
807 N. 24th St.
4269 Penn St.
4914 Bingham St.

Armed Robbery
Burglary

AUTO
1957 Chev. Sdn.
TT Grenn & White
Pa. Lic. 39609K or
1960 Cadillac
Copper & Black Vinyl
Pa. Lic. 39609K

ASSOCIATES
John Fleckenstein
George Paxos
Douglas Ehly
George Duval
Mitchell Prinski
Earl Price
Anthony DiBattista
John Hurst

FREQUENTS
Smiley's
500 East Club
J.R. Club

BARRICADE
BOOKS
Fort Lee, New Jersey

DEPARTMENT

Only)

BADGE 3672

UNIT 26th

NO.

Confessions of a
Second Story Man

Junior Kripplebauer and the K&A Gang

ALLEN M. HORNBLUM

Published by Barricade Books Inc.
185 Bridge Plaza North
Suite 308-A
Fort Lee, NJ 07024

www.barricadebooks.com

Text design by Kate Nichols

Library of Congress Cataloging-in-Publication Data
Hornblum, Allen M.
    Confessions of a second story man : Junior Kripplebauer and the K & A Gang /
Allen M. Hornblum.
        p. cm.
    Includes index.
    Originally published: Philadelphia : Temple University Press, 2005.
    ISBN 1-56980-313-7 (pbk.)
    1. Kripplebauer, Junior, 1936- 2. Criminals--Pennsylvania--Philadelphia--Biography.
3. Organized crime--Pennsylvania--Philadelphia. 4. Kensington (Philadelphia, Pa.)--Social
conditions. I. Title.

HV6248.K68H67 2006
364.16'2--dc22
[B]   2006040676

Manufactured in the United States of America

10 9 8 7 6 5 4

To my father,

Louis Hornblum,

who earned a living

the old-fashioned way,

through long hours with little to show for it.

ALLEN M. HORNBLUM is an Assistant Professor in the Department of Geography and Urban Studies at Temple University. He is a former Chief of Staff of the Philadelphia Sheriff's Office, and a member of the Pennsylvania Crime Commission. He is also the author of *Acres of Skin: Human Experiments at Holmesburg Prison.*

Contents

Prologue

We were doin' some work up in New England. You know, Boston and up, fancy houses in top-shelf neighborhoods like Kennebunk and Bar Harbor, and we're gettin' our share of jewelry, coins, furs, and things. Well, we're up in Maine somewhere, and we're doin' a big house in the woods. It's dark as a cow's ass and freezing cold, but one of the guys in the crew starts walking around the backyard. Only it's not a normal backyard; it's as big as a golf course. I tell him to get back in the house before somebody sees him and we all get arrested, but he yells back, "Hold your water. I just wanna check somethin' out."

He's gone a little while, and I go out to haul the dumb mutt inside. I see him walking around in the snow like Sasquatch or something. He's examining these little wooden sheds. He sees me and yells out, "Hey, I wanna take one of these kitties back home with me. I think they're raising mountain lions out here."

I figure the guy's finally lost it, his brain has froze. But damn if he ain't tellin' the truth. The people who owned the place musta had some kind of business raisin' cats. I mean good-sized, hairy cats. And those babies had some serious teeth. You know, like little cougars and panthers.

Well, I tell him to forget about it. We ain't working for the Barnum & Bailey Circus. The house has been picked clean. We're leaving. But he gives me an argument. After a few minutes of arguing, I just wanna shut him up, so I tell him if he can get one in a suitcase he can take it. Don't you know, that dumb jerk does just that—stuffs one of these cats in a suitcase and insists we take the damn animal with us. So here we are driving down the highway, the car's filled with enough swag that we could all get 10 years in prison, and we got a big, pissed-off cat screaming its lungs out.

After an hour of listening to clawin' and screechin' sounds, we convince Frank Buck that the kitty has gotta go. That crying and scratching was driving us all crazy. So we pull into a rest stop along the road and decide to drop the suitcase right in the middle of the parking lot. Just for kicks, though, we stick around and wait to see who's gonna be stupid enough to walk off with this suitcase holding one angry pussy. Wouldn't you know, a car filled with a bunch of niggers enters the lot, sees the suitcase sittin' there, and they naturally think they got an easy score. They start doin' a slow driveby. Just checking things out. Once, twice, and finally, on the third pass, they stop and quickly scoop up the package. But they don't put it in the trunk; they throw it in the back seat and drive off like a bat outta hell.

Well, we follow 'em down the highway and wait for the show to start. We know as soon as they crack the suitcase open all hell is gonna break loose. Sure enough, they soon begin swervin' all over the road. It gets worse. The car is hittin' the median barrier and bouncin' off across the two southbound lanes and onto the shoulder of the road. Well, we're goin' nuts. I thought I was gonna split a gut and wet my shorts. We then see doors opening, people are screaming, fur is flying, and the car goes right off the highway into a ravine and flips over on its side. We pull over laughing our asses off and see one pissed cat dart outta the car and scoot off into the woods. The niggers are laying on the snow all banged up, cursing each other out, and asking us for help. We can't stop laughing, it's almost painful, but I tell 'em we gotta go, but when we get to the next town we'll send back a tow truck.

I think we laughed all the way back to Philly. But I told the guys, "From now on let's stick with mink, fox, and sable when we're doin' a piece of work on the road. We'll grab the real pussy when we get back to some friendly joints in our own neighborhood."

—GEORGE "JUNIOR" SMITH

Part I

The Birth of a
Second Story Man

PHILADELPHIA POLICE DEPARTMENT
(Official Use Only)

BADGE 3672

UNIT 26th

ISSUED TO S. HUSIK

NO.

RANK Ptlmn

DATE 2/8/69

1. North Carolina: The Dixie MAC Machine

THEY WEREN'T OFF THE HIGHWAY more than a few minutes before Junior Kripplebauer stopped at a convenience store newsstand and purchased a couple of mundane but indispensable tools of the trade—a newspaper and a map of the city. Junior was never one to let the grass grow under his feet; the sturdy, well-groomed, six-foot-three Philadelphian was known for being all business all the time. As he and his three associates quickly continued on their way and sought out a local motel along Route 1, Kripplebauer was already examining the *Raleigh News and Observer*'s Real Estate section. His eyes carefully swooped across each page, jettisoning irrelevant articles on "Good Buys" and columns by self-proclaimed property mavens, until he discovered what he was looking for—homes selling for a half-million dollars and above. He then turned to the Religion and Sports sections to check out synagogues and country clubs in the Raleigh area. By the time the four of them checked into rooms 212 and 214 of the Best Western Motel on the outskirts of the city, Kripplebauer already had a pretty good idea where they'd be spending their first evening in town: the nearby suburb of Cary, an exclusive Raleigh bedroom community that was said to have the highest per capita income in the state.

All four were experienced professionals; each member of Kripplebauer's crew knew his job and did it. While Junior and Bruce Agnew studied the map of metropolitan Raleigh, committed streets and highways to memory, and double-checked the local telephone directory for the location of Cary's Jewish community centers and elite golf courses, Marilynne D'Ulisse and Tommy Seher took care of their assigned tasks. Marilynne, who was usually called Mickie, got directions for the closest Sears Roebuck department store. The sales clerk at Sears couldn't help but notice the cute blonde in his checkout line. It wasn't every day that a tall, shapely, blue-eyed babe in her twenties came into the hardware department to buy channel locks, pliers, crowbars, gloves, flashlights, chisels, and a sledgehammer. He would normally have offered to help the striking young woman carry the hefty assortment of tools to her car, but her cool, austere manner told him she could handle the chore by herself. After Mickie returned to the motel and Seher outfitted Junior's Lincoln Town Car with the scanners and walkie-talkies they had brought with them from Philadelphia, the four out-of-towners decided to take a ride. Although they had been to North Carolina many times before, it was their first time in Cary, and they were anxious to see the town whose affluence and natural beauty they had heard so much about.

After a short time on a four-lane highway, they left Raleigh's city limits behind and found themselves traveling on scenic country roads that meandered through some of Wake County's most prosperous neighborhoods. Upscale, well-maintained homes and impressive estates surrounded by magnificent lawns were the order of the day. The opulence of the area reminded them of the pricey, beautifully manicured properties of Philadelphia's lush Main Line. North Carolina always looked good to them. Each trip south had proven rewarding. Their expectations rose as they drove Cary's pleasant country lanes.

Kripplebauer and company agreed that they had made the right decision. It was mid-December 1975 and a good portion of the nation was in the grip of a deep freeze, but none of them wanted to stop working. New England and the Midwest were out of the question; every state from Minnesota to New Jersey was socked in under several inches of snow and ice. It was just too damn cold to work, and the snow made tracking someone a child's game. No, they needed to head south. Newspaper reports disclosed the only place within a 10-hour drive of Philly that had escaped the Arctic blast mauling much of the nation: the tidewater and piedmont areas of North Carolina. As they slowly traveled from one comfortable tree-lined street to another in the wealthy Cary subdivision called MacGregor Downs and eyeballed the regal homes of the city's professional and corporate elite—particularly those displaying mezuzahs on their front doors—they recognized the carefully landscaped Raleigh suburb as their kind of town: fat and swollen with cash.

After a short respite back at their motel, it was time for the group to go to work. With darkness falling, the men donned white shirts, conservative striped ties, and expensive Botony 500 suit jackets. Mickie was appropriately attired in a stylish white blouse and chic navy jacket and skirt. As always, she placed a black wig over her Linda Evans–blond locks and bangs. After a light meal and a few beers at a local restaurant, they were back on US 1 and headed for Cary. By eight o'clock they were in the target area and methodically driving through the plush neighborhood looking for likely marks. A large, handsome, unoccupied home was their goal, and it wouldn't take long to find one. Unwitting homeowners could always be counted on for assistance.

"The red lights of the home alarm systems were like a light beacon," says Kripplebauer. "Something like a lighthouse for distressed sailors at sea. It told us all we needed to know: there was nobody at home, and there were things of value in the house."

The group drove around for a while, checking out homes and alarm systems from a distance, and then focused their attention on a beautiful three-story house that must have been worth a good three to four hundred thousand dollars. Junior hopped out of the car, walked up the drive to the front door, and rang the doorbell. There was no response. After waiting an appropriate amount of time, he began to knock on the door, authoritatively enough for anybody at home to hear him, but not so vigorously as to disturb any of the neighbors. There was no response. He knocked again. An air of expectation built in the car as Tommy, Bruce, and Mickie watched Junior circle to the rear of the house to check further for signs of inhabitants. When they next saw him at the front door, he was trying to insert a series of keys into the alarm system. In less than a minute the crimson light went dark. The state-of-the-art alarm system had been disarmed, and the imposing structure with the small Hebrew scroll on the doorframe was theirs for the taking.

Tommy was carrying an enormous screwdriver called a "brute." He and Bruce quickly joined Junior, and all three went to the rear of the house. Mickie got behind the big Lincoln's wheel, turned on the walkie-talkie and police scanner, and slowly circled through the neighborhood. After taking the back door, the three men went to work. Tommy Seher, in his mid-thirties and a smaller version of Terry Bradshaw, stationed himself in the expansive living room between the front door and the window. It was his job to watch for anything unusual, especially the owner's unexpected return or the appearance of suspicious police officers.

Junior and Bruce, the designated searchers, raced through the house, initially to make sure no one was home and secondarily to find additional "outs" in case of an emergency. Only then could they concentrate on their real reason for being there: stealing all the swag they could get their hands on.

Bold and opportunistic, the 40-year-old Kripplebauer was a master criminal who had successfully burgled hundreds of homes and businesses from coast to coast. Raised in Pennsylvania's gritty and unforgiving anthracite coal region, he had moved to Philadelphia in his early twenties and soon after became a practitioner of "production work." For the next 30 years, scores of upscale communities stretching from Bar Harbor to Boca Raton would be left stunned and bewildered in his wake. North Carolina was a favorite stop; Junior compared the state to a huge "MAC machine" where "easy money" was always to be had. "I always stopped there on the way to Miami," he says of his periodic visits. "The state was like a drive-through bank. But at this bank you just made withdrawals."

For a half-dozen years or more, the state of North Carolina had witnessed a plague of burglaries at many of its most celebrated residences. Kripplebauer and a number of other friends from back home had pillaged the Tar Heel State as if it were their personal safe-deposit box. Dozens of Winston-Salem's, Greensboro's, and Raleigh's most fashionable private residences had been hit over the years, including the homes of a former governor and such corporate powerhouses as Zachary T. Reynolds (R. J. Reynolds Tobacco) and Fred Proctor (Proctor & Gamble). Now the inviting but unfamiliar environs of another Carolina suburb presented nothing to be concerned about. It was just another ripe piece of fruit to be picked.

The home was big—Junior figured about 15 rooms. He told Bruce he was going to find the master bedroom; Bruce could take the rest. Junior proceeded quickly but cautiously; the lavish home was modern, well constructed, and supplied with all the latest conveniences. Fearing he'd step on rugs wired for pressure-sensitive silent alarms, Junior moved around by climbing on the furniture whenever he could. He looked like a large cat on the prowl, stalking its prey and ready to strike. There wasn't a hint of nervousness or the slightest sign of apprehension; Kripplebauer was in his element.

"Once I got in a house," says Kripplebauer, "I acted as if the place was mine. All I thought about was whether the place was loaded or not. Am I gonna make a big cash score was my only concern. It was always about the money. I often felt so comfortable I would tell Bruce, 'I like this place so much I'm gonna have you change the locks and I'll move in.' "

It didn't take Junior long to discover a small safe in the closet. It was a flimsy "junk box" that could be opened easily, but he'd still need a few tools. He called down to Tommy that he had found a safe and told him to have Mickie bring the tools over. After getting Tommy's call on the walkie-talkie, Mickie drove back to the house.

Calm and composed behind the wheel, Mickie—who was Junior's wife as well as his trusted partner in all such business endeavors—was the picture of serenity. She had to be; she couldn't afford to draw attention to herself or her confederates. Though in her early thirties and the prototype for the wholesome, All-American girl-next-door, Mickie D'Ulisse was an experienced thief whose exploits and nerve rivaled that of most men in the game.

"Hell, she pulled more jobs than me, Bruce, and Tommy combined," Kripplebauer liked to brag to new partners dubious about his wife's involvement in second story work. In fact, it wasn't unusual for Junior to be having a beer and watching a ballgame on TV at his Cherry Hill, New Jersey, home and spot Mickie out of the corner of his eye putting on jeans, her wig, and a black nylon jacket, and grabbing a brute from the closet. "Hey, Mick, where you going?" he'd ask. "Oh, I'm just going for a little ride," Mickie always replied. "Well, watch yourself," Junior would advise. "I saw some state police in the area earlier this evening."

Invariably, Mickie would come home with some interesting swag—a full-length mink, a collection of fine silverware, or just a big roll of cash. For Mickie, checking out the neighborhood, perusing dignified Princeton and Moorestown homes for red alarm lights, and pulling a job or two was always more interesting than sitting at home and watching football or re-runs on the tube. In fact, she and her girlfriend Maxine cleaned out dozens of houses over the years when they were short of cash or just looking for something to do. Junior, who was no slouch himself in this department, had a hard time keeping up with her. He'd just wish her well and say, "Bring a stack of fifties back."

As soon as she pulled up to the house in Cary, Tommy went out to meet her and brought the tools inside. As he handed them to Junior, Tommy told him Mickie had already picked out several other inviting targets in the neighborhood. Junior wasn't surprised; Mickie was a workaholic. Besides, Junior had not only taught her the nuances of production work; he'd shown her how to hit a "home run" by looking for consecutive homes displaying red alarm lights. In other words, why do one house when you could knock off several in a row?

Mickie continued to circle through the neighborhood while listening to the scanner for any nearby police activity and keeping an eye out for her favorite nocturnal light show—tiny red alarm lights in the darkness. In a matter of seconds, Junior had punch-dialed the safe and opened the door. Sitting before him was a collection of cash, bank certificates, several watches, and a good bit of gold and silver jewelry. He grabbed a couple of pillowcases and began dumping the contents of the safe inside.

While Junior was cleaning out the safe, Bruce Agnew—a handsome six-footer with a prominent Fu Manchu mustache who zealously pursued other people's money—rapidly went from room to room, searching drawers, cabinets, closets, rugs, beds, anywhere somebody might decide to keep or hide something of value. Maybe there would be a valuable coin collection, a fine piece of silver prominently displayed, or just the little woman's supermarket money buried in a kitchen drawer and the old man's football winnings hidden away in an old sock. All were good to go.

Suddenly, as Junior was admiring a gold and diamond cuff link set from the bedroom safe and Bruce was grabbing valuables for all he was worth, a siren went off. Both momentarily stopped and tried to get a fix on the squawking alarm. Was it coming from the house they were in? Had one of them tripped an alarm? They were all professionals; alarms didn't rattle them. They were trained to work through such inconveniences. In fact, many of the crews from their hometown neighborhood would work right through the owners' reappearance in the house they were pillaging. Working thousands of homes over many years breeds such confidence.

Then, just as suddenly, there was silence. "It's okay," yelled Tommy Seher from the front window. "It's from a house across the street. The people were just testing their alarm. It looks like they're going out for the evening."

"Good," replied Junior, as he went back to stashing the contents of the safe in a pillowcase. "We'll do them next."

In less than 15 minutes, they had cleaned out the house. Tommy called Mickie on the walkie-talkie and told her to bring the car around; they were done. After loading the swag in the car, Mickie drove the three men across the street and the drill was repeated. Once again, it began with Junior shutting off the alarm. Seher stayed by his post between the front door and window while Kripplebauer and Agnew scavenged the house for valuables. At one point, Junior found a pearl-handled .38-caliber revolver in a nightstand drawer and promptly dumped it into a bathroom toilet tank. They were all unarmed; Junior wasn't looking for any trouble. Whenever weapons were discovered, they were quickly dispatched or made inoperative. Kripplebauer's crew was swift but meticulous; little escaped their lightning-quick inspection.

"People are creatures of habit," says Kripplebauer, who had been taught all the tricks by the creators of production work. "They hide their most precious possessions in the same place, in the same rooms. Nine out of 10 times the most valuable stuff is hidden somewhere in the master bedroom. They made it easy for us. Even a blind monkey finds a coconut if he's in the palm trees. Between the cash, silver, and gold, you can end up with a nice payday."

Twelve minutes later, Mickie heard Tommy's excited voice announce on the walkie-talkie that the swag was ready to be picked up. The big Lincoln stealthily pulled into the driveway a minute later. Mickie immediately informed them that just two blocks away were several houses in a row, all displaying red alarm lights. There were lights in a couple of living room windows, but she had passed the houses many times, and all was quiet; she was sure there were no occupants. Homes illuminated with night-lights didn't fool them. Mickie instinctively knew there was no one home.

"Sounds good. Let's go," was all Junior said as he threw the last of several stuffed pillowcases into the Lincoln's trunk.

This was "production work," residential burglaries performed as if rolled out on an automotive assembly line. The burglars' hometown contribution to crime was both revolutionary and devastatingly effective. Unlike Philly's other gifts to the nation, such as *American Bandstand*, cheese steaks, and a washed-up but sympathetic club fighter named Rocky Balboa, mass production burglaries were terribly frightening. Distraught homeowners and embarrassed law enforcement agencies across the country were routinely left slack-jawed and dumbfounded. It was if a tornado had rolled through a neighborhood, but instead of destroying the infrastructure, it left the homes intact and sucked up everything of value inside.

"Some of the guys from back home preferred the big estates, but we didn't like to do a 30-room mansion," says Kripplebauer of his crew. "It was too big for us. We liked production, house after house after house, rather than one big mansion that would take hours. We'd be in and out of a house in 15 minutes and could do five or six houses a night. We weren't looking for any trouble. We never carried a weapon on a job. And if we found a gun in the house, we'd hide it. If the owner unexpectedly came home, we didn't want a problem causing somebody to get hurt. Some other crews might spend all night in one place, but that was dangerous. There was more of a chance of somebody dropping in on you. We were interested in quantity.

"Me, Teddy Wigerman, Effie Burke, Billy McClurg, all the guys back home had it down to a science. You didn't even need to be familiar with an area to pull it off successfully. You could go into a state or unfamiliar city and know exactly where to go. We'd come into a town, check out the local paper for homes selling for a half-mil or so. And then cross-reference it with the location of synagogues and top-shelf country clubs, and you were on your way. It worked every time."

Before it was all over that cool December evening, they had done a sixth house for good measure. It had been a successful night. In a little less than two hours, they had knocked off a half-dozen houses and walked off with over fifty thousand dollars in rare coins and stamps, cash, furs, silverware, and a few pieces of artwork. As Junior said, "It wasn't anything to retire on, but it wasn't bad for our first trip to Cary." They all agreed it was worth a trip back in the near future. North Carolina's Research Park Triangle had been good to them over the years. The Raleigh, Durham, and Chapel Hill area had money, serious money. Winston-Salem and Greensboro weren't bad either, but the Triangle area was a particular favorite. Well-bred old Southern money combined with a burgeoning class of Piedmont industrial executives and the bespectacled eggheads at such academic strongholds as Duke, North Carolina, and North Carolina State generated dozens of upscale communities, plush estates, and lush country clubs. Little surprise that Junior and his friends had become fond of the area. They were not alone. Back home in the rowdy bars of Kensington, everyone spoke favorably of Wake, Forsythe, and Guilford Counties. They even felt compelled to cheer on the Duke Blue Devils and the North Carolina Tar Heels when their games were broadcast on national television. An odd sort of kinship had developed with their unwitting benefactors.

The evening's successful scores in Cary deserved a celebration, but it could wait. They didn't want to press their luck. The real party would take place when they—and the loot—got back home. After a few drinks at the motel's bar, they returned to their rooms and examined their haul more closely. Most of the stuff looked good and would move quickly, but some of it was junk or too difficult to fence and would be thrown out. They immediately began packing the swag for the trip home. Fur coats were used as suitcase liners to protect the more brittle pieces and ensure that neither the jewelry nor the silverware would rattle noisily.

No one even contemplated pocketing a fancy bauble or donning a recently procured item when their partners' backs were turned. It was unacceptable. They understood and abided by the rules. No one was supposed to keep anything for himself or herself; each member would get his or her cut when the entire haul was sold to a fence back in Philadelphia. Members of crews with looser rules or less discipline might cheat their partners and slip a diamond ring or ruby brooch or fancy onyx-handled revolver into a sock or the waistband of their underwear. Crews infected with that kind of larceny would often be paralyzed with recriminations; on rare occasions, team members would be forced to strip naked and endure humiliating body cavity examinations by their crew chief at the end of the night. Not Kripplebauer's group—Junior wouldn't stand for either the stealing or the strip searches. In addition, the crew couldn't afford to draw attention to themselves by wearing an eye-catching piece of jewelry that might be recognized by an observant cop; they were just your average tourists returning from a pleasant weekend excursion through the South.

After a good night's sleep, the crew members packed their own bags, Kripplebauer paid for the rooms, and they headed north toward Philadelphia early Sunday morning. Once again, crossing the Mason-Dixon Line had proven highly profitable. While Tommy Seher drove up Route 1 towards I-95, Bruce, Junior, and Mickie each held a package or small suitcase. They had to; the Lincoln's large trunk was stuffed with goods from three nights worth of work. On the way down to Raleigh, they had made their usual stops in the suburbs of Baltimore and Washington, D.C. The Cary scores, combined with Thursday and Friday nights' work along Stevenson Road and in Rockville, Maryland, translated into quite a nice haul, but by no means a jackpot. Those usually came when they flew into Raleigh, Greensboro, or Winston-Salem, rented a couple of cars, and worked the area for several days. The accumulated swag from such weeklong ventures would normally fill several steamer trunks or footlockers and have to be shipped back to Philly as airfreight. But despite the relatively modest haul, they were satisfied and couldn't wait to get home.

The North Carolina authorities, on the other hand, were less than enthralled with the situation. Late the previous night and all day Sunday, calls came in to the Cary and Raleigh police departments from distressed and frightened residents whose homes had been burglarized. As on earlier occasions, there were no clues as to who the perpetrators were, where they had come from, or where they had gone. The cops were mystified. Newspaper scribes cataloguing the burglars' repeated triumphs nicknamed the phantoms the "Hallmark Gang" because of their penchant for stealing only the best jewels and silver bearing high-quality hallmarks and leaving costume jewelry and silver-plated items undisturbed. It was if a team of snooty appraisers from Bailey, Banks and Biddle had gone through the homes and rejected all but their most valuable possessions. And yet a gigantic vacuum cleaner operation directed from the heavens could not have been more efficient.

Despite public and political pressure to catch the culprits, law enforcement agencies basically threw up their hands. There were no leads; there were no fingerprints; no stolen items eventually turned up; no informant ratted out a partner. Investigators were dead in the water. It had been that way for years. The perpetrators invading North Carolina's most prominent neighborhoods and breaking into some of the most expensive and highly secured properties in the state were the best thieves they had ever had the misfortune of running into.

"We had never seen anything like it," says D. C. Williams, a 13-year veteran of the Raleigh Police Department at the time. Before he could capture the thieves, he had to figure out who they were and how they were accomplishing their raids so successfully. "I had no earthly idea who was doing it. Every other weekend we'd find eight to 10 burglaries in one of our high-rent districts. It went on for years. It was usually great big stuff like silverware, jewelry, and valuable stamp and coin collections. I initially thought it was locals. There was a local family that used to do a lot of burglaries. But this was too big and smooth for them. When they ended up in jail and the burglaries continued, we knew it was other folks, but we had no idea who. The bluebloods of Raleigh were getting hit pretty hard, and the pressure was starting to build. They wanted something done."

That's what happens when titans of industry and high-ranking members of the political establishment walk through their front doors and find their homes ransacked. Mrs. Alice Broughton, for example, the wife of former governor J. Melville Broughton, walked into her Raleigh home at 929 Holt Drive on August 27, 1971, and discovered that every piece of silver she owned had been carted off. The impressive haul included a dozen gold-lined silver goblets and matching wine glasses, sterling bonbon dishes, five sterling egg holders, and 36 silver coffee spoons. More spectacular yet was the handsome silver tea service and matching tray. Though extremely valuable simply because of its silver content, the elaborate tray had sentimental and historical value as well, since it was engraved with the signatures of every member of the chief executive's cabinet, the state supreme court, and the state house and senate. It had been presented to the governor when he left office in 1945.

Though it probably provided little consolation, Mrs. Broughton had plenty of company. Many of Raleigh's finest families had taken a hit. Well-known business leaders, lawyers, physicians, bank presidents, philanthropists, academics, and wealthy heirs—all seemed to have been targeted by the burglars.

With such august—and well-connected—victims, it is no wonder that Officer Williams felt that he was "carrying a considerable load." Years passed without an arrest or conviction. "I started working weekends," says Williams. "I put together surveillance teams that worked in certain neighborhoods. We set up community meetings throughout the area to help educate residents how best to protect their homes. All the safety precautions I could think of were implemented. But nothing worked. The burglars were just too good."

Yet Officer Williams and the folks in Raleigh had not cornered the market on residential burglaries—not by a long shot. Other towns and cities across the state felt equally victimized. Greensboro, for one, laid claim to dozens of unsolved burglaries, the vast majority affecting the town's elite.

On the evening of March 8, 1975, Benjamin Cone—former Greensboro mayor and heir to the Cone Mills fortune—returned to his home on Country Club Drive from a Tar Heels–Wolfpack basketball game and found it plundered of everything of value. Over $150,000 in jewels and silver had been taken, including a rare Roman coin, a priceless museum piece. It was one of only seven such coins in the world, and the only one not on display in the Louvre.

Other Greensboro residents claiming injury and calling for action included Ralph C. Price, former president of Jefferson Standard Life Insurance Company; Joseph M. Bryan, chairman of the board of Jefferson Pilot Broadcasting Corporation; and Wilbur L. Carter, president of Southern Life Insurance Company. At least three Greensboro families had the unenviable distinction of having been hit twice by the so-called Hallmark Gang.

Winston-Salem shed few tears for the folks in Raleigh and Greensboro; the quaint southern town was in the midst of its own burglary crisis. Once again, affluent sections of town with beefed-up security patrols were the targets of the elusive burglars, who managed to escape even when caught in the act. For example, they paid a surprise visit to the home of Zachary T. Reynolds, heir to the Reynolds Tobacco fortune, on the evening of August 8, 1971. Ms. Dorothy Dean (soon to be Mrs. Reynolds) was staying alone at the residence when she saw an unfamiliar car pull into the driveway. Standing behind a curtain, she could see three men and a woman in it. The white female came to the door and rang the doorbell, but Ms. Dean, feeling uneasy about the quartet, did not answer. She then saw the woman return to the car and watched them drive to the rear of the residence. When Ms. Dean saw the car depart with only the unknown woman inside, she hurriedly called police and reported prowlers in the area.

When authorities arrived, they discovered that the residence had been broken into and an enormous collection of guns strewn across the lawn. Evidently the burglars were attempting to steal Mr. Reynolds' sizable gun collection when the police arrived and scared them off. Although they appeared on the scene in the middle of the heist and established roadblocks throughout the area, the police were unable to catch the perpetrators. The thieves had disappeared as quickly as they had emerged. All that was left was a suitcase filled with an array of sophisticated burglary tools and two walkie-talkies. Though Winston-Salem police had few, if any, leads, they knew they weren't dealing with amateurs.

These were no local kids out to score a few bucks to buy alcohol and drugs. They were up against true professionals who had the know-how, moxie, and experience to knock off some of the most important manor houses in the area.

The Raleigh, Greensboro, and Winston-Salem police departments—and the state of North Carolina in general—were not the only ones expressing frustration and an increasing sense of helplessness. In fact, the Tar Heel State had gotten off rather easy and was fairly low on the burglars' preference list. Most members of the burglary ring preferred to head north and west rather than south. And most states took even longer and suffered many millions of dollars more in damage before they even began to get a handle on who was ransacking their towns and cities.

Kripplebauer, D'Ulisse, Agnew, and Seher were the tip of the iceberg. Teams of Philadelphia burglars had worked New England and the Middle Atlantic states for decades before the state of North Carolina began noticing an outbreak of burglaries within its borders. There were lots of embarrassed police departments; the North Carolina experience was far from unique. Law enforcement folks in Massachusetts, Connecticut, Rhode Island, Ohio, New York, Maryland, Missouri, Florida, Texas, and a dozen or more other states around the nation shared that powerless, vulnerable feeling.

Eventually, the problem grew so large that the Federal Bureau of Investigation was forced to establish a special unit on the Interstate Transportation of Stolen Property. Too many state and local law enforcement agencies across the country were left dumbstruck and impotent; someone had to take over and coordinate a well-designed counterattack that was national in scope and blessed with the funds and resources to take down such a secretive and longstanding criminal organization.

"We didn't know what to tell them at first," says FBI Special Agent William Skarbek, referring to the many burglary-infested cities and towns across the nation. "We in the Bureau knew that this particular Philly burglary ring had the pedigree, that they were the best. We knew they were working here and working there. We were getting reports from Missouri, Florida, Virginia, all over the place, but we didn't know what to tell them.

"We'd be getting little pieces of information about a job they'd pull in St. Louis, Tampa, Raleigh, Westport, Lancaster, Pennsylvania. They were working the whole country. Finally, we just got on the phone and started telling these various policing agencies, 'Hey, here's what you need to do. Here's what you need to look for. Here's their MO: they work in teams with drivers, lookouts, and searchers; they'll switch cars when they're doing a job; and they use walkie-talkies and other sophisticated communication equipment. They're like nothing you've ever seen before.'"

In time, some of the victimized communities would learn the identity of the thieves. But discovering who the perpetrators were only added to the law enforcement community's shock and consternation. It was hard to imagine a more unlikely crew of successful thieves. Far from the urbane, well-educated, super-sophisticated, criminal high-rollers they expected, the thieves reaping windfall profits and wrecking havoc over much of the nation were members of something called the K&A Gang, two-fisted, beer-guzzling, ear- and nose-biting hoodlums from a blue collar, predominantly Irish section of Philadelphia called Kensington.

Despite their ninth-grade educations and inability to hold down a steady job, this zany collection of urban idiot-savants—basically, a ragtag band of union thugs, street hoods, and academically challenged high school dropouts—stole with impunity despite sophisticated estate or local police department vigilance. Whether they were pilfering a priceless collection of 70 paintings from the Woolworth family estate in Maine, stealing two million dollars worth of rare Russian coins from the Du Pont family compound in Miami, looting the ex-governor's mansion in North Carolina, or staging repeated forays into the homes of Beverly Hills celebrities, the K&A Gang proved they were the real deal, master burglars par excellence. In fact, as a group, they were unquestionably America's preeminent second story men, though the term may be a misnomer, since they had the keys to everyone's front door and usually didn't have to do any climbing. They could walk right in.

Their achievements were not lost on a law enforcement community that hunted them for decades—mostly unsuccessfully. "You've got to admire them," says one long- frustrated cop. "They were the best."

"They weren't burglars," comments another police official. "They were artists."

2. "Junior"

SLOWLY, ENDLESSLY, the plumes of gray smoke and noxious carbon monoxide and sulfur gas belch forth from the earth's spastic innards and eventually spew out of the backyards, graveyards, and barren roadsides of this long-tormented community. Combine these conditions with the howling winds that leap off nearby Locust Mountain and keep winter temperatures near zero, and no one would be faulted for thinking of Centralia, Pennsylvania, as hell on earth, or a pretty exact replica.

Centralia is a geological oddity. This aging Appalachian mountaintop community sits astride a raging inferno where temperatures hover around 2,000 degrees Fahrenheit as an enormous layer of anthracite coal is gradually consumed. For many born here during the last half-century, the subterranean flames are a painful and embarrassing fact of life.

Since the early 1960s, when the fires below began to send forth streams of dense fumes, poisonous vapors, and eye-watering smoke, Centralia has been on a deathwatch. Local, state, and federal authorities have spent millions of dollars, closed over two dozen mines, and tried an array of ingenious plans, drilling holes and flooding the burning veins of coal with everything from mud and water to flame-retardant chemical slush. Still, the fires continue to burn. The town has shrunk by over four-fifths as businesses have closed and residents have moved out or died off. Yet from its very beginning in pre–Civil War America, Centralia has watched many of its sturdiest citizens succumb to one of the most dangerous professions in the world—coal mining.

In the 1840s, when the Locust Run and Coal Ridge collieries opened, Centralia became a haven for hardworking Irish immigrants willing to risk life and limb in oxygen-short, claustrophobic mine shafts for a meager day's pay. Stoical, hearty, and desperate for work, generations of coal miners endured unimaginable privations in order to provide food and shelter for their families. By the 1930s, however, the market for coal was in steep decline, adding further misery to laid-off miners and their families. As more and more mines were closed and a once-bucolic countryside lay scarred by strip-mining, the young men in and around Centralia were forced to make a decision: hold fast to family tradition and familiar terrain and hope to obtain one of the few remaining jobs in the mines or strike out for new opportunities elsewhere. One native son, Louis James Kripplebauer, Jr., never had a doubt.

"That shit wasn't for me," says Kripplebauer of the prospect of spending the rest of his life working in a 300-foot mine shaft. "Mining was fuckin' hard work. It was brutal and could really wreck you. I had seen enough of it in my family. I wasn't gonna be another McGinley or Kripplebauer to die in a mine. My grandfather, Pat McGinley, died in a mine accident, and my father got a black-lung pension. Every day of my life I saw what the mines did to people. It either killed them outright in an accident or put a ton of coal dust in their lungs and killed them off gradually. It was like death on the installment plan."

The son of a German-American miner and an Irish-American mother, Louis James Kripplebauer, Jr., had every intention of escaping this miserable coal-cracker existence. Born in 1936 in Upper Byrnesville, a small hillside community on the outskirts of Centralia, Lou Kripplebauer—"Junior" to family and friends—never felt compelled to follow his father, grandfather, and peers into the mines. Neither the hard labor nor the meager rewards suited him. He had no intention of spending the rest of his life covered in black soot, coughing up dark, bloody phlegm, and counting his pennies.

Like many other families in the region, the Kripplebauers were desperately poor and always struggling to make ends meet. Though they and the Rileys, Sweeneys, Frugales, and Spelises and hundreds of others mined coal all day, they rarely had enough money to purchase coal for their own needs. The result was twofold: an intense and universal hatred for the company and a never-ending search for coal. Like most other children in the Appalachian hills, young Junior was assigned to gather as much coal as he could.

"We were always looking for coal. It was endless. Even during the summer, I'd be out there picking coal," says Kripplebauer. "Everybody picked coal. You'd need to grab it and stockpile it in your backyard 'cause you'd never have enough to get you through the winter. The winter months were brutally cold up there in the mountains. Having coal was a necessity. You couldn't afford to buy it. It cost too much. I was 10 or 11 years old, and all the kids in the area would watch them strip-mine the fields with these huge shovels and drag lines. When they weren't looking, me and the other kids would run out there and scoop up as many chunks of coal as we could. We'd stuff it in our pockets, carry it in our arms, and take it home and put it in the shed. Sometimes we sold it to other families that needed it. The company used to hire Pinkertons to keep us from picking up the scraps. Even pea- and nut-sized coal, which was of no value to the company, was important to us. You would have thought they were nuggets of gold the way we hoarded them. But Pinkertons would chase us off. If they caught us, they'd make us empty our pockets and tell us next time they're taking us in. They'd even come around and look in our backyards. They were always checking to see what we had. Just snooping around for the company.

"Even when we weren't out looking for coal, you'd still have the job of cracking it so it would fit in your furnace. I loved to play baseball with my friends and was pretty good. We were always looking to get a good game up, but my mother would often tell me, 'Junior, don't make no plans today. We're gonna crack coal.' I hated it. We'd be out in the backyard cracking large chunks of coal for hours. All you needed was a flat rock and a claw hammer. It didn't really require a lot of strength, but it was important to know the right technique. If you didn't know where to find the vein, it would take forever. It was a filthy job."

As Kripplebauer got older, his distaste for the company, the coal fields, and his parents' penny-pinching lifestyle only increased. His resentment was intensified by frequent trips to Philadelphia as a teenager. After losing her husband to the mines, his grandmother eventually fled the mountains and moved to a working-class section of the city called Fairmount. Junior would often visit her, especially during the summer when school was out. City life was more to his liking. Everything was different, better, grander, and the colors were so much brighter. The air was cleaner, the buildings were taller, the cars were newer and of greater variety. And there was so much to do. There were dozens of movie theaters, huge department stores, and the opportunity to watch Robin Roberts, Del Ennis, Puddin' Head Jones, and the rest of the Phillies team play baseball at Shibe Park. It all presented such a stark contrast to his grim existence back home. And, best of all, in Philadelphia there were no ugly strip mines, no faces covered in coal dust, no persistent, hacking coughs, and no Pinkerton agents watching your every move. He realized far earlier than most of his friends that his days in Centralia were numbered.

"My friends never went to Philadelphia," says Kripplebauer of the kids he grew up with in rural, upstate Pennsylvania. "They didn't know anybody in the city. It was like a foreign country to them. For them, going to Philly would be like us going to Paris or Rome, a totally different world. Although many of them were intrigued by city life and amazed by all there was to do and see in the big city, many others were scared to death of the place. They feared the niggers in Philly. Many of them thought there were one hundred thousand niggers between Centralia and Philly who were gonna rape and kill their wives. Not me, though; I had been there. That's where I wanted to be.

"I'd go to the stores in downtown Philly and walk around bug-eyed. There was just so much to do and see. And all that stuff in the department store windows you wanted to have. Gimbel's, John Wanamaker's, and Lit Brothers had everything imaginable and it all looked so good. For a kid from the mountains, the whole place looked like candy. You wanted it all. That's why I started to steal in Centralia—so I'd have money when my parents took me on trips to Philly."

Back home during the school year, his desire for money and hatred for the collieries and their oppressive working conditions led him to participate in periodic coal heists and burglaries. The company store was a favorite target. Junior and his equally disillusioned friends would steal a company dump truck after filling it with coal. The 20 bucks they received for their efforts wasn't going to make any of them rich, but as Lou always said, it was the thought that counted.

"As a kid we'd sneak on the company grounds at night," he recalls, "and steal cast iron pipes and raid their stockpiles of coal. We were only 12 or 13 years old and scooped up anything we could carry and sell. The local junkyards would buy anything. Nobody seemed to care where it came from. Crime was acceptable as long as it was against the company. As we got older, we were a little bolder, stealing trucks, breaking into the company storeroom. No one thought anything of it. Everybody seemed to agree it was okay to steal anything that wasn't nailed down, as long as the company owned it. All of us up there originally came from impoverished areas of Europe and shared the attitude that you don't tell the cops anything. No one would ever tell an official anything. You avoided officials at all cost."

Increasingly disenchanted with school, his boring home life, and his prospects in a dying mining town, Kripplebauer quit school in his senior year, said goodbye to Centralia, and signed up for a four-year hitch in the Navy. Anything was better than staying in his dead-end hometown. A chance encounter on the street one afternoon crystallized his desire to get out.

"My buddy Jimmy Spelise, who was a year older than me, went to work in the mines after he got out of high school," Junior remembers. "When he came home at three o'clock after a shift in the mines, he was so dirty I didn't even recognize him. I was coming home from school one day and passed him on the street. We were right in front of his house. I didn't even know who he was. I walked right by him. He was covered in coal dust from head to foot. His teeth, nose, and ears were caked with it. All I could really see of the guy were his eyes, and they were bloodshot. He was just another filthy miner to me. I'm tellin' you, I walked right by him and would have kept on goin' if he hadn't called my name. We both laughed at the time, but inside I was sick. I knew my friend's life was basically over. I figured he was gonna end up like my grandfather or my old man, wrecked. His life was over and he was just 18. No, I wasn't going down the same way. None of that fucking shit for me. Not by a long shot."

Rushed through boot camp because of the Korean War, the 17-year-old was shipped off to the Far East and assigned to the aircraft carrier *USS Valley Forge*. For two months Junior was part of a squad of young men who handled the carrier's dangerous catapult system and arresting gear. He also maneuvered planes above and below deck before and after their bombing runs. Though the work was dangerous and backbreaking, at least Junior and the other boatswain's mates were breathing fresh air, not swallowing handfuls of coal dust while burrowing deep inside the earth's dyspeptic bowels.

With the signing of the armistice in June 1953, Junior was reassigned stateside: first to Oklahoma for naval air technical training in hydraulics and then to the Philadelphia Navy Yard. It was in his adopted hometown that he got his first taste of prison. On a lark, Kripplebauer joined two Navy buddies and took off across country for their home in Nebraska. Displaying the daring, devil-may-care attitude that would characterize much of his life, Junior realized there would be harsh consequences for going AWOL, but he didn't care.

"I had no fear," he says. "I was young and dumb. I told myself I'd deal with that when I got back."

Kripplebauer returned to Philadelphia after a couple of months. He received a swift court martial and was sentenced to 30 days in the brig. Incarceration was not the sobering jolt it should have been. "Most of the guys in the brig were marines from all parts of the country on their way back from Korea," says Junior of his war-weary cellmates. "They had seen it all and didn't give a shit about anything. The guards were also marines. They didn't put up with a lot of shit, and the whole thing could have been an ordeal, but when they learned I was a neighborhood guy like them and lived in Fairmount, they gave me preferential treatment. My people in upstate Pennsylvania were tough. Remember, they were used to close quarters, long hours, and difficult conditions. We put up with a lot of shit. Prison wasn't all that bad considering what I was used to."

After his 30 days were up, Junior was transferred to Annapolis, where he continued to maneuver aircraft for takeoffs and landings. This time, however, he was lifting seaplanes in and out of the Chesapeake and its calm tributaries, not the roiling seas of the South Pacific. He also played catcher on the naval base's better-than-average baseball team. The squad regularly traveled up and down the East Coast playing other military teams in places like Aberdeen, Maryland; Cherry Point, North Carolina; and Washington, D.C. Whatever the location, Kripplebauer's athletic ability and leadership were clearly evident, and more often than not he ran the team. The squad wasn't championship caliber, but opponents quickly learned that the masked player with the take-charge attitude guarding home plate wasn't someone you tried to steal a base on. Two hundred pounds and a few inches over six feet tall, the former coal cracker from Pennsylvania mining country was hardy, still growing, and unaccustomed to backing down. Physical confrontations with Kripplebauer weren't a walk in the park, as a few naval base and bar-room combatants quickly found out. As Junior recalls, "I never took any shit off of anybody."

When Kripplebauer turned 21 in 1956, he was discharged from the Navy and took a job as a welder for a couple of years at a shipyard at Sparrows Point,

Maryland, near Baltimore. During the week he worked on large oil tankers; on weekends he headed back to Philadelphia and the Fairmount neighborhood, where his parents and sister had recently moved to join his elderly grandmother. Fairmount is an old working-class neighborhood cuddled up against the Schuylkill River on its western border and the row houses of North Philadelphia and bustling center city Philadelphia to its north and south respectively. Its most famous landmark was the looming presence of Eastern State Penitentiary, a huge, menacing 125-year-old fortress with 35-foot high walls and battlements more suitable for feudal lords and crossbows than for the Bible-toting Quaker social reformers who conceived of and constructed it. Many of the institution's inhabitants were from the surrounding Fairmount area, leading to some interesting exchanges between those on opposite sides of the wall.

"As soon as I started hanging in some of the bars in the area," says Kripplebauer, "I began hearing the stories about what went on and thought it was pretty incredible. There was a lot of sympathy for the guys locked up inside Eastern's walls. Neighborhood guys, for example, used to get old tennis balls or softballs and cut them in half. They'd then fill them with bennies or some other type of drug, and then stitch, glue, or patch them back up and throw them over the walls while inmates were in the exercise yard playing ball. It went on all the time. Sometimes prison guards would be in on the deal and they'd pick the balls up and deliver them to certain guys on the block. It was a well-known practice in the area. A lot of stuff like that used to go on."

Another longstanding custom was savoring a few cold beers upon release. The neighborhood's many cozy shot-and-beer joints were magnets for recently released prisoners. As soon as a prisoner served out his sentence and received his walking papers, he'd step through the prison's huge front door on Fairmount Avenue and hit the first taproom he spied. Years of inactivity on the cellblock and severe dietary restrictions produced quite a thirst—for action, as well as food and drink.

"There were a lot of criminals in Fairmount," says Kripplebauer. "The corner bars were popular hangouts for local hoodlums and those guys who just got out of Eastern. They'd come right to the bar for a drink after they walked out of the joint. These guys were away for so long they were ready to do anything. Between the beer and the freedom, they became pretty delirious. All somebody had to do was make them an offer and they were game. Just hearing a plan being discussed amongst guys at the bar would juice them up and they'd want in on it. Somebody would lay a tip down about a potential score, and half the bar was ready to walk out the door. I'm telling you, they were ready.

"There was one particular bar that seemed to have nothing but criminals and ex-cons in it. It was the Gateway Bar at 20th and Fairmount, just a block from the prison. The place was wild. It was like yard out all the time. You'd hear guys say, 'C'mon, let's go. I just got out after 10 years. I got no money and I'm in a bad way. Let's get going. Let's do something.' They were anxious to pull a job."

Junior, just out of the Navy and less than enthralled with his job as a welder, was equally anxious to get going. "All the guys in the bar were doing stuff," he says. "I started to go out with them just to see what it was like. I'd hang in the car while they pulled a job and sometimes they'd throw me a share if they did well."

The action was exciting and addictive. He soon teamed up with some of his new acquaintances and pulled a few jobs of his own. "I was playing around, having fun," he says. "I was smoking reefer, meeting chicks. I started doing stuff on the weekends, making some money, and soon gave up my job as a welder. My family had no idea what I was doing." Although Junior was a relative novice at this level of crime, he was more than willing to learn. In fact, he suggested a few scores of his own.

"I told a few guys I met at one of the local bars about a Baltimore gas station that looked like easy pickings," says Kripplebauer. "When I was stationed in Annapolis, I had a part-time job in order to make a few extra bucks and knew of this gas station that kept the money in the cash register all weekend. They never took it out. By Monday morning there was a pile of cash in there, at least a few thousand dollars. It looked like an easy score. The owner was rarely there on weekends, and there weren't any guns to worry about.

"My new friends didn't take much convincing. Me and Big Mike Savio went down there late on a Sunday night. We walked in the station, pulled a couple guns on the attendants, and then walked in the office. We put the hired help in the bathroom, took the money out of the cash register, and drove back to Philly. It was an easy $1,500 score. We just drove down and did it."

The ease with which Kripplebauer pulled a gun on some innocent store clerk shocked even him. It felt natural, totally unremarkable.

"Surprisingly," says Junior, "I never even thought about it. Putting a gun in somebody's face didn't bother me. I came from law-abiding people. Nobody was involved in crime. My family, everybody where I came from, tried to obey the rules. We hated the company and may have done a few minor things. But we were basically law-abiding. Now, I was around a bunch of guys who didn't give a fuck. They'd do anything. A number of them were packing guns. Later I began to worry that someday somebody would draw a gun on me and I'd have to shoot him. I would if I was forced to, but I sure as hell didn't want to. I knew I could be shot too and that all of this was a little risky, but I just figured it beats going to work every day."

It was shortly after the Baltimore job that Kripplebauer hooked up with his first true partner in crime—and a most unusual partner he was. Tommy Lyons was an ex-con and an ex-jockey who originally hailed from the wealthy Main Line, but after a short stint at Eastern he grew partial to Fairmount's friendly bars and the many moneymaking schemes that sprouted there. As a "baby-faced apprentice" in 1950, the 18-year-old Lyons seemed a comet on horseback as he went on a victory rampage up and down the East Coast. From Atlantic City to Pimlico and from Suffolk Downs to Hialeah, Lyons brought home a series of long shots that garnered newspaper headlines and earned the respect of his more senior competitors. Despite his youth and inexperience, young Lyons was making his presence felt on the track. Though his horse-racing future appeared bright, one thing got in the way—his passion for drugs.

"Tommy had a bad drug habit," says Junior. "I met him at Jumbo's Bar at 24th and Brown right after I got out of the service. He was a very popular guy and everybody loved him. Tommy knew everyone, and because he had traveled to racetracks all over the country, he knew the landscape as well. Unfortunately, he was always looking for drugs. A good portion of each day was devoted to getting ahold of the stuff. He had many schemes, but the one he used most often was hiding out in hospital parking lots and stealing the medical bags out of the trunks of doctors' cars. He knew every hospital in the area. I'd go with him sometimes. He'd park in a hospital's lot, and when a doctor pulled in and placed his bag in the trunk, Tommy would be on top of it as soon as the doctor entered the hospital. He got caught a couple times and did a little time. More importantly, it killed his career. He was doin' pretty well, winning race after race and upstaging a lot of famous jockeys, but when they found out he had a drug problem and had been caught selling drugs to a minor, they banned him from the track. He wasn't allowed to compete any more.

"Unfortunately, Tommy couldn't kick it; he couldn't get off the drugs. He said he got started like a lot of other jockeys by using amphetamines in order to keep the weight off; they were always watching their weight. But one thing led to another, and he quickly got into more serious stuff. He started shooting demerol and morphine. It ruined his career, put him in prison, and got him doin' stickups instead of picking up checks in the winners' circle."

Though Kripplebauer remained friends with Lyons and continued to work with him, the impact of drugs on the diminutive jockey was not lost on him. Lyons was trapped as if he had a ball and chain around his ankle, always looking for the next fix while all that remained of a promising career were faded news clips. Junior wanted no part of the drug scene; he wanted freedom, not an endless search for pills, needles, and heroin.

"Me and Tommy started to do a lot of work together. Tommy was ballsy, seemed to know everyone, and had seen a lot of the country. He was familiar with every town that had a racetrack. He also had access to guns. If we were gonna do some work together and felt we needed to be armed, Tommy took care of it. We did a lot of stuff in the Philly suburbs but also traveled out of the area. Tommy grew up in Ardmore or Haverford, so we did a lot of work on the Main Line, sometimes burglaries, sometimes stickups. We'd break into wealthy homes in Villanova and Bryn Mawr and on other occasions knock off a supermarket or convenience store. Sometimes we'd go down to Baltimore and do some work. Tommy knew the area pretty good from his days at Pimlico. Between Tommy and some other guys I was meeting from Eastern, I ended up doing burglaries at night and stickups during the day. I never let my day job as a welder interfere with my sideline."

Though somewhat primitive in their tactics, the Mutt and Jeff team of Kripplebauer and Lyons was beginning to make its mark. Junior, a strapping six-footer, born opportunist, and serial risk-taker, and the diminutive 101-pound, pill-popping ex-jockey were usually game for anything that would earn them a few bucks. Most of their exploits emphasized balls over brains, but some capers paid dividends while others paid in jail time and lead.

In 1958, for example, Lyons cooked up a scheme to rob one of America's most famous jockeys. Familiar with the inner workings of the racing industry, Lyons knew when and how employees were paid—particularly jockeys. He also knew when they cashed their track checks. Seizing the moment, they targeted Bill Hardtack, a successful jockey who was currently riding at Garden State Racetrack in South Jersey. Lyons knew the Black Horse Pike motel Hardtack was staying at and had his towering partner pay him a visit. In broad daylight, Junior knocked on the door and put a revolver in Hardtack's face when the tiny jockey opened the door. Hardtack, seeing his life flash before him, was forced to give up $12,000. He had just cashed his track checks.

The heist went down so easily that the unusual duo saw no reason to quit. "We knew these little jockeys liked to ride around town with a lot of cash in their pockets," says Kripplebauer. "It made them feel big and important. But we also knew when they picked up their checks, how they had done in the saddle the previous week, and what motels they stayed at. It was beautiful."

John Choquotte was the next unlucky jockey to get picked off. In fact, Junior and Tommy Lyons nailed four or five jockeys in this manner, including a couple at Hialeah and Gulfstream racetracks in Miami. They were nice scores, but not all of their gun-toting, moneymaking gambits went as smoothly.

That same year Kripplebauer and Lyons, along with two other Fairmount boys, were given a tip about the proprietor of a large Miami grocery store. Supposedly, the store's owner was a bagman for the mob and in possession of a considerable amount of cash, which he kept in his store's safe. The Philly crew expected a quick and uncomplicated haul. The four men walked into the store pretending to be customers. Suddenly, one of the men pulled a gun and ordered the owner and a female clerk to open a safe in the rear of the building. As luck would have it, however, a cook in the restaurant next door became suspicious when he looked through the storefront window and saw two of the robbers selling groceries to customers and pocketing the money. The cook called the police, who arrived before Junior and Tommy could open the safe.

Seven policemen burst into the store and traded shots with the robbers. When the shootout was over, both Kripplebauer and Lyons had been wounded. Junior was hit in his heel and elbow, while little Tommy had sustained serious bullet wounds to his hip and abdomen. Both men were assisted in their recovery by the Florida Department of Corrections. Junior, just 25, was serving his second prison bit, this one a four-year stint at Raiford, one of Florida's toughest penal institutions.

After serving out his sentence, Junior returned to Philadelphia in the early sixties. Eastern State and the nearby bars were still doing a flourishing business. Raiford's stern dose of southern hospitality had proven ineffectual: Junior continued to do burglaries and pull off the occasional armed robbery.

"If I got jammed," says Kripplebauer, "and had to go to prison, I just accepted it. I looked at it as if it was an occupational hazard. It was part of doing business. Make no mistake; I sure as hell didn't wanna be there. But I could handle it. Some other guys would be crippled and fold if they got stuck with a prison bit, but I learned to deal with it. Nobody fucked with me inside. I knew how to handle myself."

Shady partners, crazy schemes, and acquiring other people's money had become his life. Moreover, he was using violence and aggression over skill and guile. Strong-arm tactics had won another convert.

Gradually, however, Kripplebauer started to venture out of Fairmount for his socializing. He had grown bored with the small, somewhat depressing shot-and-beer joints that had become clubhouses for geriatric gangsters seeking a cold draft on their way out of the neighborhood lockup. Junior now started to hang out at larger, heavily trafficked bars and taprooms throughout the city that offered a more upbeat atmosphere, live entertainment, and a healthy complement of the opposite sex. The Shamrock Bar at Germantown and Erie Avenues became one of his favorites. Along with Storm Saunders and the Hurricanes—the exhilarating black house band that banged out all the new Motown hits—and the sexy women who were always on the prowl for a handsome hunk with a wad of cash in his pockets, the Shamrock also introduced him to a whole new contingent of wiseguys from all over the Delaware Valley.

One interesting crew came from Kensington, a neighborhood across town known for its many textile factories, its tough, row house Irish workers, and its fierce ask-no-quarter/give-no-quarter spirit. It was also known for a particularly savvy and prolific group of second story men, men who had the guts and guile to pull off some of the biggest scores in the area, including the legendary Pottsville Heist that took a half-million dollars from an upstate coal baron. Kripplebauer was now rubbing shoulders and sharing drinks with members of the K&A Gang.

"I started hanging at the Shamrock Bar," says Kripplebauer, "and began meeting guys like Billy McClurg, John Fleckenstine, Joe Bloom, John Berkery, Jackie Johnson, Hughie Breslin, and Charlie Devlin. They were Kensington guys, tough, ballsy, fun-loving guys. They knew how to have a good time. And they knew how to make money. One thing led to another and I started doing some work with Billy, Fleck, and Bloomie and got a real education. They taught me the real way to do a burglary; they taught me something they called 'production work.'

"The guys I was working with up till that point didn't really know what they were doing. They'd just break in a house or walk in and put a gun in somebody's face. The K&A guys were much more sophisticated. They were organized and had a system. They had it down to a science. They worked in crews. Everyone had a job. There was a designated driver who made regular scheduled stops and kept his eyes open for other opportunities, a watcher who kept a lookout for cops and homeowners, and the two searchers who went through the house or business looking for anything of value. After they were done with one house, they went to another, and then another. Sometimes they'd hit five to seven houses in an evening. It was mass-production burglary. But instead of putting the houses on a conveyor belt, we went to the houses. It was a totally different approach than what anyone else was doing. There was really no comparison between what the K&A guys were doing and what the Fairmount guys were doing. Or any other guys doing second story work, for that matter. I was now learning a new system. I learned production work.

"The K&A guys used all sorts of equipment, everything from police scanners and walkie-talkies to communicate with one another to brutes, chisels, and crowbars to open safes. But the one thing they didn't use that was the most fascinating thing for me was their decision not to use guns. The K&A guys didn't want to do stickups. They wouldn't carry a gun. They said it was a violation of all the rules. You just don't carry a gun. I thought they were kidding at first, because I, and all the guys I ever worked with, always carried a gun. I had grown used to packing a handgun when I was doing a job; it felt good. It gave you a sense of security and allowed you to believe that you were in control. But the K&A guys were serious. They argued that a gun never got them anything but a lot of trouble, and you could make more money without carrying a gun.

"I didn't believe them at first, I thought they were kidding me. They kept on insisting it was true, no weapons. I couldn't believe it. I knew they weren't pansies. The Kensington crowd was tough; they'd fight you all day and night over the slightest insult, they were incredible street fighters, but they didn't want to carry a weapon while doing a burglary. They didn't want to hurt anybody. And if you were caught, you had a lot less to worry about. The bottom line was the K&A guys were fun, really knowledgeable about what they were doing, and tough as nails. And most importantly, they were making money. I decided to put my gun down and join them."

Bill McClurg, a K&A burglar whose rap sheet goes back to the 1940s, remembers meeting the tall, striking German-Irish lad who had already done a stint in the Florida State Pen and was willing to learn the way real burglars, Kensington burglars, did business.

"That Shamrock, boy, that was really some joint," recalls McClurg, better known as Billy Blue to his friends and associates. "It attracted people from all over town, it was a jumpin' spot. Junior started showing up in the early sixties after he came back from Florida and we sort of took him in. He was a good guy, Junior—good-looking, outgoing, energetic. He just started doing some work with us. We showed him how to do production work.

"Junior was used to working with a gun, but we told him he didn't need it. It just meant more trouble in the end. All of us had guns, but we never took them on the road with us, not when we were working. We tried to be as meticulous and cautious as possible. We didn't want any screwups. We even made sure whoever was driving had papers on the car. You didn't want to be doing a house and find out your driver got stopped and couldn't show proof he owned the car. The whole thing could go down the tubes because of a stupid mistake. That's why we never carried guns on the job. We didn't want to create problems. That went for Junior as well. We weren't lookin' to hurt anybody and we didn't want to get hurt either. We wanted to burglarize houses, a lot of them. That was production work. That's the way we learned it in Kensington. It was a Kensington thing and it worked. There was nobody out there like us."

As Junior likes to say about the old working-class neighborhood's contribution to crime and the K&A Gang's reputation as America's best second story men: "The Kensington guys knew what they were doing. They totally transformed second story work. They'd do 10 burglaries a night while everyone else was doing one a week. There was no comparison."

Part II

The K&A Gang

3. Kensington

I got a call one morning that they needed another guy for a crew they were putting together to do a piece of work in North Jersey. They told me to come down to Kensington and meet them at Kellis's Bar. I walk in there a couple of hours later all decked out in my suit and tie ready to go to work, but I must be early or something, 'cause none of the guys I'm supposed to meet are there. So I order a drink and check things out. There's a couple of guys there I think I recognize, but I stick to myself for the time being. I had only been there once or twice before, but know it's a favorite of the guys in the crew. The joint is right under the Frankford El at Kensington and Allegheny and gets a lot of traffic. It's nothing special, just your basic shot-and-beer joint for local factory workers and transients who want to get lubricated.

Then a funny thing happens. A guy comes in and half the joint walks out. I mean, some of them don't even bother to finish their drinks or pick up their change off the bar. Something like this you got to take notice of. He's a big guy, pretty mouthy, and he seems to know everybody. And everyone knows him. The guy orders a beer and tells the bartender he's gotta make a call. So he's on the phone a couple minutes and then comes over to where I'm sitting and without saying a how-do-you-do picks up some of my change that's on the bar and starts putting it in the phone slot. I don't pay it no mind, but after another minute or so he does the same thing. Now, I'm looking at this guy who's paying for his call with my money.

I still don't say a thing, but I'm starting to get an idea who this guy is by the way people are deferring to him. I'm thinking this character, and he's a pretty good size, must be Charlie Devlin. I had heard about this guy for years but had never met him. Devlin is this infamous Kensington head thumper and occasional burglar who loves to mix it up. I'd heard about these classic three-hour-long bare-knuckle brawls he often got himself into. I'm thinking to myself, this is gonna be interesting.

Some guys at the bar are watching what's happening and one of 'em comes over to me and says, "You work with Jack, John L., and Effie, don't yah?"

I say, "Yeah, that's who I'm waiting for."

He tells me not to take offense with what's happening. The guy lifting my coins is Charlie Devlin, and it'd be best for my health if I don't antagonize him. "I'll straighten it out," he says to me.

I grab this Good Samaritan by the arm and tell him, "Hey, thanks for the warning and all, but I can take care of it myself."

The guy musta thought I was nuts, 'cause I ain't even five-nine and Charlie is this big lug with a well-known reputation for kicking ass and destroying people. What none of 'em know, however, is that I'm carrying a piece with me. I had already killed a couple people and had no hesitation about using it on this asshole. Most of those K&A burglars never took a gun along on a job, but I did on occasion, and I know I'll use it on that crazy motherfucker if he's dumb enough to start something with me.

Before I know it, Devlin comes back over and scoops up the rest of my change off the bar and walks back to the phone. "Hey, what the hell you think you're doing," I yell at him.

He turns and says, "You talking to me?"

"Yeah," I tell him. "That's my money you're taking. How about using your own money if you wanna make a call?"

Now it don't take an Einstein to figure out that Devlin isn't used to being challenged like this in one of these Kensington bars, and he walks back over to me stern as shit and says, "That was my money I picked up off the bar."

"The hell it was," I fire back.

He now puts his ugly mug within inches of mine and says, "Okay, jerkoff, let's take it outside."

Now I'm thinking to myself, I just came down here to meet some guys, do a couple pieces of work in North Jersey, maybe if I'm lucky make a few grand, and get out. But it now looks like somebody's gonna get hurt, and it sure as hell ain't gonna be me. I figure I'm gonna have to kill this dumb son-of-a-bitch. But that's the way it was in those Kensington bars. You could go in for a quick beer and end up fighting for your life. Some of those neighborhood joints were like gladiator schools, which is one of the reasons I tried to stay out of them.

Fortunately, this guy who had come over to warn me about Charlie steps in front of Devlin and explains to him that I'm okay. That I'm friends with Effie and the guys and I'm about to go on the road with a crew from the neighborhood. Devlin looks at me suspiciously, asks if that's true, and takes on a whole new attitude when he learns I'm working with some of the more respected burglars from the neighborhood.

The guys at the bar who are watching this little episode unfold probably thought I was a lucky fool who had just escaped a serious beating from Charlie, but in reality Charlie Devlin nearly got whacked that day. If he had touched me, I would have shot that crazy gorilla right in the head. —George "Junior" Smith

THE VERBAL CONFRONTATION at Kellis's Bar that day between Junior Smith, a handsome, preppy-looking burglar who would eventually become an accomplished contract killer, and Charlie Devlin, a legendary bar-room brawler who would quote Shakespeare as he beat your brains out, was typical Kensington: bold, brazen, in-your-face audacity backed up with gallons of guts and bravado. Most K&A guys—certainly the many burglars, roofers, and cops who grew up there—had no reverse gear. Their parents, peers, and long-established community tradition taught them to hold their ground and never back down.

Though that first meeting between Smith and Devlin at Kellis's had all the makings of your typical Kensington bar-room bloodbath, the encounter ended peaceably. However, at the JR Club, the Crescent, the Purple Derby, and a dozen other neighborhood watering holes menacingly patrolled by the likes of Cocky O'Kane, Porky McCloud, Leo Gillis, Billy McKenna, Frankie Wetzel, and Joe Cooper Smith, blood was often poured out as freely as alcohol. And Kensington, like its predatory bars, wasn't for the faint of heart. You had to be tough to survive.

LOCATED ALONG THE DELAWARE RIVER just two miles northeast of Philadelphia's City Hall, Kensington in the 1950s was a bustling collection of heavy industry, commercial strip businesses, and tiny row houses that fronted thimble-sized backyards. A struggling, Dickensian mill town in the nineteenth century, postwar Kensington was dominated by aging factories, congested streets, polluted air, and a deafening elevated transit line that bisected the community. Trees were practically nonexistent, exceeded in scarcity only by the area's few litter-filled parks and playgrounds. Religious institutions, on the other hand, were numerous and structurally impressive, but the formidable front doors of Ascension of Our Lord (Irish), Nativity BVM (Irish), Visitation of Our Lady (Irish), Saint Adalbert's (Polish), Mother of Divine Grace (Italian), and Our Lady Help of Christians (German) were open only to their own. Though they were all Catholic, each ethnic group had its own specific house of worship.

The inhabitants of Kensington took on the characteristics of the Spartan landscape that surrounded them. Firm-jawed and tight-lipped, with dark, penetrating eyes and frozen expressions, the people had a look about them—one that said, "Get the fuck out of my face, fella. I don't take shit from nobody." They projected an unforgiving, tough-as-nails nature, a personal rigidity that to outsiders appeared both proud and intimidating. As Peter Binzen of the *Philadelphia Inquirer* commented in his book on the neighborhood, Kensington was "home to a hundred thousand proud, irascible, tough, narrow-minded, down-to-earth, old-fashioned, hostile, flag-waving, family-oriented ethnic Americans." First-, second-, and third-generation Irish, Italian, German, Polish, Hungarian, Jewish, and English immigrants all settled there, but the Irish dominated, causing the soot-gray working-class neighborhood to be perceived throughout the city as a bastion of sullen, surly, and suspicious Irishmen. It also had—and some would say earned—the image of a community grounded in intimidation and ruled by menacing tough guys doing shady things. Others would argue that Kensington's Irish Catholics had every reason to be suspicious and tough-minded; their lot over many generations in the City of Brotherly Love had not been an easy one.

Kensington was founded in 1730 and named after an elegant section of London by Anthony Palmer, an Englishman and Barbados sea captain who purchased 191 acres of land north of Philadelphia's eighteenth-century boundaries in a district known as the Northern Liberties. In its earliest days, during the colonial and Federal periods, Kensington attracted immigrants for whom fishing and shipbuilding provided the stepping-stones to economic survival. Immigrants from Ireland's Protestant community arrived first, were quickly assimilated, and became shipwrights and fishermen. Over time, many adopted the anti-Catholic, Nativist attitudes of those who arrived earlier.

Irish Catholic immigrants soon followed but found a less hospitable welcome. Desperately poor and in need of work, they were gradually introduced to the "contract system" and for the most part became weavers who worked alone on hand looms in their small homes and boarding houses in the western part of the district.

Life for the more affluent, however, was still centered on the river. A local legend claims that Charles Dickens—who visited Philadelphia in the 1840s—named the area "Fishtown" because of the Delaware's abundance of shad and the large number of people employed on the river. In reality, the waterfront area at the juncture of Gunner's Run and the Delaware River was called Fishtown long before Dickens ever came to America.

As Kensington's population increased and its physical boundaries expanded to the north and west, the area's inhabitants hoped that the establishment of their own political jurisdiction would end the periodic strife between religious and ethnic groups. By 1820 Kensington had broken off from the Northern Liberties to become a separate and distinct municipality, but the decades preceding the Civil War were to be fractious and violent ones. Like other large colonial cities, Philadelphia was witnessing the first disquieting bursts of industrial development. The rapid growth of the factory system would have a considerable social impact on workers in general, and Irish Catholics in particular. New immigrants already confronted a long list of hardships: the need to adapt rural Irish sensibilities to a strange urban setting, ethnic intolerance (including "Irish need not apply" signs on factory gates), religious bigotry in the public schools and elsewhere (leading eventually to the development of parochial schools), and the lack of adequate police protection. As factories and textile mills sprang up in Manayunk, Frankford, Holmesburg, and dozens of other small towns situated along rivers and streams around Philadelphia, the inefficient production of goods in one's home declined rapidly, adding a new burden to newcomers seeking jobs as weavers.

During this period, Nativist English and Irish Protestants in volunteer militias and fire companies repeatedly squared off against Irish Catholics, hoping to turn the "alien, papist, anti-democratic" tide. Religious leaders were often at the center of the crisis, and many "pledged themselves to an unremitting ideological war on popery." More secular interests joined the fray; even publishers promised, "No theme in these textbooks . . . [is] more universal than anti-Catholicism."

This inflammatory situation resulted in a series of bloody Kensington revolts between 1820 and 1850. Violent street brawls and all-out riots lasted for days as the toll of dead and injured mounted and burned-out buildings, several of them churches, littered the landscape. An 1828 riot that took the better part of a week to contain began in a Kensington tavern when one inebriated customer made disparaging remarks about "bloody Irish transports." The anti-Catholic riots of 1844—ostensibly over which version of the Bible was to be read in public schools—resulted in 15 deaths and 50 injuries before 5,000 troops managed to quell the disturbance. A grand jury empanelled to investigate the riots and packed with anti-Catholic "Know Nothings" blamed the turmoil on the usual suspects. Embattled Irish Catholics quickly learned that the police and courts were unavailable to them and not to be trusted.

Law-abiding Philadelphians were shocked by the recurring violence and demanded a prompt resolution to the social conflagration. As one appalled citizen commented at the time, "This is the fatal evil of Philadelphia—that the riotous and disorderly are convinced of the lukewarmness and timidity of the respectable part of society, and so they take full swing upon every occasion that arises."

Though there were numerous religious and economic problems, to many the crux of the matter was law enforcement's fractured organizational structure and inability to maintain order. Most towns outside the city, like Kensington and

Southwark, had either little to no police protection or overly aggressive departments that were poorly disguised street gangs (the streets of Moyamensing, for example, were policed by a gang called the "Killers").

Consolidation of the city with its rapidly growing outlying districts had often been suggested as a way to enhance public safety, but petty political squabbles always prevented legislative action. By the 1850s, however, Philadelphia was in desperate need of more land for expansion, an extended tax base to pay for increased city services, administrative and bureaucratic simplification, and a competent police force to maintain law and order in the hinterlands. The embarrassing and deadly riot of 1844 galvanized public opinion. In February 1854 the Pennsylvania legislature passed and the governor signed a long-sought Consolidation Act that brought surrounding districts into the city and gave Philadelphia its present boundaries. Although a critical jurisdictional conundrum had been solved, Irish Catholics had little reason to celebrate. As one scholar assessed the situation, the Irish were still the most "thoroughly stigmatized white men in America," still confronted with "a labyrinth of social and class barriers" designed to thwart their progress in the city.

Yet Kensington continued to grow. Poverty, disenfranchisement, and famine back home drove tens of thousands of Irish to America—75,000 came to Philadelphia alone between 1839 and 1855, and many of them settled in Kensington. Concurrent with this influx was the rapid growth of Kensington's industrial base, due in large part to the area's close proximity to Philadelphia and its resilient workforce. Carpet manufacturing, for example, began there in 1830. By the start of the Civil War, Kensington could claim well over a hundred rug mills employing several thousand workers. The nation's first textile mill was established there and would eventually become the long-time hub of America's fabric trade. Kensington would also become home to the country's largest lace and hat factories. Shipbuilding, fishing, coal hauling, and pottery, chemical, and glass factories were all centered there and continued to flourish into the late nineteenth century. Organizations like the Salvation Army established their national headquarters in Kensington.

Despite lingering religious, racial, and ethnic tensions, some in the community prospered, allowing self-satisfied Chamber of Commerce types to proclaim Kensington an "enterprise dotted with factories so numerous that the rising smoke obscures the sky, the hum of industry is heard in every corner of its broad expanse. A happy and contented people, enjoying plenty in a land of plenty. Populated by brave men, fair women and a hardy generation of young blood that will take the reins when the fathers have passed away. All hail, Kensington! A credit to the Continent—a crowning glory to the City."

Not everyone, however, shared this glorious vision of Philadelphia's largest working-class community. Nineteenth-century industrial innovations created unprecedented advances in productivity and enormous wealth, but also vast social disruption and despair. For many in Kensington, poverty became a terrible and familiar fact of life. Unskilled factory workers received 78 cents a day in 1854, and newspapers carried advertisements for girls to work in match factories for $2.50 a week. Handloom weavers—at the bottom of the economic ladder—usually received a subsistence wage that periodic strikes did little to improve. The onset of large-scale factory work added a new pattern of servitude that widened the gap between owner and worker, accelerated downward mobility socially, economically, and geographically, and left the employee feeling anonymous even though he was now laboring shoulder to shoulder with dozens of other workers. The constant struggle to survive took its toll, and the devastating results could be easily measured. In 1856, for example, "two-thirds of the insane in the state hospital in Philadelphia were Irish born." (A century later, Kensington led the city in juvenile delinquency and was second in venereal diseases and tuberculosis.)

The long hours, low pay, periodic tribal warfare, and old European customs contributed to the growth of another business—the neighborhood taproom. The Irish had a long-established "reputation for alcoholic intake," and the saloon provided "an oasis of camaraderie for the worker, the unemployed, the troubled, and the calculating." As the nineteenth-century author John F. Maguire sadly proclaimed on his visit to America in the 1860s, "Drink, accursed drink is the cause why so many Irish in America fail." By the early twentieth century, Kensington was saturated with drinking establishments. Most residential blocks contained at least one bar, and some were said to have as many as a half-dozen. Incredibly, one seven-square-block area had 196 saloons. Appalled, two dozen churches initiated an anti-saloon campaign in 1916, but their efforts were less than triumphant. For decades to come, Kensington would be burdened with the explosive mix of tough, often angry, working-class men frequenting local gin mills and beer halls.

Despite the relentless poverty and many hardships, Kensington grew rapidly: 7,118 residents in 1800; almost twice as many by 1830; more than 50,000 by the end of the Civil War. At the start of the twentieth century, Kensington's population would top 200,000. The area's stunning growth was primarily due to one thing—work.

New immigrants and workers from across the country desperate to find jobs quickly learned that the best opportunities in Philadelphia were to be found in Kensington. Factories, warehouses, dry-docks, and other commercial establishments cluttered the mixed industrial/residential landscape and produced everything from delicate chocolate mints and fancy lace curtains to ball bearings and Flexible Flyer sleds. Three factories alone—Cramp shipbuilding, Disston saws, and Stetson hats—employed over 10,000 people. Though furniture, dye, and appliance companies all flourished there, the textile industry dominated the scene in terms of the number of plant sites and employees. Craftex Mills, Quaker Lace, Bromley Mills, Keystone Knitting, Beatty Mills, Art Loom, Robert Bruce, and Rose Mills were just a few of the over fifty textile mills that established themselves in Kensington.

By the 1920s, with a population equal to that of Washington, D.C., Kensington had solidified its position as one of the great industrial centers in the world and America's leading producer of carpets, hosiery, tapestry, knit goods, felt hats, and large ocean-going vessels. In short, Kensington was the economic engine that made Philadelphia a leading, if not the preeminent, manufacturing city in the United States.

Subsequent decades, however, would prove considerably less kind to this vital community. From the 1930s on, domestic and international events placed Kensington's socioeconomic health on a geopolitical rollercoaster whose valleys became ever deeper and more difficult to climb out of. The Depression threw thousands of Kensingtonians out of work. Scores of banks, factories, and businesses closed, with only soup kitchens and apple stands to replace them. Hopelessness pervaded the community until World War II injected a dose of manufacturing excitement back into it. Factories and shipyards were re-opened with lucrative government contracts, businesses on the avenue—that is, Kensington Avenue—once again had cash-paying customers, and taprooms were filled with upbeat, optimistic workers.

The postwar period, however, disclosed the stark human and manufacturing trends that would ultimately drive Kensington into a long, steady social and economic decline. Returning veterans took advantage of the G.I. Bill and began to recognize possibilities beyond Kensington's borders; new housing developments like Levittown offered an affordable suburban lifestyle; more and more industrialists moved their businesses south to avoid aggressive trade unions and high wages; and minorities began to encroach on the once exclusively white neighborhood. Once again, Kensington was under siege, but the majority of residents struggled on as they always had. Tough, stoical, and fiercely independent, most Kensingtonians seemed oblivious to the prevalence of alcoholism, the astronomical high school dropout rate, the foul factory odors and soot-belching smokestacks, the endless noise from train yards and manufacturing plants, and the limitations of their tiny, postage-stamp row houses.

As Paul Melione, a 78-year-old barber and life-long resident fondly recalls, "Kensington in the 1950s was a nice place to live and raise a family. You could walk down the street with your wife and kids and shop on the avenue in comfort. It was a great place to live."

"GOOD, CLEAN, HARD WORKING PEOPLE LIVED HERE," says Paul Green. "They were church-going people, mostly Irish. It was one of the best neighborhoods in the city." Green, now in his late eighties, has been a witness to Kensington's variable fortunes for most of the twentieth century. As proprietor of Economy Shoes on Kensington Avenue just below Allegheny, he has observed the area's highs and lows from the storefront window of a family business that first opened its doors in 1915. "Friday nights were really something back then," says Green. "It was family night and everybody was on the avenue. And they were all shopping. It was wonderful."

The shopping under the noisy El line was so good that it was not uncommon to find residents who had never ventured into center city Philadelphia, two miles away. The neighborhood was self-contained and relatively safe; for many working-class families, it had everything you could ever want. "It was a great place to grow up," recalls Bob McClernand. "Nobody had a lot of money, but we managed to get by. It was a close neighborhood; everyone knew each other."

"You never had any problems there," says Gil Slowe. "You could leave your keys in the car and it would still be there when you got back. Folks washed their front steps and took pride in everything they did."

"It was a very good neighborhood," adds John Kellis. "Even late at night hundreds of people would walk the streets. The avenue was busy; people were shopping." In other words, there was no need to leave the area, no need for the Bradys, O'Donnells, and Gallaghers to travel to the large department stores downtown like Gimbel's, Lit Brothers, and John Wanamaker's, or the fancy Chestnut and Walnut Street shops like Jacob Reed, Bonwit Teller, and Nan Duskin.

The businesses on Kensington and Allegheny Avenues—"K&A" to most Philadelphians—were the axis of Kensington's commercial district. Jack Bell's, Al's Toggery, DiNelli's, Mike the Tailor, Flagg Brothers, Thom McAn's, and Father & Son were just a few of the men's haberdasheries and shoe stores on the avenue. Six-foot-six, 300-pound "Uncle Miltie" Fields ran a popular sporting goods store that always offered a good deal on Chuck Taylor canvas sneakers. The Levin and Rosenthal families sold home furniture. Moe's Meats was said to have the best cuts of beef east of Broad Street. Morris Auto Parts, a shop for serious car enthusiasts, sold a surprisingly large number of sturdy, arm-length screwdrivers nicknamed "brutes" that some in the neighborhood found indispensable in their unusual line of work. Woolworth's and Kresge's 5&10s attracted neighborhood children, and the entire family enjoyed outings to the Midway, Lafayette, and Iris movie theaters (the Iris always offered military servicemen free admission). Restaurants such as White Castle, Horn & Hardart's, and the Majestic Diner, drug stores such as Samit and Sun Ray, Lee's photo store, Shalo's baby shop, a couple of Army/Navy stores, the Acme food market, and a host of other businesses were also present on the avenue and heavily patronized.

In short, for most Kensingtonians the neighborhood offered everything you could ever want—especially jobs. "If you had just lost your job, you could walk from factory to factory and get another job the same day," recalls Paul Melione. "The place was loaded with jobs; factories were making rugs, lace, clothing. Everything was being made here. The plants were everywhere." Philco, for example, which manufactured televisions, radios, refrigerators, and many other home appliances, was located just a few blocks from K&A and employed more than 18,000 workers in a complex of nine large factory plants.

But some men in the neighborhood were not enamored with an assembly-line job's long hours, monotony, and 60 bucks a week with periodic layoffs; some men longed for more and were willing to cut corners to get what they wanted. "They lasted a month," recalls Gene Pedicord. "They couldn't take the regimentation." "They didn't want to work," says another observer. "They didn't want to work at all. They just wanted to hang on the corner day and night," and still "have the girls, cars, and clothes."

As Jimmy Moran neatly puts it: "You go in a bar after a long day at work and see a couple good-lookin' chicks sittin' together and you think about buyin' them a drink, but all you got is a dollar and change in your pocket. Next thing you know, a guy from the neighborhood, a guy who ain't done an honest day's work in months, pulls up in a Cadillac, walks in with an expensive suit on, drops a hundred-dollar bill on the bar, and buys the girls a few drinks. Right off the bat, the game's over. It wasn't too hard to figure out. If you wanted the cash, the clothes, the cars, and the girls, you had to do something other than bust your hump on a lousy assembly line in a dirty, stinking factory. You had to become a burglar."

And for most, once you had become a successful second story man, there was no turning back. For row house Kensington boys who grew up in the shadow of smelly rug and textile mills and watched their fathers struggle all their lives in low-paying factory jobs, thievery—and the good life it brought—was tough to give up. Even when pressured by family members to get out and clean themselves up, the lifestyle and perquisites were just too appealing. Many found themselves, like Georgie Smith, having to forcefully educate loved ones about the facts of life.

"I told my wife to get in the car," says Smith of the unique and poignant excursion. "I said, 'We're going for a ride.' She wanted to know where we were going, but I told her we're just goin' out for a ride. I kept quiet after that. For the whole journey, I kept my mouth shut.

"She had been bothering me about it for a long time. Over and over again, she'd be pestering me to stop doin' what I was doin'. 'Why do you have to break the law? Why do you have to break into houses? Why do you have to live the life you do? Why can't we live like other people?'

"Well, I get her in the car and we drive into the city and I'm still not saying a word. She doesn't know what's up, but she soon calms down, bites her lip, and just looks out the window at the scenery. After a while I get to Kensington and start driving real slow. I just take it real easy going up one street and down the other. The streets are dirty and filled with trash and garbage. Kids, dirty and unkempt, are yelling and screaming. There's shabbily dressed people with vacant, beat expressions on their faces sitting on their front steps looking at us, and the houses are tiny matchboxes with no character, no nothing.

"This goes on for some time; I'm in no hurry. Just one street after another, and I'm not saying a word. Neither of us is. I drive her under the Frankford El, pull by some of the factories like Craftex, Robert Bruce, and Philco, and take her on a good number of streets the average nine-to-five, lunchpail-carrying factory worker calls home.

"I just got fed up with all the nagging one day and took her for a ride. We lived in a nice community in the suburbs, my kids went to a good suburban school, and we had nice, established neighbors who kept their homes immaculate. But she was on me all the time to give up what I was doing and stop associating with the guys I was hanging with.

Finally, after nearly two hours, my wife says she's seen enough, we can go home. For a good, long time after that, she didn't bring up what I did for a living. I didn't even have to say a word that day, but she got the message all right."

4. Production Work

We were doin' a big house up in Chestnut Hill one night. You know, one of those big, old, three story stone mansions set off from the road with lots of rooms and the best of everything inside. It's the usual Effie crew: me, Jack, Vince, and Effie. Well, we're tearing the place apart looking for anything of value—jewelry, furs, coins, you know, whatever we can find. We had gone through the place pretty thoroughly and know it's time to get out. We had been there a while. Effie, however, is acting strange. Something is bothering him. He ain't ready to leave, which is unusual 'cause he was always very cautious and professional. It's one of the reasons everybody wanted to work with him. He knew the business as well as anybody and made a lot of money. And better yet, he rarely got caught.

Me and Jackie are ready to go and have Vince pick us up in the car, but Effie's walking through the halls and into different rooms saying, "There's more money here. Something ain't right. I know there's more money in this house."

I told him we had gone through every room and torn the place up pretty good, but he keeps saying, "There's something here. I know there's more money here."

Me and Jack are holding a bunch of furs and pillowcases filled with an assortment of stuff and looking at each other like, what's with Effie?

Then Effie begins to storm through the house, lightly tapping on the walls and floors of the joint with one of those big 9714 screwdrivers that we used to break open front doors. He has a real intense look on his face and is completely disregarding our warnings that we better get the hell out of the place. You can hear him tapping all through the house like a crazy man, and then he suddenly calls out from one of the third floor bedrooms, "Yo, Jim, c'mon up here. I want you to hear something."

I go up to the room and Effie is still tapping away, but now he's in this huge closet. It's one we had already checked for a safe, and finding none decided to take a few furs and cashmere coats. "Listen to this," he says. He begins tapping the wall again, about every four inches apart for the entire length of the closet. "You hear that?" he says, as he travels the length of the wall once again.

Effie had discovered a hollow spot in the wall. He then starts digging at it with the screwdriver, right through the fancy wallpaper and the inch-thick wall itself. In less than a minute he broke through and into a hidden compartment that contained neatly packed bundles of wrapped money and a bunch of other things. Really ancient stuff—dusty newspapers and documents, old maps—but we grab it all.

It's not until we look at it later and take it to a fence that we learn the money was printed in the 1890s or earlier and had probably been hidden away in that house for 60 or 70 years. We figured the people currently living in the place didn't even know there was a secret compartment in the master bedroom. The money had just been sitting there undisturbed all that time. Undisturbed until Effie got there, that is. Five minutes in that place and he knew the house better than the real owners did. I'm telling you, Effie was incredible. He had a sixth sense about money and houses. There was nobody like him.   —JIMMY DOLAN

JIMMY DOLAN'S ACCOUNT of Effie Burke's extraordinary gift is no exaggeration. Effie's individual exploits and overall career accomplishments are legendary among the old Kensington burglars.

Although one of the most respected, widely traveled, and industrious members of the K&A Gang—his career stretched over three decades—he was not the first and certainly not the most famous of the K&A burglars. John Berkery, Junior Kripplebauer, and at least a half-dozen other burglars had greater public name recognition. In fact, Effie Burke, certainly assisted by the more restrained media standards of the day, had a relatively low-profile career. At loose ends and struggling financially on his return from military service after World War II, Effie Burke required the help and "professional guidance" of a fellow Kensingtonian, a tough, wily street kid who was destined to place his personal stamp on the art of burglary and ultimately become Philadelphia's "Public Enemy No. 1."

William "Willie" Sears was the youngest of John and Elizabeth Sears's six children. The family lived in Kensington, and the kids went to the Horn Public School, but most of Willie's classmates (friends called him Billy) would probably have a difficult time recalling the chubby, good-looking youngster. Apparently, Willie developed a distaste for school at an early age and rarely attended. Truancy became an even greater problem after his quarrelling parents eventually separated. In a last-ditch attempt to corral his wayward spirit, Willie was sent to the Shallcross School, an institution for "predelinquents" in the city's far Northeast. Unfortunately, his criminal proclivities may have already been well established. At the tender age of 12 , he was arrested for shooting out factory windows and automobile windshields with a BB rifle, and it soon became clear that this relatively minor infraction would not be an isolated incident.

At Shallcross, Willie was labeled "mentally normal" but "practically illiterate." Despite his intellectual shortcomings—it was said that in ninth grade he was still unable to tell time—Willie Sears was "the most popular boy at the school." Even the teachers and administrators were fond of him. "Billy was a good kid, a leader, a youngster of fine character," says Sam Glassar, a Shallcross supervisor.

Like many Kensington kids, Willie Sears was good with his hands and not easily intimidated. He won the lightweight boxing title at the school and became a standout on the baseball team. Though he had a tendency to "tease" and "needle" kids, including those older and bigger than him, Sam Glassar believes that Willie would have given any of them "the shirt off his back" if they were in need.

A natural leader, Willie could direct his followers down some troubling paths. For example, he learned how to break out of the institution and on one occasion took three fellow inmates with him. The other three youths returned to their own homes after a day on the town, an option Willie couldn't or wouldn't take. When he returned to the school the next morning alone, Glassar asked why he came back. "What could I do? Where could I go?" the boy stoically replied. "I came back to take my punishment." Willie's unexpected return confirmed Glassar's suspicion that the boy "used to misbehave deliberately so he would lose his weekend-at-home privileges."

Since the boy was unwilling or unable to adjust to the public school system and technically unable to continue at Shallcross now that auto theft was on his record, a judge decided that Willie and the community would be better served if he went to the State Industrial School at Camp Hill, better known to its unsociable clientele as White Hill. Willie was now learning the ropes from some of the most troubled and violent juveniles in Pennsylvania and on a well-worn path to becoming a career criminal. At White Hill, he honed his boxing skills, added to his criminal repertoire, and formed friendships that would be useful in illegal enterprises yet to come.

Throughout the 1940s Willie was arrested fairly regularly for everything from vagrancy and disorderly conduct to burglary and car theft, but except for a year in a Georgia State Penitentiary, he more often than not beat the case or did relatively little time. It was a lucky pattern he maintained for a good part of his career, but one that aroused some suspicion in less fortunate colleagues.

Willie Sears was not the only Kensington teenager in the forties and early fifties to reject a conventional lifestyle and employment at Craftex Mills, Stetson, or Philco for the allure of the streets and the prospect of "easy money."

Neil Ward, Bernard McGinley, Harry and Roy Stocker, Charlie McCullough, Maurice McAdams, Raymond Chalmers, Richie Blaney, Herman Cable, and other neighborhood youths were busy building their criminal resumes at the same time.

Ward and McGinley, for example, had perfected a lucrative car theft business. They'd spot unlocked cars on the street or in parking lots and steal the identifying papers from the glove compartments. After requesting and receiving duplicate titles to the vehicles, they'd go back, steal the cars, and then sell them somewhere out-of-state. The enterprise was fairly successful, though occasional business costs could make for a jarring setback. In 1948 Ward and McGinley were found guilty of stealing 20 late-model cars and selling them in nine different states. A federal judge rewarded them with a three-year prison sentence.

The Stocker boys focused on stolen checks and money orders. They, too, did well, but pinches could be painful and well publicized. One scheme, for instance, got them charged with stealing $164,000 worth of money orders from the home of an American Express agent. Charlie McCullough, on the other hand, took to carrying a gun, a rare and risky practice that most Kensington men rejected. A 1938 armed robbery that went bad proved why. Charlie was found guilty and given a hefty 30- to 90-year prison sentence.

Though not book-smart in the conventional sense, Willie Sears was no slouch when it came to recognizing an attractive business opportunity or weighing the fallout from a scheme that went bust. He also took note of guys like himself, other up-and-coming Philadelphia hoodlums, and how they were managing. He studied their criminal inclinations, totaled their successful scores, and then divided by how often they were arrested and how much prison time they did. His rough calculations, considering such factors as opportunity to work, energy expended, monetary return, and the risk of getting caught, showed burglary to be the optimum choice. Criminal penalties for burglary were relatively light; most convicted burglars were getting sentences of 11 and a half to 23 months. And it would be county time—not "the House" (Eastern State Penitentiary) or one of the other tough, ball-breaking institutions in the state prison system.

As he entered his twenties, Sears was pulling minor jobs throughout the city and quickly learned that the farther he traveled from his own Kensington neighborhood, the better he did. Initially, he and other local second story men followed the Kensington Avenue businessmen—most of whom were Jewish— back to their homes in Oxford Circle, Rhawnhurst, Bell's Corner, and other Northeast Philadelphia neighborhoods. Having learned the shopkeepers' home addresses, they would later return and burglarize the properties when they were unoccupied. However, it soon became apparent that an enterprising burglar could do even better by going just a couple of miles further and crossing into

Bucks and Montgomery Counties, two of the wealthiest in Pennsylvania. In eastern Montgomery County, for example, the lush communities of Elkins Park, Huntingdon Valley, and Rydal were a fertile field of large, posh estates filled with cash, jewelry, furs, and rare coin collections.

"We were viewed as the fat lands in the suburbs," recalls Clark Cutting, former chief of police of Abington Township, who had to contend with Sears and his K&A associates over many years.

"They were hitting the heck out of Abington," says Carl Butzloff, a former Jenkintown police chief. "They went through the walls, doors, anything. It looked like they used sledgehammers to knock down the walls. I never saw anything like it."

Sears, alone or with a partner, could cross the county line, ransack a large suburban home, and be back in a cozy Kensington bar celebrating another successful score in little more than an hour. And the same bit of larceny could go on night after night. And it often did.

Though his forays into the "fat lands" were consistently rewarding, success was not guaranteed. In fact, Willie's repeated successes were making him very unpopular in the area and attracting attention from homeowners and law enforcement authorities. This higher profile had drawbacks. On one occasion, for example, Sears and Herman "Sugar" Cable ran into some particularly astute Abington Township police officers. The episode, covered at length in the media, began when Officers Joseph Dalton and William Wagner spotted an unusually flashy Cadillac parked on the street of a fashionable Rydal neighborhood one wintry evening. Recognizing the license plate as that of a "known burglar," they ordered the vehicle's occupants out of the car, but not before one of them was seen throwing something off into the distance. Suspicious, the patrolmen called for backup and had police check homes in the neighborhood. In short order, police discovered the rear door of Mrs. Kathleen Fiege's home on Baeder Road broken open. The house had been ransacked.

Herb Mooney, former Abington police chief and the township's only detective at the time of the crime, remembers their excitement at finally nailing Sears. "They were doing one or two houses a night," says Mooney. "When we finally got him we scraped dirt and mud off of Willie's shoes and matched it with the dirt and mud found at the burglarized house."

Since Mrs. Fiege was hospitalized at the time, the police brought a relative to inspect the house. It was quickly determined that a diamond ring was missing. Police then returned to the Cadillac and, using flashlights, searched the surrounding terrain on their hands and knees until—just after midnight—they found the ring.

Adding insult to injury, on top of the prison time he now had to serve, Sears was forced to relinquish his brand new Cadillac to authorities. It seems he owed the Internal Revenue Service $18,678 for "illegal loot" he had procured over the preceding few years.

Willie's arrest, the negative publicity, and the loss of his Cadillac were obviously distressing, but it was the life he had chosen and, more important, he was doing well at it—certainly better than the neighborhood guys who had "gone legit" and were still slogging away in a dirty factory somewhere. Unlike them, he was able to purchase fancy cars and expensive suits, attract good-looking women, and buy the house a round of drinks. Getting arrested, though, was definitely a problem. He already had a lengthy string of arrests that covered everything from the discovery of 32 fifths of untaxed whisky in the trunk of his car to a holdup at the point of a gun. The real question for him, however, was how to maximize his return. Considering the risks involved, how could he increase the profit margin? Willie Sears's answer to this riddle would revolutionize the field of burglary and contribute to a lucrative cottage industry for a generation or two of Kensington crooks. In short, he would do more rather than less, but he would do it in a way that would make even corporate efficiency experts take notice.

Willie Sears's game plan was simple. He would adopt a team approach and jack up the number of residential targets on any given evening. Four men in a car would travel to an affluent Philadelphia suburb such as Merion, Rydal, or Yardley, seeking likely marks. When a fashionable home was determined to be unoccupied, three men would get out and the driver would cruise the neighborhood, returning every 10 minutes or so to see if the "swag" and his partners were ready to be collected. Of the three who entered the house, one was stationed by the window as a lookout. The other two searched the house for valuables. With military-like precision, the four-man unit would knock off six, seven, eight houses a night and 20 or more over the course of a weekend. It was a veritable gold mine. As Jimmy Laverty, one of Sears's early associates, boasts, "We transformed burglary into an assembly line process like the operations of Heinz and Ford."

Willie Sears called his program "production work," and the name stuck. For decades to come, prospective associates of Sears and other Kensington burglars would be phoned at home or furtively asked while sharing a beer at a corner bar, "You wanna do some production work tonight?" Invariably the answer was "Sure, why not?"

For some Kensington men, the offer of "doing a few houses" and the possibility of a big score was irresistible. "We'd come home with cash, coin collections, expensive jewelry, and 20 to 22 furs," says Laverty. "It would always be a hell of a haul."

Willie Sears's innovative, systematic approach to burglary incorporated precise timelines and a rigid division of labor. Crew members targeted wealthy neighborhoods, went on the road for three or four days at a time, wore conservative business attire, and avoided weapons or strong-arm tactics. The method paid instant dividends. Crew members were coming back from their jobs with their pockets stuffed with cash, expensive watches, eye-catching tie clips, cuff links, and fancy gold and silver jewelry that they often spread around to the wide-eyed, shapely women cruising the Philly nightclubs. For those in the neighborhood, it was impossible not to notice the windfall of riches and the enticing lifestyle that production work produced.

Don Abrams was one of the early observers and converts. He was soon dressing expensively and was nicknamed "the Dude" by La La McQuoid because of his penchant for $400 suits. "I saw all these guys with money, new cars, and girls," recalls Abrams. "I said to myself, I ain't gonna work for some guy and he makes all the money. So I joined Searsy. He taught me to be a good burglar. I became a second story man. I climbed like a fuckin' monkey. He taught everybody everything." It didn't take long for the Dude's mother to question his lavish lifestyle. The dramatic change in his attire and attitude surprised and troubled her, as well as the legal predicaments it got him into. On one emotional trip to the penitentiary to visit her son, she pointedly asked him, "Why do you steal? You're the only one of my sons that steals." "It's okay, Mom," Don reassured her. "I steal from the rich and give to the poor." "Who's that?" she asked. "Me," said the Dude.

Others began to take notice as well. With fashionable neighborhoods like Chestnut Hill, Haverford, Bryn Mawr, and New Hope showing a startling increase in residential and commercial break-ins, city and suburban police departments were baffled, frustrated, and under pressure to catch the perpetrators. "They wore us out," says Joseph Brophy. A Philadelphia cop for over 35 years and former captain of the Burglary Squad, Brophy had his share of encounters with Sears and his K&A crowd. "Sears was pretty darn slick. He and the gang were well organized. They were damn good burglars." Brophy, who became a cop in 1941, claims that unsophisticated deadbeats and opportunists performed most burglaries before the Kensington crews stepped into it. "Prior to the K&A guys, there was no organization to burglary. Their division-of-labor concept gave each one of them a job, and each one did his part well. It worked."

Herb Mooney, the Abington police chief whose lengthy career covered the same time period as Brophy's, has his own recollections of the K&A Gang. "I had a lot of dealings with those fellows," says Mooney. "They were professionals. They never carried guns, and I never had a problem [a violent confrontation] with them. They would never talk when we caught them, but I never had a problem with them." The gang became such a thorn in the side of Abington authorities that Mooney decided to go the extra mile and undertake some serious research. He asked a Philly detective to take him into the city and give him a tour of

Kensington; he wanted to see where the burglars came from, learn their local haunts, determine who their members were, and hopefully predict their moves. "I went to K&A," says Mooney proudly. As for what he learned, Mooney sternly declares, "They knew me and I knew them."

The information garnered from such forays had little impact on the suburban crime rate. It wouldn't be until later in the decade, when the K&A Gang took their larcenous campaign on the road, spending a week or more at a time in North Jersey, New York, New England, and the Carolinas, that Philly's suburbs could breathe a sigh of relief. In the meantime, Sears continued to perfect his craft and manage his rewarding enterprise.

According to Jimmy Laverty, Sears was the first to recognize the importance of the calendar and the impact of seasonal changes on the success or failure of a residential burglary. "Sears started doing burglaries at five p.m., and most of the work was from October to May," says Laverty. "Jobs were pulled when it was dark outside." Consequently, many burglars worked four, five, and even six nights a week right through the winter. In fact, Laverty says, the burglars' work ethic was so strong that "no one celebrated New Year's Eve. We were all working production." Such diligence enabled many of them to live the good life and take the summers off. Unless, of course, someone at Kellis's, Marty's, or the Bubble Club leaned over and whispered, "You wanna do some production work tonight? I gotta good tip."

Unfortunately for his partners over the years, Willie Sears's creative instincts called for some unusual work rules. One of the more infamous was strip-searching each member of his crew after a successful night's work so that no one could hold back on the take. Bizarre scenes like four or five nude men anxiously counting the night's proceeds around a poker table were not uncommon. Don "the Dude" Abrams was subjected to this humiliating and recurring practice.

"He stripped me balls naked," complains Abrams. "After a score we'd go back to somebody's house or apartment and check out the take. But we'd first have to strip. I mean everything. He'd make us spread our cheeks, look in our ears and mouth. It was like a goddamn medical exam. He'd then go through the pockets and cuffs of our clothes lookin' for any hidden money or jewelry. Christ, it was awful."

The Dude and many others put up with it, though. Sears was "the king of the burglars," the creator of the scam that was making them all rich. More important, the burly Sears was six-one, 220 pounds, and, as Abrams says, "a tough son-of-a-bitch, one of the toughest in the neighborhood." The beatings he dished out were memorable. Some considered him a "dirty fighter," a consummate street fighter who'd "kick you right in the teeth" if he felt it was warranted. Compared with some of the neighborhood bullies, however, "Sears was a gentleman," says

Abrams. "He didn't start fights, but he could end them pretty quick. He could also hang in there with the best of them if he had to. I saw him fight for three hours one time. They'd fight for a while, break for coffee, and then go right back at it again." The bottom line was clear; you didn't want to tangle with Willie Sears.

On one occasion, however, a frustrated Donny Abrams took a chance. He had had enough of Willie Sears and his dictatorial ways. "He'd stay in the car and the other guys would do the house. We were doing all the work. He got lazy." More important, says Abrams, his boss was cheating on the take: "He was beating the balls off me. He'd cut his mother if he could get away with it."

The routine was growing old, fast. Tired of being stripped naked every night while Sears cheated him, Donny Abrams thought of an ingenious way to strike back. He'd try to beat Willie Sears at his own game. "I carefully sliced the lapels of my shirt so there'd be room to slip something in there," he says. "Well, one night we're doin' a joint, and I come across a bunch of wallets in a drawer and they're stuffed with cash. Several wallets had four and five hundred dollars in each. So I shove 10 one hundred dollar bills in the lapel of my shirt and turn the rest in. Later, when we strip and Willie goes through our clothes and pockets, he doesn't find anything. He never thought to check out my shirt collar and lapels."

Donny was elated: he had gotten over on Willie Sears; he had beaten the master thief. Unfortunately, Donny couldn't rejoice alone; he had to share his triumph with others. Eventually, word got back to Sears. The next time they met was on a busy Kensington streetcorner. Willie, his nostrils flaring, the veins in his neck bulging, angrily stepped up to Abrams, grabbed his shirt in his large fists, and tore the lapels and collar right off. He cursed him out and let him know that if he pulled such a stunt again, there would be hell to pay. Don the Dude got the message. He started working with other crews and eventually organized a crew of his own.

OF THE MANY YOUNG MEN in Kensington who learned the burglary trade under the able tutelage of Willie Sears, Effie Burke is arguably the most professional, prolific, and respected. Revered by most of his former associates, Burke is thought by some to have burglarized more homes in America than any other single member of Philadelphia's old Irish Mob. Jackie Johnson, one of Burke's former crew members, proudly boasts, "I guarantee you Effie was in more houses than the next five guys combined." Jimmy Dolan, another Burke associate, agrees, "Effie should be in the Guinness Book of World Records for the most burglaries committed." "No question about it," adds Georgie Smith, "Effie burgled more homes than anybody." Such boasts are striking, not only for the magnitude of the claim, but for the knowledgeable and generally hard-to-impress participants making them: each and every member of the K&A Gang had broken into hundreds of houses across the country.

One of six children born to Steven Burkowski and the former Mary McFadden, Francis Edward Burkowski was a typical youth in pre-war Kensington. He displayed little interest in either school or work. The initials of his first and middle names became "Effie," and his last name also underwent some modification. His mother, an ethnicity-conscious Kensington Irish Catholic, was apparently less than enthralled with her husband's Polish heritage and eventually shortened the family name to the more acceptable and Irish-sounding "Burke."

Having dropped out of North Catholic High School in 1941, Effie Burke knocked around with some equally misguided youths and not surprisingly got himself into some serious trouble. In 1942, for example, he was arrested twice for auto theft. The second episode, in October of that year, garnered newspaper headlines. Effie, already on parole for auto larceny, stole an automobile, took it for a joyride, and then decided to pass two motorcycle policemen at high speed on Roosevelt Boulevard. When he failed to heed their order to pull over, what the newspapers called a "wild chase" proceeded up the 12-lane highway until Burke turned off at Comly Avenue. The pursuit finally ended when Burke failed to negotiate another turn at 50 miles an hour and crashed into a lamppost, snapping it off at the base. Sixteen-year-old Effie was charged with larceny, operating an automobile without the owner's consent, and driving without an operator's license or an owner's card. The joyride resulted in his imprisonment at White Hill.

In order to head off additional delinquency charges and more jail time, young Effie enlisted in the military but was immediately discharged when his age was discovered. When he turned 18, he enlisted once again and eventually saw combat in France and Germany. Discharged a second time at the end of the war, Effie Burke returned home to Kensington still lacking any enthusiasm for either work or an education. Though he was employed on the Pennsylvania Railroad for a short time, the work was uninspiring, difficult, and low paying. Street life, on the other hand, was far more exciting, less demanding physically, and, on good days, considerably more profitable.

In the late forties and early fifties, a number of Kensington crooks specialized in pilfering and cashing stolen checks. Effie, now in his mid-twenties, was attracted to the action and easy money. Joining other local grifters, he began breaking into neighborhood businesses, swiping company checks, and cashing them under various guises throughout the city. In 1952, for example, Effie, joined a floating collection of locals, including Michael Rispo, Donald Hetrick, Harry Stocker, and Thomas McGonagle, who broke into the East Thompson Terminal Corporation, the Culp Manufacturing Corporation, the Alliance Roofing and Installing Company, and the Bell Market, among other businesses. Once in possession of the company checks, they used a variety of ruses—sometimes assisted by an attractive 18-year-old girl from Buffalo, New York—to pass them. Four such burglary/check kiting schemes in 1952 alone resulted in Effie's arrest. In one embarrassing episode, he and his partner, Harry Stocker, were discovered hiding in bed together as the police closed in. Both men were buried under the covers— Effie undressed and Stocker fully clothed—when police broke into the room.

This unimpressive criminal career took a dramatic turn in 1953, when Effie came under the wing of Willie Sears, who was then in the process of revolutionizing the craft of burglary in America. Evidently, their collegial arrangement came none too soon for Burke. As some of the older K&A burglars recall, Effie was a nonentity until he met Sears.

"Effie was never nothing," says Jimmy Laverty authoritatively. "He was a nobody. He always had his head under the hood of a beat-up old Hudson while Searsy was driving a brand new 1953 Olds." Laverty, who also trained under Sears, says that Sears lived with his father for a while on Joyce Street, just down the block from Effie. Every day he'd see Effie "working under the hood, trying to fix this old piece of shit Hudson." Sears finally told Effie, "C'mon and work with me and you'll be able to get rid of that piece of shit." Effie did, says Laverty, and pretty soon Burke was buying a new Cadillac every year. They all were.

Effie spent a good couple years learning the nuances of production work from Willie Sears. The results were dramatic. He was now making more money than he had ever dreamed of, and, best of all, it seemed almost risk-free. He was burglarizing several houses a night, practically every night of the week, with impunity. He would not get pinched again until the end of the decade. (In this respect he did better than his mentor, since the police periodically nabbed Sears.)

Though never a scholar in the classroom, Effie gave his undivided attention to learning the fine points of production work. He had found a curriculum he enjoyed and excelled in. Effie quickly grasped and bought into Sears's multifaceted system: the team approach with a division of labor; dressing like businessmen with briefcases in order to blend into the best neighborhoods; going on the road for a week at a time and doing five to seven houses a night; and the prohibition against carrying weapons. The game plan worked; they were all making money and getting their kicks out of the ballsy capers as well.

Sugar Cable, Harry Stocker, Hughie Breslin, Richie Blaney, Raymond Chalmers, and La La McQuoid were also crew members for Willie Sears at one time or another and part of Kensington's free-floating criminal labor pool. They learned the business from him, eventually started their own crews (as did Effie), and ultimately became key players in the new neighborhood enterprise. But in his own quiet way Effie Burke emerged as a pillar of this cottage industry. In contrast to Sears, who intimidated, abused, and cheated many of his partners, most Kensington burglars sang Effie's praises. "It was a big deal to work for Effie," says Frank Mawhinney. "Everyone made money. He was honest. Everybody always got a fair cut." According to Georgie Smith, "Effie was a real gentleman" and possessed a "wonderful sense of humor."

Jackie Johnson, who spent years with Burke's crew, speaks of Effie's work ethic, competence, and integrity. "You put in a night's work with Effie," says Johnson of Effie's no-nonsense, workman-like approach. "Effie knew the business and was on top of every detail. He rarely put you in a dangerous situation— and if he did, he knew how to get you out of it. He was always the first to break open the front door and enter a house. He didn't centerfield it by sending the dumbest guy in the house first." Johnson also appreciated his crew chief's softer side. "Effie was an easy mark. He was a good guy, an easy touch. He'd always help you out if you were in a jam." Johnson describes the time he was out of commission with a broken leg as a result of a car accident. "Who needs a fuckin' one-legged burglar?" asks Johnson. "But Effie put me to work as the crew's driver." Effie Burke could also be all business, as Johnson found out when he came to work drunk. Effie fired him, kicked him off the crew, and re-placed him with another Kensington second story man. Burglary was too risky an undertaking for stupid blunders.

For Jimmy Dolan, Effie Burke was almost a father figure, a guy who "was generous to a fault, an expert at every phase of the game," and someone who displayed the "rare combination of being both instinctive and highly technical in the burglary field." Dolan points out that the K&A burglars were playing "a dangerous game. You couldn't make too many mistakes. And once you got some notoriety and the police were on to you, it was much worse." Effie Burke, he makes clear, knew how to handle such problems—so well, in fact, that Dolan "never got caught with Effie on a job." This was an incredible achievement, considering the hundreds of nights they worked together and the thousands of jobs they pulled. The difference between Effie Burke and the common burglar, says Dolan, is "the difference between a professor with a Ph.D. and a kid in kindergarten." The educational analogy is not that great a stretch, for Burke was indeed a teacher. "Guys would train under Effie, and after a few years they would go out on their own," says Dolan. They left to start their own crews knowing they had been trained by the best. The FBI concurred. As one special agent said of Burke, "He was the pinnacle of their operation and a teacher as well."

Even members of the general public appreciated Burke's qualities. "Effie was a guy a lot of legitimate people gave tips to" regarding cash-stuffed homes, says Dolan. "They'd come up to him all the time." And probably most important of all, according to Dolan, he was "a real standup guy." Effie would never talk; he would never rat out his partners.

As was true of just about all of the K&A gang members, however, the intense, highballing lifestyle took its toll on Burke's private life. Arlene Burke, who met Effie in 1949 when she was 19, says, "Effie was a good-natured, very easy-going guy" when she first ran in to him one day in a Kensington luncheonette. She was unaware of his prior arrests but definitely attracted to him. His friends and their lifestyle were exciting. "La La, Willie Sears, Richie Blaney, Effie, all of those neighborhood guys didn't want to work or go to school," Arlene says, "but they liked the good life." She was intrigued by all of them, but especially drawn to Effie. "Effie was very good company," recalls Arlene, fondly. "At night we'd go from bar to bar to bar. I was a quiet person, and he was really exciting."

In 1954 the two Kensington youngsters solidified their mutual attraction. Nearly half a century later, Arlene's recollection of Effie's marriage proposal and their whirlwind honeymoon still brings a chuckle. "Effie came over one evening," she recalls, "and excitedly says, 'C'mon, get your things. We're leaving.'" Arlene asked where they were going and Effie matter-of-factly said, "Mexico." Shocked, Arlene asked, "Why Mexico?" "We're going to get married," replied Effie. "C'mon, get your things. We're in a hurry."

"I knew it was crazy," says Arlene, "but I did it anyway. My mother was furious." Sitting outside in a brand new air-conditioned Oldsmobile were Willie Sears and his wife, Dolly. The five-day cross-country adventure culminated in Arlene's seeing her first bullfight. A small wedding ceremony soon followed in Juarez, Mexico. "Willie and Dolly stood up for us," says Arlene. "After the wedding, we all had a filet mignon dinner for a dollar-fifty and drove home."

Arlene quickly became disenchanted with her husband's lifestyle, extracurricular activities, and occasional girlfriends; K&A burglars were not paternal, comforting, stay-at-home types. Arlene's sister, Carole, maintained a three-decade-long friendship with Effie Burke and speaks highly of his sense of humor and fair play, but admits, "He wasn't a very good father or husband. He had a succession of girlfriends" who ruined his marriage. "My husband," says Carole, "thought Effie was Louderback Moving and Storage 'cause he was moving so often."

"Most of the time," says Arlene, "I had no idea what he was up to." News of her husband's criminal misadventures arrived in various forms. Sometimes it was the sound of police knocking on the door; on other occasions it might be an acquaintance announcing that Effie was in danger and needed help. "One night," she recalls, "a friend of Effie's came over" and ordered her to get dressed. "'Effie got caught in a house and we need to pick him up before the cops catch him. He's stuck in the woods in Jersey somewhere and needs a ride.' I had to get dressed and go with this guy. We had to look like a normal couple just out for a quiet evening drive in the country." Such impromptu excursions combined with Effie's bar-hopping and womanizing took their toll. "We separated four or five times during the next six years," says Arlene, "and I left for good in 1960." Though the couple divorced in 1964, FBI agents looking for information continued to pay her uninvited visits.

Though his marriage was crumbling, Effie's professional career was exceedingly successful. His reputation as a shrewd master burglar, a moneymaker who was rarely, if ever, caught in the act by police, was growing quickly. As the mid-fifties arrived and he broke off from Willie Sears to form his own crew, it gradually became a sign of status to work with Effie Burke. "He had a knack for knowing what house to hit," says Jimmy Laverty. "He wouldn't leave a house until money or jewelry was found." Effie had quietly but rapidly moved to the front of the class and placed his own stamp of excellence on the art of production work.

Yet the risks of his chosen profession took their toll on him, as they did on most burglars. Burglary was a crime that could land you in jail. In addition, a burglar could never be sure what he was going to find when he broke into someone's home. He could walk into a veritable gold mine or the barrel of a shotgun. And the latter happened just often enough to legitimize a thief's worst fears. The specter of such discomforting scenarios caused universal dyspepsia in the burglar community, Effie included.

"Effie had really bad nerves," says Laverty. "He was a nervous person." So nervous, in fact, that he frequently left an unusual and distinctive landmark at the scene of the crime. "Effie would crap on the lawn or the sidewalk alongside the house he was burglarizing," says Laverty. This bizarre habit allowed police to tell who had burglarized a home as soon as they came upon (or stepped in) the evidence. "We knew it was Effie's crew," snickers retired Philly detective John Del Carlino, "when we investigated a burglary scene and heard one of our guys yell, 'Damn it. It's that Polack again,' while cleaning off his shoes."

Although professional burglars are usually thought to have nerves of steel and icicles for veins, a professional, too, could have an anxiety attack while ransacking a house. As Donnie Abrams flatly states, "All burglars got bad nerves." Taking the time to visit an unfamiliar home's bathroom was a luxury a bona fide burglar couldn't afford, especially if he was the lookout man stationed by a first floor window. Such constraints produced some humorous incidents, which K&A burglars still recall with delight. Jimmy Laverty, for example, tells the story of lookout man Harry Stocker, whose nerves got the better of him while he stealthily peered out the window. As the minutes slowly ticked by, he had an uncontrollable urge to defecate. Unable to leave his critical perch by the window, "Stocker took a shit in a large fish bowl near the window and used fine lace that was set on the dinner table to wipe his ass." When the searchers had completed their haul they gathered up their relieved lookout man and exited the house, but not before one of them caught sight of a strange dark object floating in the fish tank. "Jesus Christ," exclaimed the startled burglar, "look at the size of that goddamn whale in the fish bowl."

5. Road Companies, Brutes, and Safecrackers

The three of us—me, Jackie, and John L.—are on the road doing production work in an upscale, ritzy neighborhood that's loaded with big homes and fancy mansions. But oddly enough, on that particular night we're doing a high-rise apartment building. It's the only one in the area. Most of the guys didn't really like doing high-rise work because there's too many people around and, more importantly, the difficulty in getting out of the place if the cops catch wind of ya. But we had gotten a tip on a doctor who lived there.

Anyway, we're doing this apartment and it's near the bank of elevators, which is good so we can hear if anybody is coming. We get in with no trouble and start going through the place, grabbing anything that looks of value—cash, jewelry, silverware—and then Jack whispers, "Hold it! I hear the elevator." Well, we all figure this is a 10 or 12 story building; what are the chances of somebody stopping at this floor? Don't you know, the damn elevator stops at the floor we're working on and we hear a couple people get off—a man and a woman. So we're looking at each other, trying to reassure ourselves there's no way in hell they're coming to the apartment we just cleaned out. We're listening to them walk down the hall, the side of the building we're on, unfortunately, and hope they keep going right past the apartment door me, Jack, and John L. are hiding behind. Ain't it our goddamn luck, but they stop right at our door. It's their goddamn apartment we just emptied.

We hear the guy going for his keys and putting it in the lock, but then he stops. He knows something is wrong, something doesn't feel right. Well, we ain't even breathing at this point and look at each other like, can it get any worse? We're wondering, is this guy armed? Are we gonna have to hurt somebody here?

He suddenly pushes the door open, but all we see is his hand and arm, and believe me the guy musta been a big son-of-a-bitch because his hand was huge. Right away I'm thinking somebody is gonna get hurt. Jackie and I are little guys, but John L. is pretty good size and can handle himself in a scuffle. No sooner is the thought outta my mind when the guy steps around the door, and John L. immediately gives him a forearm shiver to the throat that clears the guy right off his feet, pins him against the wall, and then drops him to the floor. His wife or girlfriend starts screaming her head off, and we grab our things and tear ass outta there. We got away, but the people in the building probably got a pretty good scare. I never did like doing apartment buildings. I did them, but they weren't one of my favorites.   —GEORGE "JUNIOR" SMITH

THEY WERE ALMOST ALL there in Kensington that morning: the smooth scam artists, the ballsy burglars, the crafty "safe" men, the hardened gunmen who specialized in "walk-ins." They were there to say a last goodbye to one of their own. The normally unruly, rough-hewn characters who survived on a fluid combination of wits, nerve, and societal indifference had gathered at Gniewek's Funeral Parlor for a melancholy farewell to a neighborhood guy, a beloved member of their criminal fraternity who had finally succumbed to a self-destructive lifestyle and a long battle with lung cancer.

Danny Gundaker, a consummate burglar, loyal partner, and trusted friend, was making one last journey. The men who had shared his zest for life (and the attraction of an unoccupied home) assembled in small groups in the building's foyer and on the pavement outside, recalling raucous misadventures, wild parties, and outrageous incidents. They recounted the time Danny was shot in the face and shoulder by police in Florida during a burglary gone bad, the time Danny broke both his ankles jumping off a roof while trying to escape from a county jail in Maryland, and the time he ran into a backyard clothesline while fleeing the police and tore the scalp off his head. Despite his recurring misfortunes, Danny was "a class act," a "standup guy," fearless, with "balls like ingots." They were all going to miss him.

After each of the nearly three dozen mourners had paid his last respects to Gundaker, and just before they closed the casket, two formidable-looking men came forward and placed on top of the smartly dressed corpse a few objects: a three-foot-long brute, a pair of burglar's gloves, and a set of home alarm turnoff keys. A few of the mourners may have missed the significance of the gesture, but most of those gathered readily understood, smiled, and nodded. They didn't know for sure where their friend Danny Gundaker was headed, but they seemed to agree that wherever his journey ended, he'd probably feel more comfortable with the tools of his trade at his side. As they all knew, Danny was all business as a burglar. And a true professional never wanted to be caught unprepared when an attractive opportunity presented itself.

One night we're doin' a bowling alley up on Roosevelt Boulevard and Adams Avenue. We're inside and decide we're gonna have to burn the safe, which takes a little time and casts off a good bit of light. We're all tense, tryin' to be as quiet and inconspicuous as possible, when all of a sudden there's a big bang like a goddamn explosion. It scares the shit out of everybody, and we all duck for cover and try to figure out what the hell happened. When we don't hear any sirens or see any cops come barging in, we look out into the middle of the building where all the dust and debris seem to be, and there's a guy lying on one of the bowling lanes moaning his head off. Once we realize it ain't the cops, we go over to see what the hell all the commotion is about. We get on the eighth or ninth lane, put our flashlights on the guy moaning in pain and the big hole that's now in the ceiling of the joint. It turns out the guy flat on his back is Steve Zagnojney. He's another burglar from the neighborhood, and we always called him Steve the Mechanic. He's screaming that he broke his leg when he fell through the roof and needs a doctor bad. What could we do? We had to forget about burning the safe and took Steve to Frankford Hospital. But that's what it was like in those days. While we're tryin' to open a safe and make a few bucks, another Kensington crew decides to burglarize the same damn bowling alley. But one of their guys, Steve the Mechanic, who goes about six-two, 250 pounds, falls through the roof while we're burnin' the safe. None of us made any money that night.   —JOHNNY BOGGS

THEY WEREN'T OFF the Delta jetliner more than a few seconds before Junior stopped at a concourse newsstand and purchased a copy of the *Houston Chronicle* and a map of the city. He was never one to waste time when working: the newspaper and map took priority over both a necessary pit stop in the men's room after the long flight and a cold beer at an airport restaurant. Junior and his three friends were in Texas on business; some things, especially a refreshing libation, could wait.

They traveled light. There was little baggage: Tommy's large suitcase and a small overnight bag for each crew member. By the time they had hailed a taxi and were on their way to a nearby motel, Junior had pretty much decided on the location of the evening's activities by scanning the *Chronicle*'s Real Estate section for quarter- and half-million-dollar properties. All that remained was to cross-check that location against the addresses of area synagogues and ritzy country clubs in the motel's telephone directory—a match and they'd be on their way.

While Junior and Bruce did their research in a Ramada Inn motel room, Tommy and Mickie went about their business; after years of working together, they had the operation down like clockwork. They first took a taxi to the nearest Avis car rental agency and signed for two mid-sized automobiles. Tommy drove one car back to the motel and immediately began installing the police scanners, walkie-talkies, and batteries he had brought with him from Philadelphia. Mickie took the second car to a nearby mall in search of a Sears or a large automotive shop. When she returned with three pairs of gloves and a collection of chisels, pliers, crowbars, flashlights, and short-handled sledgehammers, Tommy installed the same electronic gadgetry in the second car.

Their assignments complete, the four Philadelphians decided to take a ride. It was their first trip to South Texas and they were interested in seeing some of the local sights, particularly an area called the Village which the *Chronicle* declared one of the most beautiful and affluent sections of Harris County. After a brief ride along Houston's North Freeway, they turned off the highway, noticed the swift decline in office buildings, strip malls, and vehicular traffic, and began navigating through open country roads bordering expansive brown fields. Soon they were driving through quiet, attractive neighborhoods with stately homes surrounded by lush, green grass, well-tended shrubs, and the occasional gazebo and faux wishing well. Impressive, opulent mansions became more frequent, and Cadillacs, Lincolns, and sporty foreign models like Jaguars filled the driveways. The place reeked of money. Though no one mentioned it, each crew member focused on those homes displaying two items the average tourist would no doubt have overlooked: a small mezuzah and an equally small key-controlled alarm mechanism near the front door.

"I think we did okay," said Bruce to no one in particular. "This place looks like my kind of town."

"Yeah," replied Junior, "I think we're gonna be fat tonight."

After driving slowly through the area for another 10 minutes, they returned to their motel. Second story work wasn't kid's play. It was damn serious stuff, demanding more than a modicum of physical ability and nerves of steel. Though burglary was a year-round activity, those frigid January nights when fingers and toes went numb and noses and eyes ran uncontrollably were sheer hell for the Philly-based crew. At those painful times, Florida and the other Sunbelt states appeared decidedly more inviting. That was why they were now along the Texas Gulf Coast and not trudging through the snow in Newport, Greenwich, or Scarsdale. If things went well later that night, Houston might get placed right up there with their favorite winter haunts such as Miami, Tampa, and Saint Pete.

Back at the Ramada Inn, they needed to kill a couple of hours while waiting for nightfall. Mickie luxuriated in a warm bubble bath while Junior and Tommy played a few hands of poker. Bruce contented himself with a crime novel he had swiped from an airport newsstand. Finally, anxious to go to work, Junior threw the playing cards into the trash and told the crew that it was time to get dressed. The three men were attired in their customary business suits; Mickie wore a gray pantsuit with contrasting white blouse and modest bow. As always, a black wig completed her costume. With Junior and Mickie in one car and Tommy and Bruce in the other, they drove to the closest restaurant and had a light meal. Other than Mickie's comment on the number of people wearing Stetson hats and cowboy boots and Junior's reminder to Tommy to go easy on the beer, conversation was practically nonexistent.

Back in the cars, they promptly headed for the wealthy Houston suburb known as the Village. Once in the target area, they slowly traveled along Pine Forrest, Hunters Trail, and Country Squire Roads, all the while noting apparently unoccupied homes, particularly those adorned with a tiny red light by the front door. Junior finally decided that a spot along Coach Road would be the best place to park the second (or "drop") vehicle. With the whole crew in the main car, they were now ready to strike.

In a matter of minutes and with little debate, the foursome decided on a handsome three story colonial at 5927 Pine Forrest Road as the evening's first piece of work. Junior was let out of the car, walked up the driveway, and rang the doorbell. After a few seconds he could be heard knocking on the front door, and a few seconds after that he was seen moving to the rear of the structure. When he returned to the front door, he gave his partners the thumbs-up sign, and Bruce and Tommy—the latter with walkie-talkie in hand—promptly joined him. Mickie took the wheel, turned on the communications equipment, and slowly drove off. The three men would be in the house less than 15 minutes, but it was a highly profitable 15 minutes.

Among the items taken were 10 albums containing Graf Zeppelin and other early airmail stamps, as well as early plate locks; an enormous coin collection including full mint sets for a half-dozen different years and 10,000 pennies, many dating back to the Civil War; silver goblets; two diamond tie tacks; a Rolex watch; and several pieces of expensive jewelry. The owner, more than a little stunned that the thieves had gotten around his sophisticated alarm system, would later inform the FBI that the items taken were worth well over $50,000.

After Mickie was notified that the job was complete, the goods were transferred to the drop car, and Mickie drove the trio to back to Pine Forrest Road, where they entered and cleaned out another home. They walked out with 12 demitasse and 12 silver bouillon spoons, a four-piece sterling silver Royal Danish serving set, 10 pairs of gold earrings, a platinum necklace topped off with a two-and-one-half carat diamond, a gold watch with six diamonds, two mink stoles, and more.

After a quick trip back to the drop car, Mickie then took the men to 314 Hunters Trail, where they repeated the drill despite the state-of-the-art

Westinghouse alarm system with a backup directly wired to the Village Police Department.

The next stops were 1125 North Country Squire Road (cash, jewelry, silverware, and several mink coats) and 815 Creek Woodway (a heart-shaped platinum diamond band encrusted with five diamonds, a gold watch with 16 rubies and nine diamonds, a gold ring with two center diamonds, a pair of gold earrings inlaid with a diamond and pearl, and, for good measure, a tourmaline mink jacket and matching hat).

The trunks of both cars were now filled with every imaginable expensive item, from Hummel figurines and silver candelabra to fine jewelry and mink coats, not to mention the two hundred pounds of coins that stressed the automobile's suspension system. In a little less than two hours, Junior Kripplebauer, his wife, Mickie, Tommy Seher, and Bruce Agnew had broken into four homes, cleaned out at least a quarter-million dollars worth of goods, and administered a long-lasting trauma to the community's psyche. For this K&A crew, it was just an average night's work.

Their work, of course, was production work, a home burglary system that had been perfected over two decades and was still pulverizing the nation well into the late 1970s.

LOCAL AND STATE POLICE officials were pinballing between embarrassment, frustration, and annoyance. It was the summer of 1959, and communities in central Pennsylvania's hard-coal region were being ravaged by an astute and crafty group of burglars who appeared out of thin air, entered homes and businesses at will, avoided detection, and left law enforcement authorities slack-jawed and mystified. Out of nowhere, it seemed, residents of Lycoming, Clinton, Berks, Union, and Columbia Counties were being besieged as if a plague of locusts had descended on them. From the homes of prominent doctors to commercial cattle dairies, citizens all over the region were caught in the undertow.

Weeks went by before the first lead surfaced: a description of a suspicious automobile and unfamiliar, well-dressed men driving through the countryside. Finally, in early July, Pennsylvania state police made an arrest in a Williamsport motel room and confiscated several thousand dollars in cash, a rare coin collection, an assortment of expensive jewelry, and "a complete set of burglary tools." But their catch was less impressive—at least numerically—than the army they had expected to find. Instead, it turned out to be a particularly industrious "road company of four Philadelphia criminals."

It was no ordinary road company, however. It was a crew of supremely gifted and accomplished burglars: Hughie Breslin, 28; Jimmy Laverty, 27; Harry Stocker, 36; and Effie Burkowski, 33. Though the distraught victims would probably have taken little solace from the fact even if they had known it at the time, their central Pennsylvania communities had been pillaged by the best. The four Kensington burglars were the equivalent of Ruth and Gehrig's '27 Yankees in the world of burglardom.

Pennsylvania's heartland was by no means the only recipient of the K&A Gang's affection. As Jimmy Laverty says, "From the earliest days, we did jobs outside the city." "Let's go find some virgin territory" seems to have been a constant refrain of the gang members.

Initially, says John McManus, the novice Irish burglars followed the Jewish businessmen of Kensington Avenue back to their homes in Northeast Philadelphia and suburban Cheltenham. "We'd see a guy get in his Cadillac after closing his shop and follow him back to his house. We didn't have nothing against the Jews, but the Jews had a lot and we didn't have anything." The abundance of "gold, diamonds, and cash" discovered in Jewish residential targets would be the centerpiece of the gang's livelihood for many years to come.

It wasn't long before affluent communities such as Chestnut Hill in Northwest Philadelphia, Elkins Park and Rydal north of the city, and Haverford, Bryn Mawr, and Radnor along the well-to-do Main Line were also receiving the burglars' attention. "I've probably been in every house in Chestnut Hill," says Jackie Johnson matter-of-factly. Others had their own favorite hunting grounds. "La La (McQuoid) loved the Main Line," recalls Johnson. "He didn't like to travel too far."

Few others, however, had such reservations. "We'd go out on the road for a few days or a week," says Ray Mann, "and do pretty damn well." In fact, year after year more and more road companies were coming out of Kensington and traveling the new superhighways and the bucolic back roads of America, searching for "virgin territory" in some remote, pastoral corner of New England or, just a stone's throw away, across the Delaware River. "New Jersey was made for burglars," says Jimmy Laverty. "You could drive down the street of most neighborhoods and almost tell how the job would go and if it was worth it by how the houses were lit and the way the shrubs were cut." Cherry Hill, Haddonfield, Moorestown, Princeton, and other Jersey bedroom communities soon became regular haunts of K&A gang members. Some crews ventured up into Pennsylvania's Lehigh Valley and beyond, visiting Bethlehem, Allentown, Wilkes-Barre, Hazleton, and Scranton, while others headed west along the Pennsy Turnpike to Lancaster, Johnstown, and Pittsburgh.

During the 1950s, as Sears, Burke, Breslin, Laverty, McQuoid, Stocker, and company became more proficient in their chosen profession, their excursions stretched to distant locales as far west as Ohio and up and down the East Coast, from plush Connecticut suburbs to Virginia tidewater estates. But wealthy towns in North Jersey and Long Island became "favorite areas" for most Kensington crews. Jimmy Laverty, for example, was especially fond of the Oranges, Teaneck, and Tenafly in New Jersey and ritzy Long Island towns like Sag Harbor, Oyster Bay, and East Hampton.

"We were doing good in Pennsylvania," says Laverty, "but New York was a whole other story. There was little jewelry in Hazleton, Scranton, and Wilkes-Barre. It was mostly cash. How many opera houses do you have up there? Any woman up there with a nice ring probably never takes it off. In New York there'd be $15,000 in cash lying around a house, plus a safe with more cash and all sorts of fine jewelry, expensive artwork, and silverware. The New York bedroom communities were a wealth of stuff. We hit every town of consequence up there." Laverty was not alone in his fondness for the area. "We really hit Long Island," says Fancy Frank Mawhinney. "We'd look for a house that looked unoccupied and that was it." Westchester, Scarsdale, the Hamptons, and many other affluent New York towns soon became the Promised Land for a growing number of K&A road companies.

For Donnie Johnstone, a Kensington boy who learned the business in the fifties from the likes of Sears, Effie, and Jimmy Laverty, there was a comforting regimentation about the business. "We'd leave on a Wednesday and come back on Sunday," says Johnstone. "First we'd find a motel to stash our stuff and then go out and do two or three houses in a row and then move to another neighborhood and do two or three more. You'd just keep driving until you found a nice neighborhood. That was production work. Usually we'd eat dinner at three in the afternoon and then start doing production work at 4:30. We were usually done and back at a bar by nine."

K&A burglary teams quickly learned to home in on elite neighborhoods, drawn by "well-known private country clubs that were usually surrounded by large, wealthy homes," Johnstone recalls. Street smarts, experience, and a ruthless entrepreneurial spirit contributed to a sound and fruitful geographic targeting system. "We'd go into a town," says Jimmy Laverty, "and look up the private country clubs in a phone book. Most of the homes around these fancy clubs belonged to doctors. And the doctors were predominantly Jewish. All of them had cash."

"Jewish neighborhoods were good," says Jimmy Dolan. "Jewish women had to have jewelry. They loved to show their jewelry off." For many years, according to Dolan, "jewelry was the meat of the game."

Whether the goal was cash, jewelry, coin collections, or artwork, Jewish residences were considered a bonus. An impressive home with a manicured lawn and well-tended shrubs situated in an upscale neighborhood was always inviting. Add a mezuzah on the doorframe, and the Philly crews found it irresistible. "My eyes would light up and my heart would beat a little faster when I went up to the house to see if anybody was home and saw that mezuzah on the door," says Johnny Boggs. He'd curl his index finger in the crude shape of a hooked nose to signal to his partners in the car that the house belonged to Jews.

To a man, however, the gang members insist that their voracious appetite for burglarizing Jewish households had less to do with anti-Semitism than with practical financial concerns. They viewed themselves as businessmen looking for the best return on their labor. "That's where the money was," as con man and prison escape artist Willie Sutton is said to have replied when asked why he robbed banks. For the K&A burglars, Jewish homes contained the cash, jewelry, furs, expensive silverware, and other items of value they were looking for. Years of persistent, dedicated effort across large swathes of the nation had confirmed who had the goods.

"The worst thing we could see when we entered a home," says 80-year-old Billy McClurg, "was a crucifix on the wall. We immediately knew there wouldn't be anything of value to steal. The worst thing you could smell upon entering a house was wine. Italians may have money, but many of them don't keep it in the house." Known as "Billy Blue" to all his confederates, McClurg says the crews he worked with targeted "Jewish neighborhoods" almost exclusively. "We'd drive up to a town like Scranton or someplace in upstate New York and look in the phone book for Jewish synagogues. Those were the neighborhoods we wanted. That's where the money was."

In fact, some gang members sound like demographers or sociologists. German families," according to Jimmy Laverty, "had beautiful homes and substantial bank statements, but they weren't flashy and had little jewelry. They never left money lying around the house. You'll never get 10 cents out of a German's house." The homes of "gentiles" in general were less attractive to the burglary community. "She's got a diamond she's never taken off and the guy gets paid by check," says Laverty bluntly. Lawyers, surprisingly, were equally unappealing. They had all their "money invested. It was never in their house." For Laverty, as well as most of his accomplices, the homes of Jews and some Italians were the most rewarding. "They're flashy people and love jewelry. They had the money."

"Most gentiles didn't have too much," adds Donnie Johnstone. "But when you saw a mezuzah on a door, it meant a half a score at least and possibly a home run." Most of the old Kensington burglars flatly admit that Jewish homes were the core of their business, and some claim mezuzah-adorned properties represented 90 percent of their trade. "Hell, we'd cross over into Jersey," says Donnie Abrams, "get a phone book and look up the fucking Jews. And that's where we went. We'd look up all the Jews, see a mezuzah on the door, and hit 'em."

WITH THE EXCEPTION of carpenters and mechanics accustomed to working on heavy machinery, most people encountering a #9714 screwdriver might mistake it for a simple household implement bulked up by steroids. In actuality, they have come upon one of the most valuable pieces—arguably the centerpiece—of a Kensington burglar's weighty arsenal. The sturdy steel screwdriver, three feet long, three-quarters of an inch thick, was as indispensable to the Kensington burglar as a typewriter was to an author or a calculator to an accountant. Nicknamed "the brute," the hefty crowbar-like hunk of metal was an all-purpose device that could, for starters, shatter a well-built door lock (assuming that the burglars didn't already have the keys to it).

"It was the basic tool of a burglar," says Jimmy Dolan, "and one store owner got rich selling them." "We used to buy five or 10 at a time," recalls Jackie Johnson. "That was a key piece of the equipment," adds Donnie Johnstone. "Not many doors could stand up to it."

Not every hardware store bothered to carry the ominous-looking screwdriver, which could easily be mistaken for a relic of the Crusades. However, for one automotive parts shop on Kensington Avenue in the 1950s and 1960s, the #9714 screwdriver was one of the most popular items.

"We had a run on them back then," recalls Jay Tipton, who began working at Morris Auto in 1953. "Our regular mechanics who came into the store never bought them, just members of the K&A Gang." At the time Tipton didn't know the "articulate, clean-cut" customers who appeared fixated on the unusual tool, but one day in the early sixties a couple of city detectives came into the store to ask about it. "The cops said that burglars were leaving the tools at the scene of the crime and asked if we could identify any of them," says Tipton. "They had mug shots of people and I did recognize some of them." Once Eugene Steinberg, the store's owner, realized how the tools were being used, he told his staff "not to purchase the 9714 any more. It was a good seller," says Tipton, "but the boss said not to order it any more."

In fact, a professional burglar's bag contained an array of nifty tools and gadgets: gloves, flashlight, short-handled sledgehammer, crowbar, punch, L-shaped pliers, rattail files, sandpaper, and an assortment of chisels and keys. Later, walkie-talkies, police scanners, power drills, and acetylene torches would come into play. But for the 30-odd years the K&A Gang functioned, the brute was a particular favorite. In most cases, it was the first piece of equipment a burglar used on a piece of real estate. Generally, once a road crew had determined that a house was unoccupied, one of the team would go up to the front door and firmly wedge the brute between the lock and the doorframe. Within seconds of leaning on it, he would hear cracking; soon he could see wood splitting as the lock was torn away from both the door and the frame. As Donnie Johnston says, very few "doors could stand up to it."

Once inside, the men would assume their positions. As adrenaline coursed through their veins and the anticipation built, the searchers went about their individual assignments. Given a choice, most crew members would have preferred the more glamorous (and usually more rewarding) job of searcher, especially the one who had the honor of hitting the master bedroom. The expectation of discovering a cash-stuffed wallet, an envelope filled with hundred-dollar bills, a jewelry box filled with diamond brooches, or a gem-laden necklace would send anyone's heartbeat racing, let alone a professional thief's. Each home, each bedroom, each chest of drawers, each jewelry box was a new heart-thumping adventure. As Jimmy Dolan says, "The excitement of it all was tremendous. It was incredible. You never knew what to expect."

For the K&A burglar, the master bedroom was the equivalent of King Tut's tomb or a buccaneer's buried treasure—all sorts of good things were hidden there. It was where they hoped to make a big score, to get rich. "Ninety percent of the time the money could be found in the master bedroom," says Laverty. "People are creatures of habit. They love to be near their money—in the closet, the wall safe, in back of a drawer, under the mattress. But almost always in the bedroom."

Once on the verge of making the big score, like fortune seekers caught up in the nineteenth-century California Gold Rush, the Irish burglars displayed their individuality, their own personal treasure-hunting styles. Just as some 49ers tunneled deep into the mountains for gold while others sat by a stream and methodically panned for it, some K&A men were heavy-handed and destroyed the homes they rummaged through while others had a more delicate touch and tried to show some consideration for their victim's property. Jimmy Laverty, for instance, prided himself on being a thoughtful, "meticulous person." Ninety percent of his victims, he claims, "never even knew their place had been robbed. Most didn't realize until they looked for a ring or favorite brooch a few days later."

Other burglars, he says, were just interested in finding the spoils and getting out with the goods. "Effie pulled drawers open and dumped them on the bed. Everything got thrown, tossed, and trashed when Effie worked. It looked like a cyclone had hit the house. When I went through a place," says Laverty proudly, "there was never a mess." Colder-hearted practitioners would argue that the goal was to get as much as you could as quickly as you could. Neither the homeowners nor the cops were giving out merit points for neatness.

All the Kensington burglary crews were conscientious about weapons, however. No one was to carry a gun while doing production work, and a weapon discovered during the course of a job was to be discarded, preferably where no one could find it. "First thing," says Jimmy Laverty, "I would open the night table drawer, and if I found a gun there, I'd take it and throw it in the toilet tank. You didn't want the owner coming home and getting to the gun while you're in there. No one wanted trouble or a shootout."

This became a cardinal rule of the gang. "We never carried a gun," says Donnie Abrams. "If you found one while on a job, then you'd immediately hide it if you had any brains. You'd hide it behind a couch, a toilet, anywhere." Even a decade later the rule was still in effect. Jimmy Dolan, an Effie Burke recruit in the sixties, says, "It was automatic; you never carried a gun. You do and it opens all kinds of fucking doors; maybe you'll use it, maybe you'll just get more fucking time for carrying it. There was no good reason to be carrying a gun. We wanted to make money and enjoy ourselves. We never wanted to hurt anybody. We wanted to spend money, but not get anybody hurt."

An additional reason for the gang's disdain for weapons came from their growing understanding of the nuances of the criminal justice system. Getting caught with a gun meant stiffer penalties. As Jackie Johnson says, "As long as no one got hurt, you were okay and a lawyer could do something for you." "You didn't carry a gun because you were fairly sure that no one was home," brags another burglar. "You could do a hundred burglaries and you'd only get 11 and a half to 23 months back then."

The gang's "no weapon rule" became well known in the law enforcement community and was much appreciated by street cops. Though Philly and sub-urban police were being run ragged by Kensington's Irish Mob in the 1950s, they learned that its *modus operandi* excluded any form of violence. "The guys never had a gun," says John Del Carlino, a city detective who pursued the K&A Gang for over two decades. "They didn't want to hurt anybody." In fact, it wasn't unusual for the first police officers who arrived at a burglarized home to relax and holster their revolvers when they realized it was a K&A job. They knew they were dealing with the cream of the city's crop of burglars: the place was probably cleaned out, but they could be reasonably sure that no one had been hurt in the process.

Another tenet of production work that served the gang well over the years was dressing for success. Everyone, whether he was the driver who never left the car or the lookout man stuck by a window, had to be appropriately attired, preferably in a business suit. It was important to blend into the neighborhoods they were pillaging. Normal street clothes or the factory work outfits that were so common in Kensington would have been spectacularly conspicuous in upscale Merion, Scarsdale, and Sag Harbor.

Burglary garb as projected on cinema screens around the country was similarly disdained. Carole Heidinger recalls the time Effie Burke was about to take a crew on the road and a new man he was breaking in "came dressed in a black turtleneck sweater and black slacks like a Hollywood movie." Effie took one look at the guy and "rolled on the floor laughing." Real burglars—K&A burglars—were professionals, and looked like professionals.

"We were always well dressed," says Jimmy Dolan. "We looked fuckin' right. We wore business suits and even carried briefcases." "You never wore dungarees in case you got stopped," says Georgie Smith. "We wore top-notch suits. I bought expensive Botany 500 suits." "We always worked in suits and ties," adds Donnie Johnstone. "We had to look well dressed and respectable."

The ploy usually worked. A nattily attired businessman with briefcase in hand was unlikely to draw any attention walking up to a fashionable home. Why would a casual observer suspect that the well-dressed gentleman at the front door—possibly an insurance salesman or business associate—was actually the point man for an experienced, aggressive criminal organization that had just ripped off the more valuable possessions from a half-dozen families in the neighborhood?

Despite the crews' fealty to the tenets of production work, however, they were studiously opposed to any more rules or regulations than necessary and rejected the notion of modeling themselves after the other ethnic crime faction in town—the Mafia. In fact, the ever-growing number of Kensington burglary teams were nothing more than a loose confederation of mostly Irish, blue collar, high school dropouts who looked at production work as a career alternative to life as a roofer, factory worker, or cop. There was never any interest in building a rigid, hierarchical outfit as the Italians had done. Kensington Irishmen hated bosses. Installing an all-powerful Angelo Bruno–type figurehead as the *capo di tutti capi* ("boss of all bosses") of the K&A Gang would have been nearly impossible. There were crew chiefs like Willie Sears, Effie Burke, John Berkery, and Junior Kripplebauer who knew the score and had lots of experience, but an elaborate chain of command with a single overlord was against their nature. They weren't interested in constructing a strict, paramilitary-type operation where orders were given and followed to the letter. K&A men were more free-flowing and democratic. Each crew member had a vote and could veto a job if he chose to. Freedom and organizational fluidity appealed to their carefree, relaxed work ethic. If the Mafia was the model for the traditional organized crime operation, Kensington second story men were quite content to represent disorganized crime.

"WE'D WATCH THOSE MOVIES where a guy wearing a stethoscope was trying to open a safe and we'd just laugh. We knew it was ridiculous. Those of us doin' the real thing on a daily basis knew it was bullshit. It was Hollywood's version of reality. Somebody out there started that crap about burglars using stethoscopes and they never changed it. We just laughed."

Donnie Johnstone's scorn for the Hollywood safecracker gingerly turning the combination lock as he listens for mechanical levers and shifting pins is fairly representative. If a K&A burglar ever handled a physician's stethoscope, it was only because he had just rifled a doctor's home and lifted the diagnostic device as a toy for one of his children. The thieves were searching for cash, coin collections, jewelry, and furs. The discovery of a safe in a commercial or residential property only whetted their appetites. The goal was to get into it as quickly as possible. Stethoscopes were of no value to high school dropouts attacking a ponderous, 5,000-pound safe. Their game plan rested more on muscle and persistence than on faint sounds detected with supersensitive medical instruments. For real, everyday safecrackers, a sturdy chisel, a star punch, a #9714 screwdriver, and a short-handled sledgehammer went a whole lot further than any flimsy listening device.

According to Jimmy Dolan, Hollywood's stealthy, ear-to-the-safe burglar was dated at best and total baloney at worst. It was the "early safes from the 1920s, '30s and '40s that you could hear a tumbler drop," says Dolan, "but the precision safes made in later years made it near impossible to hear or detect anything. You would need space-age equipment." Dolan learned the business from the best street burglars in the country, and if they had anything in hand, it was a pair of work gloves and a brute. They'd also have a severe backache from hauling the heavy steel and concrete box to a friendly garage or deserted field where they could really get at it.

Traditionally, burglars with a specialty in cracking safes were called "yeggs" or "yeggmen," a nineteenth-century term of disputed origin that is all but forgotten today. Some etymologists attribute the word to the name of the first burglar to use nitroglycerin on a safe. Others claim it is of gypsy, Chinese, or German derivation, referring to "chief thief," "beggar," or "hunter," respectively. Many yeggmen, posing as either hobos or sophisticated dandies, rode the rails during the last quarter of the nineteenth century and specialized in robbing banks in remote but wealthy western towns. Safecracking methodologies varied. Some yeggs used cumbersome but relatively silent jackscrews to crack open a safe, while others gravitated to the dicier proposition of blowing a safe with dynamite or nitro. Though the latter would usually get the job done, the volatile mixture of table salt, sodium bicarbonate, distilled water, glycerin, and nitric and sulfuric acids could ignite unexpectedly and blow off one's hands and face.

According to experienced members of the K&A Gang, there were only so many practical ways to open a safe, and none of them incorporated the use of delicate medical equipment or unstable chemical compounds. A construction worker's tool kit or a demolition man's arsenal of gadgets was considerably closer to what Kensington "safe men" actually used. In reality, there were five tried and proven ways to crack a safe. Each had its proponents, but most burglars generally followed the same familiar drill: start with the quickest and easiest method and move through the list until they got what they wanted.

"Back-dialing would be the first thing you'd try when you came upon a safe in a home or business you were burglarizing," says Junior Kripplebauer, one of the better K&A box men. It "only worked 10 percent of the time," but it was well worth the modest amount of time and effort invested. Very simply, a burglar would slowly turn the dial on the safe's locking mechanism in a counter-clockwise direction as he gently applied pressure to the door handle. If the last person to use the safe had closed the safe door but hadn't turned the dial past zero, there was a chance, albeit a small one, that the locking mechanism had not been triggered and the safe remained unlocked. For back-dialing to be successful, one thing was required that a burglar didn't carry in his bag of tricks: the cooperation of the last person who used the safe.

Such carelessness—and it occurred in both private residences and large business establishments—was the best gift a crew could receive. "People left the dial on the last number of their combination and it would just open up when you pulled the handle," says a grateful Donnie Johnstone. He and Kripplebauer admit that when that happened—which was "very seldom"—the burglars felt that the last person who had used the safe deserved a cut of the proceeds.

Punch-dialing required substantially more time and energy, but was still one of the easier ways to crack a locked safe. The burglars would use a star or center punch and a short-handled sledgehammer to drive the safe's dialing mechanism back into the box. If done properly, according to Kripplebauer, "the tumblers would be knocked loose and everything would fall to the bottom of the safe, allowing the bars that lock the door to move. Once the bars were free to move, you could open the door." If the safe was well made or the punch-dialing was done haphazardly, it was possible to botch the job. But for a good burglar who knew his stuff, says Kripplebauer, punch-dialing would do the trick at least 50 percent of the time.

If it was determined that the safe's locking mechanism was too sound or punching it proved unsuccessful, the job then called for an exhausting, all-out wrestling match, better known in the trade as "ripping," "peeling," and "tearing" the safe apart. Peeling a safe was a physically demanding, time-consuming process—one that was more safely done in the friendly confines of a deserted warehouse or in a desolate country field (cemeteries, junkyards, and abandoned train tracks were also favorite workplaces). Taking an hour or more to rip a safe apart in its accustomed home was a risky proposition, although it was known to happen. Moving several hundred pounds or several tons of steel and concrete was no easy assignment. Many a victim's home, and many a burglar's back and automobile, were wrecked in the process.

The first step in tearing a safe open was "putting a crimp or dent in a corner of the box between the door and the frame. A chisel would then be hammered into the indentation," and, as Donnie Johnstone says, "you'd keep banging until you got a bite." Once a good bite was established, the burglars would continue along the seam, vigorously pounding chisels into the breach with "hammers and hatchets" and widening the gaps. Soon, according to Kripplebauer, "you would hear a pop, pop, pop sound; the popping sounds of rivets breaking and cracking." Burglars could now dig their brutes into the fissure, "lay back on the bar and listen to what sounded like balloons popping."

By "banging chisels in every six inches, busting the rivets, and bending the steel cover back," according to the burglars, you'd actually be "peeling" the safe apart. Once that was accomplished, a sledgehammer and brute would be used to smash and break apart the thick concrete insulation that lines all large safes. After 45 minutes to an hour of frenetic digging, chipping, and banging, everyone involved was covered in sweat, grime, white flecks of "firebrick" (a plaster cast used to insulate the safe's contents against fire), chunks of concrete, and minute slivers of steel, but the job had been completed. The box was open and the contents theirs.

Though just about all Kensington burglars employed in production work were practitioners of back-dialing, punch-dialing, and peeling a safe, only the more elite teams contained crew members who specialized in the last two safe-cracking methods: drilling and burning. Drilling a safe entailed "high-speed battery- or electric-powered drills with a variety of expensive diamond or carbon tips." The real secret, however, was not the equipment, but knowing where on a box to drill. An inexperienced, unsophisticated novice could exhaust himself turning a metal box into a block of Swiss cheese and still not get near the safe's contents.

In the absence of a helpful diagram, a hole would generally be drilled between the dial and the handle. When the hole was large and deep enough, the burglars would chop through the firebrick and concrete insulation to get to the pins and slide-bars connecting the lock, handle, and doorframe. Once again they'd use the drill to sever the exposed rods and bars and hope the door could now be opened without the combination. It didn't hurt, however, to have a little inside assistance.

Once more, K&A crews showed their ingenuity. By going to friendly locksmiths or directly to the safe manufacturers such as Mosler and Diebolt (some even used the Library of Congress), they were able to acquire schematics that fit right over the face of the safe door. "The schematics clearly showed the soft spots and specified where to drill," says Kripplebauer. "Drilling worked a good percentage of the time, but had its drawbacks. It was riskier because it's noisier and takes longer."

If the box appeared too tough or drilling proved unsuccessful, there was one last way to mount an assault: burning the safe open. Burning targeted the same strategic spots as drilling and was just as labor-intensive, if not more so. But it also carried additional security concerns, such as casting an incredible amount of light on the illegal exercise and the very real possibility of starting a fire. Not every burglar could handle an acetylene torch, oxygen tanks, or super-hot burning rods, and many, as Donnie Johnstone readily admits, "didn't have the knowledge" for such a delicate and dangerous project. Others—whether through bluster or ignorance—tried to emulate their more experienced Kensington colleagues, with often disastrous results. "I burned a safe one time," says Don "the Dude" Abrams, "and nearly all the money in it."

To prevent such a painful outcome, some of the more savvy safe men first burned a hole in the top of the safe and then flooded the contents with water. Wet money could be put in a dryer or hung out to dry; burnt money was gone forever.

Though there are plenty of boxes that resisted break-ins, there were other times when the gods looked with favor on their inept, stumbling efforts. For example, Jimmy Laverty's crew "once got a tip about a house in Jim Thorpe, Pennsylvania"—this "old couple that kept a safe filled with cash between their two beds." The burglars drove upstate to the mountainous coal-mining region one night, successfully entered the home, and immediately tried to punch the safe open, but the box was too tough. They needed to peel the safe but didn't have the luxury of doing it at the site. They'd have to lug it out of the house and back to Philadelphia—not the easiest of assignments in a small town where everyone knew everyone else and strangers were easily identifiable.

As Laverty tells the story, he and his associates drop the safe out the second story window, and it lands with a loud thud. Just as they are about to push it toward their car and make a quick getaway, a patrol car slowly pulls into the street, and the officer behind the wheel looks directly at them. The burglars freeze, visions of handcuffs, high-priced attorneys, and cold, damp jail cells shooting through their brains. Then, recalls Laverty, "the cop gives us a friendly wave. So we wave back. And what do you know? He drives away."

The burglars' luck does not end there. As they continue to "push the safe a couple more times end over end, the door flips open." They quickly empty the safe's contents on the sidewalk and hightail it back to their favorite Kensington night spots.

Junior Kripplebauer had a similar stroke of good fortune one night. While burglarizing a large restaurant on Route 1 in southeastern Pennsylvania, Junior and his partners realized they were not going to be able to open the safe. If they wanted the day's receipts, they would have to take it with them. The safe was so heavy, however, that they lost control of it as it was being eased down a long flight of stairs. It fell noisily to the bottom of the steps, putting holes in several walls and a large dent in the wooden floor, but the door flew open during its jarring decent, and they were now able to pocket the cash and drive off into the night $8,500 richer.

6. The Pottsville Heist

Pottsville was a hell of a fuckin' score. —Don "the Dude" Abrams

Pottsville, that was the biggest goddamn thing. —Edward Froggatt

Rollicking as a roller coaster, boisterous as a pirates' ball, reeking with ribaldry and as eerily and factually fatal as the cold deadlines of a LeCarre spy thriller. That is the Pottsville burglary. Big, big, big and bad. —Leonard McAdams

In my 45 years as a policeman, I've had some interesting cases—gun battles and everything. But this, this surpasses them all. It's a movie. That's what it is, a movie. —Detective Captain Clarence Ferguson

IF THERE WAS a clarion call for criminals, a sawed-off shotgun heard round the world, a signature event of villainous larceny that put the K&A Gang on the map, it was the Pottsville Heist of 1959. The story combined incredible characters, gut-wrenching drama, unpredictable twists and turns, ruthless executions, and spell-binding courtroom testimony. As one newspaper scribe wrote of the mother of all burglaries, "It was the most incredible, the zaniest, the ultra-Hitchcockian and, for a time, the largest cash haul burglary in the history of Pennsylvania." The half-million-dollar score, the dead bodies, the back-stabbing, and the blockbuster cast of wildly colorful characters made Pottsville the stuff of urban legends. And Kensington burglars had their fingerprints all over it.

Though the infamous and nearly half-century old burglary took place on August 7, 1959, our story actually begins several years earlier when Clyde (Bing) Miller, a wealthy, upstate Pennsylvania owner of strip-mining machines, first glimpsed a super-hot showgirl in the Celebrity Room, a high-end nightclub on South Juniper Street that catered to staid Philadelphia's few movers and shakers. Her name was Lillian Reis, and Miller couldn't take his eyes off her. The voluptuous, dark-haired beauty in her mid-twenties was regularly described as "sexy," "sultry," and "seductive"—many people compared her to Liz Taylor.

She was a twice-married chorus girl with two young children, and struggling to make ends meet on $60 a week. To Bing, she was a Greek goddess.

"She really made an impression on me," said Miller in a magazine interview. "She was the most beautiful girl I ever saw. When that chorus came out, you saw her—and only her. What I was spending on her was peanuts."

Miller may have thought a "refrigerator, a washing machine, a garbage disposal unit, an air conditioner, a diamond ring, a fur coat, an automobile, a Florida vacation and $200 a week" were peanuts, but few others would. In time, even Miller would start worrying about money, which is how the small mining town of Pottsville comes into the picture. Masked as Gibbsville by John O'Hara in popular novels such as *Appointment in Samarra*, Pottsville would regularly be in the headlines over much of the next decade as the setting for a real-life melodrama.

According to Miller's version of events, he and Lil were talking about her dream of one day buying the Celebrity Room nightclub when he started thinking out loud about a newspaper article on "income tax fraud" and a wealthy business associate of his in Pottsville who was known to keep extremely large sums of cash in a home safe. Miller always maintained that Lil was quick to pick up on the idle comment. Most close observers of the Pottsville saga believe that she was about to pull the plug on her weekly trysts with Bing. His business had gone south, he was running out of money, and Lil expected her social schedule to become very busy. If Miller wanted to continue the liaison, he'd have to come up with some dough.

The dough he came up with belonged to John B. Rich, a 66-year-old Pennsylvania coal baron who owned the Gilberton Coal Company. Rich, whose real name was Giovanni Battista Recchione, had come to America from Italy in 1906 when he was 14 years old. Penniless and unable to speak a word of English, he took a job as a "breaker-boy," sifting coal by hand for a couple of dollars a day. Thanks to determination, hard work, and an entrepreneurial spirit, Rich was running his own coal company by the early 1940s. He became a millionaire not long after.

For Lillian, though, the interesting part of the story was not a lowly immigrant's extraordinary climb from poverty to great wealth but the old man's cash. No slouch herself with regard to entrepreneurial endeavors, she turned to one of the Celebrity Room's numerous patrons who specialized in such logistical problems.

John Carlyle Berkery was one of many K&A burglars who, when they had just made a score, frequented the center city nightclub. In addition to attractive dancers, it featured performances by known funny men like Jack E. Leonard, Lenny Bruce, and Don Rickles and established singers like Buddy Greco, Johnny Mathis, and Ella Fitzgerald. A tall, cherubic-faced man of 29, Berkery had already accumulated a number of arrests. He had a nose for a good tip and a reputation as an up-and-coming practitioner of production work. Lil, the story goes, enlightened him about a certain Pottsville millionaire who could be sitting on as much as a half-million bucks.

Berkery liked what he heard. According to subsequent court testimony, he brought two additional Kensington second story men—Vincent "Barney" Blaney, 26, and Robert Poulson, 24—to Lil's house in South Philly on the evening of August 6, 1959, to discuss the job. After a couple of phone calls determined that Rich was out of the country —he was vacationing in Europe— and gave the crew his address on fashionable Mahantongo Street in Pottsville, it was decided that they would drive up to the coal country the very next night. Lillian insisted that Berkery take her tough, well-built boyfriend, Ralph "Junior" Staino, 27, who also worked at the Celebrity Room, to ensure that her interests were protected.

On the way up to Pottsville, the four men stopped in a Reading hardware store to pick up a few odds and ends—brute, hacksaw, screwdrivers, and hatchet. They arrived in the small mining town well after nightfall. After assuring themselves that the house was vacant, they entered and quickly discovered a flimsy safe in the basement. While Staino kept watch at a first floor front window, Berkery, Blaney, and Poulson battered the safe door open. It is said that they "almost fainted" when they discovered a wall of money staring them in the face: "money stacked in bundles of $10,000; $20,000; and $50,000. The money was in $5, $10, $20, $50, and $100 bills."

Unprepared for such a haul, they started grabbing pillowcases from all over the house and eagerly stuffed the cash into every container they could find. Suddenly they heard a loud siren that seemed to blare through the entire neighborhood. "Here come the cops," one of the men yelled. The four burglars scattered, some with bags of money, some without, and all in a panic, struggling to be the first out of the house. But when they exited the kitchen door and hit the back lawn, they realized that no cops were chasing them—the wailing siren was merely a nightly curfew warning for teenagers. The crew re-entered the Rich home and cleaned out the safe, except for what was later estimated to be $1.5 million worth of bonds and other valuable papers on the safe's bottom shelf.

The four returned to Philadelphia giddy with excitement. Back at Staino's West Philadelphia apartment at 42nd and Spruce Streets, they emptied the bags of money on his bed and counted the proceeds. None of the Kensington men was a mathematical genius, and they were well up into six figures, a numerical neighborhood they were totally unfamiliar with. Each time they reached the rarified air of $350,000, they got light-headed, lost track of the count, and had to begin again. Police would later determine the haul to be about $478,000, an unprecedented, astronomical score by the standards of the day.

By prearrangement there was to be a four-way split, with Lillian getting everything over a hundred grand (the sum they had expected to find), since she had put the operation together. Poulson and Blaney each took a $25,000 cut and an extra $1,200 or so in "pin money." Berkery was said to have walked off with $100,000. Bing Miller, the original finger man, was given $7,000 for the profitable tip.

Within hours, certainly within days, word filtered through Kensington taprooms and rug factories that some neighborhood guys had come into some serious money. "Bobby Poulson called me up and said we're going down the shore," said Don "the Dude" Abrams. "He had $30,000 in his basement, his share of the score. He took about $5,000 and we went down to Atlantic City and had a party. We got so fuckin' drunk we ended up sleeping on the beach."

Throwing caution to the wind, the group began a major infusion into the area's economy. Lincolns and Cadillacs were purchased. Berkery bought a suburban New Jersey home, and Lillian put money down on the Celebrity Room.

Back in Pottsville, John Rich had returned from his vacation to find his house burgled, his safe looted, and no idea who to blame. Curiously, Rich claimed to be missing only $3,500 in cash and $17,000 in jewelry, hardly an earth-shattering crime. Who would connect the relatively minor burglary on Mahantongo Street and some unexpected extravagance in Philadelphia? That ignominious or heroic role—depending upon your ethical vantage point—would be left to the brother of one of the criminal actors.

It was now February of 1960—a good six months after the burglary—and Richie Blaney, Vince's younger brother, had just completed his fifth week at Eastern State Penitentiary for a probation violation. He wasn't liking it one little bit. A Kensington thief and a graduate of the Willie Sears School of Burglary, Richie had also developed a not-so-secret sideline as an informant. Accounts of his duplicity were not hard to come by.

"I came home to my mother's place one night," recalls Jackie Johnson, "and the cops are goin' through the house. Somebody had tipped them off, and they're looking all through the place. Then I see Richie Blaney there and ask my mother, what's he doing here? She said, 'He came in with the cops and showed me a badge like the others.' I told her he ain't no cop. He's from the neighborhood. I told him to get the fuck out of the house. But that's what he was doing at the time, making pretend he was a cop."

"Richie was following me for days," says John L. McManus of his own run-ins with Blaney, "so I finally picked up a tire iron and told him I was gonna break his goddamn head. He told the cops I threatened him and they put the word out to beat me on sight. And they did, they got me good and put me the hospital at Moko [Moyamensing Prison, now demolished]. The nurse called the FBI and they came in and took pictures of me. They wanted me to sign some stuff and testify, but I won't rat. Not even on them."

Though being a snitch for the man didn't improve his reputation in the community, chubby, moon-faced Richie believed that his cooperation in a few sensitive areas had gotten him out of several scrapes. And he now desperately wanted out of Eastern. He sent word from his jail cell that he had information about an unsolved crime—a big score that included some neighborhood guys and Lillian Reis. The message landed on the desk of Captain Clarence J. Ferguson, Philly's version of J. Edgar Hoover.

By the time of Pottsville, Clarence Ferguson was in his sixties, had over four decades on the police force, and was a law enforcement institution in the City of Brotherly Love. Commander of an infamous 40-man unit called the Special Investigations Squad, he wore a dated porkpie hat, had a stable of snitches he kept out of jail, and had carte blanche authority to investigate any person or crime he found of interest. Blaney's incredible tale piqued his curiosity; he had heard stories of some big spending by a few K&A guys. And it was well known that Lillian had just purchased the Celebrity Room and was putting more enthusiasm than usual into her favorite refrain, "Drink it up, boys."

Richie recounted for Ferguson how his brother Vince and Bobby Poulson had arrived at his house the night of the burglary. They were beside themselves with excitement and proudly showed off their take from the caper—thousands of dollars in cash. He explained how they hid Vince's share in his kitchen oven and went out to celebrate. More important, he went on to enumerate a number of key elements of the crime that had the ring of authenticity. Over the next several weeks and months, Blaney would be ushered in and out of Eastern's formidable front gate as if it were a revolving door to a supermarket rather than a state penitentiary. He had become "Ferguson's number one informant," indispensable to the old man's intelligence-gathering system.

After conferring with Lieutenant Jesse Stanton and Sergeant Roy Wellendorf of the Pennsylvania State Police, Ferguson started putting the pieces of the puzzle together. They quickly agreed that there might be a connection between the Rich heist and the unlikely big spenders in Philly. Looking for a key link to confirm Blaney's account, they theorized that the gang's tipster was none other than Lillian's sugar daddy, Bing Miller, now a sick man and no longer a high-roller. They tracked him down to a small Jersey fishing village where, broke and suffering from cancer, he managed a motel and restaurant. Brought back to Philadelphia for questioning on April 2, 1960, within a few hours he had confessed to being the finger man for the Rich job. The next day police arrested Reis, Staino, and Poulson. Vincent Blaney and John Berkery were arrested within the week. Poulson and Blaney signed confessions "within seven hours."

If authorities thought they had put this baby to sleep, however, they were sadly mistaken. In fact, the bizarre story was just beginning.

OUT ON BAIL AND AWAITING TRIAL, the defendants might have decided to become models of propriety and stay out of the newspaper headlines, but not this crowd. Moral rectitude was and would remain an alien concept. In July 1960, for example, Lil and Junior got into a brouhaha with a young woman at an Atlantic City nightclub that resulted in punches being thrown, unflattering newspaper coverage, and additional courtroom appearances.

"I was just walking to the ladies' room at the Escort Bar," recalls Virginia Chiucarelli, who was just 24 at the time of the incident. "I didn't know Ralph Staino from a bucket of beets. He offered me a job at the bar, but I said I had a good job and started walking away and then somebody goosed me. The only one who could have done it was Ralph. I hit him and then he hit me back. I hit him again and then he really started to punch me.

"People started to yell, 'Ralph, you're such a big man, but you can't knock out that 112-pound girl.' I ended up with a slight concussion, a broken nose, and a missing tooth. He sure made a mess out of me. They had to take me to the hospital."

Things turned much grimmer that summer. Within days of the Chiucarelli incident, members of the Pottsville team started to turn up in distressed condition.

In mid-August, four months after Bobby Poulson and Vince Blaney had confessed —and a year after the Pottsville burglary—Vince went missing and Bobby was discovered staggering around the grounds of Our Lady of Lourdes Hospital in Camden by two nurses just coming off duty. In addition to being severely beaten, he had also been shot in the base of the head and stabbed numerous times. A priest gave him the last rites; no one expected him to live.

A message was being sent. Informants could have a greatly curtailed life.

"They thought they were dropping a dead body at Our Lady of Lourdes," said Herbie Rhodes. "John Berkery did that little number. Berkery did that in the back seat of his car."

Rhodes was a key member of Ferguson's squad and had a front-row seat for the lengthy Pottsville drama. "Poulson nearly died," said Rhodes, who saw him in the hospital before and after surgery, " but he wouldn't give a formal statement. He was afraid for his wife and kids."

Some believe the doers never expected Poulson even to make it to the hospital, much less recover. In fact, the perpetrators thought they had killed him and planned to bury his body in a ravine, but in typical Kensington fashion they had forgotten to bring a shovel. They dumped the body and went to get something to dig with, but when they returned the body was gone.

After his astonishing recovery, Poulson regaled police with a ridiculous story about aborting a trip to Atlantic City, being dropped off by John Berkery at a Camden transit stop, and soon afterward being assaulted by a group of men who spilled out of a car. Despite this unlikely account, Ferguson picked Berkery up and charged him with the attack. Even though the police claimed to have found blood in the back seat of Berkery's car, they couldn't make the charges stick and were forced to release him. Poulson, for his part, informed authorities that he had turned over a new leaf. He would no longer be a witness for the prosecution.

Just days later, on August 23, the crab-eaten remains of Vince Blaney were discovered by fishermen a mile off Margate, New Jersey. He had been shot in the back of the head. Trapped gasses caused the body to float to the surface despite the seven-foot chain and 37-pound industrial weight attached to it.

Some six months later both Reis and Berkery were arrested for Blaney's murder. The state's key witness was one Robert Russell, who claimed to have seen Berkery plug Blaney several times at an Atlantic City boatyard while Lil stood by laughing her head off. Unfortunately for the prosecution, Russell was not the most stable of individuals. Soon he was doing the confessing. Russell's account of the murder was pure fiction. The police were back to square one.

In March 1961, the action shifted to a Pottsville courtroom. The trial was a big deal in the small mining town, and the players and accounts of the crime were not all that clear. "It's a very puzzling case," said a county prosecutor. "It's the first case I can recall in which the thieves exaggerated the loot—in this case by more than one hundred times. It's been my experience that the opposite is usually true. Ordinarily, it's the victims who exaggerate."

Even though he had repudiated his confession, the jury found enough merit in Poulson's original statement to convict him of burglary. In May, both Berkery and Staino were convicted, and Lillian was seen to shed a few tears for her boyfriend.

With Vince Blaney dead and Bobby Poulson properly schooled in the harmful effects of cooperating with the authorities, Richie Blaney became the key witness for the prosecution. Though he hadn't participated in the heist, he claimed to know intimate details of the caper and had dedicated himself to convicting his brother's killers.

Blaney had become inseparable from Ferguson and had even started wearing an upturned porkpie hat like the captain. He grew comfortable passing himself off as one of Ferguson's officers, who were with him at all times for his own protection. As newspaper articles described it, detectives "were at his side when he drank a beer at the Coal Mine taproom in the Necho Allen Hotel . . . walking the streets of Pottsville . . . and with him until he went to bed." They even "drove him back to Philadelphia in a squad car." According to Joe Daughen, a long-time *Philadelphia Daily News* reporter who covered the trial, Richie Blaney was being passed off as "Detective McCoy" by Ferguson's squad up in Pottsville prior to his appearance on the witness stand. Few people actually knew who he was until he walked in the courtroom.

In court, Blaney was a combination of Marlon Brando and Laurence Olivier. As the "Commonwealth's crown jewel," he is said to have put on a "dramatic show" that included "strutting to and from the witness stand" and spouting off a series of witty one-liners that both entertained the jury and frustrated the defense. For example, when the counsel for the defendants asked him if his wits kept him out of jail, Blaney replied, "No . . . my lawyers." And how many lawyers do you have, he was asked. "Just one at a time," he answered. During one lengthy cross-examination, Berkery's lawyer, State Senator Benjamin Donolow, asked Richie if he was telling the truth. "If you were interested in the truth," Blaney shot back, "you'd plead him [Berkery] guilty." Donolow asked for a mistrial and complained that Blaney had been getting away with wisecracks throughout the trial. The stout second story man may have felt like the cock of the roost in court, but it would only be a matter of time before he got his.

IT WAS A SUNNY, 86-degree July day. Star witness Richie Blaney, now preparing to testify against Lillian Reis, got out of bed at his recently purchased Oxford Circle row home, picked up a day-old newspaper, and had a breakfast of scrambled eggs. He lounged around for a few more hours, asked whether his Bermuda shorts had been pressed, and at 3:30 p.m. left the house. He got into his 1956 Oldsmobile, turned the key in the ignition, and, as the *Daily News* described it, "was blown into eternity."

The explosion could be heard—and felt—throughout the quiet, middle-class community. Blaney's body received a "searing burn" and was blown into the back seat of the blue and white sedan. Police said his body "was ripped apart but his face was hardly scratched." Fenders, grillwork, and motor parts were left scattered along Alma Street. The engine hood was discovered on a nearby rooftop, and glass littered the street like "pulverized sugar." One shoe remained in the front seat, and Richie's black porkpie hat was found on the pavement some distance away.

Most living room windows along the street were shattered, and venetian blinds and curtains were now hanging at odd angles. Within minutes "some 1,000 persons" began congregating on the narrow street to see what all the noise and excitement was about. They could clearly hear the screams of anguish coming from 6011 Alma Street.

Joanne Blaney, Richie's 24-year-old wife, watched her husband leave the house, "locked the door, took her three children to the second floor and prepared to watch television." When she heard and felt the vibration of the blast, she said, "I knew what it was."

When Captain Ferguson learned of the successful assassination—it is said to have been "the city's first car bombing"—he was described as "Philadelphia's angriest man." The old detective claimed not to be surprised by the murder. "I have predicted it," said Ferguson. "I expected it. I am thankful that Blaney's wife and his children did not get into that car with him." His promises "to get these killers" were said to "flow like molten lava."

Ferguson wasn't the only unhappy law enforcement officer. "Richie was a very likable guy," said Detective Herbie Rhodes. "Personable but devious. I was one of the guys assigned by Captain Ferguson to keep an eye on him. Word on the street was that they were going to do him in. After what happened to his brother Vince and Poulson, we were assured of it. We had different guys on the detail and were stationed on Alma Street. Richard was afraid, but his wife called off the protection. Ferguson tried to talk her out of it, but they were tired of cops around all the time.

"I was on vacation down at Avalon and was in a bar watching John Facenda give the news when he reported what happened. I can't tell you how angry I was. They put enough dynamite in that vehicle to blow up several cars. Fergy went bananas. The Blaneys were killed out of sheer revenge."

The police interrogated several dozen suspects, but the most likely candidates, said Ferguson, had alibis "so pat and airtight that they must have had some knowledge that the crime was to be committed." While police searched for the killers, Lil and Junior Staino announced their plans to get married. First, however, she would have to stand trial in Pottsville and explain where she obtained the funds to purchase the Celebrity Room.

Though Lil decided not to take the stand in her own defense, she remained the center of attention in the economically distressed mountain town. The jury, particularly the men, kept track of her every movement, gesture, and glance. Women—and reporters—took note of her big-city, cosmopolitan wardrobe. "Clad in a black skirt, red and black bolero jacket . . . her high heels clicking, bangles and pink lipstick gleaming in the street lights . . . ," wrote one reporter covering Lillian's departure from the courtroom one day.

In the courtroom, Lil's attorneys portrayed her as a model of financial propriety, a consummate saver, a person who had hat boxes, cigar boxes, and valises filled with hard-earned dollars—all accumulated pre-Pottsville. Michael Corabi, her estranged husband, and Sidney Reiskin, her stepfather, a New York jeweler, testified to her thrifty habits. Though actually a prosecution witness, local boy Bing Miller provided her with unintentional support by cataloguing the gifts and cash stipends he had favored her with over the years: expensive appliances, vacations, jewelry, furs, mortgage payments, and a housemaid. All this allowed the defense to construct a viable explanation for Lil's ability to buy a Philly nightclub.

Calvin J. Friedberg, the Schuylkill County district attorney, was hamstrung by the murder or recalcitrance of key witnesses. He and John E. Lavelle, Lil's defense counsel, battled over every aspect of the case, including John B. Rich's peculiar claim that only $20,000 in jewelry and cash had been stolen.

After a "bitterly fought" 20-day trial and two days of deliberations, the jury was ruled hopelessly deadlocked and a mistrial was declared. Nearly half the jury argued that the state had not proven Lillian's connection to the burglary and voted for acquittal. They were all men.

Lillian Reis's next trial would not be for another three years. During the intervening years, Lil and her Pottsville crew were constantly in the news. For her part, "lissome Lillian" wasn't always the *provocateur* of these encounters with police and newsmen. In 1962, for example, she was arrested several times for doing the Twist. Apparently, voluptuous Lil's version of the popular dance was too much for the town fathers of Ephrata and Conshohocken. Even sophisticated Atlantic City shut down the "Queen of the Twist" and brought charges.

When Reis's attorney pointed out that the Lennon Sisters, Lawrence Welk, and Sammy Davis, Jr., hadn't been hit with the "transient worker registration law" Atlantic City had used against Lil, the town's police chief was forced to admit that, after all the trouble she had caused, he just "didn't care to have her in Atlantic City."

In fact, Lillian had not only become red meat for cops. The voracious carnivores in the Philly media market were equally exercised: she and Junior Staino couldn't do a thing without drawing attention. Her club was burgled, hit with tax liens, and charged with hiring "B-girls" to solicit drinks with patrons. Simple traffic tickets turned into major conflagrations that resulted in trips to the hospital, salacious news stories, and more court appearances. The *Saturday Evening Post* did a multi-page spread on her that resulted in a lawsuit, and a West Coast film crew came to town to do an "adult movie" about B-girls and vice rackets. Lillian, of course, had a starring role.

There was no doubt that Lil was hot—in fact, downright radioactive. James Tate, Philly's mayor, said that she and her club were "giving the city a black eye." No shrinking violet, Lil shot back when they padlocked her club's doors, "This is Philadelphia's loss. This is the last decent place a man can take his family."

IN APRIL 1964 Lillian was brought back to Pottsville for her second trial. The cast of characters was pretty much the same, except that a young and feisty Bobby Simone now represented the Philly showgirl. Cal Friedberg was tenacious as ever as prosecutor and had some memorable exchanges with Lillian, who this time decided to take the stand in her own defense. This jury came back with a verdict of guilty. Lil was stunned and wept openly, while Captain Ferguson displayed a conspicuous smile.

Simone appealed, and three years later the conviction was overturned, setting the stage for another combative round in court. Surprisingly, Berkery, Staino, and Miller faced a similar scenario. Their convictions were tossed when the Supreme Court ruled that "standing mute when being questioned about incriminating evidence" had been "made to seem a tacit admission of a crime." By 1970 the Schuylkill County legal establishment had spent over a decade pursuing the Pottsville defendants, and they were physically, psychologically, and financially exhausted. They had had enough. They dropped all the charges against Reis, Miller, Staino, and Berkery. Everyone was declared innocent, and old man Ferguson, who was finally about to retire, boiled with resentment and outrage. He died at age 75 the following year.

The saga of the Pottsville Heist was finally over, but no one who was around at the time will ever forget it. Or Lil or Berkery or Ferguson, for that matter. That goes double for those who played a role, however minor, in the drama. Al Ronconi was one of them.

"I loved the Celebrity Room," says Ronconi, who hung out at the club as a young man. "It was like going to New York City. I got to know people like Don Rickles. I remember Rickles used to ask, 'Why does everybody carry heat in here?' And when news of Lil's role in Pottsville broke in the papers, Rickles would be yelling on stage, 'Where's that money? Who's got that money?' Lillian was going crazy. She couldn't wait to get at him."

The Pottsville players left an indelible mark on Ronconi. "Lil was better looking than Liz Taylor and had a heart of gold. She was drop-dead gorgeous and had a great sense of humor, but she liked to walk on the wild side. Bing Miller used to come in and put two $100 bills on the bar, have breakfast, and just look at her. Berkery was real handsome and girl-crazy. He was a shrewd, tenacious guy and always dressed to kill. He wasn't Italian, but he was a real charmer."

About Junior Staino, Ronconi is less generous. Ronconi unwittingly became part of a money-laundering operation when Staino asked him to change some money at the bank. "He asked if I would mind converting this money that was in a shirt box. It was a whole bunch of fives, tens, and twenties he wanted changed into $100 bills," recalls Ronconi. "He offered to pay me, but I wouldn't take it."

As it turned out, the bank was limited by law to a $10,000 transaction, but it was enough to put Ronconi under suspicion. "I wanted to strangle Junior for involving me. My father was Old World Italian, and he came down on me. He was fucking mad. I was fucking humiliated. How could anybody know that money was stolen?"

Ronconi was dragged up to Pottsville four times to testify. "I finally took the stand," he says, "on the fourth trip." As bad as the court appearance was, it paled in comparison with news of the Blaney murders. "I was scared to death when people started to show up dead." He stayed away from the Celebrity Room: "I wouldn't get within 500 miles of there after that."

The Pottsville Heist was like an electrical storm that lights up the heavens. Young men in Kensington paid particularly close attention. As Billy Blue McClurg says, "Pottsville was a big thing. The guys involved were nobody until then. After that Berkery became well known and guys got to talking, 'Let's get into that.'"

Many people were captivated with the larger-than-life characters and the bizarre twists and turns, but for some it was more than a fascinating story—it presented a new way to make a living. "The Pottsville case put the word out," says Jim Moran. "There's big money to be made out there. Pottsville really gave a push to the burglar wannabes."

7. Natural Selection

I had an advantage the other guys didn't. I looked Jewish. I could definitely do things they couldn't get away with. For example, I could be up in Hazleton, Scarsdale, or New Haven and be looking to make a few scores. I'd look up the location of a few synagogues in the telephone directory or just take a drive in one of the nicer sections of town and park near a synagogue. I'd then walk in and ask to see the Rabbi. The guy wouldn't know me from Adam, but I'd be well dressed, introduce myself as a businessman relocating to the area, and request his help in finding a nice, upscale neighborhood to buy a home in.

Invariably, the Rabbi would be helpful. Excited by the prospect of acquiring a new member for the congregation, the Rabbi would take the time to suggest a number of attractive, predominantly Jewish neighborhoods. Sometimes they'd even identify important and affluent members of their congregations and supply me with their addresses and their professions in an effort to impress me. Of course, I'd always express my appreciation to the Rabbi for his time and assistance. I'd then go directly over to the homes and neighborhoods he had just suggested to me and steal the hell out of them. I took whatever I could grab. I did it all the time; it was easy. The other guys from Kensington looked like hoods and thugs. They could have never pulled it off, but I could. I looked like I belonged. It was great.

—Charles "Chick" Goodroe

We stop at a traffic light at an intersection in Spring Valley, New York. It's a beautiful little town inhabited by Hasidic Jews, many of them dressed in black with yarmulkes and long strands of hair falling off the sides of their faces. A lot of them work in Manhattan's jewelry trade. We had been beating the hell out of them for years. Different crews had been goin' up there for a while, so they must have gotten fed up and been on the lookout for us.

Well, we're up there one evening looking to do some work, and we're at this traffic light, and a group of people is crossing the street, and a couple of them are starting to take a close look at us. They're looking at our car and looking at us. All of a sudden, this one woman raises her arm, points at us, and starts screaming, "*Goniffs, goniffs!* They're the *goniffs!*" Then others start to point and yell, "*Goyim, the goyim! It's the goyim! The goyim* are here!"

They knew we didn't belong there and probably figured we were the burglars robbing the hell out of them. You can believe we got the hell out of there real quick. They were actually chasing us down the street and yelling, "*Goniffs! Goniffs!*" They knew we were thieves all right.

We wanted no parts of them. We hit the gas and got out of town.

—Jimmy Dolan

POTTSVILLE REGISTERED ON the criminal Richter scale. It was impossible for young toughs like Junior Kripplebauer not to notice the bold headlines in all the daily newspapers, the staggering six-figure score, and the animated barroom accounts of wild spending sprees by the participants. Just as Sputnik had captured worldwide attention and provided a wakeup call to American scientists and government leaders a few years earlier, Pottsville directed a spotlight on burglary as a good way to make big money without hurting anybody. Practically overnight, every street urchin, high school dropout, and neighborhood wannabe dreamed of getting in on the action and fashioning his own half-million-dollar heist. For many aspiring hoodlums in the city of Philadelphia, both young and old, burglary had renewed credibility as a lucrative criminal profession, and joining an established K&A crew was considered the epitome of success.

Jimmy Dolan and Chick Goodroe—even more than Kripplebauer—were representative of these new K&A Gang recruits. They grew up in the neighborhood; they had imbibed the aromatic mix of factory smoke, corner taprooms, and underworld braggadocio from infancy. They were Kensington boys.

A gregarious, rebellious youth, Dolan came from Fishtown in Kensington's southernmost reaches and was already well acquainted with the rough-and-tumble habits of an unforgiving blue collar section of the city. "In my neighborhood," recalls Dolan, "you wore a football helmet so you wouldn't get sucker-punched."

In 1956, at the age of 15, Dolan had had enough of ruler-swinging nuns, uninspiring priests, and strict parochial education. He left North Catholic High School in his sophomore year to join the Army. The military proved equally distasteful, so Dolan went AWOL. He did his "first bit" at Fort Lewis in Washington State and returned to Philadelphia a year later.

In no time at all, Dolan was running with a gang of teenagers and making a name for himself as newspapers chronicled his frequent arrests. One arrest—which resulted in a four- to 22-month sentence—saw Dolan and five of his teenage partners plead guilty to "taking $4,000" in the course of committing "41 burglaries." Not a particularly impressive haul, if you take into consideration the effort expended and, especially, the jail time. Though still technically a juvenile, Dolan had already bought into the revolving-door criminal lifestyle, his prison sentences growing longer with each conviction.

It was while doing a six- to 15-year sentence for burglary (the sentence was eventually cut to three to 10 years) at Eastern State Penitentiary that Dolan would come in contact with the man who would teach him the nuances and art of burglary. Effie Burke was serving one of his rare prison sentences and quickly took a liking to the fun-loving Fishtown teenager housed with him on D block. Burke was 17 years older than Dolan, but he invested the time to teach the kid the ropes of prison life, how to minimize the chances of getting caught in the first place, and how to maneuver when stuck in that pain-in-the-ass labyrinth known as the criminal justice system. Burke was released first but stayed in touch with his headstrong but affable pupil.

"He told me to look him up when I got out," says Dolan appreciatively. "He did everything for me. He provided lawyers, sent me money, and helped me get my sea legs when I got out." After doing "four years and change on the sentence," Dolan contacted Effie Burke and soon became a Burke protégé and K&A gang member.

"Right away," says Dolan, "Effie buys me a wardrobe and tells me to stay dressed all the time." He said the gang "always dressed as upstanding citizens" and even "carried briefcases" when they went to work. After a "couple of months" of watching, listening, and learning, Dolan was allowed to go on his "first job with Effie" and the other crew members—on that occasion Jackie Johnson, Michael Leo Andrews, and Bobby Schneeman. Whether or not he realized it at the time, Jimmy Dolan was being broken in by one of the top Kensington crews.

Most of Effie's guys had begun their criminal careers in the early fifties and, like young Dolan, had allowed their inexperience, general ineptitude, and unbridled enthusiasm to get the better of them. They pursued dubious schemes that usually resulted in arrest and embarrassment. Michael Leo Andrews, for example, was once caught stealing "36 pairs of women's shoes valued at $70.96," which did little to improve his street reputation and generated negative publicity, legal fees, and jail time. However, once Andrews and the other Kensington wannabes were introduced to Willie Sears, Effie Burke, Jimmy Laverty, Hughie Breslin, and the nuts and bolts of production work, their decision-making skills improved and their thievery grew more sophisticated. Almost immediately the scores became larger and there were more of them. And the odds of arrest and imprisonment diminished considerably.

Now, with Effie Burke's help, Dolan too would jump from the minor leagues to the majors. It was if Casey Stengel had just snatched a promising but wet-behind-the-ears rookie off a struggling farm team and placed him in the lineup alongside DiMaggio, Mantle, Berra, and Whitey Ford. Jimmy Dolan was now in the big time.

"I didn't have any track record to speak of. I was a young kid," he says, "but Effie knew how to pick guys. He knew what he was looking for. He'd watch you for a long time to see if you measured up. You didn't know it, but he was grading you, seeing if you were worthy. Nobody ever went bad in Effie's crew. He just had a knack of knowing what to do and who to pick. There was no room for mistakes in what we were doing. Effie would blow up at you if he saw you make a mistake. He told us all the time, burglary was a dangerous business, and if you screw up you could get hurt bad or, even worse, get one of your partners hurt. He drilled it into us. He didn't want to hear about stickups, drugs, or other criminal schemes. If there was an argument about something in the crew, he would overrule all of us. Effie said the biggest reason guys make mistakes is because they believe they know it all. They get lackadaisical. He wanted everything done the right way, the Effie way. He was a burglar-artist.

"I was excited about being with guys like Effie Burke who had all this experience and expertise. Even though they made me the window man and made me carry all the tools all the time, I was working with Effie Burke and one of the premier crews. The money was almost secondary."

Dolan's admiration is obvious, and probably well deserved. Effie Burke was the consummate professional, dedicated to putting forth your best, whether your craft was brain surgery, carpentry, or burglary. And it usually paid off. As Dolan says, no one in Effie's crew ever rolled over and informed on his partners, and none of them were ever caught while pulling a job. Both are remarkable statistics considering the longevity of the crew and the thousands of homes they entered over the years. And they made a lot of money.

"I went all over the country with Effie," says Dolan. "We did 20 or more trips a year, not counting the ones we would drive to, and we'd be gone a few days to a week at a time. We'd go up to New England, out to the Midwest, and even California a few times a year and did pretty well. The money was good. But Effie showed some discretion. He was smart. If he went to a place, he wouldn't go back for a while. He'd give it a rest even if he did real well. He didn't want to overwork a profitable area and alarm the authorities and ruin it like some other crews did. When we weren't flying somewhere, we'd hop in the car and drive. One-nighters were common. A five-hour drive to some destination was nothing. We were on the road all the time—Connecticut, Massachusetts, New York. We worked according to the money we made. If we were short, we'd head out and go where the most affluent towns were located. Maryland was a favorite stop of Effie's; there were a lot of wealthy towns down there. But Effie wouldn't go much further south than that. Effie didn't like the South. He didn't know the lawyers, and the laws down there were unreal. Hell, a midnight burglary in an unoccupied home down there was a capital offense."

Years later Dolan found out personally how tough the South could be on intruders when he put together his own crew and traveled below the Mason-Dixon Line to do a few pieces of work. It didn't take him long to discover the reason behind Effie's reluctance to work in Dixie.

"Me, Hog Schneeman, and Reds Gorman were grabbed in Virginia," says Dolan of the excruciating experience. "We were caught with a load of swag in the car. There was jewelry from five or six burglaries, maybe a hundred grand there. Schneeman offered to take the weight because he was the one caught with the swag and tools, but I told him no—we'd hang together and see if we could beat it. I didn't want him to plead guilty, even though it meant Reds and I could have walked away. Effie had taught us you don't let a partner burn. If it's a reasonable bit time-wise, okay: let the guy take the fall, and the crew takes care of the guy's family. But the Virginia thing was heavy. One guy would get buried doing that. Schneeman was a good guy and great driver, and driving was an art. Sometimes I'd have to drive and it was—oh my god, it was terrible. I'd get lost. I had a very bad sense of direction. I couldn't find a thing, but Schneeman could drive all night to a distant state he hadn't ever been to and take you right to where you wanted to go.

"I thought we'd all make bail right away on the Virginia thing, but that's when the shock came. We were told to forget about getting out of jail. There would be no bail. We were facing a capital charge and could even get the death penalty—life at the very least. I thought to myself, oh, fuck, what did I get myself into this time? We discovered that many states in the South were crazy on the subject of burglary after dark. And that seemed to go double if it was done by burglars from up North. We called back home desperate for help and found out who the best criminal attorney in the state of Virginia was. We hired him right away. His name was Hardaway Marks, and he cost a lot, but he was worth it. He got each of us a sentence of three 10- and three one-year bits running wild—33 years hard labor—and told us we were lucky at that. I couldn't believe it. Something that would have been 11 and a half to 23 months back home was 33 years in Virginia. I thought I was dead. Marks told us to hang in there; he thought he could get the sentence reduced even further." (Eventually each of the 10-year sentences was thrown out.)

"So now I'm down in Virginia doing a big bit, and I figure it can't get any worse than this, but it does. They put me to work on the fuckin' chain gang. It was unbelievable. It's hot as hell and I'm the only one of the three of us out there. Hog Schneeman and Reds Gorman are sick and kept inside the jail, but they put me on a gang doing hard labor. Well, one day we're out in the field working our asses off, and some crazy nigger decides to make a break for the woods. He thought the guard wasn't looking and he could make it. All of a sudden there's a big fuckin' bang. It was like a goddamn cannon exploding. I turn around in time to see this nigger get hit by the blast. He goes airborne, and his whole side is blown the hell out. You can see guts, shit, and blood, all fly out of him in 20 different directions. The guard hit him with buckshot and the guy just exploded. He got totally fucked up.

"I'm standing there in disbelief. I can't fuckin' believe it. I then turn back to the guard on horseback and he's aiming the shotgun right down at my fuckin' head. I throw my hands up. I'm scared shit he's now gonna blow me away too.

" 'You Yankee piece of shit,' he says to me, 'are you dumb or something?'

"I look around and I'm the only one standing. Everybody else has hit the ground. They're not only on the ground; they're trying to bury themselves in the dirt and mud. It's like they're worms trying to burrow their way down as far as they can go. So with that shotgun pointed at me I jump down too and start burrowing myself as far down as I can, 'cause the son-of-a-bitch was gonna plug me next. You couldn't believe what it was like down there. It was in-fuckin'-credible."

Fortunately for Dolan, episodes like his Virginia debacle were few and far between. Effie Burke had been an exemplary teacher; mistakes of judgment were unacceptable. Burglary was a cerebral exercise constantly testing the wits of the participants. It was the homeowners and cops against the burglars, each trying to get the better of the other. The police were always improving their game. Wealthy homeowners, as well, tried to keep pace with their blue collar adversaries. The sophisticated home alarm systems of the sixties, for example, were supposed to nullify the risk of home burglary. For the K&A burglars, however, such electronic devices presented a minor, temporary inconvenience. The electrical protection systems were quickly overcome; eventually, they offered a slight advantage to the thieves.

"It was like a game of chess with the police and the alarm systems," says Dolan. "We always had to counter what the cops and the alarm technicians threw at us. We made 'em feel they were playing chess against Bobby Fischer. The alarm companies actually learned from us. They got a real education. So many times we left 'em wondering, 'How'd they do that?' when we broke in to a place and didn't set off any of their state-of-the-art gadgets. When the alarms first came on the scene in the late fifties and early sixties, it only took us a little while to figure them out. The whole system began with a key, so we got ahold of the keys from locksmiths. We already had master keys to most front doors, so now we got ahold of the master keys to the alarm systems. We had flat keys for the front doors and round keys for the alarms. Homeowners thought they were protected, but we had the keys to turn off their alarms. There were these little red and white lights on the alarm systems—red when the system was on and white when it was off. We'd just drive down the street of a wealthy neighborhood and look for the alarm lights next to the front door. A red light meant the owners were probably out for the evening. It also meant they had something in there of value they wanted to protect.

"We'd go back to the house later in the evening, turn off the alarm, and break in. To make sure the police didn't get suspicious while patrolling the neighborhood, we'd paint the white light red using fingernail polish. This way cops on patrol wouldn't be surprised to see the alarm turned off but no car in the driveway. It worked every time. We were good, very good. We were professionals. Nobody ever panicked. In fact, we'd keep on working as the homeowners were coming in the house. We knew exactly what we were doing."

The Effie Gang, as Dolan and his crewmates came to be known, developed a reputation for professionalism, cunning, and standup behavior. In addition, they were serious money-earners. Practically every burglar in Kensington aspired to become a member of Effie Burke's crew.

"Guys were always trying to coax Effie into giving them a position on the crew," says Dolan, "but there were so few openings. Years would go by before a new member would join up. When they didn't get anywhere with him, they'd start working on me and the other guys. They were hoping to get to Effie through us. Guys I didn't even like would start to make nice to me, buy me drinks, socialize with me, butter me up any way they could in order that I'd put in a good word for them. It almost never worked. I remember Charlie Devlin needed some money and was working Effie, me, and the others for a position on the crew. He was driving us crazy. Effie finally comes up to me and asks, 'What do you think, Jim? Should we put Devlin to work? Do you think he'd be any good?'

"Charlie was on me like a bride in heat on her wedding night. He was saying, 'C'mon Jim, you know we been friends. You know I've always taken care of you. We've never had a problem. You know I'll do a good job.' It was very unlike Charlie to be kissing someone's ass, but he was desperate to become part of Effie's operation. He was out to make some money, and he knew it wasn't unusual for each of us to make $10,000 over the course of a weekend. I finally told Effie I guess we could try it, but it still made me nervous. Devlin wasn't a burglar in the pure sense. Yeah, he had done a number of burglaries over the years, but he didn't work the way we did. We knew what we were doing.

"Well, don't you know it, Effie gives Charlie a shot one night and puts me in charge of him. He tells Devlin, 'Okay, Charlie, you're in. We'll see how it goes. But I want you to take orders from Jimmy. Anything he wants you to do while we're on the job, I want you to do. You hear me?' Devlin isn't too happy with me being his boss, but he was delighted to be working with the premier crew in the area. He was looking for a good payday.

"Well, we're burglarizing this house one night and I'm driving Devlin crazy. I'm telling him to do this, do that, just driving him nuts with orders. Normally he would have hauled off and tried to hurt me, and you didn't wanna be hit by Charlie, but I was having some fun with the situation. I was really busting his chops. I made him work the window; he wasn't happy. He really wanted to do some searching. He wanted to go through the house and find the money and jewelry. That was the exciting part. He was all upset I stuck him as lookout. I could tell he wanted to give me a shot to the head, but I told him, 'Don't give me any trouble, Charlie, or I'll tell Effie. You don't do what I say and Effie's gonna hear about it.' Charlie was going crazy.

"He was going crazy for another reason as well. He couldn't take the work. As tough as Charlie was, being in somebody else's house without a gun made him nervous as hell. We were in the home for quite a while that night, and Charlie was getting increasingly edgy, really nervous. He kept on asking, 'When are we gonna get out of here? Why's it taking so long? Somebody is gonna spot us.' He just couldn't handle the pressure. Charlie would fight a dozen guys. Be in a back alley brawl for hours and be able to take an incredible amount of punishment. He wasn't afraid of anyone, but burglary took a different kind of balls. It certainly wasn't for everybody.

"The job was incredibly stressful. Anything could happen if you weren't careful, and guys knew that. You could be extremely careful and still get fucked up. I was bruting a door one time and nearly got my head blown off. We were on the road and found a house that looked pretty inviting. We started to check the place out. We had certain tricks to determine if anybody was home. We'd always go through a series of things to be sure we weren't breaking into an occupied house. Once in a great while we'd be surprised and find someone home after we entered the place, but it was rare. Well, on this particular occasion, we checked the place out, decided nobody's home, and started to go to work on the front door with the brute. I'm leaning on it, and all of a sudden there's this incredible explosion. For a second or two I thought my head had been blown off. I jumped like a kangaroo. My ears were ringing and my head felt like it was on fire it was burning so much. I saw things like they were in slow motion. I looked behind me, and there was this huge hole about the size of a softball in the front door, and that was a heavy damn door. The hole was right where my head would have been if I had been standing straight up, but I was leaning on the brute at the time and slightly bent over when the shotgun blast hit the door.

"I was picking splinters out of my head for a year. Guys began calling me 'Wooden Head' because of all the lumber stuck in my head. And I got gray hair overnight. All of a sudden I went from dark to white hair. It was incredible, but I went to work the next night. Just like a paratrooper, you got to go out.

"It was fascinating how many supposed tough guys couldn't handle the work because of incidents like that. Going in somebody else's house unarmed scared the hell out of guys. They'd freeze up. Charlie Devlin was a perfect example. He did one job with us and we never heard from him again. He had had enough. That's why so many guys went into stickups or walk-ins. It took less intelligence, preparation, and regimentation. They were cowboys. Just walk in, put a gun to somebody's head, and take the money. But who wants to put another person's life in danger? Sooner or later you're going to pull the trigger and kill somebody. The guys who were part of Effie's crew weren't out to hurt anybody. We never carried guns; it was a rule. We didn't look at it as an assault on people. We always justified it by saying we weren't hurting them physically. And we specialized in rich fuckin' people, people who were insured. Yeah, we were taking their valuables, but they were getting repaid by the insurance companies. What's the big deal? So who were we robbing? The insurance companies."

The ability to rationalize away the thought that he might be harming someone was central to Dolan's ability to carry out his job. Occasionally, however, the rationalizations and psychic protections were dramatically swept away. During the course of one burglary, the façade of indifference was revealed for what it was—a convenient lie. He was burglarizing a mansion in upstate New York when the homeowners unexpectedly returned. Hearing them pull into the driveway, Dolan and his crew fled out a back door, quickly circled around to the street, and were promptly picked up by their waiting driver. They hadn't traveled more than a few feet when a woman came running out of the house screaming. She was calling for help, asking for someone, anyone, to come to her aid and call the police.

"The woman came out screaming," recalls Dolan, "and she wouldn't stop. She just went on and on. You would have thought she had been raped or something. I thought to myself, 'Did I cause all this screaming?' That was bad. We talked about it in the car driving away from the place. It had an effect on me. I was never the same after that. It really shook me up."

Not enough, however, for Dolan to give up his line of work. The money, the excitement, the lifestyle, and the camaraderie of fearless burglars and other ballsy underworld figures had seduced Dolan, like all the others. It was too good to give up. The women alone were reason enough to stay active. "Girls were all over the place," says Dolan. "They were all over us. They were in it for the money and the excitement. I had a different girl every day of the week. There were so many I finally had to name them according to the day of the week just to keep them straight in my head. That worked out fine until one of 'em would get out of line and show up early. If it was Wednesday and Sunday came up to me in a bar, I'd get all confused. I'd get angry as hell and tell her, 'Hey, this is Wednesday. I'm not supposed to be seeing you until Sunday."

It wasn't all Budweiser and roses, however. There were definite downsides to the profession. Paydays weren't guaranteed; looting a house wasn't to be confused with a relaxing stroll through the park; and police harassment was a constant source of irritation. The last of these sometimes became so bad that Dolan felt as if he was wearing a bullseye on his back.

"The cops were always on us. For example, I'm in a bar downtown one night and everything is going good, no problems at all. All of a sudden a few guys from Ferguson's squad come in, spot me, and pull me out of there. They arrest me and take me over to Ferguson's office in City Hall. They take me in this room, and in the middle of the room is a big wooden chair that's bolted to the floor. It looks like the electric chair. All that's missing is the skullcap.

"Well, they put me in the chair and place my hands in these handcuffs that are fastened to the arms of the chair. Now I'm in this chair for hours and starting to get pissed off, 'cause they've basically kidnapped me. I start yelling at them, 'What the hell is going on here? I wasn't arrested; I was kidnapped. I want to see my lawyer; I want to see Eddie Rieff. You can't keep me locked up like this. It's not me who did anything wrong; it's you guys who are breaking the law.'

"This goes on for hours. It's nearly four in the morning now and I'm still demanding to be cut loose. They keep telling me to pipe down. They tell me the captain is coming in. I've had about all of this I can take, and next time they tell me to shut up, the captain will soon be in, I tell them, 'Oh, yeah, the captain is coming in. What's he gonna do when he gets here, blow me?'

"You should have seen their faces. For an instant they were dumbstruck; they couldn't believe anybody would say something like that about their beloved Clarence Ferguson, the most famous cop in the city. They then rushed me and began pummeling me. I'm gettin' hit all over and I can't protect myself 'cause I'm handcuffed. All of a sudden they stop. Ferguson had finally shown up.

"He says, 'What's going on here?'

"One of the detectives says, 'You should have heard what he said, Captain. You should have heard what he said.'

" 'Well, what did he say?' asks Ferguson.

" 'Well . . . well,' stammers the detective, 'I can't . . . I can't repeat it, Captain.'

"Ferguson looks at him and says, 'What do you mean you can't repeat it? What did he say?'

"The detectives all look at each other and then look at me. 'Okay, Dolan,' says one of them, 'tell the captain what you said.'

" 'I didn't say a thing, Captain. I don't know what they're talking about. And besides that, they've kidnapped me. I don't know what I'm doing here and they won't let me talk to my lawyer.' "

Dolan was eventually cut loose, but the experience wasn't unusual. Felons were considered fair game by frustrated and overly aggressive law enforcement officers, and the lumps that were dished out never sat well with the recipients. As bad as the pummelings were, however, they paled beside the burglars' chief fear and constant concern: informants. There was nothing lower or more deserving of community scorn (not to mention retribution) than a rat. The Blaney brothers' ugly demise may have offended the sensibilities of some in the neighborhood, but to others the outcome was well deserved. Justice had been served. Jimmy Dolan not only bought into this dogma; he was a high priest.

"You always had to be on the lookout for a rat," says Dolan. "Rats were around, but not on a wholesale basis. You constantly had to be on guard. Most burglars had standup reputations and the right values. Jackie Johnson, for example, would never, never rat on you. If you put him on the electric chair, he still wouldn't rat on you. There was no such thing as taking that principle too far. No way you bend the rule. It would be a breach of honor. You gotta take the blows, and sometimes it's very hard. You get the reputation of not cooperating, and the government will bury you with long prison bits. And long prison terms are killers. If you do over 10 years, you're gonna be kind of wrecked after that.

"Effie schooled me early on as to who was a rat and who had the habit of going south on his partners. He said, 'Willie Sears was a rat and robbed his partners.' It wasn't public knowledge, but guys eventually put two and two together. No matter how good you were, if you're in this life you're gonna go to prison and do some time. When a guy is working like crazy and getting pinched as often as Willie did, but doesn't do any time or just short bits, you start to get suspicious. The really good burglars stayed away from him, but the young ones were impressed by his reputation and accomplishments. Joey Cooper Smith was the same way. The burglar gentry never accepted him. He may have been a hell of a fighter, but no self-respecting burglar would work with him. You didn't want to associate with those kinds of people. They were scumbags."

Dolan's visceral distaste for informers occasionally got the better of him. Once he found himself in the company of Sylvan Scolnick, a larger-than-life grifter and so-called criminal mastermind who had engineered numerous phony bankruptcies and con games and was widely known to be spilling his guts to law enforcement authorities in the mid-1960s. Though Dolan had never had any dealings with Scolnick, just being in close proximity to such a high-profile snitch was too much to bear. At the time of their meeting, both men were under lock and key at the Philadelphia Detention Center. Even there, their paths should never have crossed, since the grossly overweight Scolnick, also known as Cherry Hill Fats, was sequestered from the general population and housed in a special wing of the prison hospital. Dolan, however, had been informed that a shadow had appeared on a chest x-ray during his intake examination. He required a followup. Guards escorted him off the cellblock and over to the prison hospital, where he met the man the *Daily News* called the "Titanic trickster."

"They bring me up to the hospital ward and there's about 10 beds in there," recalls Dolan, "but what immediately caught your eye was this incredible mound of stinkin' flesh that's sprawled out over two beds. The beds had been lashed together and propped up on a dozen steel milk cans so that it wouldn't cave in. It was the strangest sight in the world. After the initial shock of seeing such an obese thing as this, I realized who it was. Sylvan Scolnick.

"I didn't want any parts of him. I didn't even want to be in the same room as him, but I went to my bed and waited for the doctors to call me in for another x-ray. After a while I got a little bored and got up to get a newspaper that was laying on a chair. That's when he opens up.

" 'Hey, kid,' he says, 'hand me one of those magazines over there.'

"I look around and realize there's no one there but me and him.

" 'Yeah, you,' he says, 'just get me a magazine over there.'

"Now I'm thinking to myself, that fuckin' rat is talking to me. Telling me to get him something. I'll give him a magazine all right. So I go over and pick up a couple of *Time* magazines, roll 'em up real tight, walk back over to Scolnick, and start hitting that fat rat with them. I'm beating the hell out of him, hitting him on the head and shoulders, and he begins screaming like a gigantic stuck pig. He's yelling for the guards, and all the other guys in the ward are wondering what's going on. After the magazines fall apart in my hand, I tried to strangle the motherfucker but his neck was bigger than my waist. It was like trying to grip a horse's ass. I couldn't get my hands around that obese thing. It was impossible. The guards finally showed up and pulled me off him. They asked Scolnick what he had done to provoke me, but he said I must have been in the hospital because I was a psych case or something, 'cause he hadn't done a thing.

"All I knew is that he was an informer and he asked me to do something for him. The newspapers played up his credentials and made him out to be a criminal mastermind, but he was a rat. That's all he was to me, a big fuckin' rat."

Dolan practiced what he preached; the principle of noncooperation was never to be broken, even when he was the victim. A dispute with a business associate at a local restaurant got out of hand, and Dolan ended up being shot in the groin. As he lay on the restaurant floor in great pain, he looked up at his assailant and said, "Keep your mouth shut when the cops get here. Let me do the talking." When police and hospital emergency units arrived at the scene, Dolan told them he couldn't identify the shooter. Police pressure proved ineffective. Dolan remained unable to name or describe his assailant, just as a standup K&A man was expected to.

SIXTH AND PIKE, 11th and Ontario, Front and Allegheny, and 22nd and Clearfield were all prominent corners that became asphalt and concrete incubators for tough-talking, street-wise Kensington kids eager to earn a reputation. Charles "Chick" Goodroe grew up at Fifth and Lehigh, just a few short blocks from Kensington and Allegheny Avenues. He knew the corners and the various characters well. His own corner was "D" and Westmoreland Streets, and he quickly became one of the regulars. Chickie was no tough guy like Nails Mancini, Billy Crocker, George Monday, and Eddie Lucas, young, established brawlers who thrived on the corner rivalries and periodic gang wars. His father was Jewish, although Chick wasn't brought up Jewish, and he was certainly no goody two shoes "A" student or jock. As a youngster he was drawn to Kensington's dark side and its many illegal diversions.

A good 15 to 20 years younger than the neighborhood old heads like Willie Sears and Effie Burke, Chickie knew the names and the stories but showed little interest in emulating their exploits. "The guys I hung with," says Chickie, "were doing burglaries on Kensington Avenue, and I stole like crazy on the avenue too, but it was a younger crowd and it wasn't with the intention of making a career out of it." Everybody did it, it was part of growing up, and he was just another one of the guys trying to get over.

"We were just having fun, bullshitting with friends, hanging on the corner," Chick fondly recalls. He quit Stetson Junior High in ninth grade and began to spend even more time with his friends on the corner. The scheming and the actual practice of pulling off illegal capers were definitely amateurish, but also fun and exciting. He now realizes that those youthful misadventures were shaping a career path. As Chickie says, "I was graduating into a criminal lifestyle."

Chick's first serious contact with the criminal justice system took place on the West Coast. He went to Los Angeles in 1959 to live with his stepfather (his biological father was Irv Morrow, a New Jersey restaurant owner) and immediately found himself running with different crowds in Glendale, Hollywood, West L.A., and Santa Monica. Hooking up with the "Valley guys" led to a series of burglaries. "Cars were everything back then," recalls Goodroe. "We robbed a garage in Santa Monica and I got caught. I was 18 years old." Chick was lucky; he copped a deal with the prosecutors. "I got nonreporting probation with the understanding I'd leave L.A. and go back East to Philly."

When he returned, Chickie started to hang out with Mitch Prinski, John Bosak, George Foerster, and a few other Kensington guys. Fun and games were still the order of the day. "Mitchell and I went down to Wildwood in the summer of '61 and got a place on Second Street," says Chick. "We stole everything on the Boardwalk and sometimes had to sleep on people's porches when we got too drunk to make it home or didn't have a place of our own. We burgled the homes of little old ladies and stole whatever we could get our hands on. We didn't hurt anybody. Sometimes we'd just go in a house and grab a shirt for the night."

Back in Philly, Chick started to hang with some older guys at Kensington and Allegheny Avenues. Kellis's Bar and Horn & Hardart's restaurant became his new clubhouses. Even the steps of the First Pennsylvania Bank became an attractive hangout. He had "graduated" once again and was now associating with serious practitioners of "production work," men who had made theft their profession.

"If you were growing up in Kensington," says Goodroe, "you eventually had to make a choice. You could either become a burglar, a fireman, a policeman, or a roofer. The people who became burglars were basically lazy and didn't want to work. They wanted to hang at bars all day and have a good time." Chick enjoyed the lifestyle, the action, the camaraderie, and, of course, the princely wage scale. "I liked what I did. I liked the benefits."

Within a short time, Chick was following in the footsteps of his predecessors, tailing Kensington Avenue's Jewish businessmen back to their homes in Northeast Philadelphia and suburban Cheltenham. In no time at all, Chick and his friends were leaving the city for richer stakes on the Main Line, in New Jersey, and in upstate Pennsylvania. "Let's go do a piece of work" became a common refrain.

"We'd be hanging out," recalls Chick, "and somebody would say, 'Let's take a ride. Let's take a ride up the turnpike on Friday.' I don't know how many times we drove up to Wilkes-Barre and Hazleton. We used to call Hazleton 'the bank' because we always came back with money. Guys would say 'Let's go to the bank tonight' or 'Let's take a ride up to the bank.' There was a lot of Jewish money up there. Allentown had a lot of Jewish money as well. Everything was nonchalant. The burglaries were rarely a planned deal. We'd be riding down the street and somebody would say, 'Let's go grab that.'"

But when they got to their destination, they were all business: the basics of production work kicked in. "We'd get to the neighborhood around supper time, about five or six o'clock at night and go right to the Goldbergs' and the Silvermans'. We kept a mental note of people going in and going out of their houses. Who turned the lights on and who turned the lights out? We tried to remember everything."

Many affluent families unknowingly collaborated with the out-of-town burglars, showcasing their possessions by purchasing expensive home alarm systems that the original members of the K&A crowd learned to circumvent as soon as they came on the market. By the time Chick Goodroe and his cohort arrived on the scene more than a decade later, alarms were more useful to the burglars than to the homeowners.

"Those small red lights on the front doors," says Chick, "told us the people had alarms. It was as if they wanted to tell us, 'I got something to protect.' You'd be riding down a dark street at night, and all of a sudden you'd see a red light on the doorframe of someone's house. It was like a lighthouse beacon. You couldn't miss it. We knew just where to go."

Every K&A burglar worth his salt carried a set of one hundred keys, some flat and some round. The flat keys opened most front doors, and the round keys were for the alarms. It took a good burglar less than a minute to turn off the alarm system and open the front door. On those rare occasions when they didn't have the right key for the front door, they used a wrecking bar or brute to dislodge the lock from the doorframe. "Those wrecking bars and brutes really made a mess," says Chick. "It really destroyed the doorframes." Most of the time, however, they had the proper keys, resulting in a stealthy invasion and getaway. "I believe most people didn't even know I was in their house until much later," says Goodroe proudly.

Once inside, the real fun began. "I always wanted to be a searcher," says Goodroe. "Everybody kept their money in the same places. People are creatures of habit. They're basically lazy. I could hit a master bedroom in five minutes or less. Guys who took 20 or 30 minutes were retarded."

Safes presented little hindrance; in fact, they added to the excitement and heightened the expectation of a big score. "If you ran into a safe," says Goodroe, "it was basically rip and tear. Very few of us ran around carrying drills and oxygen tanks. Brute force is what we generally used. Wherever you found a seam, you worked on it. Fireboxes were even more common than safes, and they were no problem at all, almost like toys. If you did happen to run in to a big safe, you'd take it home with you and then work on it."

If there was an aspect of the business Chick didn't like, it was lugging the vast array of burglar tools around. "The bag of tools used to kill me," he says. "It must have weighed 40 pounds or more. You'd be carrying sledgehammers, wrecking bars, punches, gloves, alarm keys, screwdrivers, and flashlights. Christ, it got damn heavy after a while, especially if you were waiting in the woods on a cold night for your driver to pick you up or the cops were chasing you. You were always running in the woods, and it was goddamn cold. You'd miss the pass and you'd have to freeze your nuts off for another 10 minutes waiting for the car to come around again. The worst thing in the world was to be stuck with a bag of goods on the run in a town you had no business being in."

After relieving a few homes of their most valuable possessions, the night was declared a success and the crew headed home to examine the proceeds. "Back in Philly, we'd all go over the haul," says Chick. "Guys would be grabbing a diamond ring, an emerald brooch, or a gold watch and say, 'I'll take this piece.'

'I'll take that piece.' 'That piece goes to the fence.' 'I want that piece.' All the guys were doing well and having a good time. Everybody had money. You'd go into a bar afterwards and boast, 'You should see the score we just made.' "

By the mid-sixties, Chick Goodroe was making a "couple thousand a night" at production work. The pot would vary, however: one night could be a bust; the next, a pretty good score. Moreover, much of the stuff had to be fenced, and it could take a week or two to get paid. But Chick was in no hurry; he enjoyed scrutinizing his nightly hauls. "I would look at the stuff gradually, handle it for days. I'd play with it, examine it, and then decide what I'd keep and what I'd sell. I loved jewelry; I had a hard time parting with it."

Some of Chick's work was planned, and the crew knew they were going on the road for a couple of days. At other times it was a "spur of the moment thing." Guys would be sharing a few laughs at their favorite drinking establishment and somebody would say, "Let's take a ride." Within minutes they could be in Cherry Hill, New Jersey, looking for the better neighborhoods, the Jewish neighborhoods. "I was looking for mezuzahs all the time," says Goodroe.

Seizing opportunities was a central tenet of the trade, and Chick missed few. "I was out on a date one night at a Northeast Philadelphia restaurant," he recalls, "and during the course of the meal I went to the men's room. I noticed that the manager's office was right next to the men's room. I loided the door [celluloid cards were used to beat superficial door locks] and grabbed $5,000 or $6,000 from the desk. It wasn't planned, it just happened."

Conversely, a planned "piece of work" could generate relatively modest returns. For example, the burglary of a Main Line sports figure resulted in $200 in cash, a bowling medal, a gold ring, and 10 silver dollars. Making things worse, Chick was arrested in the apartment and had to put out a few thousand of his own money to retain an attorney.

Despite such occasional business expenses, Chick was more than pleased with his life. Compared with the majority of Kensington men, slogging away in stifling textile or carpet factories, Chick had attained the American dream. He could sleep till noon, socialize with his friends all night long if he cared to, and afford two new cars every year and any woman he went after. As Goodroe likes to say, "How many guys have made love on a half-dozen fur coats?"

His trade, though perilous, presented few complications he couldn't deal with. Chick was a natural. He took to entering other people's homes and stealing other people's possessions as a duck takes to water. "When I first started it was the camaraderie," says Goodroe of his early forays into burglary. "It was like going to a baseball game with friends. It wasn't like I was really committing a crime. It was a game. Gradually, though, I really started to get into it. I could feel the anticipation, the rush of adrenaline. I couldn't wait to get out of the car. There was a sense of excitement. What were you gonna find? What were you gonna run into in the house? Would there be jewelry, fat wallets, and expensive artwork? Cash was always nice. Sometimes you felt like a voyeur as you hid in the underbrush, searching for points of entry, looking through windows, and occasionally seeing naked people in their homes.

"From the very beginning, I never had a problem with nerves. Some guys would get a bad case of the shakes and have to take a shit. Joey Cooper Smith, the tough guy that he was, once had to take a shit right in the middle of the living room. Window men usually got it the worst. They'd just be standing there counting the seconds while looking out the window, looking for the cops or the homeowners. They weren't going through closets and drawers searching for valuables. For window men, minutes seemed like hours.

"I, on the other hand, never had a problem. Once I'd open the door of a place I was robbing, I'd make a real fast run through the place to ensure the house was empty. I'd also be making an instant survey of what was in the place. If the bedroom door was closed it could get a bit scary. You didn't know if somebody was behind that door or not. You never knew what you were gonna run into. The greatest rush, however, was opening a drawer and finding a really good piece of jewelry. It was great. You knew you had a good score."

Not every Kensington wannabe took to the craft as easily as Goodroe. Those short on stealth, brains, and nerve gravitated to what they considered an easier payday: walk-ins. Chick didn't like gunplay or violence, but friends once talked him into taking part in a walk-in. He regretted it from the first moment. "We made good money, but I didn't like it," he recalls. "I felt sorry for the person. The guy was scared to death; he was crying. I didn't like terrorizing anyone and felt guilty. I knew if I did any more walk-ins I'd always be worried somebody would get shot. I never did another one. I knew I was a burglar and a good one. Why the hell did I need to scare the hell out of anyone?"

One concern that surfaced early and remained throughout Goodroe's long career was the downside of teamwork. The crew concept was the backbone of production work, but more skeptical, independent players saw definite disadvantages in working with others.

"The first time I had to split the money," says Goodroe, "I realized I'd rather work for myself. I hated to share anything. I started doing more work on my own in the afternoon. Anything I got was mine. Besides, I never liked to work at night anyway; it interfered with my social life." But working with a crew presented additional issues. Basically, in the minds of some, the more players there were, the more problems could arise.

"There were always beefs when you had three or four guys working together. I remember one occasion we were working in the Phoenix-Scottsdale area. It was me, Bosak, Foerster, and it's dark as hell out there in the desert; you couldn't see a goddamn thing. We finally break into this big house, and while we're searching the place the guys get into a beef over something. There was always some bullshit between guys. It gets pretty ugly, and Bosak says, 'Fuck it. I'm getting the hell out of here.' He runs out of the house into the darkness, but right smack into a 10-foot-tall cactus. Bosak got nailed pretty good and we ended up pulling a bunch of cactus thorns out of him. It must have been some kind of poisonous cactus 'cause the wounds got infected right away and we had to take him to the hospital. But how were we supposed to know? We were Kensington boys; what did we know about the desert and cactus?

"Stupid stuff like that was always possible when you worked with a crew. If I worked on my own, however, there was less bullshit. And if I got caught, it was on me. I didn't have to worry about anybody else."

Working with a crew could lead to some serious problems, especially if one of the guys got caught and couldn't take the weight. Most K&A guys were notoriously uncooperative; even when squeezed by police, they wouldn't even think about ratting on a partner. A few, however, buckled under a severe police grilling and the prospect of a lengthy prison sentence. Some of the guys who were toughest physically couldn't handle incarceration.

Joey Cooper Smith was like that. A pulverizing street fighter with considerable ring experience and "arms like sledge hammers"—he once put Hurricane Carter on the canvas—he hated prison; he just couldn't take it. He was one of the first to break out of the Philadelphia Detention Center shortly after it opened, and he committed the unpardonable sin, according to standup guys, of ratting out his partners. In fact, in his desperation to avoid doing time, Cooper Smith would occasionally inform on those who weren't his partners.

"Cooper Smith was a piece of shit," says Goodroe. "He was so self-absorbed, all he cared about was himself. Guys were intimidated by his toughness. Older guys wouldn't work with him because of his reputation, but younger kids breaking into the business were still influenced by him and would work with him. Joe ratted on me in 1965. He gave me four cases I really didn't do. I was sold out by him. And my lawyers didn't help. They were putzes. I ended up getting 16 months to 10 years for stuff I didn't even do."

For many in Kensington, such a betrayal warranted severe retribution, but Chick refrained. "I was never a violent type of guy," he says (though his reputation for nonviolence would be dramatically altered less than a half-dozen years later).

Chick was further sensitized to the drawbacks of working with partners by the death of La La McQuoid during a botched burglary in Florida. In late June 1965, an elite K&A crew broke into the "swanky home" of Mrs. Lucille Ferree in Fort Lauderdale. The gang had been tipped to a stash of expensive jewelry. What they found was a deadly trap that resulted in the shotgun murder of James L. McQuoid and Danny Gundaker's being shot in the face and shoulder.

According to news accounts, the FBI had received a tip that the K&A Gang was going down to Florida to do a piece of work. The Bureau's informant was right on the money. After a two-day stakeout at 2409 East Las Alos Boulevard, police welcomed the Philly burglars with a hefty dose of lead. After the gun-smoke cleared, bloodied and mangled bodies lay strewn on the thick pile carpet as gloating officers stood over them. The event captured headlines around the country. When Captain Joseph Brophy of the Philadelphia Police Department was asked by his Fort Lauderdale counterparts to help identify the participants, he tersely replied, "They're all from the K&A Gang and they're all top men in the field. Their field is burglary."

La La McQuoid, just 36 years old, went back to the early days of the gang and was one of its best-liked and most respected members. His death at the hands of the police—his friends referred to it as an "assassination" or "execution"—shocked many in the burglary community. K&A Gang members never carried weapons on the job. Lying in wait and shooting them down like dogs was uncalled for: they considered it the moral equivalent of premeditated murder.

For Chick Goodroe, the Fort Lauderdale incident sent a sobering message: partners talk. Somebody in the gang, he reasoned, had shot his mouth off—maybe in a bar, maybe to a disgruntled wife, maybe to a friendly police officer—and now La La was dead, Gundaker was fighting for his life in a Florida hospital, and two more were in prison. The idea of working alone was becoming more attractive all the time.

In the following years, Goodroe found himself spending more and more of his time burglarizing homes by himself. He would still occasionally work with a crew of friends at night, but his afternoons were increasingly spent in Philadelphia's affluent suburbs. The change had immediate dividends. "Working by myself," he says, "was more profitable." No longer would he have to share what he had stolen, and working alone ended his fear of being turned in by a partner. More than any other member of the K&A Gang, Chickie Goodroe flourished as a solitary worker.

"I was good," says Goodroe. "I could open a door without the key faster than the owner could with a key. Attitude was also a major factor. You couldn't afford to get ruffled. You had to be able to handle yourself in all sorts of circumstances. I was doing a house one time and the owners walk in while I'm searching the place. I tell them, 'It's all fixed' as I walk out. They looked at me and said, 'Thank you.'

"And I could work daytime and the other guys couldn't. Because I was half-Jewish, I looked like I belonged. Nobody questioned me being in a Jewish neighborhood. I could park my car on the street and walk right up to the front door and knock on it. If no one answered, I'd walk around the house to determine if anybody was home and the best point of entry. There was always a protected spot where no one could see me. I also focused on stuff I could grab. I didn't worry about breaking open a safe. It took too long, and some you just couldn't open. I'd leave my house at 11a.m. and be home by 2:30 in the afternoon. Sometimes I'd just do one house, and sometimes I'd do two or three. I made $7,000 from one house one time. I left my place at 11a.m. and was back by 12:15p.m. The door to the house was open, and I found gold coins in an attaché case. It was so easy, I went back again a couple weeks later."

On occasion, however, Chick wished he had brought a partner or two along, at least for the heavy lifting. "I was doing a piece of work in South Jersey," he recalls. "The house was in a wooded area down by the shore, and on the second floor I find a safe. I figure it's loaded. I didn't have any tools with me and not a lot of time, so I decide to take the damn thing home with me and work on it. It must have weighed several hundred pounds, and I'm breaking my back dragging this thing through the house. I finally get it outside and somehow manage to lift it up and into the trunk of my car, but I can't close the trunk. The safe's too big and bulky. I tie the trunk down as best I could so it doesn't flap open on the road and drive off.

"What I don't know, though, is that somebody had seen me doing all this stuff and called the police. They immediately set up roadblocks in the area, and after I stop to re-tie the knot holding the trunk down, I drive right into one. The cop stops me and asks, 'What do you have in the trunk?'

"I start to make small talk with the guy and slowly get out and walk to the back of the car. I'm hoping I can talk my way out of it, but the cop is persistent and wants me to open the trunk. He keeps on asking me, 'What's in the trunk? What do you have in the trunk?'

"I slowly start to walk to the front of the car. While he's trying to get a better look inside the trunk, I jump behind the wheel and pull out like I'm entered in the Indy 500. I'm about 30 yards away and the cop starts shooting at me. Bullets are hitting the car, I'm weaving all over the road, and I lose control. I drive off the road and crash into a tree somewhere in the middle of the Pine Barrens.

"I'm all banged up, but I manage to crawl out of the car and drag myself deep into the woods before the cop can catch up to me. I soon hear the sirens of more cop cars pulling into the area and eventually search dogs that are brought in to track me down, but it was so wet out there it must have confused the dogs. I laid out there in the brush, woods, and sand for two days. When I didn't hear any more searchers or barking dogs, I made my way to the shore and into Atlantic City. I must have looked like a derelict who had just been beaten up in a fight, 'cause I was all banged up from the crash and crawling through the woods for two days."

Although Goodroe avoided the police dragnet in the South Jersey Pine Barrens, the cops eventually got their man. The wrecked car—containing several bullet holes and the stolen safe—was traced back to him, and he was promptly given a new case. Through the good lawyering of Steve LaCheen, Goodroe rarely did time in prison, and when he did the sentences were manageable, especially considering the amount of burglary he was doing—solitary ventures in the afternoon, production work with a crew of partners in the evening. Burglary convictions normally resulted in relatively short prison terms, and in the 1950s and '60s more serious crimes could also draw a light sentence. No better example of this exists than the shooting of Chick's wife, Mary Ellen, and his friend and burglary partner Jimmy Castor. The May 1972 double shooting, which resulted in Castor's death and the serious wounding of Mary Ellen, could have put Goodroe away for life, but he was back on the streets in a little more than a year.

"It all started," according to Chick, "about three o'clock in the morning when I was driving down Route 70 near the Garden State Race Track. I'm riding along in my Jaguar, and out of the corner of my eye I see Mary Ellen's car in the parking lot of the Holiday Inn across from the track. I know it's her brand new Grand Prix because I just got it for her. It had this really beautiful sandalwood color. It was unique; there wasn't another one like it. Now I'm wondering, what's she doing out here?

"I had this friend who owned the bar, the Garden State Grille located in the hotel, so I thought I'd stop in and see if he saw her. He was just closing down the bar for the night, but once I describe her he remembers her right away. She was a beautiful girl, only 19, and that night she was wearing this beautiful hot pink outfit. It was her birthday.

" 'Yeah, I seen her,' says my friend. 'She was in here with Jimmy Castor and they left together. I think Castor was driving his Cadillac.'

"I start driving around looking for them, and in the parking lot of the Country Squire Inn I spot Castor's Cadillac. I go over to the motel's office and tell the clerk I think a buddy of mine is staying here. He's with a good-looking bimbo in a hot pink outfit. The clerk says he thinks they were staying there but wasn't sure what room they were in since he hadn't checked them in. He lets me look at the guest log, but there's no Castor registered. He was using an alias. I gave the clerk 20 bucks, and he gives me the key to the room he believes they're in.

"When I opened the door, they were both in bed naked. The gun was on the bureau. We both went for it. There was a struggle. We start hitting each other with the gun, the lamp, and anything we can get our hands on. Then he got shot and Mary Ellen was shot. I immediately cut out."

As he fled the scene, Chick thought his life was over. He had shot his wife and her lover. Visions of life in prison—maybe even the electric chair—filled his head. He had been on the run before (at the time of the shooting he was being sought by authorities in nearby Montgomery County). He knew the routine; he knew what to do.

"I went back to my house," says Chick, "and grabbed everything of value. I threw everything in the car and drove up to Allentown. I got a place to stay, bought a new car and a new identity. I also sent Mary Ellen flowers while she was recovering in the hospital. A couple days after she got out of the hospital, she came up to Allentown and started living with me. We were okay for months; then Mary Ellen had a dentist's appointment back in Philadelphia. I drove her down, and while she was at the dentist's I thought I'd do a piece of work in the suburbs. I got caught in Cheltenham. They not only had me for the burglary, but for the murder of Castor. Sal Avena set up a plea bargain for me. I pled guilty to involuntary manslaughter and we avoided a trial. We argued that it was a straightforward case of self-defense and a crime of passion. The prosecutor went for it. I guess he must have figured it was just one hoodlum killing another hoodlum. I was sentenced to a year and a half in jail."

The shooting incident unnerved Goodroe. But it was the realization that he had taken a life and shot his wife that was so unsettling, not the fact he was forced to live like a wild animal on the run. Chick considered himself a burglar, not a killer. He never wanted to physically harm anyone. Having law enforcement authorities pursuing him was no big deal. In fact, Chick did some of his best work as a fugitive and was already being sought by police at the time of the shooting. "I liked being a fugitive," he says. "You had to be aware of everything. It made you sharper, more awake, more alive." He compared it to a natural high where all the senses were extra-responsive.

Not long before the shooting, Chick and Mary Ellen had gone off to Hawaii while local authorities sought him for several burglaries. He called it a "vacation." For several months the couple lived like celebrities, staying at plush, top-of-the-line resorts, frequenting expensive restaurants and nightclubs, and taking cruises, all of it paid for by credit cards and Chick's periodic afternoon and evening visits to other people's homes. It was a wonderful time. The idyllic island getaway would have lasted considerably longer if not for a bit of self-destructive professional bravado—Chick's insistence on showing Mary Ellen the palatial penthouse of entertainer Don Ho.

"I got restless one day," says Chick, "and was looking over the posh Hawaiian Hilton Hotel. While I'm there, a dry cleaner is making a delivery and I notice the name 'Don Ho' on the clothes. Normally I'm looking for Jewish names. However, I figure this is worth a stop. I follow the delivery guy all the way up to the thirtieth floor; it's the penthouse. Now I know that's where all the money is. The guy knocks on the door a couple times—no one answers—and then leaves the packages by the door and takes the elevator back down. It's looking good; nobody is home, and I just happen to have some celluloid with me. I have no problem loiding the door and walk into a huge apartment. There's an incredible aquarium with some serious fish, a large, sophisticated recording studio, and a tremendous view of the bay and harbor. After admiring the view, I start wandering around the place looking for the master bedroom. I figure this could be a pretty good score. But there are several bedrooms, and while I'm searching I think I hear a noise in one of the rooms. Maybe somebody is home after all, so I immediately get the hell out of there.

"That evening, Mary Ellen and I are having dinner in the Hilton, and I guess I had a little too much to drink and wanted to show off, 'cause I ask her, 'How'd you like to see Don Ho's place in the penthouse? It's really incredible.'

"We go up to the penthouse and I knock on the door. No answer. I start to loid the door, but I'm having trouble. It's not working. This is odd, 'cause I had no trouble earlier in the day. Then I think I see some movement near the bottom of the door and begin to believe somebody on the other side is holding the doorknob. I tell Mary Ellen she's got to get out of there. I quickly put her on the elevator and send her down to the lobby while I take the stairs down. Believe it or not, I'm down the 30 floors before she is. I quickly leave the building, but when I look back the hotel's security has grabbed Mary Ellen and begun interrogating her.

"She tells them she meant no offense; she was just a fan hoping to get a celebrity's autograph. They then bring down Don Ho's maid to see if she can identify her. She says the people at the door didn't look like burglars. She says the couple at the door was well dressed, and the guy had a fancy sports coat on. It's always fascinated me how people always have this conception of what burglars look like or how they should be dressed. It never squares with reality.

"The hotel's security lets Mary Ellen go, but they have our address, and I know our time is up and we better get the hell out of there. We had to get out of Hawaii, but it was three o'clock in the morning, and I had three months of collectibles I had to pack up and get out of our room. We quickly got a room in another hotel and left the next day for Vegas. We stayed there a month."

Years later, Goodroe had a startling reminder of his lengthy Hawaiian vacation. "Mary Ellen and I were staying at the Concord up in the Catskills one time," he says. "I was up there often because it was a great place to relax and work all at the same time. I could take in the shows and entertainment, and also do a bit of work up there. While everyone was in the dining room having dinner, I was breaking into rooms and stealing anything of value I found interesting. It was easy, but none of the other K&A guys could have pulled it off. I looked Jewish and easily passed as just another Jew enjoying himself up there in the Catskills.

"One night, however, Mary Ellen and I are browsing in one of the hotel's swanky jewelry stores. There's a lot of people looking over the display cases, and all of a sudden some guy standing next to us starts yelling, 'That's my ring. That's my ring.'

"He's pointing at Mary Ellen's opal ring, which I had picked up while doing a piece of work in Hawaii. I start to turn red and figure this guy is the real owner of the damn ring and now I'm in big trouble. I'm not sure what I'm going to do, and Mary Ellen is now starting to get flustered. The guy, who's well dressed and looks like money, keeps saying, 'That's my ring. That's my ring,' and then adds, 'My initials are inside. Look inside the band. My initials, "BH," are inside the ring.'

"It turns out this guy was Bernard Hammerman, a well-known jewelry designer, who recognized one of his creations on Mary Ellen's hand and just wanted to do a little boasting in front of his wife or girlfriend. He scared the hell out of me and made me think that Hawaiian excursion had come back to haunt me."

As the years passed and Chick spent more time burglarizing houses on his own, he gradually became more interested in rare artifacts and expensive artwork. Cash and jewelry were always welcome, but historical documents, fine sculpture, and paintings became an additional source of profit. This shift in emphasis furthered his education, as the ninth-grade dropout sought to learn the fine points of classical, modern, and abstract art.

"I was doing a lot of work in the Washington, D.C., area," says Chick. "I once took a whole art collection from a house in Georgetown. I started to go to the Library of Congress and the Smithsonian on a regular basis to check out the history of the painters and value of certain paintings. As time passed, there seemed to be more money in artifacts, and so I became more interested in ancient bronze statues, delicate sculpture, and quality paintings. I really liked it, but you had to know what you were doing. Some houses would tell you the paintings inside them were of some value. And usually you'd know the work of an old master if you came upon it. But you didn't want to get cheated, and some fences didn't even know what you had. Some of these guys may recognize a real Picasso from a print, but most fences wouldn't know one of the old masters from a subway conductor. That's where the problem came in. You needed a European connection, someone who knew quality stuff and how to unload it. Someone who knew how to get the most money for what you had."

8. Blue Collar Robin Hoods

Sometimes we'd get a tip that a certain house had some money stashed away, maybe a safe or a secret hiding place where a bundle was supposed to be hidden. I was always nervous about tips; maybe it was a setup and the cops'd be waiting for us. But we did a few when they sounded good. Well, it happened on more than one occasion where we'd break in a house and it immediately looked suspicious. The furniture, the rugs, the wallpaper, everything looked old, drab, and faded. We'd go through the house and there was nothing of value there. Christ, it almost seemed like the owner was a 90-year-old grandmother on welfare or something. After a while, one of us would say, "This place is a bust. The folks livin' here are poorer than us. Let's throw 'em a couple bucks and get the hell out of here." Then each of us would drop a 10- or 20-dollar bill on the kitchen table, walk out, and go to the next house.

—GEORGE "JUNIOR" SMITH

We were half of the Robin Hood myth. Yeah, we took from the rich, but we didn't give it to the poor. We squandered it. Bars loved us. Car agencies loved us. We spent it like fools. There was no sense of value there. We spent money like drunken sailors. Robin Hoods? Nah, we spent the money.

—JIMMY DOLAN

We didn't want to hurt anyone. We didn't want to terrorize people. We stole for a living. It was nothing personal.

—CHARLES "CHICKIE" GOODROE

IN THE EARLY 1960s, a growing number of young truants, delinquents, and social misfits rejected the notion of earning an honest wage in a Kensington carpet mill, shipyard, or hat factory in favor of the fast life of the streets. The riveting Pottsville drama was still being played out in the daily newspapers. Meanwhile, that alternative neighborhood career option, the K&A burglary crew, gained respect and esteem.

The gangs' exploits were well covered in the media and their lavish lifestyle was showcased at corner saloons, but most Kensingtonians went about their business and displayed little if any outward displeasure with the local high school dropouts turned hip, expensively attired men-about-town. Many in Kensington looked at gang members with envy; it was almost as if they "weren't really criminals." Some attribute this tolerance to the gang's "Robin Hood mystique."

"They didn't bother anybody in the neighborhood," argues Gil Slowe. "You never had no trouble with them," but, he further cautions, "you didn't want to give them any trouble either."

Slowe's wife, Ronnie, agrees. "I never saw them as bad guys," she says. "They were always well behaved around me." As a teenager in the 1950s, Ronnie served gang members coffee in the local Horn & Hardart's. She never once had a problem with any of them; in fact, she admits to having had a crush on one. "Effie Burke was very nice to me," says Ronnie. "He made me feel real comfortable. He never treated me anything but good."

Gil and Ronnie Slowe's almost affectionate view of the local burglary ring is not unique in Kensington. Residents did not feel threatened by the local thieves; some even thought they had a certain happy-go-lucky charm. "I don't know of them hurting anybody," says Mary Kober. Although she would often see K&A gang members driving their brand new, colorful Cadillac convertibles and big Lincoln Town Cars through the streets, or hanging out in neighborhood restaurants and bars, usually attired in expensive suits and shoes, "they were just . . . the K&A burglars," nothing to be angry or alarmed about.

Today, Jack Dempsey views the guys as Kensington's version of South Philly's "goodfellows" or "wiseguys." Instead of Italians with slicked-back hair and sharkskin suits, you had tough, hard-nosed, ruddy-faced Irishmen whose behavior could probably be chalked up to "immaturity, attention deficit, and bi-polar" disorder. "But who knew of that stuff back then?" asks Dempsey. "They were crazy and always raising hell, but they didn't really bother anybody." And besides: "They'd always help you out if you needed money." As a kid in the late forties who earned a few bucks shining shoes in local restaurants and pool halls, Dempsey knew them as "exciting characters" and "great tippers. For a 10-cent shine, they'd give you a half-dollar or dollar tip."

Joseph Edelman, a businessman whose drinking establishment is just a few feet from the busy intersection of Kensington and Allegheny Avenues, recalls the burglars as local "Robin Hoods" and "gentleman thieves." He considered most of them "pretty classy guys" who followed their own "code of honor." And as misguided as that code may have been, they were not without a social conscience, for, as Edelman says, they "helped a few people out." "They threw their money around," he admits, on parties and drinking binges, but they also showed sympathy for distressed neighbors and shoved "one hundred dollar bills on people" in a time of need.

Two factors allowed Kensington people to look favorably on the gangs. First, a community that sent "more kids to jail than college" viewed property crime as less wicked than violent, personal crime. And, second, the well-known gang members "weren't plundering anything in the neighborhood." "A lot of them were nice guys," recalls Bob McClernand, who went to school with future gang members and competed against a few of them on the athletic field. They were guys with "a good sense of humor," and many were "willing to lend you money if you were in a jam."

Maybe Brother Hugh McGuire of the Christian Brothers religious order sums up the community attitude best: "They weren't really criminals." His fond assessment was not shared by their victims or the police, but it was not unique in the community. The Kensington burglars who broke the hearts and destroyed the sense of security of homeowners from Bar Harbor to Miami, and drove East Coast law enforcement authorities to distraction, basically left most Kensington businessmen and residents alone.

"They never bothered a soul around here," says Paul Melione. A neighborhood barber for over 50 years, Melione took note of things from his storefront window on Allegheny Avenue and insists, "There were no burglaries around K&A. We had petty thieves around here, but none of the real burglars worked around here." In fact, he recalls, the gang would often act as peacekeepers. "They told folks to behave around here or they'd suffer severe consequences." Melione thought most of the gang members were decent guys; some were "gentlemen" who chose burglary as a profession only because "they didn't want to work" a regular nine-to-five factory job.

It is probably the drunken spending sprees and the generosity of individual gang members that Kensington residents remember best. "They were pretty loose with their money," recalls Joseph DiLeo, a Kensington Avenue bar owner, and they could put on quite a party. "If you needed money they'd give it to you," says Ed Froggatt, who grew up and went to school with many of the K&A guys. "Everybody trusted them. They were very generous, good, down-to-earth guys who could be a lot of fun." One day they would be "playing games against a wall with one hundred dollar bills," he recalls, and the next day "you'd see them in a club and they'd ask you for some change for a beer. They were broke." And then "the next time you'd see them on the street or in a bar, they'd give you 10 or 15 dollars" to pay you back for that 10-cent glass of beer you bought them.

"They gave money away," says Paul Melione. "They gave waitresses hundred-dollar tips. If you were a neighbor and facing hard times you could always go to them for help." Hence what Melione calls their "Robin Hood reputation."

"I'm telling you," says Jim Moran, "Jackie Johnson must have given a fortune away. He'd be sitting in a bar drinking his beers and reading the newspaper, and people would come in and give him a sob story and he'd end up giving them a 10-, 20-, or 50-dollar bill. Word would get around Kensington that Jack Johnson just made a score the night before, and he was drinking at Kellis's or the Shamrock or some other place, and all of a sudden you'd have a line of people out there hoping to get a piece of the action. It was like he had his own social work agency. I'm telling you, Jack gave a fortune away."

Jimmy Dolan is another one of the usual Sherwood Forest suspects. "Believe it or not," says Jimmy Laverty, "Dolan regularly gave money to the orphans at St. Vincent's Orphanage. He'd say 'Let's all throw in two, three hundred dollars apiece for the kids.' And if somebody was in trouble, Dolan would pull out four or five 20-dollar bills and give it to the guy. He'd give it up even though he'd be left with eight dollars in his own pocket." Such gestures were rewarded.

"Burglars were admired," says Jim Moran. "They were getting over" on the system, "but not hurting anybody. And money flowed from them to the community." This lovable-scoundrel view of the K&A burglars extended well beyond Kensington's borders. Even the men assigned to apprehend and prosecute them occasionally admit their amusement and begrudging respect. "They had fun; they were a fun-loving bunch of characters," says former Assistant District Attorney Joel Moldovsky, who established a special departmental unit in the Philadelphia DA's office to hunt them down and get them off the street. "They were princes of the city."

In probably the best testament to Kensington's romanticized notion of the gang, concerned parents would ask the older, better-known K&A burglars like Effie Burke, Willie Sears, or Hughie Breslin for help with their unmotivated or trouble-prone sons. They wanted their kids to become apprentice burglars, and who better to instruct them than established K&A guys? "I remember fathers, even mothers sometimes, coming up to Effie on the street and asking if he'd do them a favor and take their kid on the next trip," says Jimmy Laverty. "They'd tell Effie, 'He's a good kid. I know he'd work out as a driver or watcher.'" (Mothers whose sons went into the business often defended their boys' choice of profession by telling neighbors, "At least they don't hurt anybody.")

In some quarters, in fact, the K&A gang members were celebrities. Starting out as aimless misfits and oddball street urchins with junior high school educations and a bad attitude, they had achieved a certain status or flare that made them objects of interest and speculation—even adulation on occasion. "You'd go in a bar," recalls Jimmy Laverty, "and get stares from people as if you were a well-known major league ballplayer. People wanted to meet us and tell their friends. We were celebrities."

The flashy lifestyle was enough to turn heads. "Guys had money and new cars," says Laverty. "You'd go to the JR Club under the Frankford El and it looked like a Cadillac showroom. Everybody had a brand new Cadillac back then."

Not everyone bought into the idealized perception of sharp-dressing, soft-hearted burglars, working-class heroes, or homegrown Robin Hoods. Some saw the K&A Gang for what they were: thieves. Maybe they were elite burglars, maybe they were top-of-the line second story men, but they were thieves all the same. "They were just crooks," says Andrew Guckin. Guckin, a long-time Kensington resident and local businessman, witnessed the gang's growth and eventual demise. He blames the gang for giving the neighborhood a bad name and the press for hyping their escapades. "Kensington was a good solid neigh-borhood, there were some professionals, and everything could be purchased on Kensington Avenue," he says. "Most people were stable and hard working, but the press kept on writing about 'the K&A Gang,' 'the K&A Gang,' 'the K&A Gang.' The press built them up more than what they deserved. You never heard about the good people." For Guckin, all the media accounts of the gang's exploits were "nothing to be boastful about. I didn't see where it brought us any pride."

As for the gang's Robin Hood image and Kensington's lavish production of burglars, Guckin is equally unimpressed. For him, their acts of generosity do not outweigh the harm they did, and, furthermore, he doesn't believe that Kensington produced any more burglars than any other Philadelphia neighborhood. And yet as burglars go, Guckin flatly states, the K&A Gang was top-shelf: "They were the best. That's why they attracted so much publicity. Most of us try to be the best we can, and if you're gonna be a burglar, you may as well try to be the best."

9. Pugilists, Drunks, and Misfits

One of the teams had a sit-down. Somebody knew their business and was talking to the Feds. They had gotten caught with a safe. They had done a doctor's house and robbed him of $450,000, but somebody close to them had dropped a dime on them.

They think it may be Terry and finally decide they don't want Terry to hang around with them any more. Now they got to figure out who's gonna tell him. John Terry is somebody you don't really want to fool with. He and his brother Charlie have both been convicted of murder, and they've both done a lot of work, if you know what I mean.

The guys decide to pick straws to see who's gonna get the job of tellin' Terry the bad news and Frankie gets the short straw. They meet at the 19th Hole Lounge downtown, and Frankie tells John Terry he's out, the guys don't want him to hang around any more. He says some shit is going on, and somebody is talking. He tells Terry to stay away from them.

Terry gets an attitude right away and tells Frankie, that's all fucked up and you think I'm a rat. He asks Frankie if he has his shit with him, and Frankie says no. Terry then tells him, the next time I see you, you better have your shit on you.

Frankie took the threat seriously, 'cause all of a sudden he pulls a gun and shoots John Terry in the head. Customers scatter; the bartender locks the door and goes into a panic. He starts hitting the bourbon, drinking one shot after another. Frankie drags the body to his car and starts driving around looking for a good place to dump the body. In the meantime, the bartender, who's still knocking back a few, reopens for business. In an hour or so, Frankie comes back to the bar, and he still has the body with him. He says he couldn't find an alley to dump it in. They prop the body up in the men's room, have a few more drinks, and try to decide what to do.

Customers are periodically going to the bathroom, but no one makes a big deal about it. Apparently it's the type of joint nobody is surprised to see a body propped up on a toilet seat. Eventually, Frankie and the bartender decide to call the police and come up with some phony line about the shooting. In the meantime, a customer comes up and says to the bartender, "Hey, did you know there's a dead guy in the bathroom?"

The bartender, who's from the neighborhood and now pretty well fucked up himself, tells the guy, "Mind your own business, fella. Didn't you ever see a dead body before?"

The cops arrive, but right off the bat they're suspicious. When they examine the body, they notice that rigor mortis has already set in. They know the shooting took place much earlier than Frankie and the bartender claim it did.

Eventually, the bartender cracked and testified against Frankie. But he was only convicted of involuntary manslaughter.

—JUNIOR KRIPPLEBAUER

I'm talking to Bones one day in his office on York Street and he tells me he just picked up a new fighter, a young heavyweight. He says the kid's got potential, but he only speaks Spanish.

I say to Bones, "But, Bones, you don't speak Spanish. How you gonna communicate with this kid? How you gonna teach him anything? You only speak English and he only speaks Spanish."

"Whaddya mean?" says Bones. "I speak Spanish."

"Okay," I say. "Let me hear you speak some Spanish. How are you gonna tell this kid to train?"

"I'm gonna tell him to 'go runno aroundo the blocko teno timeso.'"

—JIMMY DOLAN

They really wanted to do a good thing. Their intentions were good, but as usual things got a little weird. It was like that sometimes.

Leo Gillis, one of the toughest little monkeys you'd ever want to meet, had just died, and there didn't seem to be any family around to make any of the funeral arrangements. A couple guys, Harry McCabe and another guy, decided to try and do right by little Leo, so they took his body to a local undertaker for a proper burial. Unfortunately, after the funeral director goes through the list of items to be purchased like a coffin, embalming, Catholic service, and such, he comes up with a big number. The guys are broke, they don't have any money, and the guy ain't gonna bury Leo without gettin' paid.

McCabe and this other guy then get the brainstorm of raising the money for Leo's burial. They'll just go from bar to bar in Kensington, tell guys Leo died and needs burying, and could they chip in 10, 20 bucks to give Leo a decent burial. They figure it won't be that hard 'cause everybody knew Leo and knew what a standup guy he was all his life. Leo was a real tough guy. He hit so fuckin' hard. I saw him hit a nigger in Holmesburg; he knocked the guy out for 15 minutes. I thought he killed him.

Somehow McCabe gets ahold of a refrigerated meat truck, wraps Leo's body in a large blanket, and throws him in the back with all the hams, bacon, and pork chops. Well, they're ridin' around Kensington stopping at all the bars and taverns asking for donations to bury old Leo. Now guys are chipping in, throwin' them five, 10, 20 bucks, and of course McCabe and his buddy are having a few drinks themselves as they reminisce about Leo and what a tough son-of-a-bitch he was all his life. Pound for pound he was one of the toughest guys on the street. This goes on for hours as the guys drive this truck around with Leo's body in it.

The money begins to accumulate, but the guys are also startin' to feel good about this campaign of theirs and start to offer toasts to Leo's memory and buy a round or two at each of these joints. Realizing they got a long way to go to get up to what the undertaker is gonna charge them, McCabe and his friend start selling some of the meat out of the back of the truck at various streetcorners. They're selling hams for three, four, five bucks apiece and doing okay at it. Folks were gettin' a good deal.

Along the way they start doin' business with a Greek guy who owns a restaurant or something, and he starts buying a good number of these discounted hams and pork chops. He knows these hams and chops go for a lot more than what Harry is charging him, so he's really into it.

While they're doing business at the back of the truck, he spies this big wrapped package and asks, "What's that?"

"Oh, that ain't nothin'," says McCabe. "It's just a side of beef."

"Well, how much you want for it?" asks the Greek guy, not knowing he's making an offer to buy a real stiff, little Leo.

I don't know whether the guys thought about it or not, but they sold most of the hams and kept Leo.

Now they're still on their mission, but at some point they end up spending more money at these bars than what they're getting in donations. Toasting Leo, buying rounds, gettin' drunk, by the end of the night they're nearly broke again. This goes on for several days, and Leo ain't any closer to gettin' buried and they're still nowhere near what the undertaker is asking. After the third or fourth day, they begin to panic. Leo's starting to go bad, he's beginning to decompose in the back of the truck. They now begin wondering with each additional beer what they're gonna do with this body that's going bad on them.

Finally one of 'em gets the swell idea to drive to a cemetery, so off they go in the dead of night with the truck and Leo. It's late, so they're wandering around this cemetery in the dark looking for a decent place to dump Leo. Eventually they come across a freshly dug grave. Since it's unoccupied, they carry Leo out of the truck, stick him in the hole, quickly cover him over with dirt, and get the hell out of there.

As I said, the guys sincerely wanted to do a good thing, but after more than a few drinks they ended up partyin' with a stiff. It's not exactly what they intended on doin', but things just got a little messed up. It was like that sometimes. —JUNIOR KRIPPLEBAUER

MANY CITIES AND NEIGHBORHOODS HARBOR their share of Runyonesque oddballs, especially of the gangster variety: Boston's North End, Hell's Kitchen in New York, Chicago's Near West Side, the Woodlands district in Cleveland, and San Francisco's North Beach, to name a few. Philadelphia's Kensington belongs to that loopy pantheon of working-class ethnic neighborhoods. By anyone's standard, Kensington was home to an abundance of incredible screwballs.

Overworked, underpaid, hangover-plagued factory workers trying to scratch out a living. Stressed-out Irish Catholic housewives riding herd over passels of snot-nosed children. Eagle-eyed Jewish proprietors guarding their Kensington Avenue merchandise against freckled-faced nine-year-old thieves. They provide a good beginning. Add on a burgeoning criminal element: lazy, happy-go-lucky, Budweiser-guzzling burglars, zany scam artists, cunning fences, and bold, in-your-face gunmen. The world of Willie Sears, Effie Burke, Jimmy Laverty, and the other production workers was far from dreary. And, as Philadelphia Detective Herbie Rhodes bluntly said, "There were more assholes per square foot in Kensington than anywhere else I ever worked."

Unforgettable characters could be found gulping down an endless row of beers in the Shamrock, the 197, the JR, the Pleasantville, the Erie Social, Nino's, Kellis's, and the many other bars and after-hours clubs that dotted the community. They came in all shapes, sizes, and professions: deeply tanned, weatherbeaten roofers; sneering, cynical cops; average, surly, salt-of-the-earth felons. Occasionally, they were all three. Sometimes it felt as if Kensington had cornered the market on off-beat characters.

For many Kensingtonians—both inside and outside the criminal arena—the name "Charlie Devlin" has a special ring: sort of like the ringing in your ears after an unexpected blow to the head. A Shakespeare-quoting bully who patrolled Kensington's bars and back alleys with authoritative regularity, Charlie Devlin was a menacing figure of legendary proportions who could have achieved pugilistic infamy in any city in the country. It was Philadelphia, however, and in particular the beleaguered neighborhood of Kensington, that had the singular misfortune of having to put up with his bloody shenanigans. Other overbearing, pugilistic warriors circulated through Kensington, but there was something special about Charlie. Observing the mayhem-laden landscape he created, one local offers this succinct judgment: "Charlie Devlin was a fuckin' jerkoff. He was a petty-ass thief who wasn't good enough to work with the better K&A crews, but I'll give him this, he was tough as hell." Many called him "the toughest guy in the city of Philadelphia."

Although he was not particularly imposing physically, his penchant for bloody, tooth-jarring, bar-room, back alley, and streetcorner confrontations was renowned throughout the city. A little over six feet tall and well over 200 pounds, Devlin was broad-nosed with dark, heavy eyebrows, deep-set eyes, and a receding hairline. "He was built like a pear, with huge, powerful hips and legs, but narrow shoulders. He looked unimpressive, but he could dance and he could hit." His capacity to hit was particularly memorable. "He had huge, powerful hands that could punch walls without being damaged," recalls one cellblock partner. "His hands wouldn't break no matter what he hit. His fingers were two to three times as large as those on the average hand."

A tough street kid, he perfected his intimidating demeanor and boxing skills at "White Hill" (officially the Camp Hill Reformatory), where he was sent in 1948, as a 16-year-old, for "delinquency." Imprisonment only fed his criminal and antisocial tendencies. During the next decade, Devlin was arrested from one to three times a year for "drunk and disorderly conduct," "aggravated assault and battery," and "resisting arrest." Sprinkled throughout his police file during the fifties were arrests for "larceny," "burglary," "gun possession," and at least one "shooting."

Some of his early criminal exploits garnered a good bit of press coverage. In 1954, for example, Devlin and three accomplices were caught burglarizing a neighborhood supermarket. Although local K&A boys Leo Gillis and Maury McAdams were also part of the heist, what made the story noteworthy was the fact that a Philadelphia policeman had been captured with them at the scene. It was quickly determined that the 23-year-old cop had repeatedly served as the burglary ring's driver and lookout during a series of commercial break-ins and beer hall lootings. Devlin did his time, as usual—a brief respite until he was out on the street and back in the action.

Though he would continue to dabble in burglary and work semilegitimately as a nightclub bouncer and union enforcer for the next decade and a half, Devlin's rap sheet expanded. Assault and battery and resisting arrest charges accumulated, like the welts, bruises, and black eyes on the faces of innocent bystanders, neighborhood tough guys, and district police officers. Charlie Devlin was a one-man wrecking crew, a riot waiting to ignite. His menacing reputation pervaded Kensington, and bartenders and club owners had a ringside seat for the nightly bedlam.

"Charlie Devlin was sick," recalls Sonny Ford, a long-time neighborhood bartender. "He was a sociopath. He needed people to be subservient to him. He once stabbed a bartender at 'A' & Allegheny when he didn't like what the guy was doing behind the bar."

"Charlie was treacherous," says Gene Pedicord, another bartender who had the misfortune of dealing with Devlin and his shakedown routine at various area bars during the fifties and sixties. "He'd call up and ask who was there. He wanted to know so he could come over and get some money. He traveled from bar to bar in order to get money off of people." Pedicord, Ford, and others became all too familiar with Devlin's intimidation of customers and the subsequent loss of business. Not to mention the bloodshed and property destruction. "We'd give him 10, 20 dollars at a time to stay out of the bar," Pedicord remembers.

The unusual practice of bribing customers to stay out of one's place of business may not have originated with Charlie Devlin, but he helped to popularize it. "Owners would pay him off to get rid of him," says Marty Rubin, a highly respected bar owner whose drinking establishments became a second home to burglars and cops alike. In fact, many bar owners in Kensington and surrounding neighborhoods decided that it was better to pay Devlin to stay out of their businesses than to have him as a customer. Friday and Saturday nights were particularly profitable for Devlin. He'd travel by taxi to popular bars and pick up envelopes or be handed a couple of twenties. At the end of the night, he had a pretty good haul. He'd then stiff the cabbie who had just spent the night driving him around the city. Those taxi drivers who protested quickly learned the error of their ways; Charlie enjoyed dishing out the punishment.

"I saw Charlie walk over to a guy in Magee's Bar and just beat the hell out of him," recalls one witness, still seemingly stunned by the incident. "Charlie was a no-good bum."

Devlin's attacks were unprovoked, indiscriminate, commonplace, and in plain view for all to see; he was a full-time, equal-opportunity head thumper. If you became the object of his interest, it was lights out; suicide might be a better alternative.

Tommy O'Rourke, a 30-year-man in the U.S. Marshal's Service, was the recipient of the Charlie Devlin treatment early in his law enforcement career. "I was a city cop at the time," says O'Rourke, "and after work one night I stopped in Joe Scanlan's bar for a drink. Soon after, Charlie Devlin and Leo Gillis walk in. Both of these guys have serious reputations. They're as tough as they come, but I'm minding my own business. Devlin doesn't know I'm a cop. Just my luck, he comes over to me and says, 'Hey, you have a cigarette?'

"I told him, 'I don't smoke.'

"Then Charlie puts his face within an inch of mine and says, 'I didn't ask if you smoked. I asked if you had a cigarette.'

"There was no doubt Charlie wanted to start a fight," says O'Rourke. "I'm just off duty and all of a sudden I'm in a bunch of shit."

Fortunately, some other customers familiar with Charlie's routine decided to intervene. They calmed Charlie down, bought him a drink, and persuaded him to find another watering hole. "The next day," says O'Rourke, "I'm at the station house and hear Charlie started a fight at Kellis's Bar last night and all hell broke loose. Charlie Devlin was a nasty bastard."

Kellis's, a well-known watering hole for alcoholics at Kensington and Allegheny Avenues, was a regular haunt of Devlin's—to the dismay of the Kellis family. They had purchased the Majestic Restaurant in 1952 and a few years later converted it into a bar. It was immediately popular and soon became a favorite hangout of the K&A burglars, who would often meet there before going on the road. John Kellis, the owner's son, recalls little trouble from the regular gang members. "The guys were always clean-cut looking," says Kellis. "They wore white shirts and nice suits. There were no bums among them. Jackie Johnson, for example, was a nice guy. He wasn't an animal. He was always well-dressed and behaved himself."

Charlie Devlin was a different story, a predatory Great White anxious to feed, ready to strike, always smelling blood in the water. John Kellis saw more than his fair share of the carnage. He hated Devlin.

"Charlie was an animal," says Kellis. "When he came in, the joint cleared out. I'll never forget that guy. I get chills up and down my spine just thinking of that son-of-a-bitch. He was an animal. I nearly had to shoot him one day. He came in the bar one afternoon and the joint cleared out; everybody just got up and walked out. It happened every time he came in. Nobody wanted to be around him. They were afraid of him. He killed my business. He said he was gonna break every bottle over my head, and then he grabbed my throat. I pulled a gun from under the bar and put it right in his face. He backed off real quick.

"Even the cops were afraid of him," says Kellis. "I seen cops come to pull Charlie out of here and they were scared shitless. They were saying real nice, 'Come on, Charlie.' 'Be nice, Charlie.' 'C'mon, Charlie.' 'Don't cause a problem, Charlie.' I couldn't fuckin' believe it." But Kellis is well aware that he was lucky to get the police to show up at all. Often they wouldn't even respond to his calls for assistance: too many of them required emergency room treatment after confrontations with Devlin. Riding through the district, cops in squad cars would ask the police dispatcher, "Is it Charlie Devlin?" when notified of a Kensington bar disturbance. Some cops chose to pass up the honor of tangling with Charlie Devlin. In such cases the Kellis family and other targets of Charlie's interest had to fend for themselves.

Even Devlin's good buddies came in for abuse. Jackie Johnson, for instance, was a regular recipient of Charlie's bullying, and John "John L." McManus once had to slug Devlin over the head with a baseball bat to keep Devlin off him; they were working out in a prison exercise yard at the time. Jimmy Dolan often tells his own prison story: the time Charlie twisted him into a pretzel while they were exercising in the yard at a large maximum-security state prison in Pennsylvania.

"We're playing basketball at Graterford one morning," says Dolan, wincing at the memory. "I'm 150 pounds and running around like a wild man. I stole the ball from Charlie 10 times and was scoring like crazy. Charlie was getting hotter and hotter. Finally, he snaps out and comes after me. He wants to kill me and, don't you know, catches me before I can get away. Charlie gets me in a hold and starts twisting and squeezing me. I can barely breathe. All of a sudden, I hear something snap. I can't feel my legs. I'm paralyzed below the waist. I can't feel a thing and I'm scared to death. I scream, 'I'm hurt! Let me go!'

"I'm now lying out on the court and they've got to bring a stretcher out for me and take me to the prison hospital.

"Devlin looks worried. He leans over and says, 'I'm sorry, Dolan. I didn't mean it.'

"I told him, 'I know, Charlie, but look what you done to me.'

"They carry me to the hospital and I'm thinking, I'm ruined, that damn gorilla paralyzed me for life. Fortunately, the doctor knew what had happened to me. He turned me on my stomach and pressed with all his might on my back. I heard a snap and immediately started to get some feeling in my legs. He snapped my back in place again and I was okay, but Charlie nearly fucked me up for good. He didn't know his own strength."

Devlin's reputation for "fucking people up" preceded him. Even seasoned jailhouse toughs kept their distance. Although Philadelphia's county jails and Pennsylvania's state prisons were heavily black by the mid-sixties, leading most white prisoners to try to keep a low profile, "Devlin would walk up to the niggers in the jail and if he saw cigarettes in their top pocket, he'd just take them out and tell the guys to fuck themselves if they objected. Very few guys—black or white—could stand up to him."

Most K&A men who spent any time at all in Kensington's taverns saw at least one or two of Devlin's back alley brawls and heard spellbinding accounts of many others. Sometimes, rarely—usually when he was outnumbered—Charlie endured a beating that would have killed a lesser man. As one observer said, "What would kill a horse wouldn't bother him." But even the honor of defeating Devlin was of short duration. In his book, the bout wasn't truly over until he was victorious. "If you beat him," says Gene Pedicord, "he was at your door the next day and would want to fight all over again. You could never get away from him until he won."

Jimmy Laverty witnessed a good many of Devlin's antics. "I went from first to sixth grade with Charlie," says Laverty. "He was a pretty nice fellow, a friendly guy, but prison changed him. When he entered the prison system as a teenager, I guess he figured, I'm gonna be a here a while so I better get tough."

What amazed Laverty was Charlie's capacity to absorb punishment. He seemed impervious to blows that would knock down and cripple most other combatants. "His big thing," says Laverty, "was that you couldn't hurt him. I saw six cops with blackjacks on Charlie one time. They were beating the hell out of him. Blood was squirting all over the place, but he wouldn't stop. He just wouldn't quit." The cops got the message: deal with Charlie Devlin at your own risk. "The cops were afraid of him. They'd wait till they had three or four cop cars available and a half-dozen guys before they'd try to take him on."

Numbers—as in being outnumbered—didn't seem to faze Charlie. Some neighborhood guys recall the time Charlie took on an entire football team. "One time," says Jimmy Moran, obviously still impressed, "Charlie had a beef with some guys from the Venango Bears, a local semi-pro football team. It must have been pretty bad because one day about a dozen of them tracked Charlie down to the Crescent Bar at Front and Allegheny. They weren't looking to kiss and make up either; they were carrying pipes, chains, and tire irons. Charlie got a call at the bar that they were coming down for him, but he doesn't run and sneak out the back door. He was no pussy. He rolls up his sleeves and tells the guys who are drinking in the bar there's gonna be some action soon, and he wants to know who's prepared to help him. Most guys got up and told Charlie they had to catch a plane. They got the hell out of there. They weren't gonna get killed for Charlie.

"Well, the Bears, all 12 of 'em, come in the bar. Charlie gets cornered against a wall by a dartboard. Things are looking bad. They're ready to maul him, and what does Charlie do? He yells at them, 'Okay, motherfuckers, let's go.'

"Well, the first guy rushes Charlie and is dropped immediately. Charlie gave him a right hand shot to the jaw, and the guy goes down for the count. No sooner than he's through saying, 'Who's next?' when they all rush him. I'm tellin' you, they beat the ever-lovin' piss out of him. They hurt him real bad. He had to be taken out of there on a stretcher. On the way out, though, he said to a guy, 'If they all would have come at me like the first guy, it would have been okay. I would've taken them all out.' I'm telling you, Charlie Devlin was a tough son-of-a-bitch," says Jimmy Moran. "He didn't back down from anybody."

Charlie may have had some mental problems, but stupidity wasn't one of them, say some of his old neighborhood cronies. "He was no dummy," claims one life-long associate. "Charlie was definitely smart. He had ideas. He came up with ways to make money."

Charlie's powers of memorization were renowned. He would bet bar patrons they couldn't name a drinking establishment in the area whose phone number he didn't know. Guys would come up with 20 to 30 bars, and Charlie knew every number. It was as if he had an alcoholic rolodex implanted in his brain.

Even more unbelievable was Charlie's partiality to poetry and the classics. All the time he was chasing John L. McManus around the exercise yard at Graterford Prison, he was reciting "The Raven" by Edgar Allan Poe. The dramatic rendering underscored Charlie's threatening intentions, explaining why John L. felt he had no choice but to slug the poetry-quoting lunatic with a baseball bat.

Jimmy Moran recalls the time a half-dozen factory workers and roofers nearly fell off their bar stools when Charlie started an impromptu drama festival. "We're in a bar one day," says Moran, "and all of a sudden Charlie begins to recite a Shakespeare soliloquy. It went on for several minutes. And then he did another one. Jaws dropped all over the place; everyone was dumbfounded. They never expected a big lummox like Charlie, who loved to fight and was always drunk, to come out with *Hamlet* and Shakespearian sonnets. But what people didn't know was that Charlie was well-read. A lot of those guys who did a lot of time were big readers."

Charlie was still best known as a tough guy, a ham-and-egg, bare-knuckle masher who never backed down and didn't require a sidearm or any other weapon to get his point across. On those rare occasions when he resorted to carrying a gun, however, he wasn't afraid to use it. He shot Ray Chalmers, a long-time acquaintance, and according to Jimmy Laverty, who witnessed the confrontation, it started over those staples of bar-room hostility: a woman and money.

It seems a real looker known as "Up and Down Mary" was at the Randolph Club one night and while dancing had her pocketbook lightened by 40 dollars. Mary believed Charlie Devlin, the bar's bouncer, had stolen her money and encouraged Chalmers to get it back for her. Ray Chalmers, better known as "Raybo" to all his Kensington buddies, was no tough guy; he was a K&A burglar and normally would never have approached a legitimate tough guy like Charlie over such a matter. However, Raybo had been hoping to catch Up and Down Mary's eye for some time. The prospect of being the hero who saves the day for a damsel in distress appealed to him. Unfortunately, things didn't quite work out that way.

As Jimmy Laverty tells the story, Chalmers and Devlin have a sit-down over the missing money, and things quickly get out of hand. Devlin, outraged by the accusation, threatens Chalmers, but "Raybo tells Charlie to stay seated, he says he has a .45-caliber semiautomatic under the table and it's pointed right at him.

He then tells Charlie to get the money." Devlin, not used to being bullied, leaves the Randolph, but only to get his own gun. When he returns to the club, he tells Laverty to bring Raybo outside. "Tell the skinny little bastard to apologize," he instructs Laverty. "If he doesn't apologize, I'm gonna kill him."

"Raybo comes out of the bar and laughs when he sees Charlie holding a gun," says Laverty. "He tells Devlin, 'What are you doin' with a gun, Charlie? Tough guys aren't supposed to carry guns.'"

Worked up and unused to being laughed at, Charlie sees that Raybo is unarmed and asks, where's his gun? Raybo admits he was bluffing and laughs at Charlie again. Furious, Charlie fires his gun but aims at the pavement. Shards of concrete fly up around them.

Raybo laughs again and barks, "Devlin, you're blind as a bat. You can't hit a thing."

Charlie then raises the weapon and fires it again, this time hitting Chalmers in the thigh. Stunned and nearly knocked off his feet, Raybo looks down at his leg, which is now bleeding profusely. He then, according to Jimmy Laverty, looks up at Devlin with an incredulous expression and says, "I don't fuckin' believe it. I just bought this suit."

Friends and bar patrons come out onto the sidewalk and assess the damage as the police arrive. Raybo has to be taken to the hospital, but he instructs the bartender not to take his drink away: "I'll be back before last call."

Herbie Rhodes was one of the arresting officers who responded "to a shooting outside the Randolph Club." He admitted to "not liking Charlie a little bit" and wasn't one to put up with his shenanigans. "I whacked him pretty good," recalled Rhodes. "I hit him in the head with a shotgun when I arrested him."

As usual, police had a difficult time getting the K&A men to cooperate; even the victim was close-mouthed. "Chalmers at first refused to identify his assailant" and told Rhodes that he was already paying the price in the neighborhood for being thought to be an "informant." Eventually, though, Chalmers told the full story, and Devlin was charged with "assault with intent to kill, aggravated assault and battery by shooting, and violation of parole," but such a case was far from a prosecutor's dream. Philadelphia's court system in those days resembled a crapshoot, especially when well-connected and savvy K&A guys were involved. At trial, Devlin was found not guilty, and his case was discharged.

"Charlie Devlin had nine lives," says one observer. "He was one of the luckiest guys you'd ever meet."

ALTHOUGH DEVLIN may have been the only Shakespeare-quoting bully prowling Kensington's streets and pubs, he was far from being the neighborhood's only "tough guy." Many Philadelphians from that era believe that the toughest guys in the city came out of Kensington. "There were three tough guys on every corner," says one native. Another witness to the almost daily carnage argues without hesitation, "Kensington produced the best street fighters in the world."

Police officers apparently agreed. Locking up Kensington incorrigibles was no walk in the park. "I sincerely believe K&A had more tough guys than any other neighborhood in the city," said Herbie Rhodes, a city detective who was part of the freelancing Special Investigations Squad. That job afforded him the opportunity to compare the backbones of Philadelphia's most intimidating criminals, and Rhodes is sure "the toughest guys in the city came out of Kensington. Those K&A guys were incredible fighters. They'd put people in the hospital."

Lou McCloud, Porky McCloud, Frankie Wetzel, Leo Gillis, Charlie Taggert, Joey Cooper Smith, La La McQuoid, Pete Logue, Joe Lepowski, Eddie Lucas, Nails Manginni, and Cocky O'Kane are just a few of the battle-scarred combatants who earned impressive reputations and terrorized those who crossed their paths. Although the neighborhood was said to have "a million sucker-punch artists who'd run a block to nail you in the jaw," there was no shortage of guys who would go toe to toe all night long. As one long-time observer recommended, "You better pack a lunch if you were gonna take one of them on."

Many of the Kensington bars hired tough guys as bouncers to maintain a semblance of law and order. Their reputations, physical prowess, and moxie were frequently tested. It wasn't unusual for South Philly, Roxborough, or Germantown tough guys to pay a visit to the Randolph, the Shamrock, the Bubble Club, or the Pleasantville Inn looking for some action. On any given Friday night, one of these bars or social clubs could turn into a pugilistic O.K. Corral. Blood often flowed as freely as the alcohol, and having an eye gouged out with a broken beer bottle or a nipple bitten off was not unheard of. "I saw guys fight for three hours once," says one observer familiar with the well-established ritual. "They'd fight for a while, take a break for coffee, and then go right back at it again."

One of the more curious footnotes to this rugged slice of Kensington life was the contribution of the "Hebrew Gladiator," a tough, hard-nosed professional boxer who was paid to keep order in rowdy Irish taprooms and banish troublemakers. A pint-sized Sherman tank, Marvin "Marvelous Marvin" Edelman was a classy middleweight whose record (34 and 3) earned him a Top 10 ranking in 1952. It was said that a shot in the ribs or kidneys from Marvin was like getting "kicked in the side by a horse."

Marvin's one-punch knockouts are legendary. Jimmy Moran remembers Marvin hitting a bar-room challenger in the ribs and the guy going down for the count. One, or maybe two, of the guy's ribs had been broken with one shot. Junior Kripplebauer recalls the time Marvin dropped Tommy Seher with a head shot in the aftermath of a truck hijacking. "We had just knocked off a truck hauling $600,000 in Alaskan King Crab," says Junior, "and had taken the truck to a remote Jersey farm for safekeeping while we sold the stash. A dispute rose between Tommy and Marvin over a sale, and Marvin got pissed and hit him in the head. Knocked Tommy out cold. Normally, I'd have to shoot a guy like that, but we all liked Marvin."

Trustworthy, fearless, and skilled with his hands, Edelman was a familiar fixture as doorman and troubleshooter at several popular Kensington night spots in the fifties and sixties. He worked the door of the Shamrock for 10 years and spent another 20 years directing traffic at the Randolph Social Club. Because he was a Jew and a prominent professional prizefighter, Edelman was often the target of drunken tough guys looking to make a name for themselves. Their challenges were invariably unsuccessful. Even Charlie Devlin knew better than to test him. Those who did, like Frankie Wetzel and Leo Gillis, regretted it.

"I had to knock out a guy a night for the first fuckin' year," says Edelman of those early days on the job. The recurring bar-room challenges were of no great concern: after confronting the likes of Tiger Jones in the ring, untrained, inebriated Irishmen were a minor threat. Fighting at the Cambria gym, a local Kensington Avenue blood pit, Edelman had grown used to the catcalls, the ridicule, and the rowdy patrons' desire to see the Hebrew Gladiator get his butt handed to him. "I used to pack the place," says Edelman with an amused chuckle. "They came to see the Jew get beat." But he never did and thereby gained quite a following. If there was anything blue collar Kensington stevedores and roofers valued, it was toughness, and Marvin was tough. He may have been a Jew, but he was a tough Jew.

HE COULD OCCASIONALLY be seen on an old rocking chair in the back of a bar at Front and South Streets like a weary old working-class Buddha, but his pensive exterior belied his many death-defying exploits over the years. Even most of the K&A regulars who brought him swag to move each week probably didn't realize the full extent of "Bones" Gales's criminal career. For them, he was just another Kensington fixture, a dependable, harmless old-timer, a fence who took their jewelry, furs, and silver tea sets with no questions asked. In fact, Edwin "Bones" Gale was a throwback to another era, to the roaring '20s and bloody '30s, when kidnappings for profit and mass murder by warring gangs were commonplace.

A gambler, numbers writer, burglar, bank robber, stickup man, leg-breaker, fence, and prison road-gang escape artist, Bones Gale had seen and done it all. In fact, there wasn't much in the catalogue of criminal activity that Bones hadn't done. Six feet tall, 230 pounds, Gale was a big man, a tough guy, a "muscle man," and a criminal "kingpin," as the cops liked to say. First incarcerated in New York City at the age of 14, Bones spent a good portion of his teenage years learning the ropes in Montgomery County Prison, Huntingdon Reformatory, and Eastern State Penitentiary. He was serving an eight- to 12-year term for armed robbery on a Georgia chain gang before he was out of his teens. Brutal country roadwork under a blazing sun and the ominous eye of callous guards on horseback had little appeal for him, so he escaped—not once, but three times.

Back in Philadelphia, he became involved in everything from illegal lotteries and burglary to gambling and armed robbery. A stickup at the Two Pines Inn in Media, Pennsylvania, resulted in chaos and mayhem; the establishment's orchestra leader had his leg blown off by a shotgun blast.

Gale was famous as the sole surviving member of the notorious Mais-Legenza Gang, a particularly violent crew of gunmen from the early 1930s who unceremoniously disposed of bullet-riddled bodies up and down the East Coast. Also known as the "Tri-State Mob," the gang had once kidnapped Willie "Big Nose" Weiss, a Philadelphia racketeer, and demanded $50,000 from his family for his safe return. After receiving an initial payment of $8,000, the gang decided to abort the scheme, but not before putting two bullets into Weiss's head and throwing him off a Neshaminy Creek bridge. Caught in Manhattan by an army of sub-machinegun-toting Philadelphia and New York City policemen, Robert Mais and Walter Legenza hoped to be brought back to Philadelphia for the Weiss murder, but the state of Virginia—where they had already been convicted of murder and sentenced to die in the electric chair—had first dibs on them.

Gale managed to avoid the chair, and the experience caused no soul-searching turnabout in his professional life. He remained an enterprising criminal who would be arrested over two dozen times (everything from drunken driving to knifing an adversary) and was suspected of doing some of the biggest contract hits in Philadelphia. Eventually, up-and-coming Kensington burglars of the 1960s came to know him not as an archcriminal, but as a friendly, reliable neighborhood swag dealer. "He sat in a small office at Front and York Streets," recalls one regular patron, "and chain-smoked and drank all day long while reminiscing about the old days. The old guy had a million stories."

"AS FAR AS I'M CONCERNED, Jackie Johnson is the classic example of a standup guy. The cops, the DA, the prison wardens—they all punished him beyond belief, but the guy never wavered, never showed weakness, never cracked. There's no doubt about it, Jack's the poster boy for someone with a standup reputation."

The heartfelt praise for a fellow crew member is typical of the universal respect accorded Jackie Johnson by Philly burglars. The tribute should not be taken lightly. If there was a stepladder of community values in Kensington's criminal milieu, the highest rung was reserved for "standup guys," those men who never broke under police pressure, never cooperated with legal authorities, and never rolled over on a partner. "Tough guy" and "moneymaker" were also neighborhood terms of honor, but the highest accolade was reserved for those who "kept their mouth shut" and "never talked." As one believer said, it wasn't just important—"it was everything."

"It was a big thing when we were growing up in the forties and fifties," says Jim Moran of the community standard. "You didn't tell the cops anything, especially if it was going to jeopardize other people. You don't tell the man anything. You never ratted on anybody. It was very serious stuff; people who talked were highly ostracized and often given a good beating."

The notion of keeping silent and keeping the police at arms length was instilled in Kensingtonians at an early age. "From the day you were born it was bred into you," adds Kensington native George Holmes. "It was part of the Kensington mentality; it was a great honor to be known as a standup guy. It meant always doing the right thing. If you ratted to the cops, you were a rat, and people treated you like a rat."

In a neighborhood that also honored its tough guys, it is interesting how few of them were accorded the "standup" designation. Being a feared street fighter wasn't necessarily equivalent to being a standup guy. Willie Sears, Joey Cooper Smith, and Charlie Devlin were infamous street fighters who were given a wide berth, but few in Kensington considered them standup guys. They were all suspected at one time or another of "going bad" or "going south" on their partners. As Jim Moran says, "Some of the strongest guys couldn't handle prison and rolled over. They didn't become neighborhood patsies, because they could fight, but nobody saw them as standup guys." Cooper Smith, especially, was a known rat who would do anything—including inform on his partners—to stay out of prison. He was physically formidable, but the prospect of doing time humbled and weakened him. Yet some little guys with no reputation as tough guy were psychologically strong and could do the time. They earned people's respect and were the ones "everyone wanted to work with."

Jackie Johnson was one of those guys. Five-foot-eight and 145 pounds soaking wet, Jack had a healthy head of dark hair and a penchant for dry, witty repartee. He talked out of one side of his mouth, reserving the other side for the nonstop intake of Budweiser. Johnson met Effie Burke in the 197 Bar in the late fifties and immediately became a cornerstone of an elite burglary crew. Though he occasionally came to work drunk, no one had to worry about Johnson spilling his guts to the cops if he was caught on the job. His partners slept tight at night, knowing Jack would never give them up, regardless of the physical or psychological pressure he was under.

The Devlin murder and the Holmesburg Prison riot of 1970 illustrate Jack's standup character. On February 27, 1969, the body of Charlie Devlin was found on Luzerne Street, stuffed between two steel pillars under the Second Street overpass. Dressed in a "rumpled blue suit and white shirt, the badly bruised and battered corpse" was initially thought by police to have been a victim of a hit-and-run automobile accident. On autopsy, two bullet holes were discovered on the right side of the head. Devlin had been killed execution style somewhere else, and his body had been moved to the Luzerne Street site to make his death look like a traffic accident.

Police were faced with an endless array of suspects: Devlin had terrorized the neighborhood for years, cops as well as private citizens. Just a month earlier he had been arrested for assault and battery on a police officer. It was said that spontaneous celebrations broke out in bars all over Kensington as word spread of his demise.

The first lead came with the discovery of Devlin's 1961 Pontiac station wagon in a driveway near "A" Street and Roosevelt Boulevard, the home of Jackie Johnson. Johnson, 34, had over a dozen arrests dating back to 1957. An alcoholic with a soft heart, Johnson was widely known for drinking away the hours at various Kensington bars while giving fives, tens, and twenties to local residents down on their luck, but he wasn't known for being physically aggressive. At the time of the murder, he was on probation for a prior burglary.

Cops, prosecutors, and judges thought they had discovered the weak link in the conspiracy. They knew Devlin had been killed in Johnson's home. An informant had told them that Johnson was one of six or seven people in the house at the time of the murder. Ray Brahm, another burglar, was fingered as the actual shooter, but the government's informant was shaky; his testimony needed backup. The authorities figured that Jack Johnson was their man. They figured wrong.

Johnson was brought down to police headquarters and the district attorney's office numerous times to hear a laundry list of threats and deals, but he refused to cooperate. He claimed he wasn't in the house at the time of the murder and didn't know a thing. Prosecutors threatened to revoke his probation and have a judge re-sentence him to a lengthy prison term if he didn't tell them what they wanted to hear. Johnson maintained his silence.

"Back then," says Johnson, "you were ostracized if you ratted on somebody. Police informants had to hang with each other 'cause nobody else would deal with them. There weren't many around. If I had talked, I'd have to go against everything I believed in. I couldn't do it. I wouldn't do it."

Though they knew he wasn't the shooter, Johnson was given eight to 20 years for a relatively minor prior conviction for which he had originally received probation. The new sentence would be vacated, he was told, as soon as he decided to cooperate. Even after Ray Brahm was tried for Devlin's murder in December 1970 (he was acquitted), the authorities kept the heat on Johnson.

Periodically shipping him from one state prison to another in order to make his life more difficult ("diesel therapy"), they continued to inform his attorneys that the deal was still open—Johnson talks and he walks. Jackie Johnson "could have walked out of prison any day" over the next 10 years, but he maintained his silence.

Even more than the Devlin case, perhaps, the Holmesburg Prison riot of July 4, 1970, underscored Johnson's commitment to noncooperation with the police. In the summer of 1970, radical blacks and members of the Black Muslims instigated a riot in the prison dining hall. Unprepared and outnumbered, white prisoners were beaten and knifed at will while guards and other inmates scattered for their lives. Cries of "Kill Whitey" and "Death to all honkies" reverberated throughout the chow hall as the few dozen white prisoners tried to hold off several hundred black prisoners who had invaded the scullery and gained access to an assortment of kitchen knives, meat cleavers, and heavy, bone-crushing mallets.

When Philadelphia police under the forceful leadership of Frank Rizzo regained control of the institution many hours later, scores of inmates required hospitalization. Jackie Johnson was one of them, stabbed nine times, his wrist broken, and his scalp torn open by a meat cleaver. In the riot's aftermath, city police and prosecutors from the district attorney's office went from cell to cell, methodically interviewing witnesses and victims. They were determined to prosecute all those involved in planning and participating in the bloody disturbance. A number of inmates testified in court against the riot's ringleaders, but Johnson wasn't one of them.

Though labeled "Exhibit A" by prosecutors and pressured to testify, Johnson remained adamant. He refused to provide any assistance to the authorities. He left no doubt how he felt, saying to prosecutors: "Let me tell you something. If you bring me down to court and say I was hit by this guy or that guy, I can assure you that I'm gonna say that's the wrong guy. I'm gonna tell everyone he's not the one who stabbed me."

Investigators were stunned. They couldn't believe that a white guy who had nearly been killed by radical black separatists would not relish the opportunity to get back at his tormentors. They knew there was no love lost between the Irish burglar and the Muslims, but Jack wouldn't budge. Encouraged by cellmates and pressured by authorities, Jackie Johnson maintained his lifelong principle of never assisting "the man."

HE SCAMPERED ACROSS backyards and hurdled fence posts like an Olympic decathlon champion, and his ability to scale the sides of commercial and residential buildings reminded some of a hungry chimpanzee foraging for food, but what Marty Bell really was, was a consummate second story man. Small, swift, and wiry, Bell was a gifted athlete who chose breaking into homes over pole vaulting and the long jump as vocational interests. No structure could resist Bell's reflexes, speed, and primate-like climbing ability.

"Nobody could catch me," says Bell. "I was quick and I could climb. I could enter a home or building from any floor. Even if the cops were onto me, they could never catch me. I was the best at scaling walls and fences. The cops once had me pinned by an eight-foot wall. They had chased me through an alley and thought they had finally cornered me. They fired six shots at me, but I hopped that wall in a second and got away."

Marty Bell was from an Irish-Italian family that resided in Frankford, an old Philadelphia neighborhood just a mile or so north of Kensington. His formal education ended after a two-day stint in ninth grade. A year earlier, a painful sixth-month stretch at Daniel Boone, a disciplinary school for troubled youths, had soured him on school. Life on the streets, however, presented a far more enticing educational prospect.

"I started to hang with all the guys," says Bell, "and learned the business. Burglary was the thing everybody was into, and I learned from some of the best. I learned safe work from the older guys and became pretty good at it. They taught me everything. I kept five or six safe boxes in my basement and would practice with them. The first time I did one on a job, it was a big eight-foot double-door safe in a clothing store on Frankford Avenue."

Though he never worked with the more elite crews, he still did well, his best score being a $25,000 heist from another Frankford Avenue business. Celebrating such achievements, Marty made the customary rounds of popular drinking establishments. It wasn't unusual for Bell himself to become the evening's entertainment. Rather than a dramatic rendition of "Danny Boy," however, the performance piece would be a 60-yard dash. The JR Club, in particular, always "a den of thieves and pirates," would instantly be transformed into a frenetic betting parlor while contestants and customers assembled on Frankford Avenue for the impromptu track and field competition.

"Guys would come from all over the city to challenge Marty," recalls one bar patron. "I don't think he ever lost. He was fast as hell. Sometimes he'd even challenge them to a race where he'd run backwards while they ran forwards. Dozens of people would empty out onto the street and watch the guys race under the Frankford El. Marty would be in a suit and tie and he'd be running backwards. It was the funniest thing you ever saw, but he'd still win. He'd beat them running backwards. Nobody could beat him."

BESIDES ITS STREET FIGHTERS, criminals who could keep their mouths shut, and athletic crooks, Kensington's vast collection of Runyonesque characters included noncombatants and noncriminals as well. Joe Doc was a lovable, good-natured bar-room denizen whose affability was much admired. Fairly early in life, Joe abandoned his considerable potential for a comfortable bar stool. Raised on Wishart Street just a block away from Kensington and Allegheny Avenues, Joe Dougherty spent his youth like many other neighborhood kids and eventually made the obligatory pilgrimage to Holmesburg Prison. But as time passed his interests gradually narrowed down to consuming as much alcohol as possible.

"Each morning," says Jim Moran, "Joe Doc's mother would send him out clean-shaven and in a clean, pressed shirt. She'd give him a pack of cigarettes and a one-dollar bill and he'd head over to the Crescent Bar at Front and Allegheny. He'd probably have his first beer around lunchtime and proceed to spend the rest of the day there. He just spent the whole day drinking at the Crescent, the 192 Bar, or Nino's. Beers were only 10 cents back then, so a dollar went a long way, but everybody loved Joe and they'd buy him beers and often give him money. In fact, he'd sometimes come home at night with more money than he started the day with.

"Joe just refused to work," says Moran. "He tried it once or twice, but didn't like it. He was quite bright though, and a good conversationalist. Everybody loved him, especially the burglars. If anybody got a score, they'd drop a note on him. But Joe Doc was spunky. Even though he was a skinny runt and not much more than a hundred pounds, he wouldn't take shit from anybody. He once jumped off a bar stool and punched Charlie Devlin in the face. And if he thought he was getting stiffed, he'd let you know. He read the papers every day and saw what was supposed to have been stolen from various homes. If he thought the guys were going a little light in what they were giving him, he'd blow the hair out of his eyes, step up to the guys and tell 'em, 'You know you can do better than that.' Yeah, Joe Doc was a real character."

Part III

The Life of a K&A Burglar

PHILADELPHIA POLICE DEPARTMENT
(Official Use Only)

BADGE 3672

UNIT 26TH

ISSUED TO S. HUSIK

NO.

RANK Plcmn

DATE 2/8/69

10. Keys to the Kingdom

Me, Bruce Agnew, and Don Johnstone went up to Boston to do a job one time. Donny had gotten a tip about a jewelry salesman who lived up there. In fact, he had gotten quite a few tips. He had met a guy purely by accident at a restaurant in Northeast Philly and struck up a conversation with him. The guy turned out to be a jewelry salesman from Brooklyn who was selling his stuff downtown at Jewelers' Row and a few places in the Northeast. Before long Donny has this guy drunk. They're becoming buddies, and he soon has this guy smoking pot in his car and giving up the names and addresses of other jewelry salesmen working the East Coast. A deal is arranged where Donny will give him a 10 percent cut on everything we score from his tips. The crew did pretty good. They hit the homes of several of these jewelry salesmen in North Jersey, New York, and Connecticut and are bringing in something like $290,000 at a time. It was good work.

So now we're up in Massachusetts looking at one of these guys that's been fingered. The guy was supposed to be swimming in jewelry. It sounded real good. Me, Donny, and Bruce get a motel room for the three of us to stash our things, and then Bruce and I go to the guy's house. But the place is occupied. The guy and his wife are home, so we figure we'll wait around for a while and see what happens. Each time we check, we can see they're both drinking pretty good, so we figure we'll just wait them out and take the place when they're asleep.

They finally fall asleep and we go in. We take the whole place. We took five bags of jewels, nice stuff. Everything is going great, but now we're waiting for Don to come pick us up. We're waiting and waiting. We keep looking out the window, but he doesn't show. We're wondering, did something go wrong? Did the cops pick him up? Now time is going by and we're getting nervous. We know the salesman and his wife aren't gonna sleep forever. And besides that, we're strangers in the neighborhood. Hours go by. We're fucking pissed. Bruce was tough on a score; he wouldn't stop. He's now swearing he's gonna kill Johnstone if he ever sees him again.

Just as we feared, the salesman wakes up, and we then have to put a gun to his head and tell him to relax and go back to sleep. We tie the people up, and now we've gone from a simple burglary to an armed robbery. Johnstone still doesn't show up. We're both ready to kill him.

Finally, the sun is coming up and Bruce and I have to get out of there. It looks like Don ain't ever gonna show, so we decide to take the jeweler's car and drive back to the motel. When we get there, Johnstone's asleep on the bed. Empty beer cans are lying all over the place. He was asleep all night while we're waiting for his drunken ass. He got drunk in the motel room waiting for us to take the jeweler's place, fell asleep, and while we're in somebody else's house, holding somebody else's jewelry, and waiting for him to pick us up, he's out drunk. Bruce was so pissed he wanted to shoot him right there. Fortunately for Don, he had given us a few big scores with his tips, or Bruce would have clipped him up there in Boston.

—Junior Kripplebauer

"WE WERE OUT ALMOST EVERY NIGHT OF THE WEEK," says Junior Kripplebauer of his introduction to production work in the early sixties. "I was working with Billy Blue, Fleck, and Bloomie at least four and sometimes five nights a week. We'd travel up Routes 611 and 309 into Bucks and Montgomery Counties looking for places to rob. Houses, businesses, car dealerships, whatever looked good at the time. We'd do four, five houses a night, but if the residential stuff was tied up, we'd grab a commercial operation. It wasn't unusual for us to be on the way back from a few scores at the end of the night and stop at a big car dealership along 611. We'd drive to the back of the place, and usually they'd have everything we'd need waiting for us: oxygen tanks, acetylene tanks, and all sorts of heavy tools. We'd then go to the office, break in, and start working on the safe. Sometimes we could punch it open and be out of there in a few minutes. Other times it would take a while, and we'd have to burn or rip the safe open.

"We once knocked off a Robert Hall clothing store in Bristol and got a whole load of men's suits. We walked out of there with over 200 suits. For a while there I thought I was a haberdasher. We were selling jackets, pants, and men's suits out of a garage in Kensington for weeks.

"Production work allowed you to make money, set your own hours, and have a little fun at the same time. If you were working and the first one or two houses you hit were a bust, you still had a shot that one of the others that night would bring in a wad of cash or a couple of diamond rings. Sometimes we'd make decent money. We'd whack up five, six, seven thousand dollars, so you might grab anywhere from a "G" to a couple thousand a night. If you could open safes, you could really do okay at commercial.

"Billy liked suburban Philadelphia neighborhoods like Bristol, Yardley, Ambler, Montgomeryville; he wasn't too interested in going out of state. We never took a gun. It was forbidden. You could get spooked and do something you shouldn't. Carrying a gun only caused problems and added to your sentence if you were caught."

As with most other K&A crew members, Kripplebauer also learned that bigger was not always better in regard to residential targets. "I didn't want to do the 30-room estates and mansions," says Junior. "There were too many bedrooms. It took an hour to find the master bedroom. I liked three-bedroom houses, where it was easier to find the master bedroom. This way the jewelry and valuables were all within sight. I became a pretty good searcher. Good enough that I could find stuff somebody else had passed over or not seen."

Junior quickly absorbed the craft's nuances, maybe too quickly. He learned "to go to the library to check where synagogues were located" and to "check the phone book for Jewish names" in order to ascertain where large numbers of Jewish families resided. Since his crew had the keys to most alarm systems, he learned to look for homes sporting "red lights" and that "two or three alarmed houses next to each other" equaled "a home run." And he learned the nuances of safe work, everything from "punch-dialing a niggerhead" (one of the old, large, black safes common in commercial establishments) to "burning" a two-ton Mosler or Diebolt.

Gradually, however, Junior's opportunistic, entrepreneurial spirit caused him to explore the workings of other Kensington crews and more distant geographic targets. More ominously, that edgy restlessness also propelled him to pick up a gun on occasion and explore more diverse, dangerous, and lucrative criminal endeavors.

The Randolph and Erie social clubs and the popular shot-and-beer joints like the Shamrock, Marty's, and the Crescent—all heavily patronized by a cross-section of K&A burglars and other criminal types—were greenhouses for tricks, scams, swindles, zany ideas, and screwy tips. Crews shared information, personnel, and equipment such as alarm keys, cars, drills, burning rods, and acetylene tanks. By the mid-1960s, Kripplebauer was working with a variety of Kensington teams that took a more aggressive approach to earning money, crews that targeted the homes of prominent citizens and possessed a more expansive geographic portfolio. He started going out with crews that regularly crossed the river into Jersey to loot properties in Cherry Hill, Moorestown, and Princeton. Pretty soon North Jersey, Long Island, Connecticut, Maryland, and the fashionable neighborhoods of Squirrel Hill and Fox Chapel in Pittsburgh would become staples of Junior's travel schedule. Eventually, Massachusetts, Florida, Texas, and everything in between would be included in his domain. In short, Junior Kripplebauer quickly earned a reputation as a moneymaker and consummate criminal who was not only opportunistic but prepared to do just about anything for a decent score. Even a routine trip to the local supermarket for some groceries could turn into an exciting and profitable adventure.

"One day I'm on the way home," recalls Junior, "and I stop at the local Food Fair in Kensington at "M" and Luzerne Streets to pick up a few things. I decide to give Sammie [girlfriend Sammie Baich] a call and tell her I'm right around the corner at the supermarket and I'll be home in a few minutes. Well, while I'm on the phone with her the store manager walks right by me, and he's carrying two bricks of cash. Big ones. Each must have been four, five inches high and packed with twenties and fifties. I figure there's gotta be a hundred grand there. I'm tempted to stick him up right there and make a break for the door, but there was extra security at the time because they were doing construction work on the store and had brought in extra people to keep an eye on the construction workers. I watched the manager open the safe right near where I'm standing. It's close to the store's front window so you can see it from the parking lot. In those days, big food stores like Penn Fruit and Food Fair kept their safes by the front window. They thought if it could be seen from the street, they were protecting themselves against a robbery or burglary. But I'm thinking to myself, if I got any luck at all I'm gonna be fat with cash tonight.

"Soon as I see the manager lock the money in the safe, I call Petie Masone and tell him to bring the hardware; we got a score. I tell him I just saw a hundred grand put in the store's safe. I then went out in the parking lot and sat in my car to make sure the manager, or anybody else for that matter, didn't come along and take the money out of the safe. I wasn't leaving that baby for a second.

"When Petie shows up we sat in my car and talked it over. The safe was pretty big—probably 5,000 pounds—so we can't just pick the damn thing up and carry it out. And it had round doors, which were usually tougher than the square ones to tear open. It would've taken too long to peel open and you're right out in the open by the store's front window. We talked about it for a couple hours and came up with a plan. We called Tony to come and keep an eye on the safe while Petie and I went over to see Bloomie, who worked at a garage next to Marty's Bar at Germantown and Allegheny. We got a set of tanks from him and went next door to a truck rental agency and picked up a good-sized truck with a lift on the back. We then got an eight-foot Johnson bar that's used by railroad workers to clear train wrecks.

"We sat in the parking lot till long after the store closed. It must've been two in the morning when we made our move. We go to the back door, break in, and use a hand-truck and the Johnson bar to haul the safe to the rear loading dock.

We get the safe onto the truck and take it over to a garage, where I must have spent a good two hours burning that sucker open. Then we started counting. I sort of lost count when we hit $87,000.

"But now it's getting close to sunrise and we got all this wet money. I had to flood the safe to make sure I didn't burn any of the cash. We take all the cash over to my place and hang it in the basement like it's the weekly laundry. Bed sheets and washrags all over the place. We had to dry it out. It's all over the house, on lines, on the steps, over chairs, tables, and wall pictures. I took a photograph of it, 'cause it looked so damn funny.

"Two days later, Captain Ferguson, Herb Rhodes, Tony Cristelli, and the Special Investigations Squad are at my front door with a warrant to search the house. Sammie is the only one home. They arrest her and take almost $18,000 they find in the house. It was my share of the job.

"When Sammie's hearing comes up at the House of Correction, I go there with Steve LaCheen, my attorney, and as soon as they see me they arrest me and hit me with a $50,000 bail. Now Sammie, who's just out on bail, has to bring money up for my hearing. And what do those fuckers do when they see her? They arrest her again. It went on that way four times, re-arresting us each time we were making bail for the other. They really wanted me bad. I told Herbie Rhodes, "You can break my balls, but you don't have to break hers." But Fergie was mad as a motherfucker 'cause he knew I did that job and he wanted that money.

"He never got it, though. Eventually Food Fair sued me in court for over $100,000, but they never got it either. Steve represented me in that case too. We won and I kept the money. Actually, Steve kept it. I had to pay him for representing me."

Junior's larcenous and industrious heart never skipped a beat. As long as he wasn't on ice behind bars somewhere, he was working. By quickly digesting the rudiments of production work and displaying a naturally bold, standup demeanor, Junior became a hot property. Both second story men and gunmen wanted to work with him. He was loyal, dependable, and apparently fearless. In addition, he was a moneymaker; he always seemed to have cash. Every day he listened to hot tips from prospective partners.

"More than most of the K&A guys, I went back and forth between burglaries and the occasional stickup," says Kripplebauer. "I'd usually decide as the opportunity presented itself. I made more money on those rare occasions with a gun doing robberies and walk-ins, but I liked burglaries better because it was safer. There was less chance of hurting anybody and a smaller chance of getting a big sentence if you were caught.

"If it sounded good, I'd do it. For example, in the spring of '67, Fleck [Billy Blue's half-brother, Jackie Fleckenstine] comes up to me and says he's got a great tip. It's a gigantic estate along the Delaware River in Bucks County. It's a mansion owned by the Biddle family, one of the most historic and socially prominent families in America. He said there was five million dollars in jewelry up there along the river just waiting for us to grab.

"Fleck always had a hot tip. He always had big plans, big ideas. The guy exaggerated everything. Everything he came up with always included five million in jewelry. Whatever the house, business, or institution, it always included five million in jewelry. Fleck was a bullshit artist, but I loved him. He was a tall, good-looking guy with piercing blue eyes, and he always wore a black suit and sparkling white shirt. The girls just loved him. I was always skeptical of his claims, but this Biddle thing sounded good, too good to pass up, so we put a crew together. It was me, Fleck, Mitchell, and Three- Fingers Hurst. It was gonna be a straight burglary; no one was supposed to be carrying anything that could get us in trouble.

"Once we got up there and took a look at the place, we were all pretty impressed. The house was so imposing. It had these huge Roman columns in front. It was immense. Once you saw the house, you figured there's gotta be something in there. It had money written all over it. We turn off the alarm, make sure as best we can that no one's home, and then enter the place. It's big, real big. We're searching all over, checking out all the bedrooms, but we're not finding anything. Yeah, there were fancy tea sets and silverware, but we were expecting to find cash and jewelry. And we were expecting lots of it. I jumped all over Fleck 'cause there wasn't any money and only a little bit of jewelry. I figure once again he's given me a bum steer.

"At one point I'm even up in the attic wandering around looking for something of value. It's then that I come upon an old colonial uniform from the Revolutionary War. Something Washington would have worn. It had epaulets, brace buttons, and lots of fancy gold trim. There was even a real three-cornered hat and an officer's sword to go with it. Just for the hell of it I put on the jacket and hat and march downstairs with sword in hand and yell out to the guys, 'Good evening, gentlemen. May I introduce myself? I'm General Nicholas Biddle of the Continental Army and I'd like to inform you that this is my personal residence you're standing in and you're all under arrest.'

"After being momentarily startled, the guys fell over laughing. They got a big kick out of it. All of them at some time or other had been surprised by a homeowner returning early while pulling a job, but never had they been surprised by anyone in the getup I was wearing. They wanted to try on the hat and coat. Fleck takes the sword from me and starts swinging it all over the place. He must have seen too many Errol Flynn movies. He thinks he's a soldier in Washington's army fighting the Prussians or something and starts stabbing things including a few lamps, sofa pillows, and a couple paintings on the wall. This was still in

LEFT: Junior Kripplebauer (pictured here on the right with an unidentified inmate at North Carolina's Reidsville State Prison in 1988) was a well-respected inmate who knew how to survive behind bars. He kept himself in shape with regular workouts that included both pumping iron and heavy roadwork on the prison track.

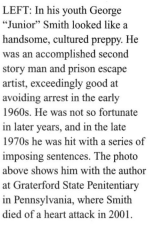

SMITH, George, R.

AKA: Richard G. Smith
Address: 5506 N. 6th St., Phila.
D.O.B.: 38 in '74;   Height: 5' 9"; Weight: 140
                     Hair: Brown; Eyes: Hazel; Build: Slender
Marks & Scars:

Reference Numbers: SBI: FBI:
                     PP: 311543   SSN: -   -

Vehicle Data: 64 V.W. Blue Reg. 03990A Pa.
Associates: Michael Rispo; Charles McCullough; John Stocker;
     Francis Walker
Hangouts: Villa DiRoma; Bars, Cottman & Algan; Phila.; Bars
     in Camden & S. Jersey
Criminal Record: Burglary

LEFT: In his youth George "Junior" Smith looked like a handsome, cultured preppy. He was an accomplished second story man and prison escape artist, exceedingly good at avoiding arrest in the early 1960s. He was not so fortunate in later years, and in the late 1970s he was hit with a series of imposing sentences. The photo above shows him with the author at Graterford State Penitentiary in Pennsylvania, where Smith died of a heart attack in 2001.

Eddie Loney, like many K&A burglars, eventually moved from production work to drugs. After relocating to Florida, he entered into numerous business ventures, both legal and illegal, and is currently a fugitive from justice. He may be living somewhere in Ireland.

RIGHT: Kripplebauer took advantage of every educational program North Carolina's prison system had to offer, and where none existed he made sure to start one. That is what he did at Yanceyville Road Camp, where this photo was taken. Intent on receiving as much earned time as possible, Junior initiated numerous projects and programs to benefit the inmate population, gaining academic degrees and time off his own sentence in the process.

LEFT: The Navy provided Kripplebauer with an escape from the coal mines. Tall, athletic, and a natural leader, Kripplebauer (on the extreme right in this photo) served on an aircraft carrier in the Pacific and on numerous East Coast naval bases; he starred on the Annapolis baseball team when he wasn't in the brig. This photo shows him at Bainbridge Naval Training Base in Maryland, prior to being shipped out to serve on a carrier during the Korean War.

Sara Lou & Teel

Happy Holidays

LOVE
JR. AND CHERYL

Cheryl and Junior made for a strikingly handsome couple, as this North Carolina prison photo shows. Though their commitment and love endured years of separation during his imprisonment, their union couldn't overcome marital discord after his release. They separated shortly after he gained his freedom in 1989. Cheryl died of a stroke in Florida in the mid-1990s.

It was not uncommon for old K&A acquaintances to meet up in prison. In this photo taken in the exercise yard at Lewisburg Federal Penitentiary (circa 1980), Chick Goodroe (center) and Tommy Seher (right) get an opportunity to discuss old times with an unidentified prisoner.

From certain sightlines, the grounds of the Allenwood Federal Prison Complex in northeastern Pennsylvania can resemble a Catskill mountain resort. In this 1993 photo, Chick Goodroe (center), Ralph Natale (on right, and soon to become head of the La Cosa Nostra in Philadelphia), and an unidentified inmate get a breath of fresh air.

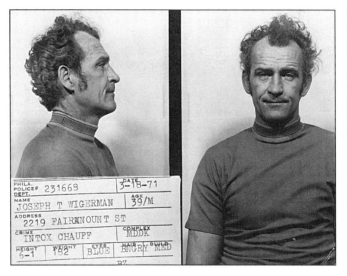

Once he became familiar with the nuances of production work, Ted Wigerman led K&A crews from one end of the country to the other. After raking wealthy towns in North Carolina for many years, he was finally caught after a crew member informed on him. To avoid a more than 40-year sentence, Wigerman became an informant as well. Though eventually freed, he never returned to Philadelphia and died in Florida in 1995.

John Carlyle Berkery was one of the most famous members of the K&A Gang. Berkery initially gained notoriety for his alleged role in the Pottsville Heist and became one of the very few members of the Irish Mob to develop close ties with Angelo Bruno and the local La Cosa Nostra operation. One federal prosecutor said, "Berkery is particularly dangerous for he combines intelligence and street-smarts with a reputation for 'muscle'..."

Marilynne D'Ulisse (here with defense attorney Stephen LaCheen) married Junior Kripplebauer after his release from Trenton State Penitentiary and immediately became an integral part of one of the K&A Gang's most productive crews. A standup crew member, loyal wife, and hard-working practitioner of production work, Mickie would eventually serve time in a North Carolina prison. She died of breast cancer shortly after her release.

The 1959 arrest and trial of Hughie Breslin, Harry Stocker, Effie Burke, and Jimmy Laverty was a big deal in Williamsport. The Kensington burglars had ravaged several pastoral Pennsylvania counties unaccustomed to such brazen criminal behavior. Though their many victims no doubt failed to appreciate it, they had been burgled by the second story equivalent of the '27 Yankees.

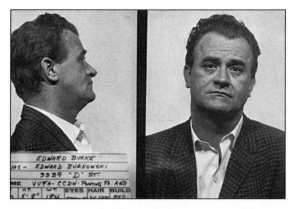

EDWARD BURKE
AS — EDWARD BURKOWSKI
3339 "D" ST.
ME VUFA- CCDW- Pushing T3 A $8
HT. WT. EYES HAIR BUILD
5' 8" 184

Francis Edward Burkowski (Effie Burke) was one of the pioneers of production work in the early 1950s. A Kensington native and disciple of Willie Sears, he captained one of the most prestigious crews of K&A burglars. He had a heart attack in the midst of a burglary in northern New Jersey in the early 1970s and never completely recovered. His health problems did what the cops could not—they kept him out of other people's homes.

BREWER, Francis James

AKA:
Address: 3301 Woodhaven Rd., Phila., Pa.
D.O.B.: 8/31/44; Height: 5' 11"; Weight: 160;
Hair: Brown; Eyes: Brown; Build: Well
Marks & Scars:

Reference Numbers: SBI: FBI:
PP: SSN: 179-34-4318

Vehicle Data: Uses U-Haul & Rental Trailers
Associates: George Young, Robert Cullen, John Stayton
Hangouts: Burlington & South Jersey, South Phila.
Criminal Record: Burglary

LEFT: Frankie Brewer grew up in Fairmount but quickly became an integral part of Kensington's revolving-door burglary teams. Handsome, tough, and fearless, Brewer worked with some of the best K&A crews and was a key member of Junior Kripplebauer's team.

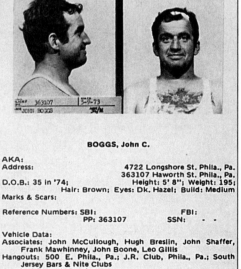

RIGHT: John Boggs, pictured here after a dispute with Philly cops, worked with a number of Kensington crews. In the 1970s a priest helped him recognize the error of his ways, and he jettisoned residential break-ins and strong-arm work for the roofers' union to become an accomplished utility man.

BOGGS, John C.

AKA:
Address: 4722 Longshore St. Phila., Pa.
363107 Haworth St. Phila., Pa.
D.O.B.: 35 in '74; Height: 5' 8"; Weight: 195;
Hair: Brown; Eyes: Dk. Hazel; Build: Medium
Marks & Scars:

Reference Numbers: SBI: FBI:
PP: 363107 SSN: - -

Vehicle Data:
Associates: John McCullough, Hugh Breslin, John Shaffer, Frank Mawhinney, John Boone, Leo Gillis
Hangouts: 500 E. Phila., Pa.; J.R. Club, Phila., Pa.; South Jersey Bars & Nite Clubs
Criminal Record: Burglary

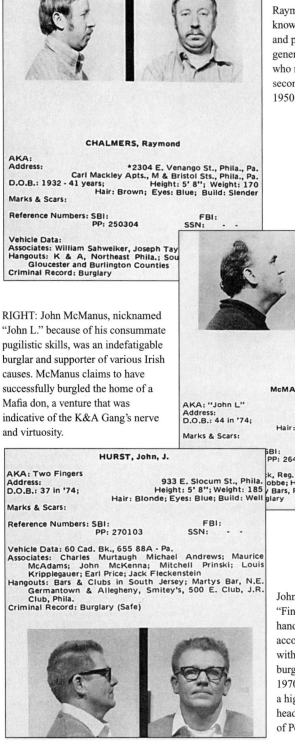

Raymond Chalmers, better known as "Raybo" to his friends and partners, was a member of the generation of Kensington burglars who revolutionized the art of second story work in the early 1950s.

CHALMERS, Raymond

AKA:
Address: *2304 E. Venango St., Phila., Pa.
Carl Mackley Apts., M & Bristol Sts., Phila., Pa.
D.O.B.: 1932 - 41 years; Height: 5' 8"; Weight: 170
Hair: Brown; Eyes: Blue; Build: Slender
Marks & Scars:

Reference Numbers: SBI: FBI:
PP: 250304 SSN: - -

Vehicle Data:
Associates: William Sahweiker, Joseph Tay
Hangouts: K & A, Northeast Phila.; Sou
Gloucester and Burlington Counties
Criminal Record: Burglary

RIGHT: John McManus, nicknamed "John L." because of his consummate pugilistic skills, was an indefatigable burglar and supporter of various Irish causes. McManus claims to have successfully burgled the home of a Mafia don, a venture that was indicative of the K&A Gang's nerve and virtuosity.

McMANUS, John

AKA: "John L"
Address: 3015 Jasper St., Phila.
D.O.B.: 44 in '74; Height: 5' 11"; Weight: 201
Hair: Brown; Eyes: Brown; Build: Well
Marks & Scars:

SBI: FBI:
PP: 264795 SSN: - -

HURST, John, J.

AKA: Two Fingers
Address: 933 E. Slocum St., Phila. k, Reg. 08851V
D.O.B.: 37 in '74; Height: 5' 8"; Weight: 185 obbe; Herman Goodwin
Hair: Blonde; Eyes: Blue; Build: Well y Bars, Phila.; S. Jersey Bars
Marks & Scars: glary

Reference Numbers: SBI: FBI:
PP: 270103 SSN: - -

Vehicle Data: 60 Cad. Bk., 655 88A - Pa.
Associates: Charles Murtaugh Michael Andrews; Maurice McAdams; John McKenna; Mitchell Prinski; Louis Kripplegauer; Earl Price; Jack Fleckenstein
Hangouts: Bars & Clubs in South Jersey; Martys Bar, N.E. Germantown & Allegheny, Smitey's, 500 E. Club, J.R. Club, Phila.
Criminal Record: Burglary (Safe)

John Hurst, better known as "Fingers" because of a deformed hand, was a trusted friend and accomplished burglar who worked with a cross-section of Kensington burglary teams in the 1960s and 1970s. One of his brothers became a highly decorated cop and the head of the local Fraternal Order of Police.

the sixties, before we realized there was money in old paintings. He thought it was funny, but I told him to cut it out. I was still pissed about the absence of any decent money and jewelry in the place. I told him to take the sword and a few nice looking shotguns we found and go kill that fucking tipper of his. The mansion was a blank. It looked great, but there wasn't much of anything in there.

"The next morning while I'm driving over to Fleck's place, I hear on the radio the report about the Biddle estate in Andalusia being robbed. They're making a big deal about it 'cause it's one of the biggest mansions in the area and was once the home of Nicholas Biddle, the founder of the Second Bank of the United States. According to the report the burglars walked off with a rare collection of hand-tooled English shotguns worth over $10,000. Now I'm starting to feel a little bit better. Maybe we'll make a couple bucks out of it after all. But when I get to Fleck's, I can't believe he's down in the basement sawing the barrels off the guns.

" 'Jesus Christ, what the hell are you doing, you goddamn idiot?' I scream at him. 'Those guns are antiques. They're worth money.'

"Now the little that we did get is worth next to nothing, and I'm bummed out again. But one thing we did come out of there with that had some value was the *Social Register.* It had all the phone numbers and addresses of all the socially prominent people in America. I was going through a desk drawer at the Biddle place looking for money, checks, anything of value, and came upon it. Once I saw what it was, I took it."

Though the Biddle estate turned out to be a huge disappointment, "the little red book" Kripplebauer had discovered was a road map to some of the wealthiest families in the country. Some of the famous families and swanky properties in the *Social Register,* Kripplebauer reasoned, must have money, furs, expensive jewelry, and other items of value. His plan to use the book never materialized, however. Just a few weeks later, Philadelphia detectives raided the apartment of Mitchell Prinski in Northeast Philadelphia and arrested all four of the conspirators. At the time, the police were unaware of the crew's involvement with the Biddle burglary. The discovery of the *Social Register*—stuffed in an old cigar box inside a closet overflowing with stolen goods in Prinski's less than regal apartment—supplied the link to the Biddle break-in. The cops had stumbled upon a mother lode of ill-gotten goods.

"We had a lot of stuff stored at Mitchell's place in the Jackson Court Apartments," says Kripplebauer. "They had no idea what they found. At least a quarter-million went down with that raid. We were packing up. We were getting ready to leave the next morning for Canada. We were going up to Montreal, where the World's Fair was being held, to unload over $200,000 in hot postal checks. Friends of mine, a crew of guys from Pittsburgh, had robbed the post office in Bryant, Alabama, and now wanted to sell the money orders they had walked off with. They had stolen the official stamping and validating machines as well. We were stamping the money orders when the detectives raided the place. We figured the Montreal authorities, with all the activity and international tourists in town, wouldn't get too suspicious about a large number of U.S. postal money orders being cashed. We had set up new IDs and had letters sent to the Canadian hotel cashing the money orders for $300 and $400 apiece. It would have worked, too, and brought in a bundle."

Besides interfering with the stolen-money-order and *Social Register* schemes, the police raid also helped uncover another creative moneymaking operation that had recently led to the collapse of a well-known Philadelphia automobile dealership.

"When the cops went through the apartment, they found the stolen checks from the Shore Brothers Pontiac Agency. We cleaned the owner's account out," says Junior, almost proudly. "Every time he made a deposit, we made a withdrawal. We had a pretty good plan. Mitchell had the ID of guy named John Barton, and we had a girl inside the Shore Brothers Pontiac dealership that was helping us. Mitchell goes to the bank to cash an $8,000 check made out to Shore Brothers. The bank teller is suspicious, so she contacts the dealership and gets our girl on the phone. She informs the teller that John Barton is a salesman for the Shore dealership down South and he needs the money, since he was leaving that day to purchase cars. He got $8,000 in hundreds.

"This happened five, six, seven times for a total of about $50,000. Every time Mitchell wanted to cash a check, we'd call to make sure there was enough money in the account. Finally, though, the owner stumbles over the scam himself. He writes a check and the bank notifies him he's overdrawn. Overdrawn by about $30,000. The guy wrote a check for something like $275, and the bank tells him he's overdrawn for 30 grand. The guy went right through the ceiling. They asked him if he knew John Barton. He didn't know what they were talking about. The bank fired their own teller, thinking she was involved with the scam, and Shore went out of business. There was no money for inventory or salaries. The bank wouldn't give him a nickel. No one figured it out until they found the stolen checks in Mitchell's place."

The takedown put Kripplebauer in some serious trouble. If the Biddle job, the car dealership theft, and the stolen postal checks and equipment weren't bad enough, he was also facing a charge of aggravated assault and battery with intent to murder. For the alcohol-sodden culture of the K&A crowd, it was par for the course. All too often the burglars' lifestyle itself—whether armed or unarmed, working or not working—got K&A guys into trouble.

In Junior's case the trouble began one evening inside the Chew Tavern, a popular watering hole in the Germantown section of the city, when he got into a dispute with Nicky Lazzaro. Lazzaro was a short, powerful man who had 20-inch arms and could bench-press 500 pounds. He bullied many in the neighborhood and kept his hand in a number of illegal endeavors. Lazzaro claimed Junior owed him money. When Junior told him he owed him nothing, Lazzaro pulled a revolver and threatened to use it.

"Lazzaro had a beef over a job me, Tommy Collins, and Petie Masone had done," says Junior. "We did the house of a wealthy tax assessor on Ridge Avenue and walked off with a big score. I think we got something like $150,000 out of there. Nicky felt he deserved a cut based on the fact that he knew the guy was loaded and he planned on putting together a crew himself and doing the job. Well, he didn't. We did. And now he wants a cut of our take.

"Nicky was very strong. He was a little guy with a complex, and he used to bully people. When he got drunk he could get really angry. He was known to put his fist right through a wall. A lot of folks were afraid of him. It got so bad, some bar owners used to pay him to stay out of their establishments. Well, he starts givin' me a lot of shit at the bar about what I owe him. He's pretty drunk and I'm not much better, but he's getting real loud and tellin' everybody my business. He starts ranting and raving about what I supposedly owe him, and pretty soon the whole joint is listening. And the next thing I know he pulls out a revolver and flaunts it in my face. He's waving it all over the place. I had my own gun on me, but I grabbed his when he turned his head. We struggled for it, and a few shots went off. The bar was crowded, and all of a sudden people are ducking and running for the door. Nicky and I are now locked in a death struggle.

"Shots were going off in every direction, and I finally manage to get the gun out of my face and pointed at his chest. Nicky's still ranting and raving, and that's when I shot him. Bing, I just popped him one in the chest. I knew I wouldn't have any more problems with him.

"But now another guy, one of his friends, jumps in, grabs ahold of the gun, and starts sucker-punching me. He hits me four or five times in the head and manages to get the gun away from me. The guy starts yelling, 'I got the gun. I got the gun.' He's feeling all proud of himself. That's when I pulled my own gun and put it right in his face.

"Fortunately for him, Fingers Hurst, a Kensington guy I did a lot of work with, was there, and he starts yelling, 'C'mon, Junior, let's go. Let's get out of here. The cops are coming. Let's go out the side door.'

"We threw the guns down and got the hell out of there. We drove over to Petie Masone's place, and I started to break out the guns. We always kept guns stashed at his place in case of an emergency. My mind was racing. I'm drunk. I figured I just killed a guy. The police will be coming after me, and maybe Nicky's friends as well. I grabbed a sawed-off shotgun and stuffed two .45s inside my belt. 'Let's go back,' I tell Fingers. 'This time I'll kill them all.'

"Fingers calmed me down, and the cops eventually picked me up."

Steve LaCheen, Kripplebauer's attorney—"legal magician" might be a more accurate description—was able to package a number of unrelated cases and cut a sweet deal for his client. It certainly helped that the shooting victim refused to testify. Every time the case was listed, Junior walked into the courtroom with Spider Haynes, a well-respected man in Germantown. Lazzaro, who required extensive surgery and had to have a lung removed, didn't want Haynes, or anybody else for that matter, to see him rat Kripplebauer out. The code of the streets—for standup men, at least—dictated that Lazzaro keep his mouth shut. He did, in fact; he never even showed up on scheduled court dates. Junior sat in the Philadelphia Detention Center for nearly two years while LaCheen tried to orchestrate a deal with the District Attorney's Office. When sheriff's deputies finally brought Lazzaro to court, he refused to testify, claiming he didn't see who had shot him. The courtroom was filled with friends of both men; it would have been too embarrassing for one burglar and "standup guy" to testify against another.

Eventually a deal was struck: two to four years for everything. In a few more months, Junior would be done with it. But not done with jail time: the State of New Jersey wanted a piece of him as well. They wanted him for a burglary in Cherry Hill and placed a detainer on him. Once he was freed from the Philadelphia Detention Center, Camden County authorities picked him up, shackled him, and took him across the river to face the Jersey charges.

Kripplebauer was no stranger to prison; incarceration was part of his professional life. Serving a few months or a few years in the joint was an understood and accepted business expense. More than most, Junior possessed the mental and physical toughness needed to endure the primitive, oppressive conditions behind bars. From the endless periods of boredom in one's cell to the periodic outbursts of violence and mayhem on the cellblocks or in the prison yard, Junior learned to survive, and in most cases to thrive. He knew how to navigate between competing prison gangs, gain the trust (or fear) of men, and always protect his own interests.

At six-foot-three and 215 pounds, Junior was no shrinking violet. Strong, athletic, and self-assured, he carried himself in a way that few mistook for weakness. He would never instigate a confrontation with another inmate, but would stop at nothing to terminate anybody brazen enough to start something with him.

Kripplebauer called on this survival instinct after New Jersey authorities took him out of Pennsylvania and placed him on ice in the Camden County Jail, a violent and overcrowded penal facility in a notoriously troubled city. The jail's racial makeup was almost 90 percent African-American. White prisoners knew it was to their advantage to keep a low profile. Kripplebauer abided by the unwritten rule, but he somehow still caught the eye of a particularly fearsome opponent.

"Hardrock got on my case big time," says Kripplebauer. "For some reason, he took a dislike to me and wouldn't let up. He was on another cellblock, but every time he saw me he'd yell, 'Hey, white boy, I'm gonna make you my bitch. Yeah, you'll be my bitch, you big honky bastard. I got something good for you to suck on.'

"This went on for some time, but I just kept my mouth shut. After a while, though, I said fuck it and started to give it back to him. I told him, 'I know you're back there sucking those kids' dicks. I read you right off, motherfucker. I know you're having a suck fest over there.'

"No one in the joint challenged him, certainly none of the white guys. He was a big guy, had done a lot of time, and was being held on a murder charge. Nobody wanted to take him, on including me, but I knew that sooner or later I'd have to do something about this asshole. Then one morning I'm sleeping in my cell, and Jack the Jew [inmate Jack Siggson, serving time for murder] wakes me up and says, 'Hey, Junior, that nigger you were having trouble with is on the block.'

"I jumped right out of bed. I didn't want to be caught unprepared with Hardrock around. I looked down the corridor and there he was, standing on a stool with his back to me at the far end of the tier, cleaning the bars. He was part of a work detail cleaning the jail. I didn't waste any time. I walked up behind him, circled just beneath him, and gave him a fuckin' shot right in the chin. I hit him with such force it lifted him up and he smashed his face in the bars. Turns out he was wearing a dental plate, and the shot I gave him drove it right up into the roof of his mouth. His teeth, blood, and the plate flew everywhere. They had to take him to the hospital to get stitched up.

"Things were a little different after that. The blacks were pretty pissed and made some noise, but kept their distance. On the other hand, the white guards were pretty pleased with me. When passing me in the corridor they'd say, 'Hey, Kripplebauer, you really shut that motherfucker up.' After seeing so many white guys get pushed around in the jail, they were tickled pink I stood up to the guy.

"I knew he'd be coming back at me so I got my shit together. I got ahold of a pair of scissors, took the pin out so I'd only have one blade, and kept it on me at all times. Next time I saw Hardrock he was cursing me and saying, 'I'm gonna fuck you up, you ugly honky devil. I'm gonna fuck you up bad. You'll be sucking my black dick yet, motherfucker.'

"I listened to him rant for a while and finally I told him, 'Suck on this, you black motherfucker.' I raised my shirt so he could see the shank I was carrying. I'd had enough of this asshole. I told him, 'I'll be in the visiting room at two o'clock. Be down there and I'll plant this iron in your heart, you fuckin' jerkoff.'

"I would have stabbed him right then and there, I was so fed up, but he never showed up. Soon after that, I hit court, was given a four-year sentence and sent to Trenton State. Things were fine for a few months, but then I got the news. Once again, Jack the Jew, who's now doing time with me in Trenton, comes up to me on the cellblock one morning and says, 'Did you hear who just came in? Hardrock was just admitted. He's down at A and O' [admissions and orientation]. Right then and there, I knew what I had to do."

"The routine is the same for everybody. A new prisoner at Trenton State is placed on "A" Block, a quarantine block. I figured that would be a good place to take him out. I worked in the hospital and had the run of the joint. I knew Hardrock didn't have anything on him yet, 'cause he just came in the joint, and I know I'm gonna have trouble with him. I told myself, let me do it now while I have the advantage.

"I was hiding in a stairwell when he was coming back from chow. I grabbed him from behind. I had one arm around his neck and started to whack him in the chest with the other. I drove the shank in his chest and stomach pretty good. He tried to protect himself with his hand and arm, but I cut the hell out of him. I really got him good four or five times. Blood was everywhere. Guys on the block started yelling; bells were going off; guards came running. I thought I had killed the son-of-a-bitch, but he survived. I don't know how, but he survived. They gave me an extra two to four for the shanking and threw me in the hole. I did most of the time in lockup. They said I was an incorrigible and put me in the Vroom Building, where they kept the nuts and the worst dudes in the joint."

The episode earned Kripplebauer two extra years on his sentence, but he no longer had to worry about Hardrock. In fact, he rarely had to worry about anybody. Such violent and decisive punitive strikes solidified Junior's reputation as a tough motherfucker it didn't pay to fool with. The prison subculture— always difficult to influence or impress—took notice. From county jails like Holmesburg in Philadelphia, to large state institutions like Pittsburgh and Huntingdon, and on up to the close-security, level-five federal penitentiaries like Lewisburg and Atlanta, Junior was known as a standup guy, a wily con who knew how to maneuver, and someone definitely worth knowing. After a few more lengthy prison stints in places like Texas and North Carolina, the name of Junior Kripplebauer would become well known throughout a good portion of America's burgeoning penal system. As one Pennsylvania lifer who never even met Kripplebauer declared, "Hell, Junior was a living, breathing legend."

His fearlessness well documented, Kripplebauer was repeatedly sought out by other desperate men to do "a piece of work" for them, but he never seriously entertained the notion. He wasn't into contract killings. "I wasn't opposed to killing somebody, but to do it for money, no way. It led to bad karma. If somebody does something to you, okay, kill him. But for money, no way."

On the street as well, Junior had earned a reputation as someone not to be trifled with. He was also seen as a "workhorse," a serious-minded criminal who was unaccustomed to downtime. Though he spent his share of time in gin mills and was often seen squiring beautiful, voluptuous women around town, he never let his social schedule interfere with his business activities. There weren't enough hours in a day to satisfy Junior's criminal appetite. He was open to just about anything and more than receptive to illegal escapades contrived by non-Irish crews—something that most K&A men generally refrained from. As one friend comments, "Junior would saddle up with an incredible assortment of people. There were so many different guys and teams. He was all over the place." His openness to outsiders was considered ill-advised, and friends tried to caution him. "Jesus Christ, it was amazing," recalls one colleague. "I told him more than once that some of these guys he was hooking up with aren't standup guys. They're not gonna step up when you need them."

Kripplebauer was even willing to freelance with one of the more active Jewish outfits wrecking havoc throughout the area at the time. Led by Sylvan Scolnick, a mountain of gelatinous flesh topped by a genius for convoluted get-rich-quick schemes, the gang included Kenny Paul, Allen Rosenberg, and Sid Brooks, a nightclub owner, burglar, and accomplished practitioner of the art of "Jewish lightning" (i.e., arson). Scolnick ("Cherry Hill Fats"), who periodically topped out at 750 pounds, was said to be a criminal mastermind of unrivaled proportions. One journalist called him "undoubtedly the fattest, probably the shrewdest, unquestionably the most deceptive, perhaps the evilest and likely the most driven criminal conspirator in modern history." Superlatives aside, Scolnick had a big body and a big brain. He and his confederates did everything from loan sharking and fraudulent bankruptcies to arson and violent stickups, but there was one significant omission in the gang's criminal portfolio: no one knew how to crack a safe.

"I was brought in to do some burglaries and open safes," says Kripplebauer of his introduction to the Jewish mob. "It certainly wasn't the first time I'd been asked to do some safes for guys outside Kensington or Philadelphia. I had already done work for a bunch of guys, including some from New York. The New York guys were all mobbed up and did stickups, heists, and bank jobs, but couldn't do anything involving a safe. They didn't know anything about it. I did a house with them one time and we found a safe. They got excited for a minute or two, but then realized they didn't know what to do. They were completely stumped. They wanted to quit and get out, but I told them to cool it for a while. They just sat in amazement and watched me work.

"The Scolnick crew got to me through Johnny Bernardo, a doorman at the Equator Lounge on 11th Street. Bernardo asked Buddy Brennan, 'Who do you know who can open safes? I need someone to help a few friends of mine.' Buddy, a Fairmount boy like myself, gave Bernardo my name and put me in touch with Paul and Rosenberg. They were immediately impressed. I remember early on we were doing the home of a prominent doctor in New York, and we couldn't find the safe. We had been there for a while and they wanted to give up, but I knew there was money hidden there. And I wasn't leaving until I found it. I'm going through everything and finally find a little toolbox hidden in a stereo speaker in the doctor's library. It contained $35,000. Rosenberg was impressed. He told Kenny Paul, 'That Junior is something, isn't he? He can smell the money.'

"I did a good bit of work with them, straight burglaries, scams, walk-ins. The K&A guys didn't want to work with Rosenberg and Paul because they were using guns. The Kensington guys wanted nothing to do with guns, but it didn't bother me. I still did a ton of work with them. At least a half-dozen times we targeted prominent citizens and posed as IRS agents. Paul and Rosenberg would knock on the door after the man of the house had left for work, show phony identification to the guy's wife, and explain that they were investigators for the Internal Revenue Service. If the woman wanted proof, they'd give her the phone number of the IRS headquarters, which was actually a phone booth I'd be standing in down the street. If she called looking for verification, I'd answer in a very official sounding voice, 'Internal Revenue Department,' and tell her the two men in her home were 'sworn government agents investigating a crime' and she was 'obligated to cooperate' with them. It worked every time. We cleaned them out.

"Sometimes we'd do a commercial operation and a safe wasn't even involved. We did the Tiffany Wig Shop on Castor Avenue in Northeast Philadelphia. Around 10 o'clock at night me and Allen Rosenberg went through the roof. We used a hatchet and crowbar to cut a hole in the roof and lowered ourselves inside the building. There was a four-room suite loaded with all kinds of wigs. We cleaned them out. We must've grabbed over a thousand wigs and hairpieces. They were pretty popular at the time and valued between fifty and a hundred dollars apiece. Wigs were something I usually didn't go after, it was a specialty item, and you'd have to know somebody who could move them. But Scolnick could sell anything. He had some important, big-time buyers."

One of Junior's more creative escapades with Scolnick's crew was the notorious PSFS Bank caper of December 1965, when the gang walked off with a cool $100,000 without even drawing a weapon. The highly publicized heist left an array of law enforcement agencies slack-jawed and embarrassed. Innovative, daring, and well-orchestrated, the scam added enormously to Scolnick's reputation as a "wheeler dealer extraordinaire" and "titanic trickster," but Kripplebauer claims that much of the hype surrounding that caper—and most of the praise for "Cherry Hill Fats" in general—was undeserved.

"Scolnick was good at con games," says Kripplebauer, "but when it came to real criminal shit he was nothing. Rosenberg and Paul figured that bank deal out; they deserve as much credit as Scolnick. The whole thing came about when Sid Brooks couldn't get his money out of the old Philadelphia Saving Fund Society. That's what started it all. One day he goes to the bank, but doesn't realize he's being followed by the cops. They had been watching him for a while. That's how they learned about the safe-deposit box. The cops thought the box contained the proceeds of various burglaries and arson jobs he had committed. They looked his name up among the owners of safe-deposit boxes, but there was nothing registered to a Sidney Brooks. He was using an alias. They then got a court order to inspect all those boxes suspected of being his. That's how they discovered the $100,000. But the government made a big mistake: they left the money in the safe- deposit box and had the IRS put a seal on it.

"Now Sid has got a problem: he can't get his money out of the bank. What's he gonna do? He goes to Scolnick and explains his problem. All of us then sat down and had a discussion, what are we gonna do about this hundred grand? How are we gonna get it out of there? It wasn't just Scolnick—there were a bunch of us trying to figure it out. It was a combination of brains. Everybody was throwing ideas out. Paul said, 'Let's just rob the bank. We'll lay them all down and rob the joint.' Others came up with other ideas. We met several times and finally came up with a plan and refined it until we all felt comfortable with it.

"It worked this way. Rosenberg went to the bank a few times and purchased a number of safe-deposit boxes, hoping that one of them would be near the box the IRS had sealed shut. The plan was to cause a diversion in the bank, get ahold of a teller's keys while people were distracted, and then switch one of the new, empty boxes with the one that held the money and walk out.

"On the day of the robbery, everything went like clockwork. Rosenberg entered the bank and moved towards the back where the safe-deposit vault was located. Paul followed him in as backup just in case anything went wrong. I then had someone drive me up to the bank's front door. I got out and threw a large cinderblock through the bank's plate glass window that faced Cottman Avenue. It sounded like an explosion. I then got the hell out of there, but as we drove off I could hear Kenny Paul yelling inside the bank. He was shouting at the top of his lungs, 'It's a bomb! It's a bomb! It's a bomb! Everybody get down!'

"It looked like a prison break. While everybody is either dropping to the floor or panicking and trying to get out of the building, Rosenberg went behind the teller's desk, got the master key that's needed to open the safe-deposit boxes, and then went to the vault. He opened Sid Brooks's box to make sure the money was there, but instead of taking the money and putting the box back and locking it, he must have got nervous, 'cause he took the whole damn box with him. He put the box inside his coat and walked out of the bank while everyone is trying to figure out what all the commotion is about. If he had locked the box, the Feds never would have known the box had been taken from the bank.

"Afterwards we let Sid walk off with $80,000 'cause it was his money, and we whacked up the rest between us. I think I came out of it with $1,800, which wasn't bad for throwing a brick."

The PSFS heist greatly contributed to Sylvan Scolnick's celebrity status and reputation as a master criminal. To serious, working criminals like Junior and his K&A colleagues, however, the tribute was severely tarnished when "Big Cherry" became an informant. Scolnick, Brooks, and the others became government witnesses against each other in an orgy of self-incrimination and mutual destruction. It was a prosecutor's dream and a nightmare for any self-respecting criminal. No standup guy would rat out his partners, but Scolnick and company dispensed with principle and decided that self-interest was the best course of action.

Scolnick alone was said to have given prosecutors "2,000 hours of testimony" that supposedly "rocked the criminal world to its foundations." Junior was not surprised by "the Fat Man's" willingness to cooperate with authorities; he had Scolnick pegged the first time he laid eyes on him. "I never felt comfortable with Sylvan," says Kripplebauer of the Jewish behemoth. "The guy was so fuckin' fat, I knew he wouldn't be able to do any time. He'd rat me out in a second if the government squeezed him and threatened him with any prison time."

Kripplebauer somehow avoided being pulled into the feeding frenzy of co-conspirators informing against each other. He was only a fringe player in a few of the Scolnick gang's projects; Sylvan didn't know his name, and Paul and Rosenberg refused to give him up, allowing Junior to stay off the prosecutor's radar screen for the PSFS job and therefore avoid both a jail term and the unwanted notoriety associated with the high-profile bank robbery. This was not an unprecedented incident: Junior did plenty of time in prison, but nothing compared with what he could have served, considering his long and industrious career. Junior was bold, some would say reckless, but he was usually able to stay one step ahead of the law.

A prime example of his brazen contempt for the odds—not to mention a demonstration of his loyalty to imprisoned comrades—was his critical role in the Graterford breakout of 1975. The largest penal institution in Pennsylvania and one of the toughest, Graterford housed two of the most dangerous felons in the state, Francis Tomlinson and John Dickel. A Kensington boy, Dickel had gravitated to armed robberies and was serving 10 to 20 years for a $50,000 robbery in Lancaster County. Tomlinson was serving a life term for the rape and murder of a 47-year-old Bucks County woman. In addition to being extremely dangerous, both men were considered certified escape artists, Tomlinson having fled the State Correctional Institution at Dallas and Dickel having done the same at Rockview. By combining their extraordinary talents, they were an even greater escape risk, despite being housed in one of the most secure penal facilities in the state.

It didn't take the two long to conceive of a plan and move on it. On the evening of October 22, 1975, Tomlinson and Dickel got out of their cellblock, ran across Graterford's expansive prison yard, and scaled its 30-foot-high wall with a hand-made rope and grappling hook. They were discovered missing the next morning, triggering a massive search. At this point Junior Kripplebauer enters the picture.

"I got a call from Troy McEntee one morning," says Kripplebauer. "He said he was in a jam and needed a favor. He told me Tomlinson and Dickel had escaped out of Graterford and it was his job to pick them up, but he couldn't find them. He said he had been driving all over the back roads that ran through the woods out there in rural Montgomery County, but all he saw were helicopters, state police, and prison guards. He was getting frustrated, afraid of being caught, and wanted someone to go along with him. I said okay and met him out there near the prison. We drove around for quite a while, skirting the prison grounds and trying to avoid the cops, who were all over the place.

"Troy finally gave up, but I continued riding around the area, looking for any sign of them, any likely place they might be hiding. Occasionally I'd stop and call out, 'Hey, Gator, you out there? It's me, Junior.' "Gator" was John Dickel's nickname. I'm doing this all over, as close as I can get to the actual prison grounds, but there's hundreds of acres of farm land out there owned by the correctional system that was used for crop production. It's tough to cover it all. The cops and state police had to have seen me, but they never pulled me over. They probably thought I was one of them, 'cause I had my German shepherd in the car with me. They must have thought I was an off-duty cop or guard trying to help out.

"I continued driving around, calling out the names of Dickel and Tomlinson, and then I hear one of them yell out. I had finally found them. I got them in the car and drove to New Jersey and dropped them off at Tommy Seher's house in Camden."

The two escapees proceeded to rob numerous area supermarkets before heading west and pulling similar jobs in California. They were finally captured while trying to rob an armored car in Anaheim. Kripplebauer was never associated with the Graterford escape; Pennsylvania state police mistakenly arrested Tomlinson's brother, Joseph, for aiding the men in their getaway.

Junior had dodged another bullet, but his luck was about to turn. Granted, he had served short bits in a number of state and local institutions, but they were minuscule in their psychological and economic impact, considering the riches and excitement he had picked up along the way. From Junior's standpoint, crime paid. In fact, it paid very well. In future years, although it would continue to pay handsomely, the business expenses would climb considerably. The FBI would become increasingly preoccupied with the activities of the K&A Gang and target them for destruction. One special agent was aiming specifically for Kripplebauer.

11. The Cops Strike Back

We were all getting hit a lot. All the cities and towns in New York and
New England were getting hit. We knew who they were. It was always
the Irish Mob out of Philly.

— DETECTIVE JIM SMITH, GREENWICH, CONNECTICUT

The K&A guys developed an expertise in stealing. They could steal the
teeth out of your mouth and you wouldn't even know it. They were the
best burglars out there.

— WILLIAM DRUM, SPECIAL AGENT, BUREAU OF ALCOHOL,
TOBACCO AND FIREARMS

FROM THE VERY BEGINNING Philly cops knew there was something novel,
something different about the K&A burglars. They were more industrious, better organized, and considerably more creative than their predecessors. Restless
thieves out of Kensington were burglarizing homes in the more prosperous
sections of the city at an alarming rate. "They were wearing us out," retired
Philadelphia Police Captain Joseph Brophy recalls of his introduction to the
K&A Gang in the early 1950s.

Earlier burglars—with no system or teamwork—had been less methodical
and certainly less productive. Now the thieves were moving with military-like
precision. It was a new phenomenon, and police were increasingly frustrated.
Residential burglaries were escalating in number, homeowners and politicians
were livid, and pressure was being exerted on the police to gain control of
the situation. In the mid-fifties even the FBI began to take notice. "The FBI
worked with us hand in glove for many years," says Brophy. "Special Agent Dave
Walker was in the squad room everyday. The FBI was particularly interested in
the criminal intelligence we were gathering and what we discovering regarding
major burglaries and truck hijackings."

Various initiatives were undertaken, from beefing up existing burglary units
to the utilization of sophisticated technology such as wiretaps: "You could do
things in those days that you couldn't do today," says Brophy. Though the

wiretaps were extremely useful, they could just as often prove dangerous. On one occasion, Brophy and his partner were discovered unconscious in a freezing attic in North Philadelphia. While trying to listen in on a burglar's conversation, "we were overcome by fumes from a space heater we were using," says Brophy, of the nearly fatal experience. "We often found ourselves in out-of-the-way places" when spying, but "when the gang moved, we were on to them."

Some taps provided a chuckle or two. Willie Sears, for example, was a central target of Brophy's intelligence unit. Police carefully charted the comings and goings of production work's creator, and so, apparently, did his associates. Sears's colleagues would call his house and ask Dolly, his wife, "Did he leave yet?" If the answer was yes, the caller would quickly reply, "Okay, I'll be right over." That there seemed to be little honor among thieves was no surprise to Brophy. Not only did they steal from each other all the time, but "all the other burglars wanted Dolly," he says. "Everyone wanted to get next to her. No sooner would Sears be out of the house and one of his buddies would be visiting his wife."

Though the wiretaps proved useful, it was another departmental innovation that resonated in law enforcement circles for years to come: the publication of a burglar handbook, a nifty three-by-eight-inch photographic dossier of the area's most troublesome thieves. "I was in the Headquarters Squad [a precursor to today's intelligence units] in the mid-fifties," recalls Brophy, "and Richard Doyle, Al Mortimer, Jimmy O'Dare, and myself would sit around and brainstorm about ways to grab these guys. What could we do to get these characters off the street? Then we came up with the idea of a hit list, a list of the most wanted burglars in Philadelphia. The concept was totally original. We just thought it would be a new and helpful twist, and it became my responsibility to keep the book updated."

According to Brophy, the "blue books" (named after their blue soft-back covers) had a dramatic impact on their prey. "They helped us put heat on the gang and drive them out of Philly." (Many K&A gang members scoff at the notion of being driven out of town. The plain truth is, they went where the money was. While affluent Philadelphia area neighborhoods were becoming played out, wealthy communities along the eastern seaboard still represented fertile fields.)

Simple but effective, the blue books provided beat cops with a handy catalogue—a pocket-sized "Rogues Gallery"—of the Philadelphia's most persistent and annoying thieves. Members of the K&A Gang dominated its pages. Along with the mug shots of Willie Sears, Effie Burke, John Berkery, Ray Chalmers, Harry Stocker, and a host of others, the book included additional information that the intelligence unit thought might be useful to officers on the street. Home addresses, aliases, physical characteristics, MOs, favorite automobiles, close associates, and favorite hangouts all gradually became part of burglars' individual profiles.

The handbooks were an instant hit. Officers walking a beat or in their squad cars could flip open their books and check out any suspicious characters who had crossed their path. As for the gang members, though some were initially delighted to see that they had earned a place in the city's pantheon of reprobates and mischief-makers, it very soon became apparent that the dubious honor was "pure trouble."

"It created more headaches for all of us," says one media-shy criminal. "It made life miserable for many of us. Any time you or your vehicle were spotted by the cops they would stop you and check to see if you were in the book. Then they'd go through the whole thing. 'Would you step out of the car, please. Would you mind if we looked in your trunk? Can we look in your glove compartment?' It just made things more difficult."

Other thieves were indifferent to the whole business. "By the time the books came along," says one, "we were doing most of our work outside of Philly. They didn't have any of the mug shot books, so we didn't have to worry about it."

Despite such negative to apathetic reviews, the blue books gradually became a bestseller—especially among the more aggressive East Coast police departments. Desperate for information about the slick operators looting the homes of their most prominent citizens, law enforcement officials sought out the Philly handbook once they learned that it was the K&A Gang that had invaded their turf. Local and state authorities from Maine to Florida began sharing information on the gang's members, tactics, and potential targets. Small-town law enforcement agencies basically conceded that they were facing a unique and unprecedented criminal onslaught. Though almost all eventually learned it was a resourceful and relentless gang of predominantly Irish thieves out of Philadelphia that was committing the crimes, they were in no position to tackle the perpetrators by themselves. Waltham, Westport, Saratoga Springs, Princeton, and Annapolis could not be expected to do the job alone. Gathering and sharing information, as well as the dissemination of Brophy's blue books, were critical first steps in law enforcement's counterattack. Within a short time, and for several decades thereafter, homemade versions of Philly's Rogue's Gallery would pop up in communities from Bar Harbor to Fort Lauderdale and as far west as Ohio, Missouri, and Texas.

For example, one helpful Maryland state trooper sent a memo concerning information gathered by a high-ranking state trooper in Delaware to a third colleague in the New Jersey state police: "I am writing you in regards to . . . the K&A burglary gang. We experienced approximately a year and a half ago a series of eleven burglaries in two fashionable sections of Salisbury. They occurred between November 1968 and March 1969 on four separate weekends, usually on Saturday evenings, hitting two or three homes in the early evening hours. In each case culprits would gain entrance to the home by prying a sliding glass door apparently with a small screwdriver. Once inside someone would pull any curtains in the front of the house and turn a chair around facing out as a lookout. A side or rear window would be opened as an escape route and any firearms would be hidden as a precaution. General ransacking in the homes resulted in fine jewelry, silverware, coin collections, and furs taken. They would pass over the poor quality items and silver plate as well as older furs. In several cases liquor was taken and some food was consumed on the premises. It is felt in most cases they were dropped off and picked up by an additional member of the gang. On the evening of September 12, 1970 we experienced two identical burglaries in the same sections. The MO is alike in every detail and we have no doubt the same group is involved."

Such missives became commonplace in small-town law enforcement offices during the sixties and seventies, and woe to the police chief who was out of the loop or dismissive of the warnings. Most took the notices seriously—especially if they had been victimized in preceding years. A Greenwich, Connecticut, police official ordered "all detective division commanders in Fairfield County" to be on the lookout for the K&A Gang. He informed his people that the gang was composed of "approximately fifty persons[,] ... operates out of Philadelphia[,]" and "was positively known to have been in Greenwich, Easton, and Wilton, Connecticut, and Rye, Harrison, Scarsdale, and New Rochelle, New York."

Police intelligence eventually became surprisingly accurate. After being hit so often, local law enforcement agencies not only learned the nuances of production work but also the names of its more aggressive practitioners. For example, one intelligence report describing the "K&A Gang's method of operations" said "members of this gang operate in groups of three or four men. They leave Philadelphia, and if operating some distance from there, may be gone for several days. They stay in motels and during the summer season and will pick out one having a swimming pool, if available. They may or may not register under their correct names. Two cars are generally taken to the first location and one will return to Philadelphia with the loot immediately after the crime or if this is not done, furs and other identifiable objects will be sent to Philadelphia by other means.

"Generally, only one car is driven to the scene of the crime. One man remains in the car and cruises around the area. The other two or three men enter the house, usually by the back door using a large screwdriver to force the door. Upon entering the house, blinds may or may not be drawn, closet lights are extinguished by breaking or unscrewing the bulb, and the refrigerator cord disconnected. One man acts as a lookout and the other men ransack the house, dumping bureau, dresser, and desk drawers. In many cases, pillowcases and sheets have been used to carry away the loot. The lookout man stations himself in the rear or front of the house, depending on the most advantageous position, and will drink beverages or eat food while so engaged. Upon completing the search, one man leaves the premises and signals the outside man, or if a radio is being used, this method is employed, who then returns and picks up the rest of the gang. If the outside man is stopped or followed by police, the other men will flee the house, steal a car, and meet at a prearranged location."

Occasionally, the police reports would veer dramatically off the mark, as did one stating that K&A gang members "are known to carry weapons and should be considered armed and dangerous." Most experienced cops knew that the gang rarely, if ever, carried weapons. Generally, though, the intelligence gathered was accurate and perceptive, as in one report that observed: "subjects have been arrested many times and experience has revealed that questioning of these subjects is useless."

Information on individual gang members was equally on target. For example, one Connecticut intelligence report describes "James J. Dolan" as a "white male, 32, 5'10", 185 lbs. Hazel eyes, brown hair, medium build, 1345 E. Columbia Ave. Philadelphia, Pa. (Mother's address). He has his vehicles listed at this address. He buys a new Eldorado Cadillac every year, Penna. Registration JJD-7. Presently has a 1969 Cadillac, turquoise. He had an apartment next to the Chapelcroft Apts. 9629 Bustleton Ave. Philadelphia, but is now living with a woman at Academy Road, Philadelphia, address unknown."

One state trooper who received and disseminated scores of reports on the K&A Gang over the years was Richard Richroath of the New Jersey state police. "They were quick and very efficient," recalls Richroath, a 27-year veteran of the force. "They'd enter a house quickly, rake it, and be gone in three minutes. They would come in a community and knock off several houses in no time at all and seven or eight over the course of a weekend." Richroath says the gang "picked on the more exclusive communities like Colt's Neck that had many impressive horse farms and communities with estate type of homes." The result was not unexpected. "Influential citizens became upset. They were really getting concerned and local politicians started to pressure us to provide better protection in those communities." Though more manpower and resources were enlisted in the fight, Richroath regretfully admits that they "never had any success in shutting down the K&A Gang." His only consolation was a general impression that Connecticut was being victimized even worse than New Jersey.

Detective Jimmy Smith of the Greenwich, Connecticut, Police Department remembers the era and the K&A Gang well. "We had a lot of house burglaries in Greenwich back in the sixties and early seventies," says Smith. "We were all getting hit a lot, all the cities and towns in New England and New York. We soon learned who was doing the jobs. It was the Irish Mob out of Philly. I think we slowed them down once we finally found out who they were and how they operated. We set up a task force in different towns and neighborhoods in New England and New York. We got to know what to look for, what type of communities they worked in and followed them around in unmarked cars to harass and keep track of them." Smith said their efforts hindered the burglars, but it "never nailed or convicted any of them. The gang was too quick and experienced. They refused to talk even when we got hold of them."

Despite what occasionally seemed like painfully slow progress, a number of East Coast communities were making some headway. The widespread distribution of blue books, improved intelligence gathering, and proactive policing had an impact. Not surprisingly, the burglars were some of the first to notice. "The blue books and some of the other things the cops did had an effect," says Jimmy Dolan. "The cops weren't dopes. They learned the routine. Cops would pull you over, look at our faces, and then turn to the blue books. All it now took was a car stop. You could be up in Connecticut or Massachusetts and your ID says Pennsylvania. You look legitimate; you're well-dressed. But then the book comes out. After a while, extreme paranoia sets in. You wanted to go to a place where the books didn't exist and the cops were unconscious. It was always a game of chess with those guys."

"THEY WERE CENTRAL CHARACTERS in our operations back then," says John Lanzidelle, who joined the Philadelphia Police Department in the mid-1950s and worked Major Crimes as a detective during the sixties and seventies. "They did a hell of a lot of work and kept us busy. A lot of those K&A guys were pretty smart. They all knew one another and shared information. They learned from each other—such as how to use burning rods to open safes—and were usually more experienced than the other guys we had to deal with."

Over the years Lanzidelle worked everything from simple burglaries to homicides and met some of the most despised and celebrated people in the news. He refers to his time on the police force as his "college education," but in a subject that few other schools of higher learning offered. "I had a ringside seat to the greatest show on earth," he says of those exciting years. The K&A Gang played a prominent role in that long-running spectacle.

"They were pretty personable guys. I never had a bad time with any of them," says Lanzidelle. "They were good guys. You didn't fall in love with them, but you wouldn't mind having a drink with them. You could kid and joke with them. Most of them had a good sense of humor and knew what the score was. And they wouldn't try to beat you over the head if you ran into them in a bar." Not that Kensington crowd were a bunch of softies. "There were some bad freakin' guys in that crowd," he says. "Guys you wouldn't want to mess with." But, he admits, there was also a charming audacity about them that made the K&A crowd something truly special.

Residential and commercial burglaries in Philadelphia during the fifties, sixties, and seventies weren't the exclusive preserve of the K&A Gang, but there was a distinctive quality about their work. Their burglaries tended to be bolder in scope, more inventive in their planning, and far more numerous than those of the others practicing theft as a livelihood. In other words, they were more accomplished, more professional; in some cases their work approached true artistry, demonstrating a real flare for originality, critical thinking, and problem solving. Other efforts recalled the original amateur hour.

John DelCarlino, a Philly police detective who worked Major Crimes through most of the sixties and seventies, spent 17 of his 27 years on the force chasing K&A's industrious second story men. It didn't take him long to become a grudging admirer of their work. "Those K&A guys were slick, sharp thieves," says DelCarlino. "They had common sense, but many of them lived in a dream world. They'd hit homes after dusk, do the burglaries, and then live like kings for a week. They would party 24 hours a day with beautiful girls, buy all sorts of clothes, and booze it up pretty good. And then when they were broke again, they'd go back out and pull some more jobs.

"They'd come up with fascinating, imaginative ways to get what they wanted. For example, they developed a really innovative scheme to get ahold of some of those expensive diamonds and gems down at Jewelers' Row in center city Philadelphia. They'd send a couple guys down to Eighth and Sansom Streets and watch the jewelry salesmen go from store to store as they sold their stock of quality diamonds. They weren't stickup men who were going to blast their way into a well-protected shop or shoot it out with policemen who patrolled the street. They were more sophisticated than that. They'd watch, listen, and learn who had what and who traveled where. In no time at all they came up with a pretty good plan. They took careful notice of the license plates of the cars these jewelry salesmen were driving and then called a crooked cop they had in their employ. They'd give the cop the tag numbers, and he'd give them the home addresses of the salesmen.

"Later that evening they'd go to the salesman's house and steal his car. They knew a lot of these guys didn't even bother to take their stash of goods into the house with them at night. Most salesmen had their car trunks wired with alarms and felt comfortable leaving the inventory in the car. The K&A guys would hot-shot the car, drive it to a garage at Memphis and East Ontario Streets in Kensington, and then go to work on the car. They knew the trunk was wired, but the fender probably wasn't, so they'd cut the metal fender, then reach in and take the sample jewelry cases. The K&A guys would then fence the stuff with reputedly legitimate jewelers. This went on dozens of times. They made a bundle using that can-opener trick, sometimes in the salesman's own driveway.

"It went on for over a year before one of our snitches gave us a call. That's how we discovered the operation in the first place. An informant tipped us off. A rat that sometimes gave us information called up John Ryan, one of our detectives in Major Crimes, and told him about a stash of hot jewels that could be found down at Nick Sama's place at 15th and Snyder Avenues in South Philadelphia. We hit Sama's jewelry store and found a dozen cases of jewelry he said wasn't his. We had a big press conference with all the jewelry laid out on a table. There were hundreds of rings, brooches, earrings, and bracelets. It was an incredible amount of stuff. We estimated there were 35 jewelry salesmen in Philadelphia alone that were knocked off in this fashion in just one year. They had a pretty good run until we shut 'em down."

Not all of the Kensington burglars Lanzidelle and DelCarlino arrested were as inventive and elusive as those who made life miserable for the diamond merchants on Jewelers' Row. Some thieves could be downright infantile in their approach; others substituted mindless bravado for brains. The results could be disastrous for all concerned. One infamous heist, for example, cost two people their lives, one of them a Philadelphia police officer.

"We were sitting down at our office at the Roundhouse [Police Administration Building] at Eighth and Race when Captain Bartley came in around mid-morning," recalled DelCarlino of the 1968 felony-homicide. "Every morning he'd hand us a slew of jobs from the night before that we had to check out. K&A guys had usually done more than their fair share of them. This time Bartley ordered us to 'get up to the Northeast. It's a bad one.'

"When we finally got up to Verree and Welsh Road, the place was crawling with cops. Homicide was there. Stakeout was there. High-ranking police officials were there. Even a few of our guys in Major Crimes were already there. Within a short time the police commissioner, district attorney, and the media would be there too. It was intense. It always is when a cop is killed on duty.

"A patrolman, William Lackman, responding to a burglary-in-progress call, was shot in the throat as he entered the home of Dr. Frank Washick. The shooter, John Seeley, was then gunned down by police as he tried to flee the doctor's home. The perps had just been taken away when we got there. Seeley's body, though, still lay strewn on the front lawn. But they missed one of the burglars. My partner found him hiding in the second floor closet as we went through the house. The guy had crapped his pants he was so scared. We were up there all day and then sent out to interview the neighbors, look up associates of the perpetrators, and find out anything we could about what had just gone down. We went to Kensington and started tracking down all the K&A guys. They all knew each other. It was a lot of legwork, but there was nothing of value."

Officer Lackman, an 11-year veteran of the force, was known as "a good hearted" soul who was "full of life" and "never had a nasty word for anybody," according to the newspaper reports. He left a young wife and a four-year-old daughter. His killer, John Seeley, 31, was out on bail for killing another policeman a year earlier. As a troubled youth, Seeley had been declared a "slow learner" and sent to a special school, preventing him from going on to high school, where he had dreamed of playing varsity football. Disillusioned and resentful, he turned to crime, building a record of nine arrests dating back to 1953. The most serious charge, the murder of a policeman, had occurred just 14 months earlier on August 6, 1967, when Seeley arrived at the home of his estranged wife and found Officer Herman J. Dietrich asleep in her bed. He killed the young officer, pistol-whipped his wife, forced her to help him dump the patrolman's naked body in an empty lot, and was nevertheless allowed to go free on $15,000 bail.

The highly publicized murder of a policeman during a burglary gone bad gave further adverse publicity to K&A burglars, but it was a misnomer. Some of the burglars involved in the Washick bust may have been from Kensington, but they weren't K&A burglars, at least according to actual K&A gang members. "Seeley was a rogue, a dangerous mutt," says one burglar. "He had a bad reputation. I seen him around once or twice in bars we hung at. He'd come in lookin' for work with any of the crews, but none of our guys would have ever picked him up. He might have done a few burglaries, but he wasn't really a burglar. He was trouble."

When pressed, even the police acknowledge that Seeley's crew were K&A imposters, impersonating their more sophisticated elders in the hopes of nailing an easy score and building a reputation. They had received a tip that Dr. Washick owned a $50,000 coin collection, but they were amateur screwups posing as veteran highwaymen. "They were Kensington wannabes," says DelCarlino. "They weren't the real deal." There is little doubt in the minds of experienced officers like DelCarlino that if serious second story men out of Kensington had done the job, there would have been no weapons, no deaths, and no coin collection. They would have picked the place clean.

As it turns out, by the late sixties, the vast majority of K&A gang members were doing very little work in the city. They were usually on the road, North Carolina, Massachusetts, western Pennsylvania, and Ohio being more likely venues for their wide-ranging operations than a single residence in Northeast Philadelphia. As one burglar says, "We wrote off Chestnut Hill, the Main Line, and the more affluent suburban neighborhoods. The elite areas around Philadelphia were burnt out, and the cops were becoming more sophisticated. There were rich people in other parts of the country."

More important, the police knew that few, if any, K&A burglars ever carried a gun on the job. And it was rare for cops to catch one of them at the scene of a burglary, much less taking part in a criminal act that resulted in anything like the human carnage at the Washick residence.

Seeley was viewed as a cowboy, a dangerous, unpredictable hooligan who often bragged, "A walk-in ain't hard for me. I can hold 20 people at bay." His partners were inexperienced dupes hoping to make a sizable score and replicate the legendary exploits of the better-known neighborhood thieves. They would pay dearly for their ineptitude: Seeley was killed at the scene, but his confederates would spend the rest of their lives behind bars. John McIntyre (23), Adolph Schwartz (22), and the so-called masterminds of the scheme, Michael Borschell (28) and William Russell (27), would receive life sentences for a burglary gone bad and the cold-blooded murder of a Philadelphia police officer.

THE LURE OF THE GOOD LIFE was strong, and K&A wannabes were everywhere. By the late sixties and early seventies, it was mostly wannabes that Philly cops were running into. The one and only time DelCarlino shot someone in his two dozen years on the force, one of these young, starry-eyed Kensington burglars was involved. "We were getting several calls a day from the same neighborhoods in Northeast Philadelphia," says DelCarlino. "Somebody was beating the hell out of Winchester Park and Lexington Park during the daylight hours. The guy was posing as a utility man or city sanitation worker. He was doing five or six houses a day, and we weren't having any luck at all. He'd wear a gray uniform like a utility worker for the gas company. He'd knock on the door, and if nobody answered and the property appeared empty, he'd break in. My partner and I decided we'd have to try something different, so we started to intercept everybody we saw who regularly traveled through the community: mailmen, UPS deliverymen, newspaper boys, folks walking their dog, anybody who regularly walked the streets of the hardest-hit communities. We told them what was happening, that the guy wore a uniform and might be using a white Ford with temporary tags, and to give us a call if they saw someone who looked suspicious going through the neighborhood.

"It wasn't long after that that we got a call around noon one day from a mailman. He thought he saw someone who looked suspicious. Henry Coshland and I went out to the neighborhood and quickly spotted the car, a white 1964 Ford, but before we could do anything the car sped off. We chased the guy a short distance when we managed to box him in, but then he took off on foot and the real track meet began. We chased him through alleys and backyards until he reached the edge of Pennypack Park [a large public park that borders Lincoln High School].

"He turned around and shouted at us while holding something black in his hand. It looked like a gun. I had him in my sights and could have shot him in the head, but I lowered my aim and pulled the trigger. The man ran another 50 feet before falling and yelling out, 'I've been hit!' "

The guy turned out to be Danny Weber, a 21-year-old Kensington wannabe, who was just following the traditional career path into burglary. Older, more sophisticated K&A burglars like Hughie Breslin, Jackie Johnson, and Jimmy Laverty would never have considered young Weber a genuine K&A burglar, but the cops did, and so did the media, whose standards were less exacting. Moreover, unlike most K&A burglars, Weber proved incredibly cooperative. In fact, he wouldn't stop talking.

"After he recovered from the gunshot wound, we took him out with us in a squad car," says DelCarlino. "We had our reports with us on previous unsolved burglaries in the area. It was incredible. We'd go up and down the streets of Northeast Philly and he'd point to houses and say, 'I hit that one.' 'And that one.' 'And that one.' 'And that one.' It went on for hours. There were hundreds of houses. I stopped counting at 400. Weber had tremendous recall and could remember every house he had ever broken into. And every little detail as to what he had taken out of there. I think he got five years or so and ended up doing the same thing for the cops in Jersey and Bucks County. He must have done a couple thousand jobs all over the area.

IF THERE WAS ONE LAW enforcement official who dedicated himself to nailing Kripplebauer and his K&A confederates, who went after the gang with the unswerving passion more commonly associated with religious crusades, it was Bill Skarbek. His commitment to their capture and imprisonment made him something of a legend within the Federal Bureau of Investigation and on the streets of Philadelphia.

A native New Englander, William Skarbek joined the FBI after graduating from law school in Florida. Though becoming one of Hoover's boys was never a driving ambition, he says, it was "always in the back of my mind." But Skarbek admits that he "didn't seriously consider it until a classmate at law school" said he had signed up to become a Special Agent for the FBI. Shortly thereafter, Skarbek wrote "Mr. Hoover a letter" expressing his interest in the Bureau, and one day, while coming off the beach, he was met by a tall, well-dressed stranger. He was an agent from the FBI's South Florida office, checking up on Mr. Hoover's new pen pal. Young Skarbek seemed to have the goods.

Preparations for the bar exam precluded his immediate assignment to FBI training school in Virginia, but a last-minute cancellation by another applicant in the following class allowed Skarbek to take one of the 50 slots at Quantico. After 14 weeks of training, the rookie agent was sent to Detroit. It was 1967, just after the Motor City had been torn up by inner-city rioters. Skarbek's cases ran the gamut from investigating organized crime figures to hunting draft dodgers to making cases against rioters. After a year he was transferred to the Philadelphia office.

Philly had "good cases, there was always a lot to do, and there was the potential of solving lots of cases because the area was so active," but the young agent was once again stuck with Selective Service work. The Berrigan brothers and a host of other antiwar protestors were active in the area, and draft board break-ins in Media, Pennsylvania, and Camden, New Jersey, had garnered nation-wide publicity and embarrassed the Nixon administration. Gradually, however, Skarbek began to be thrown some traditional organized-crime cases, a welcome but challenging diversion. Jewel thefts, home burglaries, and large-scale fencing operations were big in the area, unusually big. Almost immediately the young agent learned of the voracious criminal appetite of one particular gang of thieves: the Irish Mob out of Kensington. If you were working organized crime on the East Coast—particularly property crime—you were familiar with them.

"The K&A Gang was a special group of guys," recalls one FBI Special Agent. "They weren't as organized as the Mafia, but there was no other burglary crew as prolific or as competent. From soup to nuts, they were the best burglars out there."

"You didn't have to be on the job long to learn they were the best," recalls Skarbek. "The K&A Gang had the pedigree. They were definitely the cream of the crop and a fascinating collection of guys. There wasn't always a lot of sophistication to their work, but they made burglary a serious profession by using street-level common sense, a lot of nerve, and a good bit of ingenuity."

The FBI wasn't initially interested in jewel thefts and burglary—they thought they had more important items on their agenda—but the sheer scope of the gang's exploits put the problem on "the FBI's radar screen." As Skarbek recalls, "as soon as I started working cases in the area, I knew that Philadelphia had the most prolific interstate burglars in the country. We knew they were working the whole country. They were going up to Maine, New Hampshire, Vermont, and the rest of New England. Then they would go south and west into Virginia, North Carolina, Missouri, Florida, and Texas. They were all over.

"Their plan was simple and it worked," says Skarbek matter-of-factly. "They worked in four-man teams—a window man, a driver, and two searchers. They'd hit upscale neighborhoods, mostly Jewish homes. And the Hanukah holiday would be one of their prime periods of work. Jewish people had jewelry, but they didn't wear it to synagogue. So while the families were praying at synagogue, the burglars were preying on their homes and taking all their money and jewelry.

"The way the gang members had it set up, there was almost no jeopardy to their operations. They were slick and their operation was based on comparatively little risk. They worked from eight p.m. to one a.m. in the morning, knew when people weren't home, and were smart enough not to carry any weapons. They almost never got arrested. Schmucks get caught. Professionals like the K&A

guys didn't get caught. That's what made them so good, because for the longest time no one knew who they were. And on those rare occasions when they did get caught, they never ratted on their partners and were able to hire the best attorneys, who got them out on bail. Then they'd jump bail, not show up for trial, and the local prosecutors wouldn't pursue them with extradition proceedings because no weapons were confiscated and no one had been hurt. It was just a simple burglary charge."

Skarbek was on the Interstate Transportation of Stolen Goods detail only a short time before it became "painfully obvious the only way to make a dent in their operation was to catch them in the act and with the stolen stuff on them." It would require a major effort—in fact, a national campaign.

"Law enforcement offices at the federal, state, and local levels would have to be incorporated," says Skarbek, who vigorously lobbied his superiors in the Bureau for a full-court press on the burglars. "Initially, the other federal offices had trouble believing what we were telling them. I said if we were going to get these guys it would require better intelligence, increased resources, and far more manpower. The burglars and their fences would have to be targeted. Philly had become known up and down the East Coast as one of the top burglary and fencing operations in the United States. It was right up there with New York, Las Vegas, and Miami. The word on the street was that the K&A guys stole whatever they wanted, sold it to Jewelers' Row or up in New York if the items were particularly hot or pricey. K&A Gang operations became known to all of us because of the notoriety of the jobs, the value of the goods stolen, and the uniqueness of the pieces."

Items that were stolen in one part of the country and discovered in another had often traveled through the Philadelphia area. For example, a well-known "$85,000 brooch that was stolen from a Chicago jewelry show and recovered on Redondo Drive in Hollywood was traced back to a Philadelphia, New Hope, and New York City fencing operation."

"We kept hearing the same names: Neil Ward, John Berkery, Kripplebauer, Wigerman, Dolan. We knew guys like Effie Burke were working all across the country, but we could never get him. Burke was like the pinnacle, a teacher of the craft. And we just kept missing Berkery. He was considered the main nexus between the Northeast Irish mobsters and the Mafia. Neil Ward was said to have the keys to every hotel room along the East Coast. He concentrated on jewelry salesmen. Kripplebauer's group seemed to work with impunity from Massachusetts to Texas."

The more time Bill Skarbek spent on the burglary detail, the more frustrated he became. A bunch of high school dropouts and blue collar lunkheads were ripping the hell out of wealthy neighborhoods from Maine to Florida, and cops, and even the FBI, were clueless.

To further complicate the problem, the Philly police seemed to have adopted a minimalist approach in their pursuit of the Kensington-based burglary ring. Skarbek and his fellow agents didn't consider "the local cops all that active" under Police Commissioner Frank Rizzo, and there were rumors of a "hell of a lot of corruption" in the department. For a while there, claims Skarbek, "we didn't get involved with the local police unless it was absolutely necessary." Of course, the more time Junior Kripplebauer, Billy McClurg, Jimmy Dolan, Chick Goodroe, and the other burglary crews spent on the road, the better it was for most Philadelphians, including the cops. They could all rest easy whenever the local version of the Huns and Mongols were out of town pillaging some other folks.

Although Skarbek was supposed to focus on crime in the Philadelphia area, he didn't have that luxury. He was too busy fielding inquiries and distress calls from perturbed law enforcement officers across the country, all trying to solve a rash of high-end home burglaries: a beleaguered cop in Raleigh, North Carolina; a frustrated state police official in North Jersey; a perplexed Special Agent in Westport, Connecticut. Philly's Irish Mob seemed to be everywhere. Skarbek grew increasingly exasperated as he explained to small-town sheriff's departments the gang's history, methodology, and membership.

The more time he spent on them, the more determined he became to bring them down. Though he marveled at their ability to establish a "national network of professional burglars and fences around the country" and their knowledge of "wealthy out-of-state areas where they had legal contacts who knew the system and got them out on bail" (and thus into other people's homes) in a matter of hours, he was dedicated to ending their reign of thievery.

After considerable lobbying by Skarbek and others, combined with a deluge of citizen complaints and official requests for assistance, the FBI's national office established Operation Top Thief, a vigorous and expansive program to take down the Philly burglars. More agents were assigned; surveillance was stepped up, including the use of fixed-wing aircraft; regional meetings with law enforcement officials were increased; and the cultivation of informants was strongly encouraged.

Even with the intensive approach, triumphs by the federal agents were few and far between. The burglars weren't about to give up their brutes, alarm keys, and affluent lifestyles for something called Operation Top Thief. Never that impressed with cops in the first place, they weren't about to roll over for J. Edgar Hoover and his army of conservative, clean-cut agents. They felt they had proprietary rights on production work. No federal cops were going to take away their lucrative careers.

Skarbek's team of agents went about their business methodically. They held more information-gathering meetings with local authorities, placed a priority on tracking down leads, stepped up surveillance of the burglars and their fences, installed more wiretaps, and routinely disseminated intelligence to police agencies across the country. Most of the work was uninteresting, mundane—drudgery on the installment plan. But it was well known in law enforcement circles that such boring, time-consuming routines often paid big dividends.

A perfect example was Bill Skarbek's conversation with a young salesman for a U-Haul truck rental agency. By doing their homework, Skarbek and his colleagues pulled off one of the first and most successful takedowns of a K&A burglary crew.

Skarbek had become so familiar with the K&A Gang and their tactics that he could have formed his own crew. As he says, he started to think like them and was able to "put together their pattern of activity and knew when they were going to do something." He figured out that on many of the gang's out-of-town runs they used trucks and vans to haul away the stolen merchandise. Most of the time the vehicles appeared to have been rented from local distributors in Philadelphia. Skarbek began to visit van rental agencies throughout the city. He discreetly explained what was happening, distributed photographs of the key players, and requested the clerks' assistance. It was tedious, unsatisfying work.

One day a van rental agent called and said, "Your boy was in this morning." Skarbek was elated; it was if he had hit the lottery. The news that Ted Wigerman had just rented a van was all he needed to hear. The Wigerman takedown is one of the best illustrations of Operation Top Thief in action.

Ted Wigerman, one of the K&A Gang's most industrious crew chiefs, was tall and squirrelly faced, with a receding hairline and a nose for an easy score. That warm midsummer afternoon in 1976, he tossed back another pint glass of Budweiser, joking and slapping the backs of the usual collection of barflies at Jumbo's as if he hadn't a care in the world. Tired mill hands, heavily muscled roofers, and a few hard-edged regulars attired in flashy sharkskin suits shared drinks, macho boasts, and age-old neighborhood war stories as the strong stench of beer permeated the air and a pounding Rolling Stones song played in the background. Neither Wigerman nor his well-dressed colleagues—Michael Lee Andrews, Frankie Brewer, and Frank Zappacasta—displayed the slightest interest in the passage of time, even though they were already behind schedule on a big heist hundreds of miles away. They cherished their rye shots and beer chasers. Even the prospect of a fat, cash-stuffed safe couldn't pull them away.

Special Agent Bill Skarbek, along with a dozen other FBI agents, had been waiting for hours for the Irish mobsters to finish their beers and hit the road. After more than a year of painstaking but fruitless effort, the FBI's new task force on the Interstate Transportation of Stolen Property had finally received a solid tip, and now they had the seedy taproom under surveillance.

As the hours slowly passed, the increasingly restless federal agents sat in their sweltering cars, trying to blend into the blue collar community. Finally, just after nine o'clock that evening, Ted Wigerman, bold and bloated, staggered out of the bar. But he left alone. Moreover, neither he nor any of the other members of the gang approached the van. The agents thought they had been made once again, their stakeout blown.

Not until the next day did they realize that bypassing the van wasn't a clever ploy; it simply reflected the flip side of the gang's culture. The sophisticated burglars were also a bunch of thuggish louts who would get so tanked up in a bar that they would wind up playing darts with meat cleavers or start a bare-knuckle brawl, forgetting the jobs they were supposed to pull.

The chief of the FBI's surveillance unit gave the order to disband. But Bill Skarbek was undeterred. "I know they're going out," he argued. "At least keep a skeleton crew on overnight. I'm positive they're about to pull a job."

His superior was unmoved. "Look, Bill," he countered, "we've been out here all day. The guys are beat. We've sat around and nothing's happened. Admit it, we just got a bad tip. They're not going out tonight."

"Not tonight," pleaded Skarbek, "but maybe tomorrow morning. I'm telling you these bastards are getting ready to pull a job. I know it. I've been tracking them for years. I know their routine, their habits. Hell, I know some of them better than they know themselves. They're going out, and if we don't keep an eye on them we're going to miss it. And then we'll be kicking ourselves we gave up too soon."

Skarbek got his way, and fortunately his hunch was correct. Wigerman and his partners met at the bar the next morning and after several beers drove off in a car and the van. Three cars filled with FBI agents followed at a comfortable distance. As the caravan headed west on the Pennsylvania Turnpike, Skarbek believed the burglars were bound for Ohio or Missouri, two states the K&A Gang had recently been plundering.

Instead, the burglars turned off the highway in Amish country and drove to a residential neighborhood outside Lancaster, where they left the van in the parking lot of a small shopping center. They then drove the car directly to a large house, from which, minutes later, Wigerman and his friends were observed lugging a large safe. They placed the heavy box in the trunk of the car, where it could easily have been mistaken for a large television. After transferring the safe to the van, they headed back toward the highway.

The gang hadn't traveled more than a mile when the word was given to nail them. A wiry, six-foot-three FBI agent, whose flowery silk beach shirt and mop of blond hair made him a ringer for a California surfer dude, pulled his unmarked police car in front of the van and gradually slowed to a halt on a narrow bridge. Before the Philly thieves knew what hit them, a caravan of federal, state, and local authorities, with semiautomatics and shotguns drawn, swooped down on them, made them lie spread-eagled across the roadway, and arrested them. For many Lancaster County residents unaccustomed to such scenes, the "bodies and automobiles . . . strewn across the roadway" must have looked like a massive car wreck.

Skarbek and his colleagues were elated. This was a milestone for the FBI's new antiburglary task force, and the capture was widely played up in the media. Cynics might argue that the triumphant capture of four thieves from Philadelphia was coming 25 years late, and furthermore that there were probably a dozen or two other K&A crews continuing to wreck havoc throughout the country. But it was a signal event for both Skarbek and the burglars, especially the crew chiefs he targeted. For the first time a smart, zealous cop with resources was coming after them. Paraphrasing a famous line about another fanatical lawman uttered by Paul Newman and Robert Redford in *Butch Cassidy and Sundance Kid*, it wasn't long before the Kensington burglars collectively started asking, "Who is this guy?"

"He was a venomous son-of-a-bitch," says Junior Kripplebauer. "Boy, he wouldn't stop. He seemed to be all over the place, and he kept sending reports about me to agents and law enforcement officers all over the country. Hell, anything of value that was stolen or missing between California and Massachusetts was laid at my feet."

"That Skarbek was a motherfucker," echoes Donnie Johnstone. "He was a real son-of-a-bitch. He went after everybody like his life depended on it."

"Nobody was more successful than Skarbek," says Jimmy Dolan, referring to the federal agent's harassment of the various burglary teams. "Who the fuck is this Skarbek? He was a nut. He said he was going to get us. He took major shots at me. He was relentless."

Dolan had more than his fair share of run-ins with Skarbek. Two confrontations, in particular, were classics of aggressive, proactive police work. One involved the use of informants; the other, a well-placed wire.

"We were doing a job one night at the Oregon Diner [a popular all-night diner in South Philly]," recalls Jimmy Dolan. "We had gotten into the place undetected and were quietly going about our business. We were trying to go through a wall that would lead to where the safe was. A very slight hole had been drilled, and we were about to enlarge it just in case we had to hook up a truck and pull the wall down when one of the guys comes up to me looking concerned and whispers, 'Jimmy, I think I just heard something drop on the other side of the wall. I think there's somebody over there.'

"He's looking pretty tense and I ask him, 'Are you sure?'

"He says, 'Yeah, I'm sure. I heard something drop. Like a piece of metal hitting the floor. I'm pretty sure somebody is over there.'

"Now I'm thinking to myself, are we being set up? Is there really somebody over there? There wasn't supposed to be anybody in that part of the building. We had scoped out the place pretty good. We knew the routine. There wasn't supposed to be anybody in that room at that time of night. It was always locked and unoccupied."

"The seconds are going by, but they feel like minutes, we're in someplace we shouldn't be, and I gotta figure out if Skarbek and the Feds or the local cops are waiting for us on the other side of the wall. The wrong decision and this could get pretty ugly. I had to make a quick decision. Do we go through with it and chance the possibility we all get busted? Or do we back out, patch up the wall as best we can, pick up our gear, and get the hell out of there as fast as our legs will carry us?"

Although they were within a few feet of what they thought would prove a nice score, Jimmy Dolan's prudent decision was the right call. On the other side of the diner's flimsy wall was a whole lot of hell. Skarbek had a snitch who had tipped him off that Dolan's crew would be doing the diner that week. The FBI was just waiting to nab the burglars as they entered the room and approached the safe. The slick but impromptu getaway helped Dolan maintain his record of "never getting burned at the scene of the crime," but the federal harassment was becoming a pain in the ass. Skarbek himself was becoming a certified nuisance.

Good, solid criminal intelligence was invaluable for making a case, but for catching the bad guys red-handed, there was nothing better than a well-placed informant. Skarbek and his team of agents bent over backward to coax, encourage, harass, and threaten anyone they thought could provide them with useful information about the K&A crowd. Though the gang had a long and well-earned reputation for being uncooperative, by the 1970s there were some definite chinks in their armor. More aggressive policing, longer sentences, and the insidious psychological effects of drugs had put some holes in the once-unassailable standup ethos. Neighborhood informants were to be had, and Skarbek went after them.

When rats proved elusive or disobliging, however, the FBI did not rule out placing a listening device in someone's home, business, clubhouse, or favorite vehicle. The Feds had declared war on the burglars, and they were going to take them out by any means necessary. Once again, Jimmy Dolan was the object of their interest: the Bureau put a listening device on his home phone for 30 days.

"For the longest time," says Dolan, "there seemed to be a lot of static on my home phone, and some of the guys were telling me to get it fixed. Others said they thought the phone was bugged and that I should watch what I said when I was on the line. This goes on for a while, until one day a friend of mine comes knocking on my door, but he won't come in the house. He's got a frightened look on his face, starts whispering, and waves to me that I should step outside. I'm thinking, what's come over this guy? Why's he acting this way? We walk a few steps away from the house into the front yard and he's looking all around like he's afraid we're being spied on. He leans over and whispers to me, 'Jimmy, I'm on my scanner and short-wave radio the other night and I hear the cops talking about a house they got under surveillance. The more I hear, the more I think it's your place. They're describing the house, the bushes in front, the neighborhood just off of Grant Avenue, the comings and goings of this guy they're watching, and I'm thinking it sounds like your place. Then I hear them mention Ditman Street. Now I know it's your place. I'm telling you, Jimmy, you better watch yourself. The cops or the FBI have got their eye on you, and they probably got your phone tapped.'

"After hearing this I finally gotta take the noise on the phone more seriously and call the phone company and tell them to come out and check their equipment. Well, a repairman comes out to my house and starts to take the phone apart. It ain't long before the guy gets a perplexed look on his face. I can see he's stumped, so I say to him, 'What's wrong? What's the problem?'

"He doesn't answer right away. I can see he's searching for the right words, like he knew he probably shouldn't be telling me this, but I'm standing right over him, and he finally says, 'Sorry to tell you this, but I think somebody has put a bug on your phone. I think somebody is tapping your phone.'

"I can't fuckin' believe it. I'm really pissed. I figure it's gotta be that goddamn Skarbek and the FBI. The son-of-a-bitch breaks into my house and places a tap on my phone. I get the phone repairman to take the bugging device out of my phone and hustle downtown to my lawyer's office. I walk into Bobby Simone's office, go right by the secretary, and walk right into Simone's private office, where he's meeting with a few clients. I'm yelling and screaming about the FBI and this nut Skarbek, and Bobby asks me, 'What's that you got in your hand?' I hold the gadget up and tell them all, 'This is the goddamn bug I just pulled out of my phone. Those bastards tapped my phone.' You've never seen a bunch of guys run so fast in your life."

Jimmy Dolan always enjoyed the intellectual challenge of doing battle with the cops. It was a chess game he was pretty good at, and he usually won. But now the game was becoming more serious, and the competition was decidedly more advanced. Dolan began to lose his fascination for the game. It wasn't fun any more playing every match against Bobby Fischer.

12. Philly's Bonnie and Clyde

JUNIOR KRIPPLEBAUER'S chess match with the law enforcement community had long since become more than a simple intellectual challenge. A relentless worker who had cut an expansive swath of criminal activity across the American landscape, incorporating residential and commercial burglaries, the occasional stickup and bank robbery, plus various cons, ruses, and ploys, Kripplebauer was a one-man crime wave who was driving the nation's lawmen to distraction and bugging the hell out of Bill Skarbek. No other K&A burglar seemed so industrious, omnipresent, and bothersome to small-town sheriffs and mid-sized police departments from New England to the Gulf Coast. The list of distressed communities requesting information and guidance was endless.

The two men—each in his own way a driven soul—were destined to tangle repeatedly during the seventies. For Junior the decade began in prison, with the expectation that he would soon be back on the street. If that wasn't reason enough to be optimistic, he had also had the good fortune to meet his future wife and dependable co-conspirator while serving his last year at New Jersey's Trenton State Penitentiary. Philly's version of Bonnie and Clyde, Mickie and Junior Kripplebauer would prove a considerable challenge for the FBI and a headache for lawmen everywhere between the Canadian and Mexican borders.

"I was doing time up at Trenton State with Eddie Loney," recalls Kripplebauer of his time at New Jersey's oldest state prison, "when one day he gets a letter from this female friend of his who lives in California. She sends a photograph of herself, and Ed comes over to my cell and shows the photo to me. Boy, she was a real honey. The girl was beautiful. Tall, blond hair, blue eyes, a great figure—she was stunning. She reminded me of Linda Evans [a popular television actress] right from the start.

"Eddie saw I was taken with her and began to tell me a few things about her. Her name was Marilynne D'Ulisse, but everybody called her Mickie, and she was working as a casino dealer in Gardenia, California. She was actually a Philly girl who had been married a couple times, once to a cop, and most recently been hooked up with George "Dewey" Duval, a good friend of Loney's. Eddie explained that besides being a real looker, she was also a tough cookie.

Dewey had been arrested in Bucks County for a murder and the cops imprisoned Mickie when she pleaded the fifth. They wanted to use her as leverage against him and kept her locked up for months, but she still refused to talk. They couldn't intimidate her. She was eventually set free and Dewey beat the case, although the two of them seemed to have split after that. Between her looks and her standup principles, there was no doubt she was my kind of woman.

"Loney suggested I write her, and I did after he informed her I had fallen in love with her photo. He told her I was a real nice guy and she began to write back. We were writing to each other coast to coast for months. She told me about her young son, about her interest in athletics and that she walked or jogged every day, and her love for anything dealing with the outdoors.

"The more I heard, the more I liked her. We stayed in contact all through the spring. As I started to get short on my sentence, I told her she should consider coming back East. She must have found the offer appealing because she did just that—she came back. In fact, the first time we met was when I walked out the door of Trenton State Penitentiary. She came up with Steve [Junior's lawyer, Stephen LaCheen], who was taking me to Long Island to face a burglary charge up there. She was everything I had hoped, tall, about five-foot-eight, radiant blue eyes, real nice build. She must have brought me luck. Either that or the judge was in a good mood that day, because he sentenced me to time served and cut me loose after making me promise I'd never set foot in Nassau County again.

"We came back to Philly that night and a day or two later rented a house in Cherry Hill for $800 a month. I got money from Ben Greenberg, but knew I'd have to pay him back. Two days after I got out of prison, I told Mickie, 'Let's look around,' and that's how we started doing production work together. We went house to house in the neighborhood. I'd go up to the front door and knock. If no one answered I'd go in and clean them out. If someone came to the door, I'd tell them I just moved to the area and was lost and would appreciate directions to a street or restaurant or something else in the neighborhood. We'd then go to another area and do the same thing. It always worked; we must have done hundreds of houses in Cherry Hill and the surrounding area.

"Mickie would usually stay in the car and keep watch on things. We lived in Cherry Hill, so we knew the area well. For bigger jobs I put a crew together and Mickie would be the driver. She'd monitor the police scanner, handle communications on the walkie-talkie, and keep her eye out for cops and new targets. She was great; she had no fear, no hesitation. She was better than some of the guys I worked with. And cops rarely suspected a woman driving around a ritzy neighborhood was up to something, whereas a guy doing the same thing would draw some attention."

On June 5, 1972, two weeks after Mickie and Junior met outside Trenton's ancient state penitentiary, they drove down to Elkton, Maryland, and were married. Junior, a man about town who had had his share of vivacious, voluptuous women over the years, felt that Marilynne D'Ulisse was the one. She was beautiful, athletic, and principled, at least according to the values of the street. And if that wasn't enough, she was more than capable of doing a man's job—second story work.

Despite her wholesome, perky, bright-eyed appearance, Mickie D'Ulisse had a police record stretching back to 1962, when she was first arrested for larceny and shoplifting. But she would advance to graduate school in her association with Kripplebauer. As Junior likes to say, he "fine-tuned her skills." Both were fearless, restless; they shared an indefatigable work ethic.

"Mickie loved to do houses," says Junior; "she loved production work. She became competent at every facet of the game, and the action always attracted her. We'd go out to the movies in the evening or be coming back from a Philly or Jersey nightclub, and on the way home you'd see her closely examining each house we passed as we drove down the highway. She'd be wondering, 'Is anybody home there? Which houses have alarms? What houses appear to have something of value inside?' By the time we got home she was ready. 'C'mon,' she'd say, 'let's get our black shirts and do some work.'

"She used to tell me, 'You know, Junior, most women who come home from work or back from an evening out say, I feel like doing some cooking or baking. All I ever wanna do is put my black shirt and wig on and do some houses.'

"Even when we'd go deer hunting in Clinton and Potter Counties in upstate Pennsylvania, she'd be checking out the hunting lodges and eyeballing the bigger homes in the area. Seeing who had what and what houses were alarmed or not. Mickie was a natural."

Her husband was not blinded by love; Junior's friends and colleagues were equally impressed with Mickie's work ethic. In fact, it wasn't unusual to schedule a night on the town with the Kripplebauers and find yourself, during the course of the evening, in the middle of a burglary. Donnie Johnstone remembers a number of light-hearted evenings that were interrupted by the clarion call of production work.

"Mickie was as good as any guy I ever saw at second story work," says Johnstone admiringly. "She was really something. Mickie always wanted to work, even on social occasions. I remember double-dating with them and coming back from a club early in the morning, and as we're driving back to their house Mickie sees a red light on a home alarm system and asks Junior, 'Do you have the keys in the car?' Before you know it we're stopped by the side of the road and Mickie is pulling the Chivas Regal bag [where Junior kept his collection of home alarm keys] out of the car trunk. Yeah, Mickie and Junior were always ready to work. They never tired of it."

"She was a good student," says Junior, proudly. "I showed her how to take houses in the neighborhood that looked like good scores, and eventually she may have ended up doing more of 'em than me. Many times I'd be driving home late at night and pass a nice piece of property showing a red alarm light. The next day I'd go back and check the place out. From a distance the joint may show money but you've got to get up close and check out the driveway, the paint job, the drapes and curtains, and furniture to really know for sure. If I figured no one was home, I'd start checking the security system, and before long I'd find the right key and knew I could shut the system off. Usually, if I thought I had the time I'd take the place right then and there. But if I didn't feel comfortable, I'd just remember which key was the one and decide to come back later that night or the next time I passed the house and the red light was on. Sometimes I even left the key somewhere on the property, under a rock or piece of decorative garden ware and picked it up when I thought the owners were out. Mickie watched me do it at first and then later on would sit in the car and keep her eye out for me. Then, when she felt comfortable enough to go out on her own, she became a convert to the system and started pulling jobs all on her own.

"She was good, there was never any fear. She'd force a door with a screwdriver in a minute, though those with big door bolts would occasionally give her some trouble and I'd have to do it for her. She was as good as any of the guys. Whether it was searching a house, keeping a lookout by the front window, or driving the car, she could handle it. The only thing she didn't like and didn't want any part of were the occasional stickups where we'd go in and lay people down. She wasn't crazy about running into mouthy dogs either, but a lot of guys were equally terrified of entering a home that had a toothy shepherd or Doberman nipping at your heels. Mickie and I both loved animals and had a few of our own, including a big German shepherd, but you can't let them get in the way of business. I had a technique that always worked. If a dog came at me in a house I used a brute or an L-bar, not to hit the dog, but to break a lamp or light fixture. The explosion would scare the hell out of the dog and he'd go run and hide.

"Maybe it was because I always had her handle the police scanner and the driving that Mickie was so insistent on doing a good bit of second story work on her own or with her girlfriend Maxine. Boy, those two were amazing. She and Maxine grew up together when they were kids and both came to really enjoy second story work. They loved it. They were out all the time and would come back with some pretty good stuff. When they returned home with all this merchandise, you would have thought they were just a couple of upscale suburban housewives coming back from a wild shopping excursion at the mall. Maxine had a couple kids who were slightly older than Mickie's son, and I'd baby-sit them when the girls went out. When Mickie, I, and the crew were out for the evening, Maxine would baby-sit Mickie's kid.

"It didn't take a brain surgeon to know every time she'd come downstairs with her wig on, grab her black jacket out of the closet, and then ask me if a brute was in the car what she was up to. I don't know if production was her favorite thing to do, but it was right up there.

"And Mickie was a great driver, one of the best. She was an extra element of security. Places like Houston and Durham never saw anything like her. A female driver fronting a crew of burglars was unknown down there. Mickie often traveled with our Yorkie on her lap. Cops, especially in places like North Carolina and Virginia, never suspected a young woman with a little dog on the front seat was a key player in a burglary ring. Yeah, Mickie was something all right. She got away with murder."

Mickie also accompanied her husband on a number of bank robberies. Junior made sure she never walked into a bank and drew down on the bank guard and tellers (he suspects that she would have done so if he had let her), but she did help in the planning and execution of several bank heists, as well as the getaways. The Glassboro bank job in 1976 was a typical instance.

In his underworld travels, Junior had made friends with an assortment of criminal types. Bank robbers made up a large part of the ensemble. Though a second story man by profession, Junior was always quick to aid a friend with a plan or take part in a score that looked promising. Gene DeLuca and Bull the Greek were bank robbers out of Baltimore who were looking to expand their operations beyond Maryland's borders and make some big withdrawals from a few well-stocked East Coast financial institutions. Junior had an eye for money and never missed a private residence, business, or banking institution receiving a house call from an armored car. One day while shopping at a mall in Glassboro, New Jersey, he saw numerous bags of money being picked up by an armored car at a bank on the mall parking lot. The quiet, bucolic community bank looked ripe to be picked. He passed the tip on to DeLuca and the Greek, and they went to work setting up a plan. Mickie, never one to be excluded from a good thing or a promising piece of work, was in on the planning and execution.

Following that game plan, the Baltimore men entered the bank in workmen's coveralls while Junior and Mickie kept an eye on things from their own car in the mall parking lot and listened for nearby police activity on a radio scanner. When DeLuca and the Greek exited the bank, bags in hand, Mickie drove her car to a previously designated spot in the mall lot. The Baltimore bank robbers quickly drove up, shed the coveralls, which hid expensive business suits, and ditched the guns and money bags in the trunk of her car. DeLuca and the Greek then drove out of the area to a diner for a late breakfast while Junior and Mickie killed an hour or two food shopping at the mall supermarket while police, sirens wailing, scurried throughout the area looking for the coverall-wearing perpetrators of a local $88,000 bank heist. Later, as she slowly drove her grocery-filled car out of the mall parking lot, Mickie threw a demure smile to a concerned-looking police officer. The cop, who tipped his hat, never suspected that the cute blonde had a couple of .38s and thousands of dollars in cash among her bags of bread, milk, and frozen dinners. Junior never doubted that Mickie, if asked, would have been one of those to enter the bank: "Mickie was ballsy. She would have gone in with them."

Mickie and Junior were quite a team, as hundreds of homeowners could have testified. Though they were busy setting up house, buying furniture, and trying to earn a living—by stealing from their Cherry Hill neighbors—Junior continued to work with his regular crew and any others proffering an intriguing and potentially profitable idea. As much as Kripplebauer enjoyed working with Mickie, he was not about to jettison the many other associations and crews he had a history of working with. Some of his associates didn't like the idea of working with a woman, while some capers were considered too risky to include Mickie. Most of the time he just wanted to be with the boys. His world was filled with bar-room chatter, criminal gossip, and incessant talk of the next big score. Some adventures were well constructed and properly thought out, while others were almost laughable, right out of the grifters' edition of the Keystone Cops playbook. Typical of these years were a nice score in Bucks County and a convoluted, well-attended escapade in some godforsaken village in the hill country south of the Mason-Dixon Line.

"We got a tip about a guy in Bucks County who had once been a big politician," says Junior. "The guy's house was supposed to be loaded, both cash and jewelry. It sounded pretty good. Right away I started thinking back to the tax assessor's house on Ridge Avenue in Roxborough. We had done pretty well there, and that guy was supposed to have worked for the government. I'm thinking to myself, maybe this guy will turn out to be as good.

"Me, Tommy Seher, and Bruce Agnew go up there to take a look at the place. It was a hike from where I was living in Cherry Hill. It was in the country a good ways above Doylestown. It wasn't anything like the Biddle estate, not nearly as large, but it was still a nice, two story, brick and stone Colonial. We would have taken it that night, but we could see the place was occupied, so we decided we'd come back and hit it another night.

"It wasn't that easy. We kept on driving up there with the same result. Me, Tommy, and Bruce must have gone up there nearly a dozen times over the course of two months, but we couldn't break into the place. There was always somebody home. You could see right through the window, and they always seemed to have company. They were always entertaining folks. Whoever lived there never seemed to leave the house, and they always had an endless stream of guests. I was starting to think it was one of those country inns or bed and breakfasts that were popular in New Hope and along the river in Bucks County. It was looking more and more that we'd have to either forget about it or do a walk-in and lay them all down.

"It's late in the year now, maybe November or December, and getting cold, and we're all getting a little tired of running up to this section of Bucks County without anything to show for it. We're not out to hurt anybody, but this is getting ridiculous. We make another trip up there, and once again the place is occupied. We can see through the window and it's the same elderly couple. They're sitting by the fireplace, having one drink after another, and we're outside freezing our asses off. We look at each other and decide they're almost unconscious already. Let's just do it and get it over with.

"We had the keys to the alarm system, so we shut it down, break in, and surprise them. They're pretty old and don't give us any trouble. The old man looks like he's in his eighties and not in great shape. Instead of lying them down because of their age, we cuffed them to some chairs and started to go through the place. While I'm looking over the safe, Bruce is searching the house for anything of value. He finds a jewelry box and it's loaded. The woman loved jewelry, and it really looked like good stuff, some real quality pieces.

"I locate the safe, but I'm a little suspicious about it. I thought it might be wired with an alarm, but the woman said it wasn't. I open it and there's even more jewelry inside. Lot's of diamond rings, brooches, necklaces, some really fine pieces. We got out of there pretty quick and when we get back to Philly, I called my man, a jeweler down at Eighth and Sansom. I had been using this guy to fence my stuff for quite some time. He could be counted on to give you a fair deal. And he paid off right away, no bullshit delays. I call him on the phone and say, 'Do you want to meet me?'

" 'Sure,' he says.

" 'Bring your stuff,' I tell him.

" 'Sounds good,' he replies.

"Even though we had done a lot of business over the years, there was always some doubt. Nobody really trusted anybody. We'd meet at a motel along Roosevelt Boulevard in Northeast Philly. He would bring his scale to weigh the merchandise and I would bring the weights. That's the way we always worked it. Nobody wanted to get cheated. As soon as I showed him the stuff, you could tell he liked it. There was no junk in the entire batch; they were all quality pieces. He said he wanted the whole thing, so I gave him the stash and he took the package to New York. He sold the whole package up there, and the next day we meet and he gives me $80,000. Considering we normally made a quarter of what the score was actually worth, we must have walked out of the place in Bucks County with over $300,000 in jewelry. I gave the tipper a nice cut, maybe $20,000, and me, Bruce and Tommy whacked up the rest.

"In the meantime I read in the paper that the Bucks County home of a former mayor of Philadelphia and United States senator had been robbed and a good bit of jewelry had been taken. I didn't even know whose house it was when we did it. All I knew was that it was a politician's home and it was supposed to be loaded."

Though Junior and his crew had spent many a cold night casing the Bucks County mansion, the repeated journeys had ultimately proven quite profitable. The guys had walked away with a nice hunk of change. Not all tips were as accurate or excursions as rewarding. One escapade clearly underscored that point as well as illustrating the gang's occasional capacity for sheer stupidity.

"It was one of the craziest things we ever did," recalls Kripplebauer. "It was like a traveling vaudeville act that should never have got started in the first place. Instead, the zany scheme was taken on the road and just got worse by the hour. What a crew: there we were, 10 or 12 of us, three carloads on the highway to do a job in some godforsaken southern mining town. It was a damn caravan of drunken second story men going down the turnpike. To this day none of us can believe we actually did it.

"The story really begins when a few of us are serving time in the Burg [Holmesburg Prison], and we meet this tall, lanky Johnny Reb character with a heavy southern accent on the block who's always talking about the big scores he's been part of and what he plans for the future. The guy's a real big talker. He then starts yapping about places we should take a look at, operations down South that carry some heavy cash. He tips us off to this little mining community in the mountains right where Virginia, West Virginia, and Kentucky come together. He said there was a substantial score to be had down there. It was the miners' payroll and it added up to some pretty hefty bucks, according to him. He said the money usually sat overnight in the company's payroll office safe just before the men came in for their checks the following morning. He said he always wanted to do the job himself, but he never got around to it. The guy could have been bullshitting us, but if he was telling the truth, it sounded pretty attractive.

"Once we get out of jail we start talking about the potential score this Johnny Reb told us about, but nobody ever did anything about it. We just brought it up once in a while over beers and then dropped it. Over time guys from different crews start to hear about this tip, 'cause just about everything being talked about is overheard at the Shamrock, Marty's, or any number of other bars we hung at. It was tough keeping a decent score secret any length of time with all the Budweiser and loudmouths around. Eventually, maybe a year or two later, one crew gets serious about going down to West Virginia to check this payroll tip out, but now everybody knows about it and they want in on the deal too. We're not able to resolve who has first dibs on the score, and somehow we agree that we'll all do it, which was unprecedented and can pretty much be attributed to a hell of a lot of alcohol. Crews were normally competitive. We'd share men and equipment on occasion, but you wouldn't see two or three crews working together. It's not like we were linemen for the electric company.

"It was incredible, three cars, three different crews, and a few extra guys thrown in for good measure. I think it was me, Jackie Johnson, Maury McAdams, Leo Andrews, Billy Blue, Mitchell Prinski, Fingers Hurst, Charlie Murtaugh, Jimmy Riffert, and a couple other guys I can't remember. It was like a parade of K&A burglars heading to some little nook near Wheeling, West Virginia. We were joking in the car that if the mining company knew so many of us K&A guys were on our way down, they probably would have pleaded with us to stay in Philly and they'd agree to send us the money.

"Well, we get down there after a damn long drive and it's just as the guy told us, this little mining community in the mountains. It wasn't even a town; it was a remote little village, if that. It reminded me of where I grew up in the Pennsylvania mountains and why I was so keen on getting the hell out. We drive by the company store that shares space with the payroll office and figure it won't be that difficult a job as long as the safe isn't a problem. A couple of us check out the store while the others try to keep a low profile outside. It's a pretty big store considering the size of the town. It had a lot of appliances, furniture, and other stuff on sale for the company employees while the payroll office sat right in the middle of the store. You couldn't miss the safe; it was a good-sized one. It was pretty easy to confirm our Holmesburg tipster was right on the money; miners got off work early in the morning, about four or five a.m. and picked up their pay in cash envelopes that were kept in the safe. Christ, it wasn't even checks, it was cash money, which only made it more attractive.

"The bunch of us drove outside of town and put a plan together. We'd go in the store at one in the morning before it opened and see if we could open the safe without setting off any alarms or using the tanks we had brought with us. All of us had some experience with safes, but I was probably the most knowledgeable, especially using acetylene tanks to burn a safe open. Mitchell agreed to go with me. Billy Blue would be our driver. The other guys would drive around the area in the other two cars, listen in on their walkie-talkies, and try not to get pinched, which would take some luck. All of us were concerned that we must have stuck out like a sore thumb, 'cause these little mining towns weren't exactly Times Square and loaded with tourists and strangers passing through.

"A little after midnight, me and Mitchell go in through the roof in order to avoid any alarms hooked up to the front or rear doors. We bring the tanks and tarp with us just in case and go into the office and get a good look at the safe. It's a big, square, double-door job, about five feet by four feet, and had a trip wire attached to it. I disconnected it, but it wasn't a good sign. Maybe these hillbillies were more sophisticated than I thought. Right off the bat I figure I'm gonna have to burn this baby, but try to back-dial and punch-dial it first to make sure. Just as I feared, no luck.

"We quickly set up our stuff and I start to burn the sucker while Mitchell holds the tarp over my head so no one passing on the street notices anything unusual. It takes me about 15 or 20 minutes to burn the front panel off and a few minutes more to tear out the firewall and get to the levers. I'm finally able to move the bars that lock the door, but when I open the safe there's no money in there. I can't find the payroll, just a lot of worthless paper.

"Mitch gets on the walkie-talkie and tells the guys we got a problem, and he and I begin searching the office. We know there's got to be money there; they're supposed to be paying the workers in a few hours. We're going through the desk, file cabinets, everything that's there, looking for a cash box. Mitch gets on the walkie-talkie again and tells the guys outside what's going on, when I open an old wooden cabinet and find a three-foot by one-foot niggerhead inside. I could tell it had a pretty thick door and would be a problem. Just as I'm trying to decide whether I should try and burn it open or take it with us, the alarm goes off. The damn cabinet was wired.

"All I can hear is the fuckin' alarm ringing and thinking I now got a serious beef in the middle of nowhere. These mountain people will kill us when they find out we're Yankees from up North and were trying to steal their money. I can hear our guys yelling and cursing outside and scrambling to their cars. Me and Mitchell get the hell out of the store, hop in a car with Billy Blue, Jimmy Riffert, and Charlie Murtaugh, and drive out of there with the alarm still ringing in our ears. It's pitch black out, and we're driving like madmen along these unpaved mountain roads, and I'm cursing our lousy luck. We hadn't driven 15 minutes when I realize I'm filthy. I'm covered in metal filings, chips of white plaster, and a lot of safe dust. I can't help thinking back a few years to an earlier job gone bad in Bucks County where the prosecutor brought in a forensics specialist who testified about all the safe dust we had on us when we were arrested. I figure if the cops stop us I've had it; I'm covered in plaster and safe dust. And if I get nailed, everybody in the car with me is going down too.

" 'If we get stopped, everybody is gonna get convicted,' I tell the guys in the car. 'Mitchell and me are covered in safe dust. If our clothes are sent to a forensics lab, they can directly put us with that safe. Even if we're caught in Chicago or Pittsburgh, they can connect us to that safe. And the longer we're in this car with you guys, the greater the chance this stuff will get on you.'

"We get into a beef in the car. The guys start giving me an argument. They don't want us to take the weight. They don't want to split up. They'll take their chances, but they never had to face a courtroom grilling over forensic evidence like I did. We don't know where the other guys got to, everybody cut out when the alarm went off. The other two cars were probably halfway to Philly by now. We, on the other hand, were driving through the night on these desolate roads expecting seven cop cars to come down on us at any moment.

"After a couple of hours we've probably traveled 100 miles and come to a real town or sort of one. Something called Bluefield, West Virginia. There's no doubt in my mind the cops have been notified what's happened in that little mountain town we just disturbed and will be on the lookout for us. 'Stop the car,' I tell them just before we enter Bluefield. 'We're getting out.' They give me an argument, but they know I'm right. Me, Mitchell, and Billy Blue get out of the car and start walking towards town as the sun starts to come up. Riffert and Murtaugh take off in the car and are gonna try and make it back to Philly.

"Bill's the only one of us in a suit, so he gets us a motel room to hole up in. He then goes to a local laundry, gets his suit cleaned, and then goes out and buys me and Mitchell some new clothes we can wear. Now we got to figure out the best way to get back home. We discover Bluefield has an airport that has flights to Pittsburgh, but Bill's afraid of planes. He won't fly. Fortunately, the town also has a train station and we can catch a train to Washington, D.C. We decide to try it, although we know the cops will be on the lookout for us.

"It turned out to be the longest train ride of my life. It was only five hours, but it felt like five days. The train hardly picked up any speed between station stops and the guy driving the thing insisted on stopping at every little village or hamlet that had a newspaper and a toilet. Every time we stopped I expected the state police to come through the doors. All three of us could have used a stiff drink or two, but the train had no food service, nothing. It was like we were on a slow moving desert. It was brutal.

"We finally pull in to Union Station in D.C. and feel like we're back in the real world, civilization at last. But now we got another problem. The station is packed with people. I mean packed. It's a mob scene. The station platforms reminded me of Grand Central Station in Manhattan. We're all wondering, what the hell is going on here? It turns out there's a large antiwar rally taking place at the Capitol and people are coming in from all over the country protesting our continued presence in Vietnam. The station is loaded with kids in jeans, sandals, tank tops, bandanas around their heads and they're holding all sorts of protest and antiwar signs. Many of them are smoking pot, and some of them looked like they were on something stronger. There were thousands of them. These long-haired, hippie kids are feeling sort of bold. They're in their element. You know, security in numbers. Once they see me, Bill, and Mitchell dressed in suits on the train platform, and looking sort of serious, they automatically jump to the conclusion we're part of some government surveillance operation. They think we're undercover cops or FBI agents. Can you believe it? We're just back from a serious beef with some country bumpkins who were looking to nail us to a tree, each of us has a prison record as long as our arm, and these dirty, long-haired kids are calling us "pigs," spitting at our feet, and telling us to shove Nixon's war up our ass. It's crazy. And I can see Mitchell is getting pissed; he's having a hard time with the bullshit and the verbal harassment.

"'If one more kid calls me a pig or a stinkin' FBI agent,' barks Mitchell, 'I'm gonna deck him. I'm tellin' ya, I'm gonna drop kick 'im right on his ass.'

"That's all we need to make this debacle complete, I think to myself. A bunch of us Kensington knuckleheads traveled hundreds of miles to do a job in some backwoods hole-in-the-wall, the deal goes bust, the cops are chasing us, we get stranded in some one-horse town, have to take a hundred-year-old train back East, and now get picked up for smacking a long-haired, college kid protesting the war. All because we were mistaken for plainclothes cops."

Kripplebauer was able to restrain Mitchell Prinski from manhandling any of the youthful demonstrators, and the three broke and exhausted burglars managed to make it back to Philadelphia and Marty's Bar, where they doused their wounded egos with pints of beer and recounted the details of their grueling excursion to amused bar patrons.

Wild goose chases were inevitable in their line of work. Nothing was guaranteed, but on the whole things were going well. The two and a half years after Junior was released from Trenton State were good ones. He and Mickie were happily married and gainfully employed: production work provided a good living. But the couple was about to plunge into a maelstrom of events from which they would never quite recover. The bitterly cold winter of 1974/75 augured a dramatic shift in the fortunes of the Kripplebauers and their associates.

The decision to head south and avoid the icy grip of winter was a smart one. Everybody agreed. The Kripplebauers, Tommy Seher, and Bruce Agnew had pulled so much swag out of a fancy Houston suburb that they had to dump some of it. The large steamer trunks they had purchased for shipping the loot home were filled to the brim. Silverware had to be flattened, candelabras bent, some fur pieces and loose odds and ends discarded, and the three men labored to lift the trunks into the rental cars for the trip to the airport. Mickie was to fly back to Philadelphia with Tommy and Bruce; Junior had business on the West Coast and would meet the others later.

But it was not to be. Burglary was a dangerous game. The smallest oversight, the slightest sin of omission or commission, could result in a serious beef. As good as they were, arrest and imprisonment were always possibilities. The Houston heist had gone off like clockwork. It was a quick hitter, short and profitable, just the way the crew liked it. There hadn't been a hint of trouble. Or so they thought. But they had, in fact, made one critical mistake. Junior had told Tommy Seher on their last night in Houston to ditch the unwanted goods in a dumpster on the way to the airport. Instead, Seher had discarded a number of items in their motel's dumpster early that morning. Unbeknownst to him, Mary Esther Lee, one of the motel's maids, had been shaking out a dust rag from a third floor balcony. She couldn't help but notice a guest throwing out a couple of fur pieces, a small jewelry box, silver and crystal candleholders, several pieces of luggage, and a few paintings. "Dumbfounded," as she later told the police, she immediately informed her supervisor.

A short while after his partners had departed for the airport, Junior left his room to catch his own flight. As he walked through the motel's parking lot, he glimpsed a cop and maid talking. It was serious; he wasn't trying to make time with her. The policeman—tall, broad-shouldered, and in his mid-thirties—began walking in his direction. Junior knew he had a problem.

"Excuse me, sir," said the officer.

"Could I help you?" replied Junior courteously. He looked at the officer's name plate. D. W. Cook of the Houston Police Department.

"Are you a resident of the motel?" asked the officer.

"Yes," said Junior. "I'm just checking out. Is there anything wrong?"

"What room are you in?"

"One forty-three," said Junior. "Is there a problem?"

The officer gave Kripplebauer, his luggage, and his car a quick once-over. "Where are you from?"

"California," replied Junior.

"Could I see some identification?"

Kripplebauer handed the officer his California driver's license. It was issued in the name of Louis Bauer.

As the officer inspected it, he asked, "Are you here alone?"

"No, I'm with my wife," said Junior.

"Is she in the room now?"

"No," said Junior. "She's out shopping."

"Tell me where she's at," said Cook. "I'll have somebody pick her up."

"No," said Junior brusquely. "I can pick her up myself. Look, I've got things to do, Officer. I want to leave. Am I under arrest?"

"No, you're not. But you can't go yet."

"Look, Officer, I've got business to take care of, " argued Junior. "My wife's expecting me to pick her up. I haven't done anything wrong. Here, look in my suitcase if you want to."

Junior thought he was making some headway. The cop gradually appeared more relaxed. His posture was less rigid and his demeanor less confrontational. Junior kept talking; he was familiar with tight situations. Able to project an impressive display of sincerity at a moment's notice, Kripplebauer never lost his cool; he was a professional. Of Irish-German extraction and a lapsed Catholic of no great religious conviction, Kripplebauer could convince the Dalai Lama he was a seventeenth-century Tibetan monk preordained to bring peace and harmony to the world. Whatever was necessary to get out of a jam.

Officer Cook looked more puzzled than assertive now, but just when there seemed to be a glimmer of hope his partner drove up in a patrol car. Junior's heart sank when he got a glimpse of what the other cop was holding in his hands as he exited the police cruiser.

"I found these in the dumpster," he said, walking up to his partner. He was holding a pair of channel locks, a screwdriver, and a crowbar in one hand and a couple of cashmere sweaters with fur collars in the other. "Looks like genuine mink to me," he added, stroking the fur with his thumb and glaring at Kripplebauer.

"Did you ever see these before?" asked Officer Cook as he grabbed the crowbar out of his partner's hand.

"No. Absolutely not," said Junior angrily. "Did anybody say they saw me with them? Did someone tell you they saw me throw those things in the dumpster?"

Junior was insistent; he was fighting for his life. Cook appeared unsure. Had he nabbed a burglar or an innocent motel patron? Initially, he believed he had caught someone ripping off the motel. But the manager said the items found in the dumpster weren't his. After a quick check, nothing appeared to be missing from the motel. Perplexed, Officer Cook called the station house and told the captain of the burglary squad that they were holding "a California guy who might be packing burglary tools. What do you want me to do with him?"

"Well, we haven't had any reports of a burglary at any motels," said the captain, "but we had a bunch of others over the last few days. Looks like a few places got hit pretty bad."

He was referring to five burglaries that had been reported in just the last three days and well over a half-million dollars in stolen property. Piney Point, one of the three small towns that made up the Village community and said to be "the richest town in Texas," had been hit pretty hard. One burglary victim, according to a newspaper report, was "Harry G. Jamail, an executive of an exclusive grocery store chain specializing in gourmet food and crystal."

"Bring him in," Cook was told by the more senior officer. "Let's take a look at him."

At the station house, a detective went through Junior's pockets, wallet, and suitcase and found identification cards for a Louis Kripplebauer Jr. out of Philadelphia. That was the final nail in Junior's coffin. After running the name through the national criminal database, the captain thought he had hit the lottery. Bells, whistles, and sirens were going off. Kripplebauer wasn't any run-of-the-mill criminal; he was a certified crime wave who had done every-thing from burglary to brazen stickups and full-blown bank heists. The Houston police had nabbed the real deal.

The captain walked over to the young officer who made the pinch and congratulated him on catching one of the key players in Philly's infamous K&A Gang. He told Cook he didn't catch just any old fish; he had caught a Great White.

The captain then turned to Junior with a big smile on his face. "Hello, Mr. Kripplebauer. Welcome to Houston." His demeanor quickly changing, the captain leaned over Junior and whispered, "I got your fuckin' ass now, buddy. And I not only have you, I'm gonna get your partners as well. We know you did those houses in the Village, and we're sure as hell gonna get you for it."

The Houston authorities leaned on Kripplebauer for the names of his accomplices, their whereabouts, and the location of the stolen goods. Their efforts were futile; Junior was never a big talker. The police had Kripplebauer, but they were at a loss concerning his partners and the loot. The maid at the motel gave them descriptions of Kripplebauer's friends, but there was no sign of them or the stolen goods. The swag couldn't have just evaporated; the silver items and rare coins alone would have required several cars or a trailer to haul them away. Junior overheard the detectives saying that a million or more might have been taken.

Knowing that they had to act quickly, they immediately informed the local U.S. Attorney's Office that something unusual had gone down, that they had picked up a known burglar named Louis Kripplebauer, and that a considerable assortment of valuable goods had been sucked out of a prominent Houston suburb. Guidance from federal agents would be welcome.

When the call came in to the Philadelphia office, Bill Skarbek knew just what to do. He got on the phone with the Houston police and told them they had nailed one of the key members of the K&A Gang, the nation's premier band of residential and commercial burglars. It was a landmark—K&A guys weren't normally caught at the scene of the crime—but there was no time to celebrate. They had to work quickly if they were going to nab Kripplebauer's accomplices and get the stolen items back.

"According to what they told me," recalls Skarbek, "Texas got ripped a new asshole by Kripplebauer's crew. I told them to go to all of Houston's major trans-portation centers and check on shipments to Philadelphia. I explained to them these guys were slick and not to expect to find any of the missing items in their possession. They were probably shipping the stolen goods back to Philly in foot-lockers, and I'd be on the lookout for anything coming into Philly from Houston."

Skarbek had his agents call all the freight carriers in Philadelphia and told them to be on the lookout for any shipments coming in from Houston. When Tommy Seher, Bruce Agnew, and Marilynne Kripplebauer deplaned at

Philadelphia International Airport, they were promptly arrested and aggressively questioned. Their interrogations proved as fruitless as Junior's. Just about the time an airfreight receipt in the name of George Kuni was found on Tommy Seher, however, Skarbek received an urgent call from Eastern Airlines: four footlockers had just been unloaded. The heavy lockers had been shipped from Houston.

Just before midnight, Skarbek and two other agents seized the footlockers and took them back to the FBI offices in Philadelphia. They were opened the next morning. Inside was over $500,000 in jewelry, furs, coins, stamps, and silver. As they inspected the stolen items, the bounty seemed to fill the entire office. Jack Frels, an assistant district attorney from Houston who flew to Philadelphia to assist with the inventory, was amazed by the haul. "It just knocked your eyes out," said Frels.

The authorities now had the burglars and the goods; the Houston caper was a nicely tied package.

Back in Houston, Junior was charged with being a habitual offender and breaking into an uninhabited dwelling at night. Convictions on both counts added up to a life sentence in Texas. The cops gave Junior one telephone call, and he contacted Steve LaCheen, his attorney in Philadelphia. He told Steve he was in a serious pickle and needed the name of a good lawyer in Texas. Steve told him he'd have to make some inquiries, but he told Junior it was important to get someone immediately to fend off additional charges and ensure that his rights weren't violated. Texas justice was swift and harsh.

Junior handed the phone to the police captain, who spoke cordially with the prominent Philadelphia attorney. After a brief discussion, the captain recommended Larry Hurst, a former Houston police officer now practicing criminal law. With LaCheen's assent, Hurst was hired to represent Kripplebauer.

The initial meeting between lawyer and client was typical Junior. Kripplebauer was still in the police district lockup, mulling over his lousy luck and his chances of getting out of his current predicament. The first thing he asked for when Hurst introduced himself was a cigarette.

"Sorry," said Hurst, "I'm not allowed to bring cigarettes into the jailhouse. It's the rules." This response did not engender confidence in his client.

"For Christ sakes," replied Junior, "if you can't even get me a damn cigarette, you sure as hell can't do for me what I really need done."

The message evidently got through, for Hurst immediately turned, left the interview area, and exited the building. A few minutes later he returned holding a brown paper package and handed it to Kripplebauer. It contained a carton of Kools Menthol. Now the two were on the same page.

Not long after, Kripplebauer was transferred to the old Harris County Jail, a foul-smelling, overcrowded facility that Junior, an eminently qualified judge, considered a "horrendous, terrible joint." Torn mattresses and other makeshift beds were strewn everywhere. Inmate housing areas had migrated into the dining hall, the exercise bullpen, the corridors—the place was a stinking, noisy, wall-to-wall pigsty. Junior was brought in chained to several other prisoners, but something quickly distinguished him from the other newcomers entering the institution, and it wasn't the Philadelphian's habitual no-nonsense demeanor. Kripplebauer was a celebrity.

"I hadn't taken more than a few steps in the joint," he says, "when some of the inmates started yelling, 'That's him! That's him! That's the guy on TV.' They were raising an incredible racket. All through the jail, wherever I went. You woulda thought I was Napoleon or Grant after Vicksburg. I finally got to an area where they had a television on the wall and I realized what all the hoopla was about. There I was on the news. Reports were being broadcast throughout Texas that I had pulled off some of the largest and shrewdest burglaries Houston had ever seen. We were supposed to have walked off with millions. There were some TV accounts saying it was a $5 to $10 million heist."

Kripplebauer was instantly anointed a serious player, a heavy-hitter, some-one who deserved a wide berth.

"A guy walks up to me, an inmate," says Junior, "and points to the television and says, 'Is that you up there?'

"I said, 'Yeah, but I woulda looked a lot better if I'd've known the cameras were on me.' "

Between the media coverage and the rare and valuable carton of cigarettes in his hand, Kripplebauer was a star. When a guard escorted the famous burglar to his bunk, an unappetizing slot in a trash-littered corner of a crowded cell, another inmate (the one who had inquired if that was Junior on TV) came up to the guard and said, "No, not there. He's taking that one." He pointed to a much better bunk that was off the floor, but already occupied. With the prison guard looking on, the inmate ordered a fellow prisoner to find a new home. Junior Kripplebauer was moving in.

Over the next few days Junior was introduced to the more serious dudes in the jail. Junior's case intrigued them. It wasn't often that Yankee gangsters came through the Lone Star State wrecking such havoc. They cautioned him that the "habitual criminal tag" could draw a "life bit." If he had the cash, they suggested that he hire the best attorney he could. The name of Richard "Racehorse" Haynes kept being dropped.

"Short, classy, and in his mid-fifties," Racehorse Haynes was currently "the man" in Texas legal circles. He was in the midst of a highly publicized mur-der case involving T. Cullen Davis, a well-known and eccentric millionaire. Racehorse didn't normally handle burglaries, but when burglars were able to come up with a $125,000 retainer fee he was more than happy to call them clients.

Haynes and Hurst were able to get Kripplebauer's bail reduced to $75,000. It wasn't easy, given the court's distaste for Yankees who came South to invade the homes and plunder the savings of righteous Texas citizens. The injustice of it all was amplified by what was happening up North. Kripplebauer's confederates— Bruce Agnew, Tommy Seher, and Mickie —were cut loose with little more than a wink and a nod. Once they hired Steve LaCheen and Neil Jokelson to represent them, the court set bail for the trio at the eminently reasonable sum of $1,000 a person.

According to Junior, "The Texas authorities went crazy when they heard the incredibly low bail that was given up in Philly. They started screaming, 'They rob our homes, steal our money, pay off those corrupt judges up there, and get out of jail for next to nothing. They're all connected to the Mafia up there.'"

Jimmy Dolan arranged for a Miami bail bondsman to post bail for Kripplebauer, and after a month's stay in that filthy hellhole of a county jail, Junior left the great state of Texas and flew home. His wife and friends met him at the airport, and a wild party ensued at the Stadium Hilton Hotel in South Philadelphia. But the good feelings didn't last. Less than a month later the FBI, led by Bill Skarbek, came knocking at the Kripplebauers' Cherry Hill home. The federal government also wanted a shot at the larcenous quartet. Junior and Mickie were placed under arrest, taken to Philadelphia, and charged with aiding and abetting the interstate transportation of stolen property for the Houston heist. Though bail was a relatively modest $3,500 per burglar, Skarbek's surly attitude signaled a far more ominous threat: the Bureau's determination to take Junior and his crew out of circulation.

Recognizing the severity of the situation, Junior lined up some of Philly's best legal minds as defense attorneys, including Steve LaCheen, Bobby Simone, and Dennis Eisman. All were crafty, experienced, and usually victorious. They were also expensive. It was a testament to Junior's reputation as a moneymaker and his uncommon work ethic that such high-priced legal talent would come on board. Once the federal case was added on to his Texas troubles, which required periodic trips to Houston for scheduled arraignment hearings, Junior was shoulder deep in a costly legal quagmire. Around-the-clock production work would be needed to pay for it.

The cost was secondary, however. Junior's real concern was Mickie. He didn't want her to go to jail. He related his fear to Bruce and Tommy, and there was no disagreement. If things seemed to be going badly in Federal District Court, they would try to cut a deal that would keep Mickie out of jail.

The Feds brought in their own stable of heavy hitters. Jeffery Miller and Joseph Fioravanti were "ruthless, cut-throat prosecutors" who rarely lost a case. At first the defendants thought they'd get "most of the charges thrown out." Instead, they "got banged on everything." Every pretrial maneuver was denied;

every courtroom stratagem was defeated. Judge Daniel Huyett began to look as if he was on the prosecution's payroll. Despite some impressive legal argument-ation and innovative tactical gambits by the defense, Junior had been in enough courtrooms to read the signs: "We were going to lose."

After discussing the situation and their options with his co-defendants and their attorneys, Junior decided they should see if they could "work a deal." Reluctant, but in agreement, they each pled guilty. Junior received seven and a half years; Bruce and Tommy, five years each. Mickie was given five years probation and sentenced to do two years at the Metropolitan Correctional Center in New York. Even their best efforts didn't save her from doing time in prison. Judge Huyett, surprisingly, then gave the defendants 30 to 60 days to straighten out their personal and business affairs before reporting to prison. It was not an unusual courtesy in nonviolent cases such as the Houston job, but the judge's postsentencing latitude presented the newly convicted crew members with a window of opportunity that good second story men couldn't pass up.

Junior had no intention of reporting anywhere, much less a federal prison. "Fuck that bullshit," he remembers thinking. "As soon as I report the Feds will try and take me down to Texas so that they can try me for the same shit. They want to bury me. Hell, no, I wasn't reporting anywhere."

Kripplebauer, the only member of the crew to be hit (so far) with state charges in Texas, was prepared to go on the run. The prospect of life as a fugitive was vastly more appealing than years, possibly decades, behind bars in a series of unforgiving federal and state penitentiaries. Junior had always been about freedom. If he had wanted to be in a grim, stifling environment, he could have stayed in the dreary coal mines of upstate Pennsylvania. Though his prospective time behind bars looked less onerous, Bruce Agnew agreed to bolt as well, and go on the lam with Kripplebauer. They planned to live off the fat of the land, and if anybody could do it, Kripplebauer and Agnew could. Opportunistic, brazen, and resourceful, they were urban survivors. In fact, Junior had always prepared for such an eventuality.

"I knew I had to find a safe place to keep my money," says Kripplebauer. "Just in case I had to get out of town quick. There'd be times when I'd have a good bit of cash or some valuable jewelry, and the cops and Skarbek were always likely to come through the front door at any time and vacuum the place. I couldn't keep it in a bank, and there was little chance I'd be safe leaving it with a friend or relative. I finally decided on the perfect hiding place—a local graveyard. I went to a very old cemetery on the northern edge of Cherry Hill, called Colestown. I went to a remote section of the graveyard that was near a rarely used parking lot and was hidden by an ivy-covered fence. I found a headstone that looked like it hadn't had any visitors in quite a long time and dislodged it so that I could dig a good-sized hole beneath it that would hold one of those large metal milk containers. I then got a thick plank of wood, put a couple of inches of turf over it and replaced the grave marker. It worked perfectly. I'd visit the grave at night every so often when I wanted to make a deposit or withdrawal. I must have kept anywhere between $10,000 and $30,000 in that steel cylinder over the years. I kept an assortment of guns in there, too, just in case."

About a month before they expected Skarbek and company to come and pick them up, Kripplebauer and Agnew lit out. It was a momentous decision for both men. For Bruce it was the beginning of the end. As for Junior, it would be many years before he was a free man back in the Philadelphia area, and it was also, for all practical purposes, the end of his marriage to Mickie.

Part IV

The Desperate Years

PHILADELPHIA POLICE DEPARTMENT
(Official Use Only)

ISSUED TO J. Hosik

RANK Plcmn

DATE 2/8/69

BADGE 3672

UNIT 26Th

NO.

13. On the Run

KRIPPLEBAUER AND AGNEW traveled west to Pittsburgh, where they re-established friendships with former colleagues, men like Mike Mullen, owner of Jeff's Bar in Pittsburgh's West End, and Richard Henkel, the bar's manager. Henkel, who had a nose for money and a growing appetite for the big score, would play an increasingly significant role in Junior's criminal machinations.

In order to reduce their profile, the two Philadelphians eventually rented a cabin outside the city, in the town of Cannonsburg. During their five months in the area, there was a noticeable increase in burglaries in swanky Pittsburgh neighborhoods like Fox Chapel, Sewickly, and Squirrel Hill. K&A men had been feeding off upscale homes in the city for years; the terrain was certainly familiar to Junior and Bruce. Although residential burglaries provided a comfortable living, their best score was a well-stocked Squirrel Hill jewelry shop. The job was particularly noteworthy, not just because of the size of the score, but also because of the masterful workmanship involved in pulling it off. In fact, the heist was so professionally accomplished that local police and private security company officials were left in a state of sheer puzzlement, when they weren't accusing each other of complicity in the crime.

Henkel, whose criminal resume included a stint at Marion Federal Penitentiary for bank robbery, realized that he had made a good move by befriending the two men on the run. It wasn't every day that a couple of accomplished K&A burglars fell into your lap. Henkel knew Pittsburgh, he knew where the money was, and he wasn't bashful about going after it. But finding the right crew to pull it off was another thing. Anybody could grab a gun and do a walk-in—Henkel himself had such proclivities, as time would show. But in addition to moxie it took skill and know-how to pull off sophisticated jobs—and in some cases to foil intricate alarm systems—without getting anybody hurt or caught.

Henkel told Junior and Bruce about a big-ticket item, Lee's Trading Post, a seemingly nondescript second floor business in the fashionable Squirrel Hill area. Located down a mundane hallway in an unassuming four story corner building, Lee Trading had an exclusive clientele and trafficked in some of the highest-quality jewelry in western Pennsylvania. The place represented a huge payday, but it wouldn't be easy—the establishment was known to have an extensive and highly sophisticated security system.

The more Junior heard, the more intrigued he became. Henkel's description of the diamonds, emeralds, rubies, and endless chains of gold and silver on display throughout the store must have seemed like the menu of a four-star French restaurant to a starving sailor. Rarely intimidated by the odds of failure or capture, Junior immediately liked the idea, but the alarm system was nothing to sneeze at. Over the years, security companies had become more astute, developing super-sophisticated security devices and stepping up their efforts to thwart mayhem makers like the unschooled but ingenious idiot savants from Kensington.

Kripplebauer and Agnew went out to Squirrel Hill to check out the landscape. Normally one of the crew would have posed as a customer and cased the establishment from the inside, but Lee Trading was very selective: employees opened the door only for known, well-heeled patrons. Still, the job looked doable, provided they could "turn down" the sophisticated security system the business had in place. A potential score of this size might have tempted them to do a walk-in, but Junior and Bruce used strong-arm tactics as a last resort. They didn't relish the prospect of hurting anyone, let alone engaging in a full-scale gun battle with the cops if things should go awry. Bold but not suicidal, they never felt any desire to replicate the James Gang's Northfield, Minnesota, raid of 1876. Kripplebauer and Agnew were the crème de la crème of burglars; stealth was their game. They'd figure out a way.

Months went by as schemes were suggested and rejected, but gradually they put together a plan. It wasn't elaborate, but it did require more than the two of them could deliver, especially in terms of high-tech capability. They'd need a four-man team: Junior and Bruce, an additional man from Philly with commercial experience, and, most important, a competent "turnoff man." Turning down the alarm system was the centerpiece of the plan.

Fortunately, one of the best electrical men in the nation lived in the vicinity. Calvin Wayne Shook was part of the Youngstown Gang, a busy and menacing crew of northeast Ohio criminals and burglars who rivaled the K&A Gang in their competency and enthusiasm for second story work and regularly picked the pockets of wealthy midwestern communities. Known as "Jake" on the street, Shook was in his mid-forties and, although physically unassuming, was an unparalleled heavyweight when it came to gadgetry and technology. A connoisseur of complicated electrical systems, he studied intricate electrical engineering manuals as a hobby and developed a lucrative business freelancing his skills to other enterprising businessmen like Kripplebauer.

With Junior's credentials well established, Shook signed on to do the electrical work, and a fourth man, Bobby Dougherty, was flown in from Philadelphia.

Numerous forays were made to the site until Shook discovered the location of the building's phone lines in a tunnel beneath a heavy metal grate in a back alley. He then went back to Junior's Cannonsburg cabin and spent the day constructing an intricate cross-wired electrical board for the heist. The next night the crew went back to the alley, helped Shook re-enter the manhole and drop into the tunnel, and stood guard for a couple of hours while he tested various lines with an ohm meter to determine which ones originated in Lee's Trading Post. Once that critical chore was completed, they went back to Cannonsburg and Shook reconfigured his electrical cutoff board to silence the jewelry store's alarm system.

On the evening of the burglary, the four-man team arrived in two cars. While Dougherty stayed with the vehicles, monitored the police scanners, and kept an eye out for anything suspicious on the street, Kripplebauer, Agnew, and Shook went to the back alley, where they would do battle with the building's electrical system and, more important, its security system. The grate was unscrewed and removed, and Shook entered the hole with his tools and cutoff board and went to work. Within minutes, Lee Trading's alarm system had been turned off, and the jewels were good to go.

Junior and Bruce broke into the building and proceeded to the second floor. Shook was sent off to take a walk around the neighborhood. The Youngstown electrical wizard was too valuable to the underworld to keep at the site. Junior was always protective of precious resources; he didn't want to risk losing Jake if anything should go wrong.

With the alarm system neutralized, Junior had the luxury of taking a crowbar to Lee Trading's front door. He broke open its heavy locks in less than a minute, stepped inside, turned on the lights, and felt a sudden chill.

"My first thought was fear," he recalls. "I didn't think we had brought enough duffel bags. The place was loaded. Jewelry was on display throughout the shop. There was fancy shit on shelves behind sliding glass doors and on tabletops and counters. Everything was wired to alarms, but Jake had already taken care of that. Diamond rings, huge ruby and emerald brooches and pendants, gold earrings and necklaces, everything you could imagine. The back room was filled with huge rolls of gold chains, 14k, 16k, 18k gold, each weighing 25 pounds or more. I had to lift some of them on my shoulder they were so heavy. It was all an incredible haul. The real problem was whether we had brought enough suitcases and duffel bags. It broke my heart to think we might have to leave some good stuff behind. I think we immediately started to take the diamond rings out of these fancy jewelry boxes and throw the boxes away. There just wasn't enough room. There was too much stuff."

Kripplebauer and Agnew worked at a businesslike pace, but it took almost an hour and a half to inspect and package the awesome volume of goodies.

When they had crammed the two suitcases and four duffel bags they brought with them, they exited the building and loaded up their cars, but not before Kripplebauer did something that would befuddle law enforcement personnel for years to come. He climbed down into the hole, removed Shook's cutoff board, and replaced the metal grate. The store's alarm immediately began to wail, but Kripplebauer and his colleagues were well on their way out of the area before the police arrived at the scene.

From their initial entry into the building and for months afterward, "bafflement" best describes the condition of store owners, security company reps, and law enforcement. How was it possible for a jewelry store of that size to be stripped clean in the short time it took police to respond to a burglary alarm? It wasn't humanly possible. The cops came to the conclusion that the Lee's Trading Post heist was an inside job. Somebody with a key and ties to Lee emptied the joint and then tripped the alarm on his way out. Either that or the alarm company was in on the crime and froze the alarm until all the goods were pulled out. Outraged at the insinuations, the security firm fired back that it must have been crooked cops who cleaned out the store.

For Kripplebauer's crew it was sheer delight. They not only walked off with a huge score—a million or two at the very least—they left their adversaries dazed and confused. The Lee Trading Post job had been a brilliant piece of work.

Unable to go back to his fences in Philly, Junior called his moneymen and informed them that he had made a big score and the items were for sale. He sent Dougherty back to Philly with the jewels and had the goods displayed to underworld figures like Johnny Calabrese, who picked out the pieces they wanted and could pay cash for them. The stash brought in well over $600,000—a considerable haul. Junior figured he must have walked out of Lee Trading with over two million dollars in diamonds and gold. It was a nice piece of work.

After each of the participants got an end—Henkel, the tipper, got a 10 percent cut—Junior decided it was time to take a break and get out of Pennsylvania for a while. It would be a good time to go to the West Coast. An old cellmate, Jack Siggson, was living in the L.A. area, and maybe they could put together a couple of big scores. The Lee Trading job had whetted his appetite for jewelry stores, and, thanks to Jake's technical proficiency, alarms were a minor concern.

Between his cut from Lee's Trading Post and the other work he and Bruce had been doing in and around Pittsburgh, Junior was flush with cash. He went to California and checked out Los Angeles, Anaheim, and Garden Grove, where "Jack the Jew" was living. He cruised some beautiful areas like Laguna Beach and Newport, but finally settled on an apartment overlooking the ocean in Huntingdon Beach and began touring upscale commercial centers for likely jewelry stores that he, Jake, and Bruce could rip off.

Kripplebauer and Siggson did some second story work out there, but Junior was hampered by the weather and the absence of his regular crew. The climate wasn't conducive to break-ins: people hung out on their front lawns and porches all evening long.

Things began to look up when Bobby Dougherty came out West to visit Junior at about the same time a tip came in on a possible big score in Palm Springs. A wealthy jewelry salesman had a place on the town's famous golf course, which was about to host the Bob Hope Classic. The house was said to be loaded; it sounded like a good payday. The plan was simple and it worked perfectly. While thousands of people traversed the course during the contest and Siggson kept watch, Junior turned off the alarm and then he and Dougherty tore through the house in search of jewels and gold. Unfortunately, they found neither. The handful of gems they found were crap, mostly insubstantial stuff that knowledgeable fences would pay little for. Kripplebauer was no Sansom Street gemologist, but over the years he had accumulated some street smarts about the four "C"s. Jewels, especially diamonds, were judged on the basis of their weight (carats), inclusions (clarity), shape (cut), and light reflection (color). After handling millions of dollars worth of gems and negotiating with shady jewelry dealers for so many years, Junior didn't always need an expert to determine that a stone was flawed because of light leaking out its sides, drab coloring, or an unattractive cut. When your income depended on knowing the merchandise you were selling, it paid to know what was top quality and what was junk.

The few grand they came out of the house with was a sobering reminder that not every hot tip resulted in a windfall.

Though the Palm Springs job had proved a bust, Junior could still afford to take it easy and live the good life. He bought an expensive Olds 98 and decided to break it in by driving up the California, Oregon, and Washington coastline. He had never been to Vancouver, but had heard good things about the Canadian town. The scenic route by the ocean was delightful, as were the grand old hotels and quaint little B&Bs he stayed in. Many times he thought how Mickie would have enjoyed such an excursion, but she was far removed from such pleasures—she was serving time in the Metropolitan Correctional Center in New York City. Mickie's incarceration and her separation from her son tore at Junior, even though it was the life they had chosen and they had known the risks involved. Though she had enjoyed the life, she was now "jackpotted," and Junior blamed himself.

He called her every few days to see how she was doing. Mickie was a trooper, a standup broad; she did her time and rarely complained. Junior sent her money and occasionally sent her son some cash as well to help pay the bills. He also had friends like Jimmy Dolan drive up to New York from Philly to visit Mickie and lay a few hundred bucks on the prison commissary books for her. In their cross-continental phone conversations, Junior never mentioned the exhilarating drive up the Pacific Coast Highway and the great towns and wineries he was visiting. He always said he was doing all right, getting by. "I didn't want to break her balls," says Junior. "I didn't want to make her more miserable than she already was." The only saving grace was the knowledge that she'd be getting out soon.

Though he relished his current freedom, had a large knot of hundreds in his pocket, and was happy he wasn't behind bars like his wife, he had few illusions that he could sustain such a lifestyle forever. He tried not to think about the various federal and state law enforcement agencies that were after him, but he knew there was a pretty good chance that he would eventually face the same fate as Mickie.

Then, during one of their periodic phone calls, he received a terrible shock. Bruce Agnew, his long-time partner, "had gone bad" and was talking to the Feds. The news that Bruce was negotiating with Skarbek and the FBI leaked out when an assistant U.S. attorney told Joe Bloom, another K&A burglary defendant, that a conflict had come up in his case and he'd have to get a new lawyer. Bloom and Agnew were both being represented by Neil Jokelson in an earlier burglary case. Being told that he would have to get a new lawyer could mean only one thing: "Bruce was looking to talk and was about to become a witness" against him and probably others. Junior quickly checked the information out with friends back in Philly, who confirmed the bad news. Bruce was talking and looking to make a deal.

Junior found the news about Agnew hard to believe, but it wouldn't be the first or last time a trusted friend and partner had gone south on him. Rats were part of the business. You just tried to keep your distance from them and to be selective about whom you hung out and worked with. The immediate thing to do was to cut his ties and let others know that Bruce was probably an informant. Agnew was still in the Pittsburgh area. Richard Henkel and a few others were in jeopardy and had to be notified.

It was on his drive back from Vancouver that Junior learned about Agnew's fate. He called Henkel one morning to see how things were going and heard him say, "Don't worry about that problem. It's been taken care of." Junior didn't have to ask. He knew Bruce was gone. It would be many years before his body was discovered in a shallow grave with two bullet holes in his brain.

Not long after his return to his comfortable Huntingdon Beach pad, Junior started to get edgy. Things didn't feel right; he was becoming more suspicious. In fact, he should have been more upbeat. Mickie had been released from prison after doing five months, although she was unable to join him on the West Coast because a parole stipulation prohibited her from leaving New Jersey. But something was definitely wrong. Sometimes he thought that he was being tailed, that someone was observing his apartment. One morning, when he and Bobby Dougherty were walking from the apartment to the parking lot, he said, "You know, I got a bad feeling."

"Junior, you're just imagining things," said Dougherty.

"No, something's not right," replied Junior. "Yesterday, I saw the manager of the apartment house checking out my car. And just in the last few days that helicopter has been buzzing around here. I'm telling you something is up. They're looking for me."

"You're just getting paranoid," said Dougherty. "No one is looking for you out here."

Junior was unconvinced. "I'm tellin' ya, they're looking for us."

The two men drove to Jack Siggson's house in Garden Grove, and once again Junior mentioned the helicopters flying overhead. As usual, Dougherty made a dismissive comment about Junior's growing paranoia. They left Siggson's after a short time.

As they walked to the car, suddenly, from out of nowhere, came a raspy shout: "Hold it right there, Junior. Get down on the ground or I'll blow your fuckin' head off."

Kripplebauer turned to see who it was.

"Down, motherfucker, or I'll blow your goddamn head off," said a man in a suit as he moved closer, his finger on the trigger of a shotgun.

"Kiss my ass, jerkoff," replied Junior, trying to gauge his chances of escape.

"Down or you're dead," said the man with the gun.

"Junior, we better do as he says," advised Dougherty.

Kripplebauer raised his hands but refused to go down. He was weighing his chances for a break while trying to determine whether the man with the shotgun was alone. Both questions were answered in a moment. Just as the shotgun-toting agent ordered Junior down for the fourth time, additional officers seemed to come out of nowhere.

As Junior bent down on one knee, about two dozen agents came rushing toward him, handguns and rifles all aimed directly at him. He was forced to his stomach, arms and legs spread-eagled on the ground. Two agents grabbed his ankles while two others stood on his hands.

"Get off my hands, motherfucker," Junior screamed at them. "Get off my hands."

They eventually did, but only after the FBI agents had thoroughly checked him for weapons.

Kripplebauer was taken to the Orange County Jail, where he proved uncooperative and refused to sign extradition papers. After three days he was transferred to the Los Angeles County Jail. Once again he was met with an awesome display of television equipment and a flotilla of news reporters.

"I said to myself, " recalls Junior, "this can't be for me. I haven't even done anything of significance out here. I don't warrant this kind of coverage."

He was right. The media had staked out the county jail hoping to get some live shots of Christopher Boyce, a handsome young spy who had just been caught selling top-secret Defense Department codes to the Soviets. Boyce, who inspired the movie *The Falcon and the Snowman,* was a fish out of water in the prison. Even for Junior, relieved not to be the center of media attention, the L.A. County Jail was a "madhouse." Thousands of loud, combative black inmates, the Nazi-like L.A. County sheriffs screaming, "Shoulders against the wall, shoulders against the wall"—it made the jail in Houston seem like the Ritz-Carlton. Junior was repeatedly taken to court for extradition proceedings and repeatedly refused to sign the papers. He wasn't interested in helping the man. Nor was he in any hurry to go to a federal penitentiary.

On one of his bus trips to court, he was placed next to Boyce, the accused spy and instant media celebrity. They were the only white inmates on the sheriff's van. Boyce thought he had a natural ally in the tall, well-built prisoner with the funny last name, but he was wrong.

"Boyce asked me for a cigarette while we were being taken to court," says Kripplebauer. "I looked at him and told him to kiss my ass. I said, 'If you want a cigarette, get it off the Russians.' He didn't say a thing the rest of the way to the courthouse. He knew the score. He knew I'd break his jaw if he talked to me again. Look, I'd rob anybody, but I'd never betray the country. No way. I didn't have many scruples, but I had some."

Eventually, worn down by the jail's zoolike atmosphere, Kripplebauer said, "I'll sign—just get me the hell out of here" and agreed to extradition proceedings. He was shipped back to the Detention Center in Philadelphia and pled "not guilty" before Judge Huyett, despite having been on the run and despite being captured with $25,000 in his possession, some of it in counterfeit bills. Huyett had little time for this prodigal burglar. He hit Kripplebauer with an additional four years for the escape and had him immediately taken to Lewisburg Federal Penitentiary.

Just prior to his transfer to Lewisburg, Junior had a brief visit with Mickie at the Philadelphia Detention Center. Unable to embrace each other, they talked through a Plexiglas and steel partition and joked about their lousy luck. Their lives had been topsy-turvy since the Houston debacle: when she was incarcerated Junior was out; now that she was out, Junior was behind bars. The young married couple was no longer living high on the hog in Cherry Hill and cruising through fashionable nearby neighborhoods looking for red alarm lights. They joked and tried to reassure each other that the situation was bound to improve. But it didn't. It would only get worse.

Junior prepared himself for a long stay at the tough level-five institution in north-central Pennsylvania, but it was not to be. Early one morning, less than a month into his sentence, Junior was awakened in his bunk by a correctional officer prodding him with a broom handle.

"What the fuck do you think you're doing?" shouted Kripplebauer at the guard.

"I gotta see some skin, fella," said the guard. "I'm taking count and you're all covered up. I gotta see some skin."

Unimpressed with such institutional practices, Kripplebauer shouted back, "Listen, asshole, you keep poking me with that stick and you'll see plenty of skin."

The guard and inmate went at it for some time until additional guards arrived, took Junior out of his cell, placed him in the hole, and charged him with "conduct that disrupts, threatening a staff member and interfering with the taking of count." Seeing him as a "major crime figure, a captain in the K&A Gang," and a troublemaker they could do without, Lewisburg authorities put Junior on a prison bus in June 1977 and shipped him south to another infamous level-five institution: Atlanta Federal Penitentiary. On his arrival at the old facility—which was having its own problems with violent skirmishes between prison gangs and inmate-guard confrontations—Junior was immediately taken to a sit-down with the assistant warden.

"Listen up, Kripplebauer," said the official sternly. "We know about that shit you started up at Lewisburg. We don't like troublemakers around here. You talk like that to one of my correctional officers and we'll teach you a lesson you'll never forget. We'll tune your ass up but good. You hear me?"

"Listen, that business at Lewisburg wasn't my fault," replied Junior. "As long as the guards don't go poking me with a stick at 4:15 in the morning there won't be any problems out of me." Junior meant what he said, at least for a time.

One of the first inmates Junior met at Atlanta was Alan Reid, the national leader of the Aryan Brotherhood. Reid came over to Junior's cell one morning shortly after his arrival, introduced himself, and asked if Junior had a package for him. He did: articles of clothing that a Lewisburg prisoner had asked him to take with him to Atlanta. Junior had no idea the clothing was for a significant and feared player in the federal prison system's most violent white-supremacist organization. Reid was the model of cordiality and asked if Junior would like to join his group. The Kripplebauer name denoted German origins, a favorable signpost for Aryan recruiters. Junior, however, respectfully declined. He was a seasoned con who knew that the early days in a new penal facility were a critical testing period. He'd keep his distance from all but former friends and acquaintances. Besides, Junior wasn't into the Aryan line; some of his best friends behind bars over the years were Jews, Hispanics, and blacks.

Reid was not offended by the rejection. In fact, he supplied Kripplebauer with a piece of jailhouse advice. "He asked me if I planned on going out to the yard that night," recalls Junior. "I said yeah, I probably would. He then asked if I planned on going early or late. I said I wasn't sure, but probably late.' His demeanor took a serious turn and he looked me square in the eyes and said it'd be better if I went late. He then walked away. I took his advice, but a bunch of us never got exercise that night. They shut down the joint during the first yard out. There was a fatal stabbing in the exercise yard. Vinnie Pappa, a New York Mafioso, was shanked repeatedly in the yard. The Aryans had been paid to take him out."

Atlanta was going through a particularly violent period when Kripplebauer arrived at the institution. Stabbings and gang violence were everyday events. Life was cheap; even guards were at risk. You didn't have to throw caution to the wind in order to find yourself in a world of shit. Talking to the wrong people, dissing the wrong people, offending one of the many gangs that menacingly prowled the cellblocks, could get you hurt.

"I was told of an incident that occurred just before I got there that described the mood of the place pretty well," says Kripplebauer. "A guy was brought in the joint about eight o'clock at night, and when he was spotted he was immediately recognized as an informer. Guys were calling him a rat on the cellblock, and it looked like he was going to have to be taken to a protective custody unit where they kept all the rats, child molesters, and other examples of human waste. But the authorities were too slow; by 10 the next morning he was dead."

A couple of members of the Dixie Mafia, one of the largest gangs in the institution, approached Kripplebauer early on requesting a favor. They wanted him to buy them some items at the prison commissary. They claimed to be short of cash at the time, but said money was expected to be put on the books any day. Junior would get paid back. He had seen the con worked dozens of times over the years, and he was too savvy to be played, but he wasn't out to make enemies during his first days in the institution.

"These three guys, Southern Rebel rednecks, came up to me and said, 'Aren't you going to the store tomorrow? Will you get us a carton of Pall Mall and we'll pay you back on Friday?' I told 'em no. I won't do it. I said I was low on cash myself and couldn't do it. I was civil, but direct. I wasn't gonna fall for that con. I wanted them to know I was hip to that game and wasn't gonna play. You were always being tested. Everybody had their eye on you, watching for any weakness. You were always being measured. You had to set people straight from day one, or you were gonna be miserable your entire time there."

Gradually, Junior established himself in the 5,000-man institution. He knew a number of inmates from past prison stints and tended to walk with some serious people: Joe Dougherty, another Kensington boy, a huge, lumbering bank robber who had pulled off some dazzling scores, usually by first kidnapping the bank manager the night before the robbery and then holding his family hostage until the goods were delivered; Henry Alemon, a Chicago contract killer who worked for the mob and was said to "have had more hits than the Cubs and White Sox combined"; and Joe Havel, another big-time bank robber and prison escape artist, who was said to have a few bodies to his credit (one a fellow inmate whose head he had cut off). They and Junior walked in the yard, smoked reefer together at night, and tended to watch each other's backs. Though small in number, they were experienced standup guys who had been around the block a few times and knew the score. It wouldn't be perceived as a smart move to develop a beef with any one of them, much less all of them.

In addition, Junior was on good terms with another crew of heavy hitters who tended to be given a wide berth in prison: the Philadelphia branch of the Black Muslims. Killers all, a number of them had been part of an assassination squad recently convicted of wiping out seven Hanafi Muslims—including five children, four by drowning—at the home of Kareem Abdul-Jabbar in Washington, D.C. Given their well-established reputation for brutality and cut-throat bloodshed, most other Atlanta prisoners made every effort to steer clear of the Philly Muslims. In short, Junior Kripplebauer was connected; he wasn't someone you wanted to toy with.

Not too long after Junior arrived at Atlanta, his former partner, Tommy Seher, was brought through the institution. Seher said he was concerned about his mounting legal troubles, the spiraling cost of attorneys, and the prospect of Texas authorities picking him up for the Houston disaster. He expected to be taken down there and charged at any time. Junior tried to buoy Tommy's spirits, saying they were all in the same boat and encouraging him to make sure Racehorse Haynes accompanied him every step of the way through the Texas legal system. Junior had paid good money—including a good chunk of the Pittsburgh jewelry store score—to acquire the best legal talent the Lone Star State had to offer, and he directed Seher to make sure they got their money's worth.

Tommy said that he would and that he wanted Junior to know how sorry he was about the jam he had gotten them all into. "If I had it to do all over again," said Seher, "I'd cut my legs off before I would throw those suitcases in that Houston dumpster and put you and Mickie in this jackpot." Junior bit his lip and didn't reply, but thought to himself he'd have cut Tommy's head off if it would have prevented his lazy partner from disobeying orders and committing such a stupid blunder. But the damage was done now. They just had to put up the best defense they could and do the time. There was nothing else for standup men to do.

As Seher had feared, he was soon pulled out of the penitentiary in Georgia and taken to Houston. Kripplebauer, on the other hand, settled in for the long haul at Atlanta. Gradually, his natural creative and entrepreneurial skills began to surface. There was money to be made in such a large prison, but one had to be slick—very slick. Smuggling contraband took a high degree of originality and fearlessness, especially if you planned on moving drugs.

Although he kept his distance from illicit substances while he was on the street—other than alcohol, of course—inside the joint was another matter. Junior had been deeply sensitized to the damage drugs could do while hanging around with Tommy Lyons in the late fifties. The little jockey's promising career had been shattered by drug use, and his constant fixation on feeding his addiction was unnerving. Junior grew exhausted just observing his partner's endless quest for mood-altering junk—morphine, demerol, and dilaudin pills stolen from hundreds of doctor's bags. Kripplebauer swore he would never let the drug monkey climb onto his back.

Prison was a different story. Junior dealt drugs whenever and wherever he was incarcerated. Whether it was a county jail in Philly, a tough state prison like Huntingdon in Pennsylvania, or a maximum-security federal penitentiary like Atlanta, Junior always rose to the top of the criminal food chain; he knew how to circumvent institutional impediments and get over on people. His schemes for getting the stuff inside the walls and razor-wire fences of highly contraband-conscious penal facilities were nothing short of ingenious.

For years—decades, in fact—Kripplebauer smuggled drugs into prisons throughout the country using the most mundane of gimmicks—Philly newspapers and the U.S. Postal Service. Little did the authorities know that daily tabloids were bringing not only local and national news into their institutions, but also substantial quantities of uppers, downers, and anything else a prisoner might want to ingest to speed up or ameliorate the slow and mind-numbing passage of time behind bars.

Junior learned the newspaper scam from Tommy Lyons, who had learned the rudiments from Noisy Baker, a legendary con at Eastern State Penitentiary. Noisy, whose real name was Jacob Wright, may have thought up the ruse himself or been cut in on the deal by older cell partners during one of his many trips through the Fairmount fortress. Regardless of the originator, the scheme—if smartly executed—was a guaranteed winner. Elegant in its simplicity, it was designed to snooker all those lazy souls who judge a book by its cover. In this case, however, it wasn't a book, just a Philadelphia newspaper.

"We were doing time in the Dade County Jail in Miami," says Kripplebauer of his 1959 incarceration for robbery, "when Tommy showed me a sweet little trick. Back then all newspapers delivered through the mail like the *Philadelphia Daily News* came folded in a plain brown wrapper and stamped with an official newspaper logo on the outside. The prison guards never bothered to inspect the papers, figuring they were clean and had arrived straight from the newspaper's distribution center. Tommy said we should carefully unwrap the newspapers, make sure the logo seal was undisturbed, and send the brown wrapper back home to one of our friends. They'd then repackage it and send it back to us with some presents inside. Guess what? It worked like a charm. So well, in fact, I was able to run the scam for 30 years. In fact, they may be still using it today. By the time Tommy and me were out of Miami and doing our state bit at Raiford [Florida State Penitentiary], we were hip deep in pills.

"Each time I got a *Philadelphia Daily News* sent to me from home, I'd mail the wrapper back to Tony DiBattista or one of my other friends in Philly. He'd then tape an assortment of pills, maybe 30 to 40 of them, between various pages of the paper. Place the paper in the official wrapper, make sure it looked company-packaged, and mail it back to us fourth- or fifth-class mail. A guard or inmate would come down the corridor each morning handing out the mail, and our stash of drugs would be dropped on our bunk. Every other page in the sports, business, and entertainment sections would come taped with pills: uppers and downers, all sorts of stuff. We were in business. It was that simple.

"Initially we were just getting bennies [amphetamine pills] sent to us, but we were still making two, three, four dollars a pill. Everything was tough, if not impossible to come by in prison, and getting real drugs inside the joint was quite a coup. Everybody smoked cigarettes and they were the coin of the realm, but drugs were really something special. And getting a few dollars a pill was big money back then. Everybody inside wanted them, but you had to have money.

"Over the years, the newspaper con continued to work. Just about every place I was at was dumb to it. Even when the newspaper distribution centers went to plastic wrappers instead of paper or when I was in some tough, level-five federal institutions, I could still pull off the pill scam. For example, at places like Lewisburg and Atlanta there were probably 4,000 to 5,000 inmates, and they were getting maybe 2,000 to 3,000 newspapers each day from around the country. The guards on all the cellblocks were supposed to open the papers and make sure nothing was being smuggled inside, but they were lazy. They just handed them out. They never inspected them. The guards were too stressed, too busy; there wasn't enough time to do everything. So I got my newspaper and my daily supply of drugs thanks to the newspaper industry and the U.S. mail."

Most men on ice for extended periods of time manage life as best they can. Some reminisce about the good times and daydream about the good times they hope to have again, once they get out. Some can't handle the monotony, the close confinement, the never-ending threats from fellow inmates and guards, and they fall into deep depressions and have to be kept under close watch to prevent suicide attempts. Others cope with the oppressive conditions in various ways, such as throwing themselves into vigorous exercise and becoming fanatical joggers or weight-lifters. And some even blossom despite the iron bars and concrete surroundings. Junior was among the latter. He thrived. His restless, imaginative mind was always working, always looking to get over on the man, always looking for the best escape route, always making an extra dollar or two through some scam. Invariably, he would become one of the most successful prison entrepreneurs wherever the authorities chose to incarcerate him. Just as he was an indefatigable money-earner on the street, he was similarly motivated to make a buck while behind bars. The newspaper con was a staple of Junior's imprisonment portfolio. Other scams were worthy of an Academy Award for brazenness and creativity. His drug operation at several tough federal institutions was a classic example.

"I always took notice of the way things worked," says Kripplebauer modestly. "Each jail has its own culture, unique characteristics, ways of doing things. While I was locked up at a joint, I realized that with the right help and proper game plan some interesting stuff could be pulled off. I kept my eyes and ears open and eventually hooked up with the young clerk in the chaplain's office. His name was Mark. He was a tall, good-looking kid who was attracting a lot of attention. He was doing his first serious bit in a place like Lewisburg and a lot of the wolves in the joint wanted to cozy up to him bad. He was pretty nervous about the situation 'cause Lewisburg had some hardcore dudes, so I made him a proposition he couldn't resist. I'd protect him from the wolves, and he'd do a couple favors for me in the prison chapel.

"I told him I wanted a sticker from one of the boxes that were coming into the chapel. The prison chapel was regularly receiving donations from various religious organizations around the country. Things like books, magazines, and other religious paraphernalia were always being shipped in by concerned groups looking out for the moral welfare of the inmates. It gave me an idea.

"Well, one day Mark comes up to me with a present. It's the sticker and brown wrapping paper used by the Maryknoll Sisters out of Baltimore to send shipments of religious items up to the penitentiary. The official emblem of the world-renowned missionaries brought a smile to my face, and in no time at all I had that baby in the mail and on its way up to friends in Philly. They followed my instructions and repackaged another box of goodies for me and the other God-fearing guys at the facility. But instead of the usual Maryknoll goods such as Bibles, old copies of *Reader's Digest,* and boring Psalm books, there were 30 pounds of grass, meth, cigarettes, and a wide assortment of pills. It was quite a bounty, a pharmaceutical treasure chest. As an added touch they threw in a hunk of provolone cheese and a Genoa salami.

"Tony drove the box down to Baltimore from Philly and put it in the mail with the Maryknoll sticker on it. When the box arrived at Lewisburg, it didn't draw a bit of attention from the guards. Religious stuff from the Maryknoll Missionaries and a dozen other groups were coming in all the time. No one paid attention or gave it a second thought. The chaplain, a Catholic priest, went down to the prison mail room, picked up his mail and my box, and brought it back to the chapel storeroom, where there were a dozen or two just like it stacked up along the walls waiting to be opened. These boxes could sit there for months before inmate clerks would get to them and distribute the goods to those few inmates who were really looking to be saved. But this box from Philly had something more valuable than King James Bibles and religious songbooks. My man Mark got to the box and started passing the goods on to me. The place was higher than a kite for a good month. I even had the good sense to have Tony pack a primo bottle of Scotch for Phil Ristelli, the head of one of the New York families, who was in Lewisburg at the time. He appreciated the gesture, which put me in good with him and his Italian crew.

"The authorities, on the other hand, were livid. They knew something was up, but they were totally dumbfounded as to where all the shit was coming from. They thought there must have been a breakdown in the visiting room or possibly some guards to have gone bad for so much shit to surface.

"And they stayed pissed, 'cause the place remained high for months. Mark and I hooked up the scheme so that it ran for months. We brought in another eight boxes of goodies this way, each weighing between 25 to 35 pounds. I had so many different drugs, cigarettes, and other goodies coming in I was beginning to think I was the proprietor of an outlet store for SmithKline and R. J. Reynolds. It was quite a franchise. Hell, I had as much stuff as some neighborhood pharmacies."

In order to fully appreciate the monetary windfall the Maryknoll Sisters sticker scheme brought in, consider the income earned from one minuscule segment of the booty. Rexall nasal inhalers were a hot item in prison. The more inventive inmates had discovered that the cotton swabs inside the inhalers were laced with enough amphetamines to generate a quick high. Some men broke the inhalers open, put a piece of the cotton in their coffee, and stayed awake for days. Banned by the prison authorities, the inhalers drew premium dollars. Ever the shrewd entrepreneur, Junior would crack open his cache of inhalers, encase the cotton swabs in wax paper or plastic wrap, and carefully slice each one into numerous smaller units. Junior made a buck a slice, or $25 from one Rexall inhaler.

The marijuana stash was doled out on a small wooden ice cream spoon. One spoon was worth $10, or whatever the customer had of equivalent value. Some men traded commissary slips for reefer. Two spoons of reefer could get you a $25 commissary order. Though prohibited by the authorities, most prisoners had money for a cash sale. Money was usually smuggled in during contact visits with friends and relatives. Guys on the block were always looking for change of $100 bills. It generally cost $10 to break a hundred. Junior says a person "could make a good living just breaking hundreds."

While most prisoners lamented their predicament and fought off chronic boredom, fear, and depression as best they could, Junior was becoming the Jay Gould of the barbed-wire set.

Many prisoners took notice. Some of them Junior definitely preferred not to deal with. Prison gangs, lethal by any definition, were both admiring and envious of his various operations. They were generally willing to do anything to get a piece of someone else's action, but they never moved on the well-respected Philly burglar. Junior was "good people," no wimp, and he had a lot of friends.

14. Courtrooms and Prisons

KRIPPLEBAUER WAS DOING HIS TIME, staying out of trouble—at least not getting caught—when a brief phone conversation with folks back home on June 21, 1979, threw everything into turmoil. It heralded another frenetic chapter in his war with law enforcement and added another item to his already impressive criminal portfolio: that of prison escape artist.

"Phone calls were hard to make at Atlanta," says Kripplebauer. "Maybe you'd get five minutes once a month. They were just plain difficult to acquire. Well, here I am on one of those rare occasions, I'm making a call on a Friday night, and looking to get some good news from back home and look what I get—the Feds have arrested Mickie. I couldn't fuckin' believe it. I was furious. She just got out of prison and was trying to keep her nose clean when they bang her again. I had called Dottie Cavenaugh, a girl from Jersey I had started to see while Mickie and I were apart, and she says, 'Did you hear? Did somebody tell you? Is that why you're calling?'

" 'Hear what?' I say to her. 'I haven't heard a thing. What the hell are you talking about?'

" 'They arrested Mickie,' said Dottie.

" 'They *what?*'

"She went on to tell me that the cops came to Mickie's house with a search warrant and went through her place. She said Tommy Seher had flipped and started cooperating with the government. Not in Texas, but in North Carolina. He told the authorities that he had done a lot of work in Raleigh, Winston-Salem, and Greensboro over the years with Mickie and me, and there was a lot of stolen property in Mickie's place in New Jersey. She was arrested and taken to the Camden County Jail. The government wanted to take her back to New York's Metropolitan Correctional Center, but Mickie was fighting extradition. She had even cut her wrists with a razor in order to delay the extradition hearing. The more I heard, the angrier I got. It was all based on Tommy's statement that we had done work down there in North Carolina and supposedly substantiated by some crystal ashtrays they found in Mickie's that belonged to a rich woman in North Carolina whose house had been burgled. Dottie said some cop named

Larry Davis from North Carolina and an FBI agent called Skarbek were with the Jersey cops when they went through the house.

"I was so fucking mad. Tommy had been my partner for years. And he had worked with Mickie for a long time as well. We had done a thousand jobs together. More important than that, Mickie had been a good friend to Tommy. When he would hook up with a woman, they would stay at our place in Jersey. He liked our company. Mickie would cook big meals for them and clean up after them. She had been a damn good friend to Tommy for a long time, and then he does something like this to her. He became a no-good fucking rat. I wanted to kill him.

"When I got off the phone with her, I immediately got one of the other guys in line to give me a piece of his phone time. I called Troy McEntee in Philly. I quickly told him what had happened and I planned on coming out. I needed someone to pick me up at nine o'clock the next morning. I told him I'd be at a McDonald's restaurant that was right outside the federal prison reservation. Troy understood and said, don't worry; he'd have somebody down there to pick me up.

"It took me only a few minutes to figure it all out. I guess your brain never stops working. Even though you're locked up and separated from society, you're still thinking about things, especially how to get out. I must have been consciously and unconsciously thinking about it as soon as I hit Atlanta. It's only natural—when you feel like a caged animal you want to get out. That's all you think about.

"I had been at Atlanta for a while and had been given a job where I got to go outside the walls on occasion. It was a maintenance job where I worked with a crew of guys to fix up and maintain the homes of top prison personnel like the warden, the doctor, the psychologist, the maintenance supervisor. Everything on the reservation that needed fixing was ours. I had got the hang of it pretty quick and would periodically leave the four-man crew I worked with for a few hours in the afternoon and hit a motel in the area. Though I still loved Mickie, we had grown apart since all the crap hit us. The cops, the legal beefs, the separations had taken their toll. Dottie, another Philly girl I had grown friendly with, would come down periodically for a visit, and we'd share a few pleasant hours together and then I'd go back to work.

"I knew it would work; I had things planned. As a backup, I told Boston Blackie [Frank Rossi], a friend of mine from Boston who celled with me on the block and ran the dental lab, to call for me at one p.m. so there would be no suspicion when I didn't show up for count on the block. They had counts several times a day at Atlanta, and if you didn't show up on somebody's count you were considered an escapee and the whole place would shut down. By having them think I was down at the dentist's office, it gave me a few more hours to play with before they started looking for me.

"I went to another friend on my block and told him I was in a jam and needed some money. He came up with a hundred dollar bill.

"The maintenance crew used a pickup truck to get around, and we were always dressed in prison khakis so I had to quickly come up with something else so I wouldn't be recognized on the street as someone who just walked out of a maximum-security federal prison. It was June 22, 1979, and it was hot as hell, just as you'd expect Georgia to be in mid-summer. Underneath my khakis I wore a pair of jogging shorts and a tank top. As usual, I'm wearing a pair of sneakers.

"It's around 8:30 in the morning, and we've been doing some work on the prison grounds, and I have the guys drop me off near the McDonald's. They don't think nothing of it. They give me a wave and a smile and figure Junior is on another one of his afternoon delights at the local motel. I decide to shed my prison clothes and sit tight behind some bushes near the restaurant so I can check out everybody who pulls into the McDonald's parking lot. I don't know what the guy looks like who's supposed to pick me up, Troy never told me who he'd send down, so I'm taking a serious look at anybody who drives in. Finally, I spot a guy who drives in the lot, sits in his car a while, and then goes in the McDonald's for a cup of coffee. He comes back out, sits in his car, and doesn't look in any particular hurry. I decide I've got to take the shot; this could be the guy. I walk out from the bushes. Wouldn't you know it, just as I get near the car door the guy turns on the ignition and drives off. I'm left there standing like a naked cigar store Indian and have to run back to the bushes and hope no one saw me.

"Now time is going by, it's getting hotter by the minute, and all I can think of is that they already started looking for me. People are coming and going in the parking lot, but none of 'em look like they're there for me. They're more interested in Egg McMuffins and cheeseburgers than a guy looking for a quick ride north. I'm beginning to think Troy wasn't able to set it up and no one is coming for me. I'm now getting nervous and begin thinking I better take the hell off or I'm not gonna have the chance.

"After an hour or so, I decide that's it. I'm outta here. I start jogging up the street. I only get a block or two when a car pulls up next to me. 'Hey, you,' the guy says. 'Did you just come off the reservation?'

"Just my fucking luck. I can't tell for sure if he's a neighborhood do-gooder or some kind of government agent. He's not in a government vehicle, but his attitude is definitely more assertive than an average citizen. 'Hell, no,' I tell him. 'I live over there,' and point to a nearby housing development. 'I'm just out for some exercise.'

"The guy doesn't buy it. He turns out to be a federal parole agent. He opens the car door and says, 'I think you came off the penitentiary reservation.' He then reaches for something in his back pocket. I figure it's a gun. Maybe a badge or a set of cuffs, but I can't take the chance. I tell him, 'I don't give a fuck what you think,' kick the door closed on him, and run like a bat out of hell down the street into a housing project.

"I figure I'm fucked now and they're definitely gonna be coming after me. I'm running like a son-of-a-bitch and trying to stay off of the streets just in case he wants to be a hero, starts tracking me, and is keen on taking me in by himself. I dart through a new housing development, between houses and down driveways, and after a few blocks run up to a guy in a car who's just pulled up at a stop sign. He's a black guy about 50 years old and doesn't know from nothing. I came up on him so quick, I scared him half to death.

" 'I need a favor, buddy,' I tell him. 'I been out jogging and I'm getting chest pains. I need to get to a hospital.'

"He looks at me suspiciously; he doesn't buy it. I'm sweating bullets, but I keep talking. I explain I'm okay; I'm a salesman and live in the neighborhood just a few blocks away. He's still reluctant. I tell him I'm a legitimate businessman and show him the $100 bill I'm carrying. The guy finally lets me in and drives me to a local hospital, where I get out and he goes on his way. I spot a bank across the street and decide to go in and break the hundred. The bank is part of a small strip mall, which includes a clothing store where I buy a red T-shirt, an Atlanta Braves baseball cap, and a pair of jeans. I then go behind the store where there's a wooded area and change into the stuff I just bought and bury my sweat-soaked tank top and shorts. I know they're going to be looking for me and informing all the local train, bus, and cab companies in the area to be on the lookout for me.

"I'm trying to figure out how I'm gonna get to downtown Atlanta. I gotta make a couple calls and find out if Troy sent anybody down for me or if I gotta get a car or train to get back up North. Just as I'm trying to decide if it's worth it to call for a cab, a black car pulls up near this phone booth I'm standing in.

" 'Hey, buddy,' I say to the guy, 'Can you help me out? I'm in a jam. I'm late for this interview downtown at the Hyatt Regency. If I don't get down there pronto, I'm gonna lose this job and I need it bad.'

"This black guy is now looking me over. I'm sweating and sure as hell don't look like I'm ready for any kind of interview.

" 'Look man,' I say as I reach for my money, 'I'll give you $20 if you drive me downtown to the Hyatt.'

"His expression changes big time. 'Hell, for $20,' the guy says, 'I'll take you downtown or any other town you wanna go to.'

"When we get downtown, I get out of his car and give him the twenty. I then give the guy a serious look and say, 'I was never in this car, understand?'

" 'Friend,' he says, inspecting the money, 'I don't even know what you're talking about. I ain't never seen you before.'

"He drives off and I go in another store and buy a white T-shirt this time and a quart of beer. I want to keep changing my appearance just in case they're putting my description out on the street. I couldn't resist buying a beer; I hadn't had a real one in years. I then get to a phone and call Dottie in Jersey. I tell her to tell Troy I'm on the run down by Peach Tree Street in Atlanta and ask what's going on. What about my ride? What the hell happened? She tells me Troy did send a guy, but he got stuck in North Carolina. There's a gas crisis going on around the country, and the guy got held up down there in one of these long gas lines. But don't worry; he's still on his way.

"I go into this public park and begin sipping my beer. It's good to be free, but I feel exposed and see all these cop cars driving by. People seem to be looking at me. Maybe it's my imagination, but I don't like it. Now I'm starting to think it's better if I get the hell out of town and find someplace that's less congested. I go in a store and buy a map of the area. After looking it over for a couple minutes, I decide a place called Stone Mountain sounds good. I buy a ticket, get on this bus, and head out to Stone Mountain, Georgia. All the way I'm taking notice of the hardware stores we pass just in case I have to get some tools—gloves, screwdriver, pliers, L-bar—anything I may need to break in a joint or jump a car. I finally get out at this little place that has a garage and car lot next to a 24-hour waffle house. I make another call to Dottie, describe the place, and tell her I'll be waiting in back of the joint, where there's some heavy weeds that separate it from a small housing development. I tell her to have him hit the horn twice and I'll come out.

"I'm out there for hours, but the guy finally pulls in at two in the morning and we take the hell off. He was only a kid, but he must have been a stock car driver in an earlier life, 'cause he's running about 95 miles per hour all through Georgia and South Carolina. I'm thinking to myself, I just escaped from a federal institution, a thousand state and local cops are after me, Skarbek will probably have every FBI agent between here and New York looking for me, and I got no identification. And because of this kid I'm gonna get nabbed and sent back to Atlanta and given an additional 10 years, all for a dumb speeding violation. I repeatedly tell the kid to slow down, but he's incapable of getting anywhere near the speed limit. I finally tell the kid, 'That's it. I've had it. Give me some money and take me to the closest city where I can catch a train.' He drives me to Charlotte, North Carolina, where I hop out at the train station and take Amtrak back to Philly."

The long train ride up the East Coast went quickly, but not uneventfully. Junior always had an eye for the ladies. That day he had the good fortune to sit next to a particularly friendly female passenger who took a liking to the tall, brash stranger, a gentleman who, unbeknownst to her, had just hours before walked out of a federal prison complex. She and Junior grew quite cozy on the ride north and eventually had sexual relations. It was a first for him—doing it on a Metroliner going 80 miles per hour. Yes, it was certainly good to be free again, free of the clanging bars and metal gates, the barren, cement walls, and the daily strife caused by thousands of angry, imprisoned men. But as the train traveled through the Maryland and Delaware countryside and approached Philadelphia, reality began to set in. Junior gradually lost interest in the high-speed romantic interlude; he had more important things on his mind. He was on a mission. He was going to kill Tommy Seher.

LIKE A NUMBER of other K&A journeymen in the burglary trade, Tommy Seher grew up in a working-class section of Philadelphia and gravitated to Kensington as a young man. In addition to the many bars and lively nightclubs that flourished there, the bustling blue collar neighborhood was where second story men congregated and looked for work, much as card-carrying teamsters or longshoremen would go to a union hall. An experienced, dependable thief with a good reputation, Seher floated in and out of several burglary teams, as was the custom of certain K&A men in search of the next easy score. It was just such loose, lackadaisical working arrangements that led to his downfall and, eventually, that of his friend and crew chief, Junior Kripplebauer.

For years, Seher drifted between crews, but spent most of his time with burglary teams captained by Teddy Wigerman and Junior Kripplebauer. Both men were smart, experienced, trustworthy leaders, whose crews profited because of it. Mistakes were rare, and the scores were always good. But even in such elite, well-traveled crews, mistakes were committed—such as Tommy's decision to ignore Junior's orders in Houston and discard identifiable items in a motel's dumpster—and they could prove disastrous for all concerned. A seemingly minor indiscretion by a Wigerman crew member led to a string of prosecutions, the ugly specter of standup men turning government informants, and ultimately the demise of two prolific and celebrated K&A burglary teams.

It started far from home, in North Carolina—a state that had been a favorite target of the K&A Gang for years. Cities like Raleigh, Winston-Salem, and Greensboro might as well have been juicy plums on a fruit tree. Prominent homeowners—including top corporate executives and high-ranking elected officials—were caught in the criminal undertow and more than a little distraught over the loss of precious possessions that never seemed to surface again. Law enforcement authorities, unable to stop the pillaging, were left embarrassed and bewildered. The disturbing phenomenon, which ran from the late 1960s to the mid-1970s, became a colossal statewide mystery.

"We had no earthly idea who was doing it," says D. C. Williams, a veteran Raleigh police official, who spent years trying to track down the Hallmark Gang, named after their penchant for stealing "only the very best" silverware. "Great big stuff including silverware, jewelry," and the like was being taken, and it was happening "eight to ten times a weekend during certain seasons. Most of what was getting hit was old Raleigh money. The bluebloods of Raleigh, people that had been in the area for generations—top citizens, an ex-governor, lawyers, doctors, professionals." Precautionary measures, including stepped-up patrols, greater law enforcement networking, citizen education efforts, and a host of other programs, proved of little value. Even occasional clues—like the discovery of a piece of paper with the hand-written names, addresses, and phone numbers of homeowners on the same street as a recently burgled home—had no tangible impact. The Hallmark Gang, whoever they were and wherever they came from, stole only the best, and they stole with impunity.

On February 16, 1976, a significant break in the North Carolina mystery occurred hundreds of miles away in the form of a seemingly unrelated drug arrest at the Jersey shore. Steven Edward Schrieber, a 24-year-old Mays Landing resident, was picked up on a minor marijuana charge. In his car, however, police found a .22-caliber handgun. A routine check of the weapon through the FBI's computerized National Crime Information Center disclosed that the gun had been stolen from a Raleigh home just a month earlier.

D. C. Williams was ecstatic, for in all the many years that he had worked on the Hallmark Gang thefts, no stolen item had ever resurfaced. "I had been after these guys for years," says Williams, "and this was the first break. We were never able to recover any of the stolen property. Nothing ever turned up. When I got a call that a pistol had been recovered in Atlantic City during a drug search, I was jubilant. The gun belonged to John Holloway, a prominent Raleigh architect whose residence had recently been burglarized. It was a great break. I went to Atlantic City that very day and searched the guy's house and found luggage and a ring that belonged to Holloway's wife." The North Carolina cop also learned that Schrieber's handwriting matched that on a note found at the scene of one of the crimes.

The discovery of the recently burglarized merchandise started an avalanche of pain and hefty penal sentences that young Schrieber could never have expected. The novice burglar had broken one of the cardinal rules of the trade: never keep any of the stolen goods. No matter how unique, attractive, or valuable a gun, a diamond ring, a tie tack, a bracelet, may be, it is not to be kept. All valuables are moved and fenced as soon as possible; nothing is to be retained.

Kripplebauer was adamant about such rules. He knew how enticing an expensive Rolex watch or piece of fine jewelry for a wife or girlfriend could be, but he also knew the legal quagmire it could get you in. "I told everyone who ever worked for me that we keep nothing for ourselves," he says. "It all goes in the pot, and we then sell it to a trustworthy friend who we've done business with before. I said we were in somebody else's home to make money, not to hurt anybody or to keep interesting trinkets that caught our attention. I didn't care how much somebody wanted a fancy watch or a rare coin or a neat-looking pen; you don't keep it. I told them you only grab something for yourself if you catch me doing it. And I didn't do it." And his team followed the rules. Besides knowing it was the right thing to do, Junior wasn't someone you wanted to cross.

But young Stevie Schrieber was part of Teddy Wigerman's operation.

Wigerman had come to second story work much as Kripplebauer and so many others had over the years: early in life he acquired a taste for money and a profound distaste for an honest day's work. He was born in the small upstate Pennsylvania town of Danville, but his alcoholic father moved the family to Kensington when the steel mills closed in the Susquehanna Valley. Teddy Wigerman was a rebellious youth, and gangs, hanging out on streetcorners, and joy rides in stolen cars were his introduction to the second story lifestyle. A short stint in the Air Force let him avoid a bit in a reform school, but the Kensington tradition of going AWOL landed him right back on the streets around K&A. Wigerman joined a gang, stole cars, and stuck up stores on Kensington Avenue. Arrested in 1949 at the age of 17 as the ringleader of the Blue Dragon Gang, Wigerman was nailed with a bitter 10- to 20-year sentence.

Back on the streets 10 years later, Wigerman attempted to make a go of it as a conventional wage-earner. He got married, did construction work, and tried to make ends meet. He was soon supplementing his wages with a few burglaries on the side. He didn't set the world on fire at either profession. One night, after picking up nothing but chump change in a few burglaries in the Northeast, Wigerman stopped in at a popular after-hours club. There he ran into Maury McAdams, an accomplished and experienced K&A burglar who seemed to be swimming in money. After a few hours and more than a few drinks, Wigerman accepted an offer to fill a vacancy in McAdams' crew. By the end of the following week, Wigerman was hooked. Production work had seduced another Kensington street kid. Wigerman was making money like never before.

"That was the end of me," Wigerman told a newspaper reporter years later. "I never went back to work again."

Wigerman learned to appreciate the rudiments and subtleties of production work, but like many of his predecessors he believed he could do even better as a crew chief and eventually went out and put together a crew of his own. He developed a stringent work ethic, burgled hundreds of homes a year, and traveled to Massachusetts, Michigan, California, and Florida to practice his craft. North Carolina, too, was a recurring and lucrative part of the itinerary.

Regrettably, Steven Schrieber, a new member of the Wigerman team, was tempted to pocket a few attractive baubles there. Trusting his team members to understand the importance of following the rules of the game, Wigerman never strip-searched them after an evening's work, as the devious Willie Sears used to do. He never knew about the items Schrieber held back from his partners. They and others would pay dearly for their fellow crew member's deceit and the cross-pollination that was so common among K&A Crews. (Some K&A men have suggested that Wigerman hired young, neophyte burglars because they would be more easily cheated out of their rightful cut from a score. More experienced players would know the value of merchandise and would be less gullible if Wigerman understated what the fence had paid him.)

Wigerman gave Schrieber money to hire an attorney. It was imperative that he fight extradition back to North Carolina. A New Jersey judge, however, saw things differently and allowed Officer Williams to take Schrieber—who had no record at the time—down South to face burglary charges. During the long drive to North Carolina, according to Williams, "Schrieber didn't want to talk," and the officer didn't press him. He extended several courtesies to his prisoner, and ultimately cop and captive developed a rapport. By the time they reached the county jail in Raleigh, Schrieber must have been having serious reservations about a career as an outlaw. His first night in a southern prison, along with the knowledge that North Carolina had some of the harshest burglary laws in the country, only underscored those concerns. A second-degree burglary (breaking into a vacant house after dark) could reward the convicted perpetrator with a life sentence. Moreover, in North Carolina there was no statute of limitations on burglary. Such draconian sanctions have a way of capturing the attention of even the most hardened criminals.

It must have been a sleepless, soul-searching night for the young man, for when Williams returned to the jail the next morning he was given a five-page, handwritten account of Schrieber's six-month career as a burglar. The prisoner named Wigerman as his crew chief, identified the other members of the ring, and detailed their exploits in North Carolina and Missouri. With the help of the novice burglar, the tide had turned.

A ripple of concern shot through the Kensington burglary community with Schrieber's arrest and extradition. His willingness to cooperate only exacerbated the concern. Junior was one of those put on notice that a significant problem had arisen.

"I got a call one day from Steve LaCheen," says Junior. "He says to me, 'Do you know Stevie Schrieber?' I say no, so he tells me, 'Are you sure, 'cause you got a problem with him. He's implicated you in 20 to 25 burglaries.' That's bullshit, I tell him. I never even heard of the guy. It was true. I had no idea who he was."

Fortunately for Junior, Schrieber's information was all hearsay. The young burglar had heard numerous stories about Kripplebauer and knew that the much esteemed second story man had torn through North Carolina like a 150-mile-per-hour Nor'easter, but they had never actually worked together. In fact, they had never met. Law enforcement authorities would need something more concrete as corroborating evidence if they were going to bring Kripplebauer in and charge him with burglary. Unfortunately for Junior, young Schrieber wasn't the only one willing to talk.

As Bill Skarbek of the FBI has said of the critical event, "The dominoes began to fall at that point and would keep on falling for some time. Schrieber was the missing piece of the puzzle. He provided the corroboration and the smoking gun. He was it."

Because of Schrieber's arrest in New Jersey and the gang's extensive operations around the country, authorities in North Carolina allowed the FBI to prosecute the burglars in federal court for the interstate transportation of stolen property. The government cut a deal with Schrieber: if he testified against his former associates in front of grand juries in Raleigh and St. Louis, he'd be admitted to the federal Witness Protection Program and relocated to another part of the country.

In fairly short order, Schrieber's confederates were arrested and either forced to cut deals and talk or brought to trial and banged with incredibly stiff prison terms. For example, George Llanos, another novice burglar, chose to cooperate and received a lenient five-month sentence. Anthony Roche, a more seasoned practitioner of second story work, was loath to rat out his partners. He decided to fight it out in court and was hit with a staggering 40- to 60-year sentence. Wigerman put up a good fight at his trial in St. Louis, but was convicted and given a 12-year sentence. By the time the authorities in Raleigh put him on trial, he was out of both cash and energy. He pled guilty and was handed an additional five years.

Wigerman thought his ordeal was over, except, of course, for the time he had to serve, but the cities of Greensboro and Winston-Salem wanted their shot at the Philly burglars as well, and particularly crew chief Joseph Theodore Wigerman. Each town had suffered dozens of burglaries over the years and wanted a little revenge of their own. They took no solace in the fact that the wily Kensington burglar had already been convicted in St. Louis and Raleigh. Moreover, the federal penalties were thought mild in comparison with what the state of North Carolina could dish out. More than one Tar Heel town wanted to exact justice on the Yankee invaders. D. C. Williams calculated that "60 to 80 burglaries in each of North Carolina's four major cities . . . were attributed to the Hallmark Gang just between 1971 and 1975." For Wigerman, the disaster he feared when his young crew member was arrested and lost his extradition hearing in New Jersey had come to pass.

Faced with additional burglary charges and the corroborating statements of Schrieber and Llanos, Wigerman—now in his mid-forties and serving a lengthy sentence at Atlanta Federal Penitentiary—was looking at spending the rest of his life behind bars. Reluctantly, this K&A man who hated informants agreed to cooperate and talk with the authorities.

The significance of getting one of the main culprits in North Carolina's annual burglary festival to flip was not lost on the state's law enforcement community. As Wigerman identified the many affluent properties he had burgled and named associates who had worked with him over the years, police officers had difficulty hiding their satisfaction. After a decade of frustration, they couldn't be blamed for enjoying the moment.

As D. C. Williams says of the event, "Wigerman rolled right quick when he saw what was facing him in terms of a series of life sentences. He wanted to be first on that train out of the station."

Wigerman's willingness to name names was about to set off a new round of prosecutions, for one of the people he offered up was a Kripplebauer crew member. His name was Tommy Seher.

WHEN JUNIOR ARRIVED at Philadelphia's 30th Street Station, he was met by Troy McEntee, who drove him to a safe house in North Philly where he would hide out for the next two weeks. On the short drive to the mostly African-American working-class neighborhood, Troy brought Junior up to date on Mickie's case. Steve LaCheen had gotten Mickie out of jail by putting her Cherry Hill home up for bail. Texas and North Carolina were both seeking to extradite her for an array of outstanding burglary charges. Tommy Seher, now being held in protective custody in some North Carolina prison, had given both of them up on a silver platter. No one was sure when the extradition hearings would be held. That and bail had given Mickie a window of opportunity if she wanted to take it.

McEntee went on to say that cops and federal agents were aggressively moving through Philly neighborhoods searching for Junior. He had become a desirable catch, a big-ticket item for lawmen hoping to raise their visibility and departmental profile. Texas and North Carolina were extremely anxious to get their hooks into him as well—especially North Carolina. Learning that the infamous Hallmark crowd was actually the K&A Gang out of Philadelphia, nailing one gang member after another, including Wigerman, only whetted their appetite for Kripplebauer, one of the perceived instigators of North Carolina's annual theftcapade.

Junior was pleased to hear that Mickie was back on the street but dismayed that the extradition hearings were as yet unscheduled. His plan to get Seher depended on the rat's appearance at the extradition hearing. Without that information, it would be difficult to impossible to determine where the Feds were holding Tommy for safekeeping.

Junior quickly arranged for a brief liaison with Mickie at a Jersey motel. Although events of the past year had strained the marriage and he had begun seeing other women, he still cared deeply about her and blamed himself for getting her into such a mess. He believed he had wrecked her life. Junior knew that the FBI would be vigorously looking for him in the Philly area, especially anywhere near his wife. He wasn't wrong; the Feds had him high up on their priority list.

"Kripplebauer was a major problem," says Bill Skarbek. "His escape from Atlanta didn't really surprise me. Nothing really shocked me about Kripplebauer. He was that kind of guy. In fact, for that whole group [the K&A Gang] it was par for the course. The FBI had spent a lot of time on him and now he had broken out of prison and was on the street again. When I was notified he had walked out of Atlanta, I basically said, 'You gotta be shitting me.' We had done our job and now we've got to do it all over again.

"Earlier, when the federal judge had made the mistake of giving him 30 days to get his affairs in order before reporting to prison, he jumped bail on us. His case was one of the very few times someone had been prosecuted for jumping bail, but we eventually got him. Now he had gotten out again. We wanted to bring all the pressure we could muster to get him back. He was one of the top jewel men in the country, a real main player. We couldn't afford having him back on the street again.

"We immediately notified our cooperating witnesses [informants] on the street to keep a lookout for Kripplebauer. We told people to be careful. Although Junior didn't have the reputation for being a violent, dangerous felon, he wasn't exactly a docile person. He could do some serious damage if he wanted to. He had broken out of Atlanta, he was on the run, and we knew his connections to some nasty folks in Pittsburgh and Youngstown. He wasn't going to be brought in that easily."

Junior met Mickie at the Sandman Motel in Bordentown, New Jersey, a small roadside inn where they stayed after their wedding in Elkton, Maryland, just a few years before. The atmosphere was infused with both tremendous joy and lingering sadness. Their universe had spun out of control; they had changed from the fun-loving couple who relished both the excitement of pulling hundreds of burglaries together (not to mention the occasional bank job) and the good life it brought to desperados forced to hide in the shadows of an ever-grimmer world. Junior was a desperate fugitive on the run, and Mickie was facing terrifying trips to Texas and North Carolina. Long prison terms and years apart were assuredly in their future.

Conversation drifted from reminiscences of better times to Junior's insistence on getting Tommy for ratting on them. His mind was concentrated on one task. He wanted Seher.

"I'm gonna take him out," said Junior. "I'm gonna kill him."

"Don't be ridiculous," said Mickie. "There's going to be agents all over Tommy. You'd never get within 50 yards of him."

"I'm gonna bomb the courtroom," said Junior matter-of-factly.

"What are you talking about?" Mickie was unsure she had heard correctly. She, unlike her husband, was resigned to her fate and skeptical about any plan to get Seher, her one-time friend, periodic houseguest, and partner in crime.

"I'm gonna kill him," said Junior. "I'm gonna bomb the courtroom."

"And how are you going to do that?" asked Mickie incredulously. "They're not gonna let you get inside the courthouse, much less inside the courtroom. Forget about it. It's done."

"I'm gonna kill him," repeated Junior.

"How?"

"When your extradition hearing date is set," said Junior, "I'm going to find out what courtroom it's scheduled for. The day before the hearing I'm going in the building. I'm going to find a hiding place, and then during the night I'm gonna plant a bomb under the witness chair. I'll have it wired so that when Tommy is called to testify, I'll flip the switch and blow his lousy, rattin' ass to pieces."

Though Mickie certainly had no love for Seher, who was going to put her away for more years than she cared to think about, she felt that Junior's plan was a stretch at best. She never underestimated her husband, and she appreciated his single-minded resourcefulness, but she saw no benefit in making the situation worse. The burglary charges were bad enough; they didn't need a murder charge on top of them. Besides, she reasoned, they had only a few brief hours together; who knew when or whether they'd have a rendezvous like this again? She didn't want those fleeting but reassuring moments colored by anger, talk of revenge, and plans to exterminate a one-time friend.

They both realized that the Feds and local police would use Mickie as a magnet to capture Junior, so he would have to stay away from her. They briefly discussed her joining him on the run, but abandoned that idea. She would have to stay and fight it out in the courts. She had a son and did her best to be a good mother. Mickie expected to spend some time away in prison, but at the end of it she could return home. The life of a fugitive was endless worry, never any downtime. And a prison cell or the cemetery always awaited you at the end of the run.

"I knew what I was facing," says Junior of the lengthy Texas and North Carolina prison sentences he could expect. "Texas was gonna try me as a habitual offender. I was looking at a life sentence. For Mickie, it was different. Besides, she had a kid to take care of. We both knew she couldn't cut out."

With no date set for the extradition hearing and Seher in protective custody somewhere in North Carolina, the decision was obvious: Junior would have to leave the area. Hanging around the Philadelphia vicinity would only guarantee his capture—sooner rather than later. Junior said he'd keep in touch, send her some cash periodically, and come back when Mickie's hearing date was set. Though events had fractured their relationship and he was now involved with another woman, he wouldn't abandon her. Nor would he abandon his goal of getting Tommy Seher.

JUNIOR GOT A FRIEND, Georgie Flynn, to drive him out to Pittsburgh. He told Richard Henkel, the tipster from the Lee's Trading Post burglary, that he was in a jam and needed a place to hole up for a while. Henkel drove him to Youngstown, Ohio, where Henkel's elderly uncle lived alone. Junior could stay there and help take care of the old man. It didn't take Junior long to reacquaint himself with Jake and the other members of the Youngstown crowd.

Junior and Jake did dozens of burglaries together, mostly upscale homes in suburban Ohio communities. Occasionally, they'd hit a jewelry store and once would have pulled off a score equal to the Lee heist if an electrical failure hadn't tripped the alarm system and forced them to abort what could have been a sizable payday.

Sometimes Henkel would join them on these break-ins, but he had long ago embarked on far more grandiose and deadly moneymaking schemes. Burglaries were okay for pocket change, but he was after the big score now. And as Junior would eventually learn, Henkel would do whatever it took to get it. The K&A principle of never hurting anyone was totally alien to the Pittsburgh bar manager. Over the years a number of Henkel's associates and acquaintances were discovered in a permanent state of rigor mortis, but Junior was either oblivious to Henkel's connection to the carnage or wrote it off as part of the collateral damage that results from choosing a life on the edge.

A perfect example of Henkel's ruthless moneymaking schemes was his plan to kidnap Art Rooney, Sr., the beloved owner of the Pittsburgh Steelers. Henkel would often see Rooney at the Meadows, a racetrack in a suburb of Pittsburgh, and it got him to thinking. The prospect of picking off and holding for ransom the affable and affluent team owner was more than a little intriguing.

Impervious to the practical obstacles and legal consequences of such an undertaking, Henkel mulled over plans for some time until he came up with what he thought was a sure-fire winner. Sophisticated, audacious, and multifaceted, the plan was indicative of a criminal mind that had severed itself from legal boundaries and moral restraints.

Henkel planned to scoop Rooney up one afternoon as he left the racetrack. Once off the racetrack grounds, they'd transfer the old man to a specially adapted van, securely restrain him, and place around his neck a bomb designed to explode if anyone tried removing the device without precise directions and the required technical know-how. They would then drive their valuable human cargo to a safe house in a mountainous and uninhabited section of upstate Pennsylvania, contact the FBI, and demand $5 million for the team owner's safe return.

Henkel put together an experienced crew to pull off his high-risk, high-stakes gamble: Henry Ford, Gary Small, Glenn Scott, Jack Siggson, and Roy Travis. Gary Small was a Pittsburgh police officer, with obvious advantages as far as access and maneuverability were concerned, but Roy Travis was the key player. A former Marion inmate originally from Vancouver, British Columbia, Travis was an electronics expert with an impressive technical portfolio, including superb bomb-making capabilities.

There was one additional member of the team—Louis Kripplebauer, Jr. Recognizing Junior's steadiness under pressure, relentless work ethic, aversion to snitching, and ever-present desire for the big score, Henkel asked him if he wanted in on the dicey venture.

"I was skeptical," says Junior. "I thought to myself, this isn't stealing someone's property any more. This isn't production work; this is some serious shit. Besides that, I thought, who has the ability to lay out five million bucks? I said, who are we talking about here? Where and how are we gonna do something like this? I told him what I thought, and he said don't worry, he had it all figured out. Henkel then laid out his plan. He said the target would be Art Rooney and explained how we were gonna pull it off. When he mentioned Art Rooney, I backed up. Wow, I thought to myself, he isn't messing around. The Rooney family certainly had the money, but I knew it was gonna cause a lot of shit."

Henkel wanted Kripplebauer on board and presented his plan in considerable detail. He also made mention of his assistance to the Philly fugitive on his arrival in the Pittsburgh area, putting him up at a relative's house and introducing him to his Ohio and Pittsburgh friends. Appreciative of all Henkel had done for him, Junior listened carefully to the sales pitch and then said okay, he was in.

Such an inherently violent and dangerous undertaking was a radical departure for a professional thief. His willingness to buy in was symptomatic of his desperation. Junior was now a hunted man—an escaped convict on the run. As a career criminal facing many years—possibly decades—of imprisonment in Texas, North Carolina, and the federal prison system, with a loyal wife who was about to be hauled back to jail, and the expectation of a rendezvous in the near future with a former friend turned rat, Junior was prepared to go for broke. Hell, he thought to himself, what did he have to lose?

Henkel's intricate extortion plan impressed his co-conspirators. According to Junior, Henkel examined every aspect of the undertaking, even going so far as to calculate how much $5 million in one hundred dollar bills would weigh and how many bags would be needed to hold the alluring bundles of cash. Additionally, he had a lead-lined box built into the van to disable any tracking devices the FBI might try to conceal in the money. He even planned to notify the Army Corps of Engineers to stand ready to take directions for the removal of the bomb around Rooney's neck after the exchange took place.

For some time Henkel and members of the team practiced detonating various devices in the Pennsylvania countryside. As the target date neared, however, Henkel surprised his associates by informing them that he was having second thoughts about Rooney. The old man was too high-profile, too respected by Steeler fans in the area. Henkel substituted the name of another racetrack aficionado, Edward M. Ryan, as their target. A prominent homebuilder, Ryan had recently sold his business, Ryan Homes, Inc., for one billion dollars. Henkel seemed to know a good bit about the builder, including where he lived.

The switch in targets had little impact on Henkel's confederates. The less notoriety, the better the chance of success, they rationalized, as long as the family of the kidnap victim had the money. Some might suspect that Henkel was getting anxious. In fact, he was not the kind to come down with a case of nerves: as would soon be discovered, Henkel was quite comfortable pulling off risky ventures and terminating the lives of those who got in his way. Bruce Agnew, Kripplebauer's long-time partner, had gone missing and was presumed dead by those in the know. And Deborah Gentile, Henkel's girlfriend, was found murdered in Room 239 of the Greater Pittsburgh International Airport Hotel soon after she had taken out a $750,000 insurance policy on herself with Henkel's mother as the beneficiary. Sasha Scott, a buxom barmaid, also met a violent end, as did her husband, who had made the mistake of offending Henkel one day.

A host of Henkel's former friends and associates would turn up dead. Some were blown up by bombs; others were repeatedly shot and stabbed to death. At the time, however, not only Kripplebauer, but Pittsburgh media outlets as well, attributed the escalating death toll to organized crime factions competing for control of Pittsburgh's lucrative massage parlor industry.

Surfacing only when he had to and preoccupied with his own problems, Junior was slow to connect the dots. In fact, as part of Henkel's inner circle, his own life was now at risk. When Henkel told the group that he had decided to scrap the plan and suggested that Siggson return to California and find another kidnapping candidate out there, Junior was perplexed. He wondered why Henkel had pulled the plug on the extortion plot, but his confusion was short lived. Something of greater importance had taken precedence: he got word from friends in Philly that Mickie's extradition hearing had been scheduled. He had to return home and keep a date with a former friend who had turned government informant.

KRIPPLEBAUER PROMPTLY CAUGHT a flight back to Philadelphia. As usual, there was little in the way of luggage, but now Junior was carrying something he had never hauled around before. He had obtained C-4, a plastic explosive, from Dick Henkel and had Roy Travis show him how to use it. Tommy Seher may have thought things couldn't get any worse now that he was cooperating with the police, ratting out former partners, and facing years of imprisonment, but he was wrong. Junior planned on giving Tommy a lightning-quick ride to the morgue.

Junior spent his first night back with Mickie at the Sandman Motel in Jersey. They briefly discussed her legal strategy and Steve LaCheen's suggestion that she file for divorce in order to show her intention to separate herself from her husband's nefarious influence. Junior approved and tried to reassure her that everything would be okay, but they both knew it was a fiction. He made no mention of the gift he meant to deliver to their former friend. His plan remained the same: get into the courtroom prior to the hearing, plant the bomb, and give Tommy the ride of his life when he took the stand. No easy feat, but Kripplebauer knew the Camden County Courthouse pretty well, especially the sixth floor cell house. He had spent more time in the building than he cared to recall.

The next morning Junior went to Jeanette Donnelly's house, having planned to meet up with Troy McEntee at a nearby convenience store. Junior walked to the 7-Eleven for coffee and cigarettes and found Troy already in the parking lot, sitting in a brand new Cadillac. Junior had just climbed into the Caddy and gotten a whiff of the rich leather upholstery when two figures wearing blue FBI windbreakers approached the car. Junior immediately had a snubbed-nose .38-caliber revolver pointed in his face. The other agent shoved a sawed-off shotgun through the driver's side window.

"Shut the goddamn engine off and get out of the car," screamed the female agent.

Junior, ignoring the command, turned to his friend and asked, "You got your gun?"

Troy was silent.

Both agents were now screaming orders at them. Junior asked Troy again if he had his weapon.

"No" was Troy's surprising reply.

"I could see on his face that something was wrong," recalls Kripplebauer. "I had always known Troy to carry a gun and now he's not packing one. I couldn't

230 · CONFESSIONS OF A SECOND STORY MAN

believe it. I'm staring at him, the cops are barking orders, and all of a sudden we're surrounded by what looked like 37 officers carrying all sorts of artillery. They dragged us out of the car, threw us on the ground, and I'm griping at the bitch who first came running up to me. I'm tellin' her she should be ashamed of herself, harassing law-abiding citizens and stickin' guns in their faces. I told her she should be home taking care of her kids. But all the time I'm thinking I was set up, and it doesn't take a genius to figure out who had done it. I can't believe Troy ratted me out.

"They threw me in the back seat of one of their cars and put Troy in another one, but we're not going in the same direction. Right away I can tell by the route they're traveling they're not taking me to Philly or the Camden County Jail. One agent asks the other where they're gonna put me, and the guy says the Mercer County Jail just north of Trenton. He said he wanted to be sure I was nice and secure and far away from any of my Philly friends."

Kripplebauer's days on the run as a federal fugitive were now over. During the next several weeks he would get reacquainted with the Federal Bureau of Prisons' diesel therapy program and be abruptly shifted from one penal gem to another: from the Metropolitan Correctional Center in New York City to Lewisburg, on to Atlanta Federal Penitentiary, and then back to Lewisburg.

His brief stopover at Atlanta, the institution he had walked out of eight months earlier, was designed to show the institution's other malcontents that the Prison Bureau always gets its man. Unexpectedly, however, his fellow captives treated his homecoming like General McArthur's return to the Philippines. As Junior was escorted down the long Atlanta cellblocks by grinning guards, proud of their catch, admiring inmates lined the tiers and corridors and celebrated the hero's return. Mafia hit men, long-haired and tattooed bikers, wily drug czars, and seasoned bank robbers leaned over the railings to welcome home a slick, ballsy member of the fraternity who had accomplished what they all dreamed about: getting beyond Atlanta's fearsome walls for more than a New York minute. Applause and shouts of encouragement and appreciation echoed through Atlanta's cellblocks. "Hey, J. R., you made them look like fools." "Yo, Junior, how was the vacation?" "Hey, Junior, nice shot, fella." "You gave them a nice run, J. R." "Did you have a drink for me, Junior?"

"I had a drink for everybody," replied Kripplebauer with a wave of the arm and an appreciative nod. "Glad to see you guys missed me."

Junior's escape and unrepentant return added another chapter to the Kripplebauer legend.

The Philly burglar was placed in the hole and sat on for some time by the authorities, but the weeks of isolation and restraint were secondary to his real concern. Mickie had lost her legal battle and had been shipped to North Carolina.

She was being held in the Guilford County Jail in Greensboro. Junior knew a trip to the Tar Heel State was in his future as well.

JUNIOR AND MICKIE kept in touch through the mail. "She'd write me all the time," he says. "We'd often tease each other about our situation. I'd write her, 'Did you get a daddy or honey in there yet?' And she'd write back, 'Did you get a punk yet?' She did admit that all the dykes were cracking on her and she broke bad on a couple of them. She said she had to straighten a few of them out."

Many months later, on January 31, 1980, Kripplebauer was transferred to North Carolina and housed in the Guilford County Prison. Though he wasn't eager to face another legal battle or the prospect of an additional lengthy term of imprisonment, it was an opportunity to be reunited with Mickie, who was being held in the women's section. It also allowed him to hook up again with friend and former partner Frankie Brewer, another K&A burglar who worked with both Wigerman and Kripplebauer and had recently been brought in from Graterford State Penitentiary in Pennsylvania to face similar burglary charges. Besides their strong bonds of friendship, it was important to formulate a legal strategy that would minimize the damage the prosecution had in store for all three of them.

Media coverage didn't help. Once again, the trial of the Hallmark Gang drew considerable public interest. The earlier trials of Wigerman crew members had become something of a criminal soap opera. Now it was the Kripplebauer crew that would receive center stage treatment. Bold headlines—"Trial to begin Tuesday" and "Burglars Put Mark on the City"—announced the forthcoming show and recounted the gang's activity over the years. The Greensboro news media, like the city of Raleigh before them, didn't have to work hard to build up interest in the trial. Communities from one end of the state to the other had been bedeviled by the Philly burglars for years, and now the final chapter was about to be written. A North Carolina newspaper estimated that over "200 Hallmark burglaries had been committed in the state between 1968 and 1976," meaning that just about every city and town had a story or two to tell. Greensboro alone had several dozen burglaries during the seventies. Some particularly unlucky families like the LeBruns and the Lavietes had had the misfortune of being hit twice by the Hallmark burglars; they would become centerpieces of the prosecution's case.

As the trial approached, news articles described the horror of coming home to find your house ransacked and precious items taken. The LeBrun family, for example, "returned home from dinner at the Greensboro Country Club . . . to find all the lights on and doors standing open. The cabinets were gaping and the bedroom had been ransacked." Silverware, crystal decanters, mink coats, and jewelry had been "scooped up" and the house left a disheveled muddle. Even the few objects of value remaining, it seemed to the owners, had been defiled. "You feel like the things are dirty," Mrs. LeBrun said.

Such personal testimonies combined with the scope of the statewide victimization led to great public interest in the Hallmark story. "The trials of Louis Kripplebauer and the other Philadelphia-area burglars were big news in North Carolina in 1980 and 1981," says Martha Woodall, now a reporter for the *Philadelphia Inquirer.* "I wrote a six-part series about the burglars for the *Greensboro Record* in the spring of 1981. The tales of the Hallmark Gang, their exploits and eventual capture produced so many letters and requests for additional copies that the *Record* reprinted the series in a booklet. Readers from across the state and beyond ordered copies. It was the first time the paper had produced such a reprint."

Now that the northern invaders were about to get their long-awaited comeuppance, everyone took notice. The law enforcement community had the most invested in the outcome. For more years than they cared to recall, they had felt helpless, even humiliated. The district attorney of Guilford County called the Hallmark Gang "the most sophisticated criminals that the Guilford County district attorney's office had ever ushered into prison." Yes, the perpetrators were obviously "very sophisticated" and "the manner in which they handled the stolen property was neat," but craft aside, they were predatory criminals who needed to be taken off the street and punished.

Their intention was clear. "We were gonna give everybody time," recalls Judge Harold (Rick) Greeson, who was the Guilford County district attorney's chief assistant at the time. "We were gonna get 'em. We had receipts from the motel where they stayed, the cars they rented, and the restaurants they ate at. It was like shooting fish in a barrel."

And, not surprisingly, Skarbek was still lurking around, providing counsel, evidence, and strategy to the North Carolina constabulary. Skarbek, always Skarbek: no matter where they were or what jurisdictional authority was involved, Skarbek would surface. He had become a regular part of Junior's nightmares.

The situation was looking bleak, and the Kripplebauer team knew it. Junior had his North Carolina attorney, Locke Clifford, file a "motion for change of venue" in early March 1980. Claiming that "the news media (newspapers, radio, and television) in this area and surrounding counties have given very prominent, intense, widespread, and almost continuous publicity" to the alleged break-ins and the "organized, monolithic ring of thieves" that perpetrated the crimes, he contended that it was impossible for any defendant to receive a fair and impartial trial.

Clifford argued in his change-of-venue motion that "the *Greensboro Daily News* and the *Greensboro Record,*" along with "WFMY-TV in Greensboro,

WGHP-TV in High Point, WXII in Winston-Salem, WBIG radio station in Greensboro, WCOG radio station in Greensboro, WGBG radio station in Greensboro, and WFMR radio station in High Point," among others, had "given similar and prejudicial coverage concerning the so-called Hallmark Gang."

Not surprisingly, the motion was rejected. Guilford County was determined to give the Yankee burglars their day in court.

The stage was set for the state to exact a heavy penalty, as it had done earlier to Anthony Roche and Pete Logue. Junior, Mickie, and Frankie Brewer were to be tried together. All three were held in the Guilford County Jail to await trial. Each was an old hand at doing time, even Mickie. "Mickie," as Junior proudly proclaims, "was a tough son-of-a-gun" who handled life behind bars like the professional she was. Husband and wife were not allowed to meet—except at Sunday morning church services—but they communicated on a daily basis by way of the Guilford telegraph: the prison's air duct system.

"We'd get on the pipe every day and speak to each other for a half-hour or so," says Junior. "It only worked through the prison's bathroom air vents, so each of us would have to chase people out of the men's and women's bathrooms, then stand on a toilet or sink and stretch our necks up to the vent so we could speak to each other. It wasn't Ma Bell, but it worked. We'd tell the other inmates to take a shower or whatever they had to do later in the day so we could talk. Sometimes Frankie would chase guys out of the room and tell them I had to speak to my wife about something important."

As far as courtroom preparation went, Junior tried to "take the weight and relieve Mickie" of as much of the blame as possible. He maintained prior to and during the trial that Mickie was the victim of her husband's criminal vices and demands. "I said it was me who pushed her into stealing," says Junior. "She was just a devoted wife who was obeying her husband. It was the marriage that forced her into it. She never would have done anything like this on her own. To further that argument, Steve [LaCheen, her attorney] told her it would look good if she filed for divorce and separated herself from me as much as possible. By the time of the trial, I believe we were legally separated, if not divorced."

Not surprisingly, Robert Johnston, the Guilford County district attorney, was unimpressed with this line of argument. Kripplebauer, he claimed, was a wily scam artist as well as a burglar. And Mickie "wasn't a woman blindly following her husband. She was an integral part of the robbery team and didn't deserve any leniency."

The DA's aggressiveness toward Mickie really burned Kripplebauer. "On more than one occasion," recalls Junior, "I wanted to throw that little weasel right out the courthouse window."

Junior's strategy sessions with Frankie Brewer were slightly different. Brewer, a no-nonsense Philly boy who decked more than one overbearing redneck while celled in North Carolina, wanted to fight it out and make the state prove everything in court if they wanted to get him. Junior considered such a conventional game plan the legal equivalent of suicide. He knew that the prosecution had them over a barrel, and North Carolina's draconian criminal sanctions would bury them under under 50-year sentences.

"I told Frank he was fuckin' nuts," he recalls. "I told him you got Teddy [Wigerman] and Tommy [Seher] testifying against you. You got no chance playing the game straight up. They'll give you a life sentence down here.

"I must have argued with him a couple days. We chased guys out of the dayroom on a number of occasions so we could talk. I said, 'Frank, this ain't the time to be a tough guy. They'll knock you out of the box. Plead guilty and cut the best deal you can.' "

Curiously, however, Junior wasn't going to follow his own advice. He knew that the cards were stacked in favor of the house, but he was no novice when it came to a tactic fundamental to both the gambling den and the halls of justice: the bluff. Well versed in the law and the nuances of the criminal justice process, and maintaining a cantankerous disposition toward the sentencing authorities, Kripplebauer wasn't going to give up without a fight. Though the evidence and the incriminating statements of former partners made for a solid case against him, Kripplebauer was going to try to thwart the state of North Carolina by any means possible. He'd marshal what few resources he had and somehow try to make a contest out of it and then cut the best deal he could. He was horrified at the sentences that had been handed out to other K&A men who had proven uncooperative. Pete Logue, for instance, had been given 40 to 60 years. Since Pete was 50 at the time, Junior saw his friend shackled to a death sentence; he was therefore willing to try any legal maneuver that might save him from a similar fate. The North Carolina criminal justice system might eventually bang him with a big number, but they were gonna know they were in a fight. And if he was lucky, he just might pull off a sentence he could live with.

Junior and some friends who formed the backbone of the Lewisburg Penitentiary Law Clinic came up with a battle plan that Clarence Darrow would have been proud of. He'd force them to deal by burying them under an avalanche of legal gimmicks, constitutional technicalities, and courtroom gymnastics. Essentially, he hoped to crush them with prosecutorial costs and public safety concerns.

Junior designed a defense based on an endless supply of witnesses—almost three dozen—who would testify to his presence in other locales when the crimes were supposedly committed. In addition, many of them would swear to the boundless mendacity of the prosecution's chief witness, Tommy Seher. "They'd testify I was with them in Philly or New York or Boston and couldn't possibly have been in North Carolina at the time of the burglaries," says Kripplebauer.

"They'd also swear to Tommy's repeated comments that he'd say and do anything to stay out of jail."

What made the tactical maneuver so interesting—and so appalling to North Carolina authorities—was that the vast majority of the witnesses Kripplebauer was requesting were presently incarcerated in state and federal prisons across the country.

Kripplebauer's friends, men with serious reputations like bank robbers Joe Dougherty and Joe Havel and prison escape artists John Dickel and Franny Tomlinson, were currently under lock and key at such tough maximum-security institutions as Marion in Illinois, Leavenworth in Kansas, Atlanta, and Lewisburg. There were even a few aging Puerto Rican lifers on the witness list, nationalists who decades earlier had tried to take out President Truman in a celebrated assassination attempt. Junior had incorporated a pantheon of infamous criminal talent into his legal defense. Buried under unbelievably long sentences, Kripplebauer's buddies would have enjoyed nothing better than long, scenic road trips that provided numerous opportunities to escape—not to mention the prospect of being housed in a relatively small and unsophisticated county jail during the course of the trial.

When the Guilford County sheriff saw Kripplebauer's witness list he nearly had a coronary. In motions court, he pleaded for some judicial relief. "Your Honor," he told the judge, "we can't bring all these guys here. They're all extremely dangerous men and significant escape risks. It would break the county to bring in all of these people. This is an impossible thing we're being asked to do."

The judge assigned to rule on pretrial motions was not unsympathetic. He readily recognized that the mere cost of transporting these men to Guilford County would be prohibitive. The public safety issues inherent in such an undertaking were a whole other matter—one he shuddered even to think about.

As the DA voiced his vigorous objections to assembling the defendant's witness list, Kripplebauer gradually grew more agitated, fearing an outright rejection of his request. Realizing that he had to stem the rising tide of opposition, Junior jumped up as if unable to contain himself and shouted at his nemesis, "Your Honor, the DA wants to send me to jail for life without any opportunity to mount a defense. He'll do whatever it takes to put me away. And he doesn't care if any constitutional guarantees are sacrificed in the process." Junior then turned his attention to the judge: "Hell, why don't you just sentence me to life in prison and forget about the damn trial?"

Offended, the judge lashed back. "Mr. Kripplebauer, don't you get sarcastic with me, or you'll get your wish."

He then ordered that the defendant's witnesses were to be brought to court and that the trial should proceed as scheduled, causing the county sheriff an acute case of angina. "But, Your Honor," he said, "there's no place to house these men in the county."

Shortly thereafter, when Judge William Z. Wood gaveled the trial to order, he quickly realized that the defendant's novel defense strategy had placed the state in an untenable position. Judge Wood listened to the bickering for only a few minutes before calling it to a halt: "Everybody take a few minutes and figure this out. We're not proceeding with this trial until there is some agreement here. When you all come back I expect everybody to be on the same page."

The ruse had worked. Guilford County and the state of North Carolina were forced to deal. Kripplebauer had gotten over on them.

"They wanted me to accept an 18- to 20-year sentence like they had given Tommy Seher," says Junior, "but I wasn't gonna plead guilty and take the same sentence that little rat took. He was so stupid he couldn't even get a decent deal, and he turned over for them. I told them I wouldn't take an 18- to 20-year sentence and that I wanted my day in court. And I wanted my witnesses with me there as well. They said they'd depose them at the prisons they were being held at, but I said, 'No way.' I wanted them in court with me. We had researched the law. We had them."

The last thing the state wanted was to let Junior Kripplebauer off easy. But he now had them; they'd have to cut a deal with him. Incredibly, Kripplebauer, who refused to name names, who fought them to the end, and who was the one law enforcement agencies wanted more than anyone else, was given a relatively modest 12 to 20 years. Moreover, it was to be concurrent with his federal sentence. In the end Kripplebauer didn't walk, but he wasn't buried under a decades-long sentence either.

Mickie, now his former wife, was also dealt with leniently and handed a flat 10-year sentence (and Junior made sure she'd be eligible for parole after serving one year of it). Frankie Brewer, who chose to plead guilty like Junior, but without the courtroom histrionics and creative legal gamesmanship, was given 18 to 20 years. Though all three were going to reside for some time in North Carolina prisons, their sentences paled in comparison with those dealt out to some Hallmark burglars with very similar cases.

Soon after the deal was struck and the sentences were handed down, Junior was shipped back to Atlanta and Frankie Brewer to Graterford to finish their respective federal and state sentences. Mickie began serving her sentence at North Carolina's women's prison in Raleigh.

REASONABLY PLEASED WITH the results of the North Carolina proceedings, Kripplebauer was returned to Atlanta Federal Penitentiary on July 15, 1980 with only the Houston case hanging over his head. Though he knew the Texans would eventually be coming for him, raising the prospect of another knock-down-drag-out legal battle below the Mason-Dixon Line, there was something else to occupy his time.

Cheryl Lee McConnell was a drop-dead gorgeous brunette in her mid-thirties who had started seeing Junior prior to his departure for North Carolina. The curvaceous, raven-haired vixen with the killer smile was one of five sisters who shared not only the middle name "Lee" and a love for money and excitement, but also a striking natural beauty that caught the eye of males from Florida to Maine. Originally from South Florida, she had recently relocated to the Atlanta area. As soon as she was introduced to Kripplebauer by a friend of his who was also serving time at the institution, the two seemed to click. It was a welcome diversion for both of them, but especially for Junior.

There was an impediment to the nascent love affair, however. Cheryl was married, and her husband was one of Junior's best friends. Mike "Mac" McConnell was a bank robber of some repute who had done a slew of work with the likes of Charlie Allen and Frankie Del Piano. He and Junior had developed a strong friendship over the years, intensified by their shared time at a "cold stop" like Atlanta Federal Penitentiary.

Junior was excited at the prospect of a relationship with Cheryl, a gorgeous woman with an outgoing, radiant personality, but the fact that she was the wife of one of his best friends put a serious crimp in his dreams of a life together. On scheduled visits to see her husband, Cheryl also spent some time with Junior in the prison visiting area. Kripplebauer often had his own girlfriend down on visits, and sometimes the two couples would share an afternoon together, but when she was alone with Junior, Cheryl would admit to her marital difficulties. The marriage had been going south for some time, and her husband's lengthy incarceration hadn't helped. Initially just a concerned friend, Junior gradually became more emotionally involved and eventually found himself somewhere between enchanted and mesmerized by the comely Mrs. McConnell.

Even after he was shipped to North Carolina, they continued to correspond, and she even visited him a couple of times as he waited for his day in court. There was no doubt that a bond had formed. Kripplebauer decided that he couldn't move on a buddy's wife and he dealt with his dilemma the only way he knew how—head on. He managed to get a call in to McConnell at Atlanta one day and opened, "Mac, we gotta talk. You should know that things are getting pretty involved here between Cheryl and me. I think she's a great girl and I'm finding myself more and more attracted to her. I want you to know that I never expected anything like this to happen. I just wanted to be a friend, but . . ."

McConnell cut him off: "Hey J. R., don't sweat it. Things are over between me and Cheryl. It's been played out. The relationship is dead, it's over. You wanna take a shot at it, go ahead. But you should really consider if you can handle it. Cheryl's a handful. Anyway, man, I appreciate you coming to me. Don't worry about me. Junior, I know she likes you. Good luck."

Given the green light, Cheryl and Junior became an item and continued to write, call, and see each other whenever they could. As Junior was transferred from one prison to another and tackled his varied legal problems, Cheryl stayed supportive and filed for divorce from Eddie McConnell.

Even while he was doing battle with an assortment of political jurisdictions stretching from North Carolina to Texas (not to mention the federal government), and even though he seemed fated to remain behind bars and cut off from making any real money for at least the next decade, and quite possibly for a hell of a lot longer, there was no shortage of female suitors. Junior had the goods. Who cared, women seemed to say, if they visited him in Atlanta and Lewisburg federal penitentiaries as opposed to South Beach or Acapulco?

Yet other concerns intruded on Junior's busy love life. And some of them were deadly serious.

"I got word that my friends in Texas would be coming for me the following day. I was pretty damn nervous and sure as hell didn't wanna go down there. If they were successful they could bang me for two life terms—one for burglarizing an unoccupied home after dark and the other for being a habitual offender. Texas was like the last place I wanted to do time. I would've been killed down there. The place was just rotten through and through. The Texas prison system was like the last stop on earth. The prison gangs down there were extremely violent and constantly at war with each other. The Aryan Brotherhood, the Black Guerilla Family, and the Mexican Mafia dominated life inside those walls as much as the authorities. Even the Crips and Bloods had gained a foothold in there. The whole goddamn place was loaded with competing armies. As soon as a new fish walked inside one of those joints, he was being pressured to join up. You could hardly avoid it. And if you were by yourself you were totally fucked. Even the average Joe doin' time was forced to adopt a cut-throat attitude.

"I wasn't any virgin. I knew the score. While I was at Lewisburg and Atlanta bodies were falling all the time. It seemed that every day somebody was getting shanked. Me and Mac were playing cards in my cell one day when we saw a few ABs pass by. Next thing we hear, somebody is getting whacked pretty good. You could hear the thump, thump, thump of the shanks being rammed in the guy. They killed him right on the spot. Another time I'm heading out to the yard, and just before I leave the corridor I see a black dude pull a four-foot piece of metal out of his pants—the size of a samurai sword—and jam it in another black inmate. Shoved it right through him. The guy went down and just bled out all over the fuckin' hallway. I figured there'd be that stuff and more down in Texas. Yeah, I didn't want any part of Texas.

"They finally came for me, put me on a plane, and stuck me in the Harris County Jail to await trial. I must have been there two months, and you better believe I dreaded every minute of it. I was worried about a life sentence and repeatedly expressed my concerns to Racehorse [Haynes]. He kept on telling me to relax; he was working on something. He said he'd take care of it.

"The guy was a real character. Racehorse was fairly short and just an average dresser except for the cowboy boots he wore all the time, but he knew everyone and everyone knew him. Earlier, when I was out on bail and had met him at the courthouse coffee shop, it was tough to get a word in with everybody constantly coming over to him to say hello. Even though he was in his sixties and nothing special to look at, he was like a local celebrity. And now I was about to go to trial, but I was really small potatoes on his plate. He was in the midst of defending Cullen Davis, a prominent oilman, for a series of high-profile murders. It was the talk of the state. I felt for sure I was gonna get lost in the shuffle and end up with a bad bit.

"The court date is getting closer, and even though my attorney is supposed to be the main man and tellin' me to take it easy and relax, I'm feeling pretty uneasy. I've already paid him some big money to take care of me, but the DA wanted me real bad. The burglaries had been big news in Texas, and nailing me was a good way to get some free publicity. I'm even thinking about not showing up, if you know what I mean.

"The morning of the trial I tell Racehorse I'm not feeling good about this, and he says, 'Don't worry. It's a done deal.'

" 'Whaddya mean?' I reply.

" 'I worked a deal,' he says. 'You're gonna do seven years. And I think I can get it to run with your federal time. Ya think you can handle that?'

"I was dumbfounded. It was too good to be true. When I walked into the courtroom, I was still skeptical and expected to be nailed, but I did as Racehorse told me, pled guilty to the charges, and held my breath. The judge then sentenced me to seven years and had it run concurrent with my federal time. I tell you, I was jubilant. It was unbelievable. Haynes really had it worked. He was the man down there. I had paid him a hell of a lot of money, but I got what I paid for. I don't know how he did it, but he did it."

BACK AT LEWISBURG, Junior did the best he could under the circumstances. Though technically just another convict doing his time, Kripplebauer had a knack for making the best of a bad situation. Whether it was his stoical coal-mining background or a professional criminal's realistic outlook on life, Junior handled the blows of penal servitude. As his friend, Jimmy Dolan says of him, "Junior was a standup guy. No matter where the prison was located or the length of the sentence, he'd do his time without moaning and groaning about it. And more importantly, without ratting out a partner, or anybody else, to get out of a jam. If Junior caught a bad break, he'd just learn to deal with it and do his time like a man."

Kripplebauer still owed the federal government several years before he'd ever be taken down to North Carolina to serve out his state sentence. His various schemes and scams at Lewisburg were doing well, and the pervasive institutional violence fortunately stayed away from him, but a new worry appeared on his radar screen. An avid reader, Kripplebauer received newspapers from a number of cities, including some in western Pennsylvania. Alarmingly, the *Pittsburgh Post Gazette* and the *Pittsburgh Tribune Review* were running a series of high-profile articles on a recently discovered plot to kidnap Art Rooney. Richard Henkel, Gary Small, and Henry Ford had been picked up by the police, and there was reason to believe that Jack "the Jew" Siggson and possibly Tommy Seher were spilling their guts to authorities. For die-hard Steeler fans, the owner of the local gridiron team was a hero, making the extortion conspiracy a front-page story. The growing list of dead bodies tied to Henkel, the plan's mastermind, increased public interest.

Kripplebauer feared that it was only a matter of time before he'd see his own name connected to the plot and Allegheny County authorities paying him a visit. Everything he had ever done, it seemed, was coming back to haunt him. He wondered if he would spend the rest of his life in courtrooms around the country fending off new criminal charges. It was worse than a nightmare; it was real. Junior's life had become a never-ending legal struggle and an involuntary tour of America's federal, state, and local prison systems.

As he had feared, Kripplebauer received a memorandum from his Lewisburg case manager on October 9, 1981: the Allegheny County District Attorney's Office had requested "temporary custody" of him to face charges of "criminal conspiracy."

As usual, Junior threw himself into the legal thicket, researching the formal complaint, the Interstate Agreement on Detainers, writs of habeas corpus, motions to suppress and dismiss, and a half-dozen other complex substantive, procedural, and jurisdictional issues. A master of the nuances of the legal trade, Junior barraged the Lewisburg warden with a mass of paper, legal precedents, and well-researched arguments to block his transfer, but it was to no avail. Junior was shipped to Pittsburgh on November 10, 1981.

Compounding his predicament was the fact that he would be forced to ask the court for legal assistance. He needed representation but lacked the funds to pay for an attorney. His prison scams brought in a few bucks, but nothing that approached what a first-rate, well-known lawyer would demand to handle such a case. No longer a high-roller who could afford the likes of Racehorse Haynes,

Kripplebauer was destitute and had to throw himself on the mercy of the court and file *in forma pauperis* to attain competent counsel.

Michael J. Healey, a congenial Pittsburgh barrister in his early fifties, was appointed Kripplebauer's attorney. Lawyer and client got along well, mostly because, as Junior likes to say, "he did everything I told him."

Housed in the Allegheny County Jail, Junior spent as much time as he could in the prison law library researching various aspects of the still-developing case. Henkel, hip deep in bodies, was cutting deals and divulging the whereabouts of various corpses (including Bruce Agnew's) to avoid the death penalty. Small and Ford looked to be going down as well. Small had already lost his job on the police force, and that appeared to be the least of his problems. He was headed to prison, and so were a few others. Junior was still a bit player in the unfolding drama but had been named as a participant by at least one co-conspirator, Jack "the Jew" Siggson. (Interestingly, Siggson's testimony revealed that Junior had been on Henkel's hit list as well.)

In an effort to block Siggson's testimony, Kripplebauer provided his attorney with several well-researched strategies, including the argument that "convicted perjurers were incompetent to testify in trials in Pennsylvania." Hence, "the Jew's" testimony was highly tainted and should be thrown out. Junior also investigated other aspects of the case: prosecutorial misconduct, statute of limitation questions, and specific failures of the Investigating Grand Jury that had started the probe.

Weeks and months passed without his being brought to trial, and Kripplebauer gradually began to focus on a procedural issue that had the potential of being a legal thunderbolt—a veritable strike from the heavens that could win his freedom. He began to concentrate his energies on this rarely applied point of law.

Junior had first become aware of the critical importance of "speedy trial" issues as he watched the North Carolina prosecutions unfold. The point had implanted itself in his brain when Teddy Wigerman beat one of his cases because the local authorities waited too long to bring him to trial. It had caused a minor political uproar in Guilford County when a "Hallmark kingpin" had to be let off the hook and sent back to federal prison without ever facing the many individuals he had victimized. (Ultimately this embarrassing prosecutorial oversight got the Guilford County district attorney kicked out of office.) Kripplebauer, an accomplished jailhouse lawyer, was impressed.

As the days ticked away with no scheduled trial date, Junior was encouraged to ponder the chance of the same scenario happening in Pennsylvania. Could he beat the Allegheny County District Attorney's Office through a procedural technicality the same way Wigerman had beat them in North Carolina? Just in case, though, Junior started to line up potential witnesses as he had done earlier in Greensboro. The bluff worked once, he thought to himself; why not again?

Meanwhile, Junior spent days examining pertinent features of the Interstate Agreement on Detainers. He quickly recognized the document as "a powerful tool in the hands of a knowledgeable defendant," one that enabled prisoners to "get detainers off their backs." Specifically, according to Kripplebauer, "articles 3 and 4 of the Interstate Agreement made it mandatory that a detainee be tried within 120 days." If the prosecutor's office didn't move within that time frame, the defendant had to be set free.

"I thought I had them," recalls Kripplebauer, "but you can't ever be sure. Going into any courtroom was always somewhat of a crapshoot. I can tell you, though, it was the longest 120 days of my life. I watched those 120 days click by and feared they'd come for me one day and that would be it. They caught their mistake and I was in the soup. But they never did. They let those 120 days run out. Like I always say, the government can really fuck things up."

Kripplebauer still remembers the reaction of his attorney when he first let him in on his little jailhouse research project. "Healey came to see me at the prison one day to go over a few things," says Junior, "when I asked him to take a minute and look at a 'motion to quash' petition I had put together. He said he didn't have time; he'd read it later. He said we had a few more important things to discuss regarding the impending trial. I told him, 'We ain't gonna have a trial. I got Kim Riester [the Allegheny County Deputy District Attorney] by the nuts. Read the petition.'

"Healey's reading and reading, and you can start to see his eyes grow more focused and an intense expression come over his face. Then he looks up at me with this wide-eyed grin and says, 'I'll be a son-of-a-bitch. I think you got 'em. You got 'em by the balls.' "

A similar scene was played out a short time later, this time in an Allegheny County courtroom in front of a Common Pleas Court judge. As soon as Judge Ralph Cappy gaveled the courtroom to order, attorney Healey stood up and said, "Your Honor, my client would like to file a petition before the court."

Judge Cappy agreed to examine the document and began to read the six-page petition. He showed only modest interest until he reached page four, at which point he raised his eyes from the document, looked carefully at the defendant, and then glanced at the prosecutor.

The judge's reaction was just what Junior had hoped for. "I totally blindsided them," says Junior. "They had no idea this was coming."

Judge Cappy could do only one thing—Junior had quoted what the Interstate Agreement on Detainers prescribed in such situations: "the judge having jurisdiction must dismiss with prejudice."

Kripplebauer had beaten them again. Of course, the Allegheny County DA appealed the decision, which kept Junior on ice in Pittsburgh for many more months, but the Sword of Damocles was no longer hanging above his head. His research was flawless and his arguments factually sound: the law was behind him. Others in the Rooney conspiracy took a fall and did time, but Kripplebauer had extricated himself from a bad one. He wasn't a free man—he was going back to Lewisburg to finish his federal sentence and faced a lengthy term in North Carolina after that. But for the moment there was reason to celebrate. There was one less prison sentence to do.

AFTER YEARS IN THE LEGAL wilderness fighting off the best prosecutors Greensboro, Houston, Los Angeles, and Pittsburgh—not to mention the federal government—had to throw at him, Junior thought the end was in sight. He had dragged out his Lewisburg stay as long as he could in order to avoid spending any more time than he had to in shitty Tar Heel prisons, but once that ordeal was completed he'd be out, a free man again. As distant as that prospect once seemed when he was the target of varied, multistate criminal indictments, he realized that North Carolina could be his last stop (if no one else dropped a detainer on him, of course) and that attaining parole was the quickest way to advance his release. It wouldn't be easy, considering that authorities throughout the state believed he had gotten away with a far lighter sentence than he deserved. He approached this critical window of opportunity in typical Kripplebauer fashion—methodically, but with relentless determination and sparkling originality.

The Philly burglar first set up shop in the prison law library, developing a plan and researching everything he could get his hands on that dealt with the state's parole laws and good-time statutes. He was pleased to discover that whereas criminal sanctions there could be nothing short of draconian, the state also provided for a liberal amount of earned time credit. In other words, good behavior and accomplishments such as educational credits could be translated into a certain number of days off one's sentence per month. Junior wasn't going to miss out on a single opportunity. In fact, he even created a few credit-earning vehicles of his own.

As he settled in for what looked like a long haul in North Carolina, Junior was fortunate to have the support of many friends, both old and new. One of the latter was Cheryl McConnell, Junior's new flame, who had obtained a divorce from her husband and continued to nurture her evolving relationship with the magnetic and accomplished Philly burglar. She wrote, phoned, and visited Junior often. Sometimes she was flown in by John Stayton, one of Junior's friends from Philadelphia, who was now piloting his own aircraft. Stayton, also known as Gallagher on the streets of his hometown, had cultivated one of the larger shoplifting operations in the Delaware Valley until the lure of even bigger money in the drug trade caused him to switch fields. Like many others in the seventies, he did well in the meth business and was rolling in money.

Some of the cash was used to pay off guards at the various North Carolina institutions where Kripplebauer was imprisoned. A little private time with the attractive brunette or some extra phone time was worth a couple hundred dollars. Money always talked and Stayton's largess allowed Junior to do a lot of talking (as well as a few other things).

Stayton always offered Junior money during his visits. Appreciative but not greedy, Junior sometimes declined the friendly gesture. On one such occasion, Stayton surreptitiously passed a fistful of cash to a Reidsville Road Camp inmate to give to Kripplebauer at a later time. Stayton made a couple of mistakes during the transaction, however. He pulled the cash from the wrong pocket, thereby giving considerably more than he intended, and he compounded the mistake by giving it to the wrong inmate. The prisoner, a well-known snitch in the camp, was staggered to count out $2,800, which he dutifully passed on to Kripplebauer. Unfortunately, he also told one of the road camp captains about the transaction.

Soon after, a captain confronted Kripplebauer in the exercise yard. "Okay, Kripplebauer," he barked, "strip down."

"Whaddya talking about?" asked Junior, who was running laps on the track.

"You heard me, Kripplebauer. Strip. I want everything off."

"Like hell I will," said Junior, who had no intention of getting jaybird naked while dozens of men were exercising in the yard.

"Kripplebauer, I'm ordering you to strip down," said the increasingly agitated officer. "Are you going to disobey a direct order?"

Junior knew as well as anyone how unusual such a command was. In some prisons such a public affront to a prisoner's manhood was unthinkable; it could get a guard killed. He knew that the captain had grown frustrated trying to locate the money from Stayton. The captain had already rifled Kribblebauer's bunk, locker, baggage, workplace, and anywhere else he could think of. He was desperate to get ahold of the money and now looking to see if it was secreted on Junior's body.

Reluctantly, Kripplebauer shed his jogging shorts, T-shirt, underwear, socks, and track shoes. "You know this ain't right, man," he said. "This is some serious shit you're causing here." The captain then performed a body cavity search right there in the prison yard, for all to see. It was humiliating experience for Kripplebauer, but once again, the captain failed to find the money.

Blood had been spilt over less serious personal insults in the yard, and Kripplebauer wasn't timid about repaying debts, but this time he chose to be diplomatic. He had gotten over on the officer, he still had the money, and, more important, he wanted to get the hell out of North Carolina. He was building up parole credits, getting visits from Cheryl, and didn't want anything to derail his game plan.

Oblivious to his near-death experience, the captain kept a close eye on Kripplebauer. Junior had initially hid the knot of money below ground on the Reidsville complex but then removed it and distributed the cash among trusted members of the prison population. The institution had a rule that an inmate could have up to $25 in his possession. Junior doled out the money and gave each man a dollar a week for his services. Officers thought it unusual that some perennially broke prisoners were now loaded with cash, but they never got a handle on the source of their sudden windfall.

Despite the many years Junior still owed North Carolina and Cheryl's desire to find a romantic partner who wasn't in jail, their attraction to each other was strong and genuine. They were not blind to the insanity of it all; they just chose to downplay the hurdles and improbabilities. They were in love.

Junior felt fresh and alive knowing that a beautiful woman like Cheryl was in love with him; he was as happy as he could be, considering he had been behind bars for eight years and was facing that much and more in the future if the authorities got their way. He still kept in touch with Mickie, but they were no longer husband and wife. She was trying to get her life back together and raise her son in Cherry Hill. The adjustment had not been easy. Even though she was a woman, and even though she was eligible for parole, the North Carolina authorities were in no mood to hand a "get out of jail" pass to a member of the Hallmark Gang. Mickie had suffered in prison, and it had taken a toll on her health.

With marriage on his mind, Junior had to get his divorce papers, and Mickie was the one who had them. It wasn't a phone call he delighted in making, but it had to be done. He needed the paperwork if he was to marry Cheryl. When Mickie asked why he needed the documents, Junior told her he had met someone and wanted to marry her. Mickie was momentarily silent and then began to cry. Though they had been divorced for several years and each had become involved with someone else, there was still a bond between them. Mickie was shaken by the news.

Junior tried to explain. Tough cookie that she was, Mickie quickly regained her composure, wiped away the tears, and joked, "She's not one of the bulldykes from Central Prison, is she?"

Once he assured her that he hadn't developed an interest in any pushy, tough-talking North Carolina lesbians, Junior began to talk about Cheryl—how they had met, their growing fondness for each other, and her strong support, despite his lengthy incarceration and constant transfers between institutions.

Mickie listened and understood, maybe better than anyone else in the world could. She had gone through a similar experience with the handsome, self-assured Philly burglar. In fact, just over 10 years ago she had fallen for him and come East without even having met him. Their mutual attraction blossomed through correspondence and a couple of worn photographs. Mickie understood why women were attracted to Junior, and also why a person locked in a concrete box for years needed somebody on the outside.

Junior could tell that something other than his planned marriage was bothering her. "Mickie, what's wrong?" he asked. "Something else is going on, isn't it?"

"I'm not good," said Mickie. "I guess all that shit is catching up with me."

"Whaddya talkin' about?" asked Junior.

"Remember I told you about those lumps I had? It's breast cancer."

Taken aback, Junior waited before replying. He didn't like where the conversation was headed. He wanted to ask how serious it was, but could only come out with, "Was it from the implants?"

"No, I don't think so," said Mickie. "I knew I had a problem down in North Carolina. I could feel the lumps and told the prison authorities I had a problem and needed to see a doctor at a hospital, but they just passed it off. They should've checked me out and taken care of it down there."

"What are you gonna do?" asked Junior.

"The doctor's talking about taking my breasts off," said Mickie.

"It's that bad?" said Junior, for the first time realizing the seriousness of the situation.

"Yeah," said Mickie, "it's pretty bad."

Mickie's condition frightened him. He felt helpless. It was hard to picture his old partner—spirited, cute, full of energy, the physical equal of most men he had ever worked with—in such bad shape. He told a couple of captains and sergeants about his former wife's condition, and they allowed him some additional phone time to check on things periodically. The conversations grew shorter and more ominous.

Calling for an update one day, Junior heard the terrible news. Mickie's breasts had been removed; she had had a radical mastectomy. "The doctor said if he didn't take them off, the cancer would spread," Mickie told him. Junior felt instantaneously drained, as if a large vacuum had just sucked the life force out of him.

Their next conversation was equally bleak. "My luck is still the same—bad," said Mickie despondently. "It's spread. It's in my lower back now. It's getting worse. It's probably going inside and if that happens it's all over. They can't take my insides out like they did my breasts."

"What's the doctor say?" asked Junior, who had had an indication that things weren't going well when, in an earlier conversation, Mickie had said her hips were bothering her.

"He wants to put me in the hospital and give me radiation and chemo," she said.

"What's that gonna do?" asked Junior.

"Hopefully arrest it," said Mickie.

"You're getting arrested again?" Junior said in mock horror, trying to inject some humor into the painful conversation.

"Yeah," she replied, trying to put up a good front, "now I'm getting arrested by doctors."

The attempt to lighten the mood was fleeting, however. "The doctor has given me 20 months," she said. "Maybe two years."

"I felt terrible," recalls Kripplebauer. "There was nothing I could do for her. She was in terrible pain and slowly dying and I was locked away in a series of shitty little prisons with little prospect of getting out anytime soon. Yeah, we were quite a couple.

"I could tell how weak she was getting. It was pretty bad. She would tell me how horrible she felt and admitted that if she had known it was gonna be this bad, she wouldn't have taken the chemo and radiation."

Their next—and last—phone conversation was arranged by their friend and attorney Steve LaCheen. "I was notified by Carl Jackson, a close friend of Mickie's, that she was in bad shape and hospitalized at the University of Pennsylvania," recalls LaCheen. "After work that evening, my wife and I went to see her at the hospital. A nurse told us what room she was in, but when we entered there was just a little old, bald-headed man laying there unconscious. I told Helen we must have entered the wrong room, but she said we had the right numbered room. I still thought there had been a mixup, so I went back to the nurse and said there must be a mistake. Someone else was in that room. We're looking for Mickie D'Ulisse. She told me we were in the correct room; that unrecognizable figure lying there in a fetal position was Mickie. She didn't have long."

LaCheen hurriedly got on the phone with North Carolina correctional authorities and later that evening arranged for Junior to talk to Mickie by phone. As Steve wrote of the incident many years later, "I held the phone to her ear, and could hear Junior telling her that he loved her, that he had always loved her. There seemed to be a barely perceptible change in the expression on her face. I thought it might be the trace of a smile; but that was all."

Steve and Helen held Mickie's hands as Junior spoke of his eternal affection for her. Though it may have been only wishful thinking on their part, the LaCheens believe Mickie's grip tightened slightly during Junior's tender monologue.

Later that night, Mickie died. It was February 20, her birthday. She was 40 years old.

ONCE AGAIN KRIPPLEBAUER'S LIFE turned around quickly. Now things were moving in his favor. He was getting married and making some history in the process, for it would be Reidsville's first wedding ceremony. The December 1, 1984, event was the talk of the penal institution. As Junior likes to say, "They had never seen anything like that at the camp."

John Stayton, a connoisseur of clothing, flew in from Philadelphia with a slick new suit for the groom and was promptly appointed the best man. Junior's sister and brother-in-law also flew in from Philly. A Baptist preacher from the local town was hired to perform the afternoon service, and Cheryl brought in five maids-of-honor to walk down the makeshift runway with her. The camp cooks prepared a special meal and baked an impressive layered wedding cake. It was quite a lavish ceremony for the dusty old eyesore of a road camp, and wide-eyed prisoners sat transfixed by the highly unusual slice of normality and wholesome excitement in their midst.

The new Mrs. Kripplebauer planned the entire event and wasn't the least bit deterred by the unusual location or the lack of historical precedent. "Cheryl knew how to get what she wanted," says Junior. "She was a very strong-willed, controlling person and was always able to get people to eat out of her hand." That included Reidsville's tough-edged captain. "She came up for the event several days early to ensure her plans were carried out properly," says Junior, "and was initially met with a series of 'no's' and 'can't do that' answers by the captain. But she would turn on the charm and flash that gorgeous smile and before long she was getting everything she wanted. The captain just couldn't resist her."

And what she couldn't get by charm, Stayton's money could usually buy. That evening, after the wedding reception was over and most of the 50 or so guests had departed, including the captain, a well-paid sergeant allowed Junior to take his new bride to the road camp's marital suite—the captain's office. There, Junior promptly cleared off the cluttered desk and consummated the marriage with the new Mrs. Kripplebauer. (Not long after, Cheryl called from Fort Lauderdale. "Guess what?" she asked cheerfully. "You're pregnant," replied Junior without missing a beat. "How'd you know?" asked Cheryl. "I know," said Junior. "Believe me, I know. After all the years I been locked up without any sexual activity, I could get a gas range pregnant." On June 21, 1985, three pound, three ounce Shannon Lee Kripplebauer was born in a Fort Lauderdale hospital.)

Despite his new marital status, Junior was still the property of North Carolina and had to adjust to life inside the camp. At Reidsville he had what he called "the worst fucking job in the world" as the unit's "television man." It might seem to be a piece of cake compared with working on a road crew in 96 degree heat (as an escape risk, Junior wasn't allowed to work outside the prison compound), but the job of scheduling what prisoners could watch on television had some definite drawbacks.

"My unit had a few dozen men, but only two TVs," says Kripplebauer. "Fights occurred all the time over what shows the guys were gonna watch. The blacks wanted to see things like *Dallas, Dynasty, Soul Train,* and soap operas while the whites were into movies and sports. Things could get damn nasty if somebody was insistent on watching a program that was different than what the majority wanted to watch or what I had scheduled. Democracy and voting had nothing to do with it. Fights between competing television enthusiasts were a regular part of the daily activities. The TV man scheduled what could be watched, so I'm being threatened and bribed all the time. No matter what I did, there were always guys who were angry and pissed off at me. It was a real pain in the ass, that job.

"The only time I really gave a shit what was on the tube was when Villanova played Georgetown for the NCAA basketball championship in 1985. I told them all to go to hell, that's what we were watching. If they didn't like it, they could get the hell out and pound sand."

Though Cheryl's visits were a nice respite and the money he received from friends kept him well supplied with reefer and other forms of contraband, Junior's high-profile status in the road camp drew some envy. Not surprisingly, a couple of inmates looked to gain an advantage by ratting him out. An investigation resulted in a shakeup at the facility and Kripplebauer being disciplined and shipped back to the state's maximum-security penitentiary in Raleigh. It wasn't the best of times for Junior.

"When I was transferred to North Carolina's Central Prison from Reidsville Road Camp," says Junior, "they treated me like shit. They never missed an opportunity to bust my chops. I was given the worst jobs, the lousiest assignments, and the guards made it clear they were out to get me. Basically, my life wouldn't be worth shit for as long as I was there. I finally confronted one of the guards and asked, 'Why the hell is everyone out to fuck me over? What had I ever done to anybody at Central?'

"He didn't mince any words. He called me a lousy rat and said I ratted on a guard at Reidsville and cost the guy his job. He said they hated rats at Reidsville and said they were gonna fuck me over every chance they got.

"I couldn't believe it. I told him he better go check my jacket again. I told him I didn't rat on anybody and that was a motherfuckin' fact that was known to every cop, FBI agent, and prison guard in North America. I told him I was transferred to this shithouse of a prison because I wouldn't talk. I had a good thing going at the road camp, a real good thing, but somebody ratted on me and the officer who helped me set it up. The authorities wanted both of us to talk, admit what had gone down, but neither of us would cooperate. The officer quit on his own because he wasn't gonna talk. They punished me by shipping my ass out to Central Prison.

"I must have made an impression because he did check things out and things changed big time right after that. From that time on I had it pretty good. They treated me pretty damn well after they realized me and the sergeant were okay and somebody else had informed on us."

It was a temporary respite, however. Throughout the 1980s Junior was periodically shopped around from one North Carolina prison to another, transfers without rhyme or reason—sometimes a high-rise, maximum-security institution; at other times a less restrictive road camp. From Central Prison in Raleigh, which he considered "a nightmare," he was moved to Reidsville Road Camp, then back to Central, and then to institutions in Ashville, Salisbury, and Yanceyville after that. It sure seemed like North Carolina's version of diesel therapy.

For Kripplebauer, the Ashville experience was particularly bad, not so much for its harsh conditions as for its location. It was out in the sticks and a horrendous trek for his new wife. "You had to take four planes to get there from anywhere," he claims . "I didn't want Cheryl making that exhausting trip from Fort Lauderdale to Ashville. I wanted out of there bad, so I just shut it down. I stopped participating in everything. It caught their attention pretty quick."

Playing a risky game of chicken, Junior decided not to report to his work assignment on the laundry detail. The captain sought him out. "Kripplebauer, you haven't reported for work in three days. What's the story?"

"I'm sorry, Cap," said Kripplebauer, "but I don't belong here and I'm not gonna do any work here. I wanna be transferred out."

"You want what?" said the captain in disbelief.

Junior explained where he had been, the years he had in, and his willingness to work any job, but not in Ashville, North Carolina.

The captain got a kick out of the Yankee's brazen attitude. He could have dealt the recalcitrant prisoner time in solitary or a good old-fashioned thumping, but he decided to check out the inmate's jacket first. It proved to be a good move for both of them. Kripplebauer's folder was impressive. The state was still quite interested in the leader of the Hallmark Gang and directed that he be kept under close watch and separated from enemies (Seher and Wigerman) as well as friends (Roche and Logue). The file also explained why he was moved around the state so often: it was at the request of the FBI. Joe Dougherty, a bank robber par excellence and one of the FBI's most wanted fugitives, was on the loose, and some at the Bureau believed he was planning to break Kripplebauer out of prison. Realizing that the straight-talking burglar might be more trouble than he was worth, the captain shipped him out on the first bus the very next day.

WHATEVER HARSH OR dilapidated penal institution he called home, Junior always directed each day's activities to improving his case for parole. He wanted out bad.

"I spent hours in the law library going over anything that had to do with the parole process," he says. "Some things like five days a month for participating in an educational program were well known and heavily bought into by the those inmates looking for the quickest way out. But there were a few others that were on the books that hadn't ever been utilized or had just plain been forgotten about over the years. For example, I discovered that captains of the guard had the power to make good-time recommendations over and above what various programs offered. I asked a few officers about it, and they thought I was trying to get over on them.

"Even though they didn't seem to be aware of it, I came up with a plan to grab that extra time off. I was gonna paint the entire Yanceyville prison complex and make myself indispensable to a certain captain I had in mind. I told Captain Rodgers, 'You supply the paint and I'll put a crew together. I'll paint the entire place and you'll end up looking real good to your boss.'

"Captain Rodgers, a real old-timer, was skeptical. He thought I was trying to con him. He came out and said, 'Kripplebauer, you son-of-a-bitch, if you get me fired I'm gonna kill you. I'm tellin' you, I'll come up to Philly and get you.'

" 'Hell,' I replied, 'you should know better than to come up to the big city looking for me, Captain. Your family would never see you again. Besides, you let me do this project and you'll probably get a merit raise. Maybe bumped up to warden.'

"When we were done painting the joint, I asked him for 30 days for six months. He nearly fell over, but he eventually signed the papers."

Another earned-time vehicle for Kripplebauer was participation in educational programs. Although this was a widely accepted form of good time, not every prison in the North Carolina battery of penal institutions offered such programs. This presented a definite problem for inmates set on accruing as much time as possible through their schooling. Kripplebauer had the additional problem of being shopped around—a year or two at Reidsville and Yanceyville road camps and a few years at Central and Salisbury state prisons. Not to be deterred, he decided to start educational programs where none had existed before. He was on a mission, and North Carolina's lack of programmatic and rehabilitative initiative wasn't going to stop him.

"When I was transferred to Yanceyville," he says, "I was disappointed to learn that the only educational program they offered was a welding course provided by the Piedmont Community College and Technical Institute. There were no liberal arts courses of any kind, and only a few guys at a time could get into the welding program. I was really upset and considered threatening them with a class action suit, but I figured that would take years to go through the courts. Then I thought of another way to jump-start things. I began having a number of conversations with administrators from the college and the road camp. They basically gave me a bullshit story that they couldn't offer any college courses at the prison because they didn't have enough interest. There weren't enough guys with high school diplomas to take college-level courses. I told them they'd have those guys if they offered a GED program at the camp.

"I guess they thought I'd get off their backs if they threw me a bone, but they never expected me to run with it. They let me start a high school equivalency program, but said they didn't think it would fly because I'd need 15 students to start a class. I got guys to join up by telling them that they could further their education, get a diploma, and five days a month on top of that. To the administration's surprise, the program took off, and pretty soon we had the bodies we needed for Piedmont Technical to offer college courses. Unfortunately, the college had problems getting qualified college instructors to come into the camp and teach us anything but psychology courses. I ended up taking so many damn psych courses I was beginning to think I was Sigmund Freud. I didn't really care, however, 'cause I was really after the good-time credits. Five days per month added up, and I wanted out of North Carolina."

Another component of the parole campaign was Kripplebauer's letter-writing effort. No friend or influential authority went unsolicited. Letters from teachers, counselors, social workers, lawyers, his wife, future employers, and a host of other cronies and contacts flooded the North Carolina parole board. One would have thought the middle-aged second story man was a beloved rock star as opposed to a common thief trying to get out of doing additional time.

Letters spoke of the parole applicant's "invaluable service to the educational program," a wife's "complete faith and trust" that her husband "would never return to prison life," and a Philadelphia store manager's commitment to provide him with a job if he was set free.

Kripplebauer's own letter to Walter Johnson, Jr., the chairman of the North Carolina Parole Commission, was a classic. In the highly diplomatic missive, Junior transformed himself not only into a model prisoner but also into a champion of moral rectitude, a proponent of sober reflection, and a shining example of the rehabilitative powers of the North Carolina prison system.

The two-page single-spaced letter spoke of a "48-year-old individual" taking stock of his life and recognizing that this was his "last shot" in a "country [that has] become hardened toward crime and criminals." Kripplebauer admitted to being a "complete failure," a "thief" who "stole other people's property and got caught numerous times." Now, he argued, "I have decided that if I quit being a thief and stop stealing, I can live outside in society, free from crime." Reflecting on his many failures, stating that he was "free of criminal associates over the last seven years," and recognizing that he "must change" his life, Junior announced, "This is it!" He was finally prepared to go straight, "live under parole rules . . . and not violate any trust the Commission would place in [him]."

Letter-writing campaigns were a standard part of the parole process for proactive petitioners seeking the earliest possible release date. Letters from prison staff extolling the virtues of felons born again as law-abiding citizens were nothing new; teachers, counselors, and case managers had been writing them for years. Junior added a new wrinkle to the practice, recruiting a hitherto untapped arsenal of supporters: prison guards.

Turnkeys had always been thought to have too adversarial a relationship with the inmates to comment favorably on a prisoner's parole petition. Junior, however, was on a mission and unwilling to leave any stone unturned. Screws, too, were drafted to participate in the "free Junior" campaign. The results were impressive. One correctional officer who also claimed to be a "minister" found "Louis to be a good influence upon the other inmates, especially the younger ones that are sometimes more in need of a guiding hand." To this morally concerned officer, Junior was "kind and courteous . . . spent much of his time reading and writing" and was usually "constructively" engaged "both mentally and physically."

Another CO claimed that Kripplebauer was "personable, responsible," and always displayed a "mature and good attitude." For another uniformed officer, Junior was "kind and courteous" and a good bet to do "very good on the outside." Letter after letter underscored his many good attributes, positive contributions to his surroundings, and favorable prospects for adapting to the free world. Reading the officers' complimentary letters, in fact, one wonders what such a magnanimous figure was doing in prison in the first place.

The parole board must have been impressed, if only because they were hearing from their own front-line troops for the first time. If the more discerning members of the board detected a certain uniformity in terms of vocabulary, style, and syntax in the letters, there was a good reason. Kripplebauer had written them all and then had the guards affix their signatures to the positive commentaries. If nothing else, he was creative and industrious.

"I had good relations with a number of guards," he says, "and asked a few of them to write something in my behalf for the parole board. Most of the guys said they'd like to help, but didn't feel comfortable writing anything. They weren't really writers, if you know what I mean. They said, 'Junior, you write something good that won't get us in trouble and we'll sign it.' So that's what I did."

Though Kripplebauer's demeanor was exemplary and his multifaceted, military-style campaign to gain parole was nothing short of remarkable, he was repeatedly denied parole. And maybe he shouldn't have been surprised. For years the Hallmark Gang had been an extraordinary problem in the state, and Junior had become an exceptional case, something of a prized catch. Not only was he one of the ringleaders of the gang, but he was also a tough nut to crack. He didn't snap when they squeezed him as Wigerman and Seher had, and he

wouldn't hear of informing on his partners. Moreover, he had fought government prosecutors and lawmen every inch of the way and always appeared to be
getting over on them, manipulating the system for his own benefit. They weren't
going to make it easy for him to gain parole, especially if one dedicated North
Carolina detective had anything to say about it.

Larry Davis, a good ole boy from Greensboro had made catching the Hall-
mark Gang something of a crusade. He took the gang's annual raiding parties
through the state as a personal affront and was determined to nail them, to
force them to see the error of their ways, to make them pay and repent. In fact,
North Carolina's version of Bill Skarbek did his FBI compatriot one better:
Davis converted gang members into Bible-thumping, toe-the-line citizens. Both
Tommy Seher and Teddy Wigerman had been miraculously transformed into
God-fearing church-goers by the Greensboro cop. Detective Larry Davis was
somewhat scary. Like Captain Ahab setting out to capture the great white whale,
he was more than a little interested in making sure Louis James Kripplebauer
never led another marauding party through his state again.

As Locke Clifford, Kripplebauer's North Carolina attorney, wrote him in
December 1983, "it appears that we are a long ways from getting you paroled."
Despite the massive effort to influence them, parole board members considered
Junior "not parole material," and Davis had a good deal to do with it.

Three months later, Clifford wrote to his client, "I am convinced that in
order to get you any favorable consideration by the North Carolina Parole Board
anytime soon we are going to have to get a recommendation from . . . Larry
Davis, the detective who was in charge of the investigation." Clifford said that
Davis' "basic problem" was "fear for the safety of some of your former colleagues." And if Junior wanted any hope of getting out of prison, he'd have to "belly
up . . . and put yourself in the same boat with their people."

In other words, Detective Davis feared that Kripplebauer would terminate
the lives of Tommy Seher and Teddy Wigerman if he got out of prison. In order
to preclude that possibility, Davis hoped to keep Junior behind bars as long as
possible. And the only way to escape this harsh scenario was to rat out his friends
and partners and become a government informant like Seher and Wigerman.
Clifford asked his client to "think it over and let me know if you want me to
arrange a meeting."

Several days later, Junior ripped off a note to his friend and legal advisor back
home in Philadelphia, attorney Steve LaCheen, telling him about the "terrible
letter" he had received from Locke Clifford. Though he didn't go into great depth
regarding the "freedom for cooperation" deal, he didn't have to. LaCheen knew
what Junior's answer would be. Never a big communicator, Junior wasn't going
to start now. He just wasn't made that way. Beginning his eighth consecutive
year behind bars—with many more to go if Larry Davis had anything to say

about it—Junior just tightened his belt, did his time, smoked reefer, perfected his handball game, and continued to work toward his release.

Parole efforts continued, and in late spring of 1984 Kripplebauer received another letter from his North Carolina attorney. According to Clifford, Detective Davis "has agreed to get off your back and recommend your parole . . . if we will set up the following procedure . . . to prevent you from coming back to North Carolina ever again to bother anybody." The deal required Junior to "provide a detailed description of some crime that you have committed in North Carolina, e.g., conspiring to hijack a cigarette truck." Moreover, the "confession statement" had to contain "sufficient details" for successful prosecution and would be held by Clifford indefinitely. Unless, of course, Junior returned to the state and Davis nabbed him, which would oblige Clifford to turn over the incriminating letter.

Clifford stated his discomfort with being a middleman in such an unusual deal and asked for his client's reaction. Once again Junior was unimpressed but asked Steve LaCheen to contact Clifford so the two attorneys could discuss the matter.

LaCheen told Clifford the offer was "somewhat surprising." Why, he asked, couldn't they all "avoid a whole lot of aggravation" in addition to a "1,000 legal questions" by just making it part of Kripplebauer's parole that "he not return to North Carolina?"

Later, in a memo to himself, LaCheen attributed "Davis' paranoia" to the detective's investment in getting "both Seher and Wigerman out of jail, living and working in Greensboro, and attending his own church. They have become personal friends and he personally guaranteed their safety." Davis' concern, according to LaCheen, was simple. "He presently feels certain that Junior will in fact try to kill one or both of them."

LaCheen planned to discuss these issues with Clifford and Davis during a previously scheduled visit to North Carolina to see his imprisoned friend. After returning from his May 1984 information-gathering trip, LaCheen penned another memo for his own personal file: "Davis will not let up nor will he just let events take their normal course." Davis communicated that "the only thing that would really satisfy him would be for Junior to give somebody else up."

The memo also mentioned Locke Clifford's belief that Davis was "absolutely paranoid" about Kripplebauer, and it wasn't just due to his concern for "Seher and Wigerman, but about himself as well." Clifford also stated that the "head of the Parole Board is a good friend of his, but absolutely refuses to stick his neck out unless Davis backs off."

LaCheen was struck by Detective Davis' fear of Kripplebauer and his determination to "harass" him at every opportunity. The North Carolina law enforcement officer might well "be waiting at the prison door whenever it is that Junior is released" in order to re-arrest him. Considering the parole embargo and less than impressed with Clifford's representation of Junior, LaCheen believed it was time to discover whether another attorney might "be interested in this matter" and also time to examine the "parole law" to see whether "the board is abusing its discretion" in this case.

Over the next few years, a new attorney was hired, new strategies were pursued, honor-grade status was attained (normally a prerequisite for parole), and letters continued to be written on Junior's behalf (including one from Tommy Seher). Still there was no relief. Kripplebauer was buried. North Carolina had him and didn't want to give him up. Unwilling to name names, perceived as a threat to lawmen, and of no great interest to the parole commission, Junior watched the months of the calendar pass over and over and over again. Though he did not give up hope or stop working toward his release, Junior recognized that he was paying dearly for his former forays through North Carolina as part of the Hallmark Gang.

THE LONG-AWAITED event occurred on December 11, 1989, and was as un-expected as it was unceremonious: a haggard Yanceyville correctional officer barking out, "Kripplebauer, get all your gear together. You're discharged."

"Whaddya mean I'm discharged?" said Junior, anticipating another prison transfer. "Where they sending me now?"

"Wherever you want," the officer replied.

"Whaddya mean, wherever I want? Just tell me where they're sending me."

"They're not sending you anywhere," said the sergeant. "You're out. Your sentence is over. You're done."

You couldn't blame Junior for initially believing he was being transferred to another miserable, overcrowded North Carolina penal institution, since such abrupt and unsettling transfers had become commonplace over the last decade. But this time it was different; he was being released, his time was up. He had maxed out.

It had been quite a stretch: nearly a decade and a half of his life, a couple dozen prisons, and the years from 1975 to 1989 a shadowy blur of dirty cell-blocks, harsh overseers, and lost opportunities. Junior was still afraid it was all a big joke or, more likely, a ruse—that the FBI would be waiting outside the prison gate to re-arrest him for the Rooney caper. But, in fact, the seemingly interminable ordeal had finally come to an end. He was a free man again.

Cheryl, always one to make the most of a jubilant occasion, sent a Mercedes to collect Junior at the prison's front gate and deliver him to the Raleigh airport, where an expensive suit and a ticket to Fort Lauderdale awaited him. Upon land-ing in the Sunshine State, he was met at the terminal by Cheryl and her equally beautiful sister, Suzanne, who was driving her fancy red Cadillac convertible.

They drove him to a big party in his honor. The next 24 hours were a blur of back-slapping, joyous celebrations and introductions to Cheryl's family and friends, but through the euphoria something was starting to eat at him. The next day at Joe Zonka's, a popular restaurant in Miami Beach, Junior half-heartedly listened to the upbeat chatter and words of encouragement from Cheryl's well-heeled friends. He appreciated the toasts and good wishes and luxuriated in no longer having anyone order him around. The freedom to move about was exhilarating. But one concern weighed on his mind: "What am I gonna do now?"

15. From Burglary to Drugs

CHERYL, A COSMETOLOGIST, was renting a nice house in the Pembroke Pines area and painting nails at an upscale beauty salon that drew a fairly comfortable crowd. Junior, keeping to his prison regimen, was up early every morning and jogging through the tony neighborhood in an effort to maintain his excellent physical condition, one of the few redeeming features of life behind bars. His reaction to the lush new environment was not surprising.

"You couldn't help but notice the wealth that was all around," he says. "I said to myself, it looks like I'm gonna be doin' some work here." But there was one problem; he lacked a partner. Junior had long ago bought into a team approach to residential and commercial thievery. During the halcyon days of the K&A Gang in the 1960s, a four-man crew was a staple of production work. He and Mickie often worked together as a smaller but equally efficient unit, but two was his lower limit. He just felt more comfortable with a partner. Junior was no Chickie Goodroe: working alone wasn't his thing.

While he was away many things had changed on the outside, including home alarm systems. Companies had caught on and dispensed with operating keys and red alarm lights. Junior was unsure of himself as well as the new technology and believed he needed a partner if he was going to come up with some good scores and tackle what appeared to be more sophisticated home security equipment. New to the community, unfamiliar with the local criminal talent pool, and not wanting to get "totaled out" just after being released from prison, Junior was uncharacteristically cautious. Feeling pressed to bring in some money to support a wife who wanted the very best, Kripplebauer did something quite extraordinary: he went straight. He got a job.

"I saw a sign one day for the Fruehauf Trailer Company near Miami and decided I'd give it a try," says Junior. "I walked in cold and said, 'Do you need any help here? I need a job.' The boss asked me what I knew about big rigs and trailers, and I told him I had a lot of experience. I told him I could do anything he needed done, repair a wreck, stretch a trailer, whatever he needed."

The episode was the dream of parole officers around the world: a career criminal deciding to become a productive member of society. But there would be no storybook happy ending here. Although the work was hard, hot, and dirty—Junior called it nothing short of "backbreaking"—and paid a measly $4.80 per hour, those were not the reasons for his ethical relapse and sudden departure after only three months of work. That can be chalked up to something equally commonplace: marital difficulties.

"We were beefing bad over money," says Junior. "Cheryl was definitely high-maintenance and had to have the finest of everything. Things she didn't even need or really want became big purchase items. She must have thought I was gonna be rolling in cash and jewelry like I was in the old days. But now I'm breaking my back every day on busted trailers for little more than my pop was earning when he was working in the mines.

"It got so bad we couldn't pay our bills and they turned our water off. I remember I came home from work one Friday and gave Cheryl my paycheck and told her to go to whatever utility companies we still owed money and pay them off. She came back later that night and I asked her if she had taken care of the bills. She said no. I said, why not? She then hands me a large shopping bag containing five telephones, the latest, most expensive models. We now had a new, stylish telephone for every room in the house, but no running water."

Kripplebauer didn't threaten his wife or yell; he did what any self-respecting ex-con would do. He gave Fruehauf notice that he was quitting, called his sister in New Jersey, and asked her for an airline ticket back home. He had had enough of Florida and Cheryl. As far as he was concerned, the marriage was over. Though they had been an ideal couple while he was incarcerated, three months together in the free world put the kibosh on their union.

Back in Philadelphia Junior quickly got a job helping Lem Byrd, an old friend, in the trailer business. Though the work was hard and the pay less than impressive, it kept him busy and let him send a weekly check to Cheryl. It wasn't long, however, before Junior got the itch and started to look around for a crew. There was only one problem; there wasn't anybody to work with any more. It was like one of those science fiction films where the hero wakes up one day to find the streets of the city deserted and everybody gone. Junior's nightmare reflected the profound changes that can occur with the passage of time. Just as Kensington's once-thriving textile industry was gone, so were the K&A thieves—gone to prison, gone to the cemetery, or gone into the drug business. Some, believe it or not, had even cleaned up their act and gone straight. Junior felt like a relic from some bygone era, the reprobate equivalent of the neighborhood iceman or milkman. He wondered if he wasn't an ancient artifact that belonged in a museum.

Junior inquired about old friends and past associates; there must be some-body out there doing production work. The news was depressing. Jimmy Dolan told him straight out, "It's over, Junior"—the K&A Gang, hitting the road, doing a half-dozen homes a night, it's done. It's over. Production work was a thing of the past.

Pressed to come up with names, Dolan could think of only one decent crew still working, but he told Junior he probably wouldn't want to join them. Blackie Battles had a crew of about eight to ten guys. Some were okay, but others were incompetent lunkheads. Jimmy told him he'd know some of the guys and be welcome, but Junior could see the downside. Hell, he didn't need any more rats in his life. And there were already too many guys in the crew. They'd need two cars to go anywhere, probably drink a case or two of beer along the way, and require help getting out of the car by the time they got to their destination. Blackie's team sounded more like a vaudeville act than a polished unit, and having just gotten out of prison, he wasn't interested in doing any more time because of a slipshod operation. After giving it some thought, Junior decided "to pass on the opportunity."

The pull of production work and the need for money didn't dissipate, however. Kripplebauer broke into a few homes in New Jersey and Pennsylvania, but the experience wasn't all that satisfying. He was setting off alarms and having to abandon his searches before he had copped anything of consequence. Motion detectors, heat sensors, and other high-tech security devices confounded him. He discovered that many of these systems could be neutralized by cutting the phone lines, but it wasn't the same; the world had definitely changed. Burglary was a different ballgame now; it was no longer the fun and familiar enterprise it had once been.

Ever so slowly, Junior started to consider other moneymaking ventures, the kind that he had always refrained from, but that now seemed progressively more attractive—drugs. Junior weighed the pros and cons of the drug business, but he always came back to the same issue: he needed the money.

Buried in a dozen different prisons and out of commission for almost 15 years, Junior still recognized that drugs had transformed the criminal landscape. Even before he went away, some of his friends were encouraging him to get into the game. They were all doing well. But he resisted. "I knew what was going on," he says of the transition from burglary to drugs, "but I wasn't aware of the incredible amount of money that was being made. I heard stories about Hughie Breslin, Maury McAdams, Jackie Kirby, and John Berkery, but I didn't want any part of it. I didn't see where I could make the money. Who was I gonna sell it to? The people I knew buying it already had a distribution network. I didn't have anybody to sell it to. I knew guys who were selling meth to anybody and everybody. I wasn't gonna do it. With my luck, I knew I'd get ratted out.

"Burglary was dangerous, but drugs had the potential of being an even more violent world. A lot of people got hurt, but there was no real work to it. For older guys you no longer had to worry about running across lawns in freezing weather, carrying a 40-pound bag of burglary tools, or finding a buyer for what you stole. Drugs made you a hell of a lot of money. I'd say 90 percent of the K&A burglars got into drugs, and 50 percent of those got caught and did time. But the money was phenomenal."

Historically, K&A guys had very little interest in drugs; alcohol was their thing. Some guys in the fifties and early sixties had started taking diet pills and "eating bennies" because it gave them a little boost and could keep them awake for extended periods of time, a valuable commodity when you were driving across the country and then hitting a series of homes over successive nights. "You could drink for days on end without getting drunk," says one appreciative burglar.

Methamphetamine only increased their awareness, staying power, and sense of invulnerability. "Guys wanted meth," recalls Kripplebauer of the powerful stimulant. "They'd be driving, stealing, and drinking for days. Along with the euphoria, you felt like you could do anything. You felt invincible."

Years later, the burglars realized that meth could do more than keep them awake for extended periods; it could make them millionaires. As Junior said of the drug's "flood-like attraction" during the seventies, "I didn't know anybody who didn't want to get into the wholesale or retail end of it."

PHILLY COPS FIRST take notice of a new drug hitting the streets in the mid-sixties. In the beginning they're perplexed; some are even dismissive of this unfamiliar substance that seems to be centered in the black community. Frank Wallace, a retired Philadelphia police inspector, recalls an African-American informant telling him and members of the Narcotics Squad about "monster" and its incredible "effect on people." "It was 1966 and completely new," says Wallace. "Nobody knew what the guy was talking about. We told our lieutenant what we were hearing, but he wasn't interested. He told us, 'We're interested in heroin. That's what we should be looking for.' "

Within a year, however, Wallace and the Narcotics Squad would bust their first meth lab on Powelton Avenue (he recalls it as a "crude setup" that resembled something out of a "Dr. Frankenstein movie, with beakers, flasks, glass tubes, and wires all over the place") and watch the drug cross over to the white community. Within a few years meth—or what former "Five Squad" Lieutenant John Wilson called "the poor man's cocaine in the seventies"—was "moving quickly" through the city and developing quite a reputation. "There was a definite market for it on the street," says Wilson. "People were quickly getting into meth. It cranked you up and gave you a greater kick than anything else out there." Appropriately nicknamed "speed" in the white community, the drug could also be "produced easier" than most of its illicit competitors being manufactured and sold on the black market.

Methamphetamine is an artificial stimulant that releases high levels of the neurotransmitter dopamine into the brain, producing euphoria and increased energy, often lasting over 12 hours. But meth can just as easily produce paranoia, delusions, and memory loss, as well as symptoms of physical degeneration such as rotting teeth. Meth users are known to addiction counselors as some of the hardest drug addicts to treat.

Meth dealers—and the labs they needed to manufacture the product— cropped up first in South Philadelphia, then in Fishtown and Kensington. The labs were rudimentary and easily transportable; they gave off a distinctively foul odor that most people said smelled like "cat piss." Soon dealers and labs alike could be found throughout the city, enabling the Drug Enforcement Agency to label Philadelphia "the meth capital of America" during hearings before the U.S. House Select Committee on Narcotics Abuse and Control.

During those early years of the drug's evolution, the prominent names associated with it were Stevie Vento, Victor DeLuca, Salvatore Soli, and Ronald Raiton. As meth grew in popularity in the seventies and eighties, however, the surnames associated with its production and sale took on a different ethnic flavor. Pennsylvania Crime Commission reports begin to identify Hugh and David Breslin, John Berkery, Edward Loney, Maurice McAdams, Carl Jackson, Edward MacEntee, and Roy Stocker as key players in the meth business.

Though many drug gangs ultimately moved to cabins in the Poconos or other rural areas to do their "cooking," any garage or basement would do. In fact, as one meth cooker said, "All you really needed was electricity" (for the fans necessary to expel the odor and the lingering combustible fumes). A batch of methamphetamine required phenyl-2-propanone (P2P), mercury, alcohol, aluminum foil, hydrochloric acid, and monomethaline (heavy water), along with a large vat and filter, pyrex dishes, electric hot plates, and a fan or two.

P2P, or "P" or "oil," as it was also known, was far and away the most difficult of the ingredients to acquire. Without it, the manufacture of methamphetamine was impossible. Banned in America, the liquid chemical was almost worth its weight in gold, and people went to great lengths to acquire it in Europe and smuggle it into the country.

The manufacturing process began by mixing the alcohol, mercury, water, oil, and aluminum foil in a 15-gallon kettle and stirring until the foil dissolved, the temperature rose, and the chemical reaction got underway. The cooker had to stir constantly, take the temperature of the kettle's contents every 10 minutes to ensure that it didn't exceed 150 degrees, and add hydrochloric acid at the right stage. Explosions were not uncommon, and the 24-hour cooking process was physically demanding, necessitating the use of dependable personnel as neighborhood alchemists.

After a filter had cleared off the residue and impurities, the desired pH was obtained by adjusting the alcohol and hydrochloric acid levels while the liquid was kept warm on electric hot plates. When removed from the heating elements, it would quickly crystallize into the illegal and highly profitable drug.

In addition to the fear of explosions and lengthy prison terms if caught, freelance cookers had to contend with the nasty after-effects of the manufacturing process. "The stench was so strong," says Donnie Johnstone, "you couldn't stand yourself. The odor and chemicals seeped into all your pores and there was no way to get it out. I took five showers a day for four days and the odor was still there." And cookers remained high for days. "You were literally speeding," says Johnstone. "I couldn't sleep for three days."

It wasn't a fun job, but meth cookers were well paid. Johnstone says he once cooked a gallon and a half of oil over 26 hours, yielding 18 pounds of meth. At $6,000 per pound (wholesale), the final product was worth over $100,000. His share was approximately $15,000 for one day's work. Some cookers made up to $2,000 per pound.

The meth trade was extremely lucrative for everyone involved in the production and distribution of the drug. As the Pennsylvania Crime Commission reported in 1990, "vast profits" could be made. "The price of a gallon of P2P in France or West Germany in the early 1980s was $135 to $155. Once the drums reached Philadelphia, a gallon typically sold for between $2,500 to $7,500 at the wholesale level, a mark-up of between 1,800 and 4,800 percent. In the mid-1980s, a gallon . . . was selling for as high as $28,000 in Philadelphia." During the course of the decade as the price of the finished product climbed, "a gallon of P2P . . . could translate into gross profits of $60,000 to $120,000."

FOR THE KENSINGTON CROWD, the transition from burglary to drugs wasn't an overnight phenomenon, but it wasn't glacial either. It was more of a gradual, steady shift in product line spurred on by a panoply of societal, technological, and market forces. Improved policing, more sophisticated alarm systems, the greater use of personal credit cards, and the advancing age of the burglars all prompted the shift. For most, however, it just boiled down to dollars and cents. As any good businessman would tell you, go with the goods that will earn you the most money with the least amount of effort. And the K&A crowd did. Drugs had it all over second story work: you could make 10 times the money with 10 percent of the effort.

It was almost impossible for the hard-working burglars not to notice. As Donnie Johnstone says, "There was such good money in drugs you couldn't resist it. Just about everybody who wasn't away [in prison] or dead got into in it. And compared to burglary, it was no effort at all."

"The money was phenomenal," agrees Marty Bell. "Why should I take a shot breaking into places and the chance of getting caught for a couple grand when I can do a deal and make a quick hundred Gs?"

"It was incredible," says Jimmy Dolan of the rapid growth of the drug business. "The burglary business dried up in the seventies. There was nobody to work with any more. I made up my mind it was over. And for a lot of guys drugs were a million times easier and much more lucrative. It was tough to turn down a package of money when you're hurting. They were living large and getting a new Cadillac every five months. My God, they had so much money."

Though the attraction was great, it wasn't necessarily an easy progression for everyone. Some had reservations. For Jackie Johnson, who spent the seventies in prison, re-entering the underworld labor market in 1980 was quite a revelation. "No one was doing production work any more," he says. "I couldn't find a crew to work with, but guys like 'One Eye' [Maury McAdams] were constantly coming up to me and telling me all the fuckin' money they were making. C'mon in, they'd say, there's money enough for all of us."

Johnson, like many others of his milieu, resisted for a while. Drugs went against their ethic. True K&A burglars never wanted to hurt anybody and therefore never carried a weapon when they entered a private residence; they just wanted other people's money. But the need for money, and the flash and glitz of their friends trading in drugs, were like the gravitational pull of the earth. Before long, Johnson would be like so many others, arguing that if he "didn't do it somebody else would." They'd also be hip deep in money. (When he was arrested in 1983, after being ratted out by the close friend who had gotten him into the business, Johnson had over $630,000 hidden in the ceiling of his home. The Feds got him and the money.)

NOT ALL K&A MEN fell under the spell of drug dealing and the big money that came with it. Jimmy Dolan is probably the best example of a K&A burglar who resisted the temptation to make a quick fortune by peddling meth to a rapidly growing consumer market. Though he well understood the attraction of easy money, he couldn't partake in the human damage it caused. Yes, he could ransack a home without thinking twice about it, but pushing drugs was over the top. It went against his nature.

"The money was so overwhelming it was almost impossible to turn down," says Dolan. "It was like a tidal wave, an irresistible force. The growth of the drug business was incredible. It was a million times easier and much more lucrative. I saw so many guys get into it. Guys specialized in P2P in order to produce meth. Meth was the fucking poison that ruined everything. About 70 percent of the guys got into it. But I couldn't do it. I'm no fucking angel, but I just couldn't do it. It's just how I was raised. I watched neighborhoods disintegrate, turn into shit, because of drugs. They were ruining the lives of all these fucking kids. These kids are this country's future, and they were being ruined. It was awful.

"Yeah, I burgled homes, but we specialized in rich fucking people. Plus they were insured. So who were we robbing? The insurance companies. There were some stiff penalties if you got caught with drugs, but the real charge should have been treason. Cities lie in ruins today because of drugs. It's a terrible thing. Nothing of any good comes out of that shit. You're destroying our own people.

"It was hard talking to guys who were wearing $1,500 suits and driving a $30,000 Mercedes. I told some of them they were in the wrong fucking business. I said they'd rue the day. Some of them nearly got violent with me. They didn't want to hear that shit. Their attitude was drugs are already here and if I don't do it somebody else will.

"Drugs were the downfall of everything. I never robbed one of my partners and I never put any one in jail. Effie was drug-free. He never did a drug deal in his life. I was the same way. I couldn't do it. Even though the burglary business was drying up in the 1970s due to better alarm technology, movement sensors, cameras, and all that other shit, I decided I wasn't going the way of so many others. I wasn't gonna get into the drug business. I made my mind up it [burglary] was over. There was nobody to work with. Yeah, the young kids were into drugs and you could make big money, but they were getting ruined from it. I decided it wasn't for me. I wasn't gonna be part of it."

JUNIOR KRIPPLEBAUER CHOSE to take a different course. "I needed the money," he says. "The bottom line was, I was willing to move drugs even though it meant I'd catch hell if I got caught."

While still working on trailers during the day and beginning to do some part-time work as a limo driver between Philly and the Jersey shore, Junior fell into a position where he could make some quick and easy money moving P2P. It appeared simple and relatively safe; a trusted friend wanted to buy it, and another good friend wanted to sell it. As middleman in the transaction, he could bring in a good bit of cash.

All he had to do was move a gallon of the oil a few blocks: literally from one side of Philadelphia's Benjamin Franklin Parkway to the other. The eight-minute transaction would earn him an easy six grand, since he was buying the "P" for $34,000 and selling it for $40,000. Junior knew the hit he could take if caught with the oil, but he decided it would be "no problem." As he succinctly says, "I knew who I was getting it from and who I was selling it to."

Kripplebauer admits to a certain amount of nervousness, especially during those early transactions. He'd meet his supplier in the parking lot of the Ben Franklin Motor Lodge, place the gallon container of P2P in his car, and then drive south across the flag-festooned Parkway to the Park Town Place Condominium, where he would transfer the oil to the buyer. To minimize exposure and thwart government surveillance, he'd get a room at the Motor Lodge near the parking lot, watch for the arrival of his contact, and just flick the remote on his car trunk to allow the oil to be placed in the vehicle without even being present for the transaction. The Park Town Place transfer would take place just a few minutes later in the high-rise structure's underground garage, well out of sight of curious passersby. Money would be exchanged later, usually at the foot of Allegheny Avenue by the Delaware River on the deserted grounds of the old Cramp Shipyard. The delayed financial transactions—an oddity in the drug business—were possible because of Junior's close relationship with both the supplier and the buyer. He orchestrated over two dozen such deals during the early to mid-nineties. Sometimes they were multi-unit transactions, with five gallons of oil going for $175,000.

Junior was doing well. He was now driving limousines for a living during the day—mostly as a front—and bringing in the serious cash doing his periodic drug deals. He was back in business and no longer concerned about when the next dollar was coming in or where it was coming from. European vacations, new cars, expensive suits, and fancy restaurants were once again the order of the day. He was now involved with Hannah O'Brian, an attractive woman from his old Fairmount neighborhood, and the prospect of marriage was being seriously discussed. (Cheryl had died of a stroke in a Fort Lauderdale hospital on Labor Day, 1994.)

His fortunes had definitely turned. "My biggest concern," he says in all seriousness, "was where to hide all the money I was making." Banks were out of the question, and he was always worried the Feds would come busting into his new home, a beautiful house by a lake in Collingswood, New Jersey, that he paid for in large part through drug deals. Stacks of money could be found in the strangest places in the Kripplebauer household: buried under trees in the backyard, stashed behind fake walls, or hidden in restaurant-size containers of mustard and mayonnaise in the pantry. Junior even began to put a good bit of money out on the street; he had it and friends needed it.

The party came to an end, however, when his friend the oil supplier was scooped up in an FBI sting in 1995. His decision to deal only with trusted, standup friends paid off when his friend held up under pressure from prosecutors and refused to talk. It is unlikely that the authorities were ever aware of the legendary second story man's involvement with P2P. Nevertheless, his days in the meth business were over.

The loss of income did not go down well. "It was over $10,000 a month down the drain," says Kripplebauer. "When they arrested my friend, it collapsed the whole fucking deal. I was told of some other contacts, particularly a guy in North Carolina who could supply all the oil I wanted, but I said no way. I wanted no part of it. If I didn't know the people or think they were standup, I'd pass on it."

Surprisingly, Kripplebauer rebounded rather well, and in a most unexpected fashion. His next moneymaking venture was legitimate. Money attracts money, and the ever-resourceful entrepreneur stumbled into a deal with friends who were connected down at the Port of Philadelphia. He and his new partners procured a lucrative contract to pick up iron ore that had just arrived on cargo vessels from South America and move it to a nearby location. The logistics couldn't be simpler: haul the ore, which belonged to U.S. and Bethlehem Steel, from Pier 19 on Delaware Avenue to a Conrail yard near the Philadelphia Navy Yard using a fleet of dump trucks. Contracted to do at least 10 ships per year, the partners earned $1 per ton, or $70,000 per ship.

After a year in the freight-hauling business, Kripplebauer's fortunes turned once again. Infighting among the partners resulted in an ugly and irresolvable split. Junior and another partner were cut out of the deal, precipitating a series of lawsuits and countersuits, and the potential for more serious retaliatory strikes. Junior was eventually talked out of seeking revenge, and his rage over the hauling contract shenanigans was more appropriately directed at another bit of treachery that occurred at approximately the same time.

Junior had developed a stake in a Kensington card game run by his good friend Jimmy Dolan. Though neither of them was getting rich running a neighborhood poker table, it supplied them with income that they didn't want to share with someone just because he had the unilateral temerity to declare himself a partner. The would-be partner was Joey Merlino, *infant terrible* of the local Italian mob, who had appointed himself to fill the leadership void left by the lengthy imprisonments of mob bosses Nicky Scarfo and John Stanfa. Seeking a portion of the proceeds from every loan-sharking, extortion, and illegal gambling operation in the city, Skinny Joey had his street soldiers let it be known that a new street tax was in effect, and woe to those who refused to pay it.

When Merlino's emissary brought to Jimmy Dolan the bad news that he now had to pay "$500 dollars a week" tribute to run the card game, he was met with a flood of indignation and four-letter words. "Jimmy was apoplectic," recalls Junior. "He went ballistic." But that was mild compared with Kripplebauer's reaction. Already seething from the loss of the waterfront contract, Junior wasn't in a mood to get financially spanked again, especially from an upstart gangster half his age. He opted to deal with the matter in his own inimitable way.

Following a pattern developed on the streets of Philadelphia and refined in some of the toughest prisons across America, Junior planned a pre-emptive strike. Rather than request a sit-down with the young Mafia chieftain to plead their case, Kripplebauer decided to do a walk-in, a bold in-your-face confrontation in the most public of places, a fashionable riverfront restaurant. Notified that Merlino would be at the upscale La Veranda restaurant on Delaware Avenue on a certain evening, Junior staked the place out and walked in on Skinny Joey's dinner party. Attired in a dress jacket that hid a semiautomatic tucked into the small of his back, he diplomatically requested a minute of Joey's time, and the two men walked off to a quiet section of the restaurant near the bar.

"What can I do for you, Junior?" said Merlino, slightly taken aback at the unexpected visit.

"How's my credit?" asked Junior.

"Okay," said Merlino. "How much do you need?"

"Five hundred dollars," said Junior.

"Yeah, that's fine," replied Merlino, somewhat surprised by the modest figure. "Is that it?"

"Five hundred a week," said Junior, more authoritatively this time.

"Five hundred dollars a week?" said Merlino, now a little confused. "What do you need $500 a week for?"

"I need it for when they come to collect on our card game."

"What the fuck you talking about?" said Merlino, genuinely confused.

"What I'm fuckin' talkin' about," said Junior, his voice rising, "is my card game with Jimmy Dolan on Allegheny Avenue. Your boy came around wantin' $500 a week."

"Oh, I got it," said Merlino. "That game's been running a long time, and we ... "

"Forget it, Joey," said Junior cutting him off. "My partner said no and I say no. We ain't paying it."

Merlino started to shake his head and explain the way things were gonna work now. Kripplebauer wanted none of it; he hadn't come there to listen to a lecture. He was going to do the explaining.

"Listen to what I'm gonna tell you," said Junior, the veins on neck starting to bulge as he stepped closer to the young Mafioso. "This conversation is over. We're gonna walk out of here and that's gonna be the end of it. We ain't ever gonna talk about this again, you hear. Now listen to me carefully—I didn't come here without thinking of the consequences. If this is not settled now, nobody is walkin' the fuck out of here. You understand? Nobody is leaving."

"Hey, Junior," said Merlino, "take it easy. Nobody is looking to pressure you guys."

"We're not paying any street tax, Joey," said Junior. "Remember, this is our city too."

As it turned out, everybody walked out of La Veranda that evening on his own two feet. Kripplebauer had been prepared to go to war, having brought in a couple of serious players from North Carolina, friends he had made during his many years of imprisonment there. The men were stationed outside the restaurant and armed with two Mac 10 automatic pistols. They also had at their disposal two .22 caliber revolvers with silencers, two bombs, and a menacing-looking street-sweeper. For weeks afterward, one of the North Carolinians sat in a car outside the Allegheny Avenue card game just in case there was any trouble. Though many others around the city were grumbling about having to cough up a weekly payment, Dolan and Kripplebauer never paid any tribute to the boys downtown.

KRIPPLEBAUER WAS STILL driving a limo between Philly, Atlantic City, and the Big Apple. He was also keeping his eyes open for promising economic ventures; he was anxious to make up for the loss of the waterfront hauling contract. It wasn't any big surprise that a good many of his Manhattan customers and well-heeled AC gamblers were recreational drug users and always willing to pay well to score a favorite mood-altering substance. Whenever he could, Junior tried to please his wealthy clients. Most were into coke, and Junior knew where to get it; he had friends. The deals were relatively small, and the extra cash they brought in was almost insignificant.

It wasn't until he got hooked up with some serious out-of-state drug suppliers that his drug trafficking became a real moneymaking operation once again. Junior discovered a contact in North Carolina who could supply him with grass, and his old friend Eddie Loney, who had relocated to South Florida, had established business relationships with some well-stocked South American coke dealers. Junior had buyers who were interested in both grass and coke. He was well aware of the hefty penalties involved if he was caught with coke, but he rationalized that his solitary, low-level operation would fall below law enforcement's radar screen, and figured that he could pull it off if he did most of the work himself and kept the number of contacts down to a minimum. He took comfort in the fact that he had previously moved gallons of P2P without the slightest problem.

Kripplebauer went down to Florida to visit Loney and explore the idea. He was introduced to a wealthy Colombian who said he could supply whatever Junior wanted: top-shelf stuff in whatever quantities he desired. It sounded good. Junior immediately saw how he could recoup the losses from the demise of his P2P operation and ore-hauling contract. The weekly limo paycheck and the receipts from Jimmy's poker game just didn't cut it.

Kripplebauer got together $22,000 to buy a key of coke from the Colombian and decided to move the stuff himself. He didn't trust the longhaired young hippies who usually got the job of being airline pack mules. Poorly paid kids on the fringe of the drug business drew attention to themselves, were mistake-prone, and could be counted on to screw up and rat out their partners when faced with prison time. No, he'd do it himself. Junior had always done the heavy lifting; he wasn't like some insecure crew bosses who always sent the dumbest, most malleable member of the burglary team to brute a front door.

The transaction went smoothly, though Junior sweated bullets throughout the episode. He decided to minimize his exposure at the Fort Lauderdale Airport by taking possession of the package at the very last instant before he boarded the plane. Just as the boarding announcement was made, Junior hurried to the men's room, met his contact, and had the tightly wrapped package of coke placed in the bottom of a shopping bag that contained newspapers, candy, and T-shirts he had just purchased at an airport newsstand.

There wasn't a whiff of suspicion or hint of trouble from airline personnel or airport security. A well-dressed businessman in his fifties carrying an open package of souvenirs for his family set off no alarms. Moving a kilo of coke up the East Coast went smoother than he had expected. Junior was in business.

Kripplebauer quickly sold out his supply of cocaine, but not before he cut it. Eddie Loney had shown him how to maximize his stash by watering it down with inositol, a white powdery substance normally used as a vitamin supplement. The quality of the cocaine was so good he could cut it significantly without his buyers' having the slightest notion that the product had been diluted. Junior was buying an ounce of coke for $900 and selling it for $1,200. A five-ounce buy for $4,500 could turn a $1,500 profit after he "whacked it up" with inositol. He was making between $5,000 and $8,000 a key. For Junior it was a "no hassle" proposition like his earlier P2P transactions. "It didn't really have much risk to it," he says matter-of-factly. "I knew where I was getting it and I knew who I was selling it to."

Before long he was making regular round-trip excursions to Florida on Spirit Airlines out of Atlantic City. Being his own pack mule, though physically taxing and time-consuming, not only cut out the chance of loose-lipped or incompetent intermediaries being picked up by authorities; it also gave him a chance to visit with friends and soak up the South Florida party culture. He took note: South Beach was someplace he could settle. The women were beautiful, the drinks were strong, and the living was easy. Sometimes Junior wouldn't disembark in AC on the return flight but would fly straight on to Boston. Frank Rossi, an old Atlanta cellmate and all-around operator, had become one of Junior's better customers.

Rossi, also known as Boston Blackie in the criminal community, was impressed with the quality of cocaine Junior was running. He had always appreciated Junior's track record for reliability. After several such transactions Rossi told him that they could supply all of Boston if he could get the product in large enough quantities. Could Junior supply 20 keys per month? The request was music to Junior's ears, like the constant ringing of a Vegas slot machine on a big payout. "The Rossi deal really whetted my appetite," he says. "If that went down, I knew I'd be fat again."

Rossi introduced Junior to Bobby Luisi, an up-and-coming Boston mobster who was a serious money-earner and seemed to be connected to major players throughout New England. He was a big talker and liked to put on a show, but Junior didn't mind a little braggadocio if the Beantown Mafioso could back it up. Luisi said he could move whatever Junior brought him and promised lavish financial rewards for everyone concerned.

The shared excitement of an attractive and highly profitable new venture was short-lived, however. While visiting Kripplebauer in Philadelphia to solidify their new relationship, Luisi was introduced to and quickly seduced by Joey Merlino and the Italian Mob. A night on the town that started at Dangerous Curves, a Northeast Philly strip club, and gravitated later in the evening to some center city nightclubs, led Luisi to believe he could do better with the South Philly Mob as his coke connection than with Kripplebauer's one-man operation.

Kripplebauer was incensed by Luisi's defection, but what could he do? Merlino had a crew of soldiers and Mafia lineage. They were not much more than South Philly street hoodlums, but they had the imprimatur of the Mob and Junior was a lone wolf trying desperately to stay off the FBI's radar screen. As it turned out, Luisi's decision to abandon Kripplebauer and go into partnership with Joey Merlino proved quite costly. The Feds had cultivated a number of informants in the Merlino organization who wore wires and captured numerous conversations between the Philly and Boston wiseguys regarding drugs and other illegal businesses. They would all end up doing time.

Kripplebauer, meanwhile, kept to his more modest drug business and did relatively well. He was making some money, avoiding missteps, and occasionally enhancing his operation with new gimmicks that either streamlined it or made the drug transactions more efficient. For example, Ed Loney told him how to ship the coke by Federal Express and avoid the hassle of flying back and forth to Florida.

Shipping the coke by Federal Express was a simple and usually reliable way of doing business until the highly sensitive nose of a drug dog got a whiff of one of the packages at the Fort Lauderdale Airport. Confiscated by the Drug Enforcement Agency, the package contained half a kilo of pure cocaine. Not surprisingly, the DEA took a quick interest in Louis K. Bauer of Philadelphia and in the Fort Lauderdale car dealership where the FedEx package had originated.

The DEA weren't the only ones interested in the package, though; so was Louis James Kripplebauer. "When the FedEx package was late, I knew something was wrong," he says. "I waited for the Feds to come and wondered whether I should inquire about the missing package. After giving it some thought, I called Federal Express and asked the shipper what happened to the package. He started asking me all sorts of questions: Who was I? Where was I calling from? Who in

Fort Lauderdale sent the package? I knew the Feds had gotten to this guy. They were looking for me.

"I told Eddie we had a problem and that he shouldn't sign or accept any packages that came to his house. I figured they'd tap our phones and put surveillance on us, particularly me. It got to the point that I couldn't sleep and was expecting them to come busting through the house at any moment, even though I knew the government was always capable of making mistakes and not following up. They were really stupid when you think about it, because they had me. All they had to do was deliver the package and wait for me to pick it up."

Junior couldn't count on the government's tendency to screw up an investigation. His nerves started to get to him. Then, in a significant bit of luck, at least for those at the Florida end of things, the individual whose name appeared on the FedEx package at the car dealership was arrested for an unrelated charge. While in prison, he committed suicide, forcing the FBI to concentrate their efforts on one Louis K. Bauer in Philadelphia.

The waiting game eventually took its toll, and Junior finally decided to cut out. He said goodbye to Hannah, whom he had recently married, flew to Boca Raton, and stayed with Eddie Loney for a couple of weeks. Loney was doing well and had a number of businesses running, both legitimate and illegitimate, including a telemarketing operation. He hired Kripplebauer as one of his time-share salesmen. Between his legal salary selling time-shares and his illegal income moving drugs, Junior was doing rather well also. He got a place of his own, bought a foreign sports car, picked up an attractive girlfriend half his age, and became a regular at fashionable South Beach restaurants and nightclubs. In short, life was good.

Epilogue

Hannah and I had gotten into a real bad beef, so I decided to get out of the house for a while and drove over to Wings Field and got drunk. I'm still feeling pretty good, so I drive over to Philly and go to a bar on Aramingo Avenue. I don't mind the drive 'cause I had just bought a beautiful new Pontiac GT and that baby could really move.

Well, I'm over at this bar until closing, and the bartender offers to drive me home, but even though it's three a.m. and I'm feeling whipped, I tell him I'm okay and can drive myself. Wouldn't you know it, I'm in the middle of the Walt Whitman Bridge when I notice I'm being followed by a cop. I look at the speedometer and I'm doing 70 miles an hour and the bridge sign says 45 miles an hour is the maximum speed. I know I gotta problem.

The cop puts his lights on, and I pull over to the curb. He asks me if I'd been drinking. I told him I had a glass of wine at dinner and hadn't had a drink since, but I was really totaled. He asks me if I had a good reason for going 74 miles an hour, and I told him I had just bought the car and was still getting used to it. It may have been more powerful than I expected.

The cop asks me to take a breathalyzer test, but I refuse. I got $8,000 in my pocket and don't wanna spend any more time with this cop than I have to. I know if he finds the money I'm gonna be in for a long night. He starts asking me a series of questions: How far did you go in school? Can you read and write? Do you know your "ABC"s? I'm starting to get a little pissed now. I ask him, is this a sobriety test or a stupidity test?

Now he's the one getting pissed, and he tells me to get out of the car. He wants me to go through the drill and touch my nose, my ears, walk a straight line. I can't remember if I did it right or not, but he says he's taking me back to the station for a sobriety test. I say to the cop, don't you wanna ask me anything? Don't you wanna tell me my rights? Now he doesn't want to talk.

They throw me in a drunk tank and keep me there for a couple hours, but never check my pockets and don't find the money. After a while a cop comes around and tells me I can go, but somebody has to pick me up. They're not gonna let me drive.

I call Hannah and wake her up. I can tell she was in a deep sleep. I tell her I need a favor. I got picked up for drunken driving, and they're holding me in the jail by the bridge. Can she come pick me up? She says yeah, but it will take a little while. I tell her it's okay, I ain't going anywhere.

About an hour goes by and then the next thing I know a cop comes over to me and says, "I got some bad news for you." "Yeah, what now?" "Your wife just got picked up on the Ben Franklin Bridge. She's drunk and causing a disturbance. We had to arrest her. She sure as hell shouldn't be driving. You got anybody else you want us to call?"

—JUNIOR KRIPPLEBAUER

THE INTERSECTION OF KENSINGTON and Allegheny Avenues is still busy, with pedestrians and motorized vehicles competing for space. However, the sights, sounds, and smells of the community are considerably different from the social and economic landscape of a half-century ago. Popular Kensington landmarks of that era, like the Midway and Iris movie theaters, Horn & Hardart's and Wimpy's restaurants, and a host of family-owned retail shops are long gone, replaced by no-frills discount houses, dollar stores, or in some cases, empty storefronts. The once-mighty Kensington industrial community is also gone, with only barren, trash-strewn vacant lots to show that multistory factories like the Robert Bruce textile mill and Philco electronics once thrived there.

McCarthy's Pool Hall, the Cambria Gym, the Bubble Club, the Purple Derby, and the Randolph Social Club are also now part of history and the fading memories of septuagenarians. Once Irish/Polish, the community is now mostly black and Puerto Rican, with a broad sprinkling of other Latin American subgroups. The percussive beat of Manny Oquendo & the Libre All-Stars is far more likely to be heard on Kensington's gritty streets than anything from the Clancy Brothers or Bobby Vinton. And while there are still many honest, hard-working families living there, syringes and crack vials are all too commonly found on the sidewalks. There are days when violent crime and arson appear to have the beleaguered community in a stranglehold.

Not that the Kensington of old was always a model of traditional family values and respect for the law. Though the majority of residents during the third quarter of the twentieth century shared those ideals and tried to instill in their children a strong work ethic and a sense of fair play, there were a good number who didn't. And it was one group of men in particular who gave the neighborhood a completely different reputation—a reputation that was spread far and wide.

IT DOESN'T TAKE A BRAIN SURGEON to recognize Junior Kripplebauer, Jimmy Dolan, Chickie Goodroe, and the other members of Philly's old K&A Gang as natural-born rule-breakers: social miscreants who for all their charm, panache, and boundless nerve just couldn't conform to the dictates of society. Part rebel, part mischief maker, the Kensington second story man found an occupational niche that allowed him to thrive economically, flout convention, and satisfy his passion for excitement and a good time. Failures in the classroom, temperamentally unsuited for assembly-line factory work, and unsuccessful in traditional nine-to-five blue collar jobs, gang members gravitated to a profession that offered the right mix of challenge, reward, and exhilaration. Drawn to other people's money and possessions as moths are to a bright light, they relished the intellectual challenge of entering a locked home, thwarting a state-of-the-art security system, and circumventing the best efforts of well-funded but clueless law enforcement agencies. Without question, they loved the life.

Though they repeatedly squandered the spoils of their far-flung exploits, drowned themselves in whiskey and women, and presented the dysfunctional mirror image of a smooth-running, hierarchical criminal organization, the K&A Gang knew how to do residential and commercial burglaries as well as, if not better than, any other assemblage of social misfits and scoundrels in American history. Contracted by organized-crime elements in other American cities to do jobs the Mob couldn't or wouldn't attempt, they wowed "made men" in New York City with their knack for opening heavily secured safes and impressed Boston bank robbers with their ability to enter private residences undetected and, most surprisingly, unarmed.

It goes without saying that if Richard Nixon had been as smart as the mobbed-up elements in the Big Apple and Beantown and used the K&A Gang instead of his appropriately named "plumbers" for the break-in at the Democratic National Committee offices in June 1971, no one would ever have heard of "Watergate" and he wouldn't have been forced to relinquish the presidency. E. Howard Hunt, E. Gordon Liddy, and the other three bunglers involved in the DNC break-in may have been Nixon loyalists willing to commit any crime for their commander-in-chief, but when it came to the art of burglary they were rank amateurs compared with Hughie Breslin, Jimmy Laverty, John L. McManus, and the rest of the K&A crowd.

Boisterous, reckless, and argumentative, K&A burglars could destroy a Kensington drinking establishment in a matter of minutes and leave all in attendance shaken and scared to death, but they were also capable of sublime artistry when picking the collective pockets of well-heeled towns and cities across the country. Their flamboyant lifestyles, legendary accomplishments, and widely covered run-ins with the law elevated them to mythic status: home-grown, neighborhood heroes for many cramped, row house denizens who saw them as contemporary Robin Hoods, beer-guzzling, ruddy-faced, happy-go-lucky, artful outlaws following in the footsteps of such illustrious American misfits as Billy the Kid, Butch Cassidy, and John Dillinger.

Like their better-known predecessors, they were done in by a confluence of factors they neither controlled nor understood. They were devoted to an in-the-moment lifestyle that traded many tomorrows for a little action today, but their zest for the big score was blown off course by the turbulent and unpredictable winds of time.

Law enforcement agencies around the country gradually adapted, learned the K&A game plan, and implemented surveillance techniques and response procedures that eventually caught up with their elusive quarry. Home alarm systems grew more sophisticated, as red lights on the front door—the siren call for every K&A burglar—were removed and replaced by a befuddling array of heat, light, and movement sensors. And the age of plastic allowed credit card carriers to dispense with the practice of keeping large sums of cash in bedroom drawers and safes. In short, times had changed.

Probably most important of all, however, was the influence of drugs. As Jimmy Dolan says, "It wasn't the cops or better alarms or anything else that killed the K&A Gang. It was drugs. Meth was the fuckin' poison that ruined everything."

Standup guys, guys who had a reputation for honesty and integrity, who never cheated a partner or cooperated with authorities, were now suspect, willing to give up a partner to stay out of jail, willing to send a buddy to prison to get their next fix.

That was particularly true after the federal government instituted new drug sentencing guidelines in the early 1980s. What had once been a three-to-five-year stint in a state prison became a 20-to-40-year bit in a federal institution. Not everyone could handle such a lengthy jolt. As one Kensington burglar/meth cooker said, "Rats increased tenfold because of the new penalties. There weren't many rats before the federal guidelines, but afterwards it was like Monte Hall—let's make a deal."

"It was like tumbleweed," says Chick Goodroe of the growing list of infor-mants. "Tough guys rolled, and underlings started to say, 'Hey, if they can do, it so can I.' In the old days being a standup guy was everything, but that was when sentences for burglary were 11 to 23 months. Five to ten years was considered a big bit. With meth it was now 20 to 40 years. Some guys caught a life bit. It was awesome."

Steve LaCheen, who began his legal practice defending K&A burglars in the early 1960s and developed strong personal relationships with many of them, saw it all. "The drugs corrupted them," he says. "It was like a virus. They were like pigs at the trough."

Not everyone, however, made the conversion from burglary to drugs. Some, in fact, didn't live long enough even to witness the transition, much less take part in it, while others turned their back on the lucrative but stigmatizing enterprise. Still others got out of the game completely. They went legit.

Willie Sears, arguably the inventor of production work, was gunned down in his Cadillac while stopped at an Atlantic City intersection in the early morning hours of February 21, 1964. A Kensington tough guy who revolutionized second story work, he watched his pupils like a hawk while occasionally skimming the best items from a score for himself. It is generally believed that his sudden and violent demise was due either to a friendlier-than-called-for relationship with the local police or to cheating one of his partners once too often.

Effie Burke, a Sears disciple who injected a bit of pride and professionalism into the guild and became something of a role model for many of his students, suffered a severe heart attack in the early 1970s while working a job in north Jersey. Effie was always nervous during break-ins despite his many years in the business, and the coronary left him unsure whether he could still handle the physical and psychological stresses of this most demanding of criminal occupations. Unwilling to deal drugs and unable to handle the rigors of residential break-ins any more, Burke became "reclusive" and "ended up tapped out," according to a former colleague. He died in 1980.

Roy Stocker, 80, was released from Graterford State Prison in 2004 after serving 14 years of a 20-to-40-year sentence, only to find that the feds wanted an equally long part of him. When he was convicted of running a $52 million methamphetamine ring in 1990, the judge hit him with the maximum term allowed by law after accusing Stocker of ruling his organization with "fear and force" and referring to the "victims of his drug trade" as "uncountable."

Carl Jackson, convicted in 1987 as a "producer and pusher" of methamphetamine, was sentenced to life in prison under the federal drug kingpin statute. Now 68, he has just completed his sixteenth year in a federal penitentiary. It was said by a journalist "that Jackson's profits rolled in so quickly that he did not know what to do with all the money."

Bill "Billy Blue" McClurg is now in his eighties and requires dialysis treatments several times a week. An owner of several bars, McClurg has done well financially. His share of a quarter-million-dollar score at the home of a wealthy plumber many years ago was used to launch a successful loan-sharking operation. He, more than most of his neighborhood compatriots, planned for the future.

Marty Bell, one of the most agile of second story men, was shot by an off-duty police officer during an altercation on December 12, 1976. Bell, who was widely known for his "quickness and climbing ability" and, in fact, fitted the stereotype of the athletic cat burglar, was paralyzed below the waist by the gunshot and has been confined to a wheelchair ever since.

George "Junior" Smith died of a heart attack in Pennsylvania's Graterford State Prison in 2001 after serving nearly two decades behind bars. By that time he looked more like Rip Van Winkle than the handsome second story man he was when he started his criminal career. Junior, with a white beard stretching down to his chest, became a devotee of Eastern and Buddhist philosophies in order to escape the confines of his tiny prison cell and a sentence that offered no hope of parole eligibility until the year 2024.

Don "the Dude" Abrams got out of production work in the 1970s when alarms started to go high-tech. He spent many years as an employee of Progress Lighting. Though he began his burglary career with Willie Sears in the early 1950s and claims to have done thousands of homes over the years, including those of Sammy Davis, Jr., and Eddie Fisher, he can be found today walking along Kensington and Allegheny Avenues. Unlike most of the other members of the K&A Gang, Abrams remained in the neighborhood his entire life.

Johnny Boggs eventually met Father Peck, a priest with a mission and a persuasive personality, who gradually convinced Boggs that he still had time to straighten out his life, save his marriage, and become a contributing member of society. An enforcer for the roofers when he wasn't breaking into houses, Boggs decided to "shy away from crime" in the mid-1970s, stay clear of drugs, and clean up his act. Today, he is an accomplished handyman who repairs houses for a living.

Donnie Johnstone did several prison bits during the 1970s and 1980s for burglary and receiving stolen goods. Although he had a hand in the meth business, he was never arrested for any drug-related crimes and left prison for good in 1991. Today, Johnstone tends bar and frequents quite a few others as a patron.

Michael Lee Andrews, a renowned driver who could steer a crew of burglars from one end of the country to another without relief or a map, was found murdered in the trunk of his car after a drug deal gone bad.

Mitchell Prinski, who did second story work with Junior Kripplebauer and Chick Goodroe, among others, was nailed with a 30-year prison sentence in the 1990s for his role in a methamphetamine ring. He is currently at Allenwood Federal Penitentiary and will be eligible for parole in 2017.

Eddie Loney relocated to South Florida and made a considerable living in the drug and telemarketing businesses. He is currently a fugitive from justice and being sought for his role in a multimillion-dollar time-share scam. It is thought that he may be in hiding somewhere in Ireland.

John Berkery, considered one of "Philadelphia's most clever and fascinating criminals," by police and crime reporters was another of the many K&A burglars who gravitated to drugs. Berkery was convicted of "distributing 24 pounds of methamphetamine and possession of more than 200 gallons of P-2-P, the contraband chemical used to make the drug in 1987." This came after he had been a federal fugitive for over five years, much of which he may have spent in Ireland. Commenting on Berkery at his sentencing, federal prosecutor Louis R. Pichini said, "The defendant's unlawful activities exhibit a cunning cleverness and sophistication that has little equal in the Philadelphia criminal community." Now back on the street, Berkery is studying law.

Jackie Johnson was released from federal prison in the early nineties after serving six years of a 10-year sentence for his participation in a methamphetamine ring. Notification that his parole period had finally expired in 2003—the first time he had been off parole since he was nine years old, he claims—inspired a celebration by K&A oldtimers. Known as a "standup guy" all his life, Johnson can still keep a secret, tell a good story, and serve a stiff drink. He currently tends bar at a Tacony shot-and-beer joint.

Chick Goodroe was a federal fugitive for 10 years before serving five years at Lewisburg, Danbury, and Allenwood penitentiaries. Released in 1992, Chick has worked as a marble and granite countertop salesman for the last eight years and has gradually become accustomed to "getting up at six a.m. and doing a full day's work." He now spends his days assisting homeowners in upscale residences he would formerly have burgled.

Reflecting on the irony, Goodroe says, "I'm working homes in Princeton, New Jersey. They're $3 to $10 million homes and I'm thinking about my life. I never expected to be this old. I never saved any money. I never thought it would end. Back in the day, if you were sitting with 10 people for dinner and you picked up the check for $2,000, it wasn't a big deal. You'd work the next day and make it up. None of us were rocket scientists, but we knew how to make money."

Though his lifestyle has changed dramatically, he now claims to be enjoying "the American dream" for the first time. "I have a job, two mortgages, two car payments, health insurance, and a young girlfriend," Goodroe says proudly. Yes, he sometimes tires of the drudgery and long hours, but he's finally bought into the program. Old habits die slowly, however, and flashbacks to an earlier time periodically peek through the mist of conformity. "Every time I approach a house and see a mezuzah or a red light on a door," says Chick of his sales appointments at some of America's most fashionable homes, "I get a rush."

Jimmy Dolan made and lost several fortunes as a thief but "made up my mind it was over when the burglary business dried up in the late 1970s." As he says a bit sadly of the changes that occurred at the time, "there was no one to work with any more." Dolan isn't reluctant to admit that he "should have stayed in school" and made something of himself, but he's "really not ashamed" of his years as a K&A Gang member. "Oh, sure, I've got a ton of regrets," he says, "but there's no turning the clock back." And even if he could, working as a Kensington second story man isn't one of them. "I met some interesting people, guys who became good friends. They were the only standup guys I ever knew. The people whose homes we hit weren't getting hurt. Nobody got robbed [at the point of a gun]. And the insurance companies were usually paying off anyway."

"There were some bad gangs out there," says Dolan of the many crews that either did things they shouldn't have or flipped on their partners when the pressure was applied. "I caught a break; I never worried about getting ratted on. Thank God, they were all standup guys. In the early days all the burglars were standup, but as time passed a lot of them rolled. In the end it was a flip of the coin."

Dolan kept his hand in a few business ventures—both legal and illegal—over the years, including a couple of successful Northeast Philadelphia nightclubs that fronted lively backroom poker games. He is a natural raconteur whose humorous stories of brazen gangsters and big scores captivate young and old alike—his current Tacony-based card games are attended as much for his wit and wisdom as for the chance to make a few bucks at the poker table.

The prototypical gangster with a heart of gold, Dolan never forgets those still doing time. He occasionally visits, writes often, and is usually the first one to rip off a few twenties from a pocket billfold to ensure that a friend "still buried" in America's vast network of federal and state prisons has some money on the commissary books.

AS FOR LOUIS JAMES KRIPPLEBAUER, Jr., it didn't turn out exactly as he or anyone else would have expected. As luck would have it, the arc of his full and varied criminal life came to a sudden stop on July 18, 1999, on a typically sunny Florida morning. Junior and his girlfriend Sherry had just completed a vigorous lovemaking session and now lay in bed discussing what each of them had scheduled for the day. Junior finally got out of bed, showered, dressed, and was prepared to start making his rounds when Sherry asked, "Feel like stopping at the store?" She was hungry.

Junior said sure and drove his Maserati convertible a short distance down Oakland Park Boulevard to the local Cuban deli. While the proprietor made the two hoagies he had ordered, Junior quickly polished off a sweet tasting Yoo-hoo and a pack of crackers. After paying for the sandwiches, he retraced his route back home. He had a terrible need to urinate.

"I had to take a piss," recalls Junior of the event that would change his life forever. "I pulled into the driveway of our apartment and hit the remote to open the garage door. Nothing happened. I hit it again. Nothing. And then again.

Nothing was working. I thought the battery was dead, but kept on hitting the remote."

Observing this odd situation, a neighbor cautiously came up to the car and asked, "Are you okay, George?" (Kripplebauer was known as "George Bain" in Florida). "Are you in pain? Are you all right? You don't look good."

"No, no, no," replied Junior, his body slouched to the side and his head lying against the head rest. He was still trying to manipulate the remote control for the garage door.

"Something's wrong," said the neighbor, his concern increasing. "You don't look good. Do you need help?"

"I'm all right," said Junior. "The door won't work. I can't get the garage door to open."

Now taking notice of the situation below her window, Sherry came outside to see what the problem was.

"He's having a stroke," said the neighbor.

"I'm all right," said Junior. "I'm okay."

"He's not okay," replied the neighbor more assertively. "I think he's having a stroke."

Sherry and the neighbor decided to get Junior out of the hot South Florida sun and helped him out of the vehicle and into the basement of her town house. He was still insisting he had to take a piss, so they helped him into the bathroom and stood by him so he wouldn't fall.

When the ambulance crew arrived at the house, they immediately laid Junior on the floor. He was still arguing that he was okay and didn't need all the attention he was receiving. It was then that the medical technician said, "Pal, you're having a stroke. This is my business and I'm telling you you're having a stroke."

"It didn't process," recalls Kripplebauer. "They kept on talking stroke but I didn't comprehend what was happening. As I'm in the ambulance I heard them discussing somebody's condition and they keep on mentioning stroke, what they should do, what medicine to inject, but I didn't think it was for me. I kept telling them I was okay; I wasn't having a stroke."

In fact, Junior was in the midst of a massive stroke, one that would come close to taking his life. It was payback time: he was now paying for his bad crack habit. Dealing drugs, hanging with a fast Miami crowd, he had joined their lavish, self-indulgent, reckless lifestyle. He was smoking crack several times a day after becoming addicted to the "intense marijuana high" he got from the drug. Hospital toxicology tests showed he was on the verge of "narcotic poisoning; his blood system was full of it," doctors told him.

"When I woke up the next day," says Kripplebauer, "I looked around and saw a guy in bed with an IV and tubes in him and another guy who was hooked up to a sophisticated monitor, and I knew I was in the hospital. I finally realized I was in bad shape. I couldn't move one arm or a leg. I thought that maybe I had been in a car accident 'cause that was the last thing I remembered, driving the car. I felt my arm and head to see if plaster casts had been placed on me. I didn't know what the damage was.

"I had to take a terrible piss, but had trouble moving and getting out of bed. I didn't understand why I couldn't stand up; it was very difficult. When I finally got up, I immediately lost my balance and tried to reach out for the bed with both hands, but only one arm worked and I crashed to the floor. One of the other patients saw me go down and rang for assistance. When the nurse came in she started screaming, 'What do you think you're doing? You shouldn't be trying to get out of bed.'

" 'I was walking to the bathroom,' I told her.

" 'But you can't walk,' she replied.

" 'What do you mean I can't walk? I can walk.'

" 'No you can't,' the nurse shot back, 'you're paralyzed.'

"It was then that I learned just how bad I had been jackpotted. It affected my whole left side. I couldn't swallow, my speech was slurred, and even my face was affected."

Doctors theorized that if Kripplebauer hadn't maintained his rigorous workout routine from his days in prison, which still included running five miles a day, the stroke would probably have killed him. As it was, his recovery was partial at best and the struggle long and arduous. He was in Fort Lauderdale's St. Luke's Hospital for months, relearning the simplest human functions, how to swallow, talk, and perform rudimentary tasks with one side of his body useless, completely shut down. There would be only pureed food for the first three months of his hospitalization, hours of painful rehab that wasn't all that successful, and familiarizing himself with his new vehicle—not a Lincoln Town Car, Cadillac de Ville, or foreign sports car, but a cumbersome wheelchair that he could barely manipulate.

Eventually, his sister and niece thought it was time to bring him home and had him transferred to a rehabilitation facility in Camden, New Jersey. More exercise, counseling sessions, and therapy were in store for the once-formidable physical specimen who was now a broken shell of his former self. The upstate Pennsylvania coal-cracker had come full circle: from his youthful dreams of escaping the filthy, stifling coal mines to confinement in a facility for aged, crippled residents who can no longer survive on their own. Between those extremes, however, Louis James Kripplebauer, Jr., lived life on his own terms.

Though Kripplebauer must have been tormented with self-doubt and regret during his lengthy recovery, he assumed the role of team captain, an upbeat, therapeutic cheerleader encouraging his wheelchair-bound roommates and other physically handicapped residents to work harder, keep the faith, and not fall prey to despondency and defeatism. Better times were ahead, he'd counsel the 85-year-old ladies who received few family visits, and their male counterparts who had little but their meals to look forward to each day. They would overcome their current difficulties, he'd argue, and make the gains that would allow them to leave the medical facility. Yes, he'd counsel them—they'd enjoy life once again.

At both the Camden rehab facility and the assisted-living community he would shortly be transferred to in Voorhees, Lou—as he would now be known—was undoubtedly one of the most popular and trusted members of the residential community. Upbeat, concerned, and always desirous to provide a helping hand, Kripplebauer was a friend to all and kept the door to his room open around the clock just in case he was needed. More like a benevolent mayor looking after a valued constituency than a needy patient requiring assistance, Junior was no doubt thought to be a retired physical education teacher or social worker, and certainly not what he really was—a bona-fide and extremely accomplished second story man who ran law enforcement authorities ragged all over America.

Now in his sixty-eighth year and confined to a wheelchair at a South Jersey assisted-living facility, Kripplebauer looks forward to visits from friends and family, periodic excursions to the shore to enjoy a pina colada on the beach and play the slots, and the generous kisses of a gentle and loving border collie pup who pays scant heed to her friend's age or infirmities.

Ironically, the door to his room is now closed. The fabled burglar who may have pillaged more homes than Genghis Khan, and who preoccupied law enforcement officers 10 times as long as John Dillinger, had fallen victim to thieves; money and personal items had gone missing. Was it a cruel turnabout for an infirm and well-liked senior citizen or just deserts for an inveterate career criminal? Alas, the master thief who ran roughshod over affluent communities from the Canadian to the Mexican borders, and from ocean to ocean, is now the one on the alert.

Thieves beware—one of your own is watching.

Acknowledgments

THIS BOOK could not have been written without the assistance of scores of individuals in Philadelphia and around the nation who were willing to be interviewed—many times over, in some cases. Not surprisingly, the great bulk of the interviews that make up this historical investigation are with criminals—specifically burglars—and the federal, state, and local lawmen who chased after them. If it had not been for the willing cooperation of both thieves and cops—many of whom were talking on the record about sensitive subjects for the first time—this project could not have been undertaken, much less completed.

I must initially thank Jimmy Moran and Jackie Johnson for providing the inspirational spark that led me to tackle this subject. Until now the K&A Gang has only been whispered about late at night in the safe confines of neighborhood taprooms across Philadelphia's river wards. Though it was my original intention to research an unrelated criminal justice story, the entertaining accounts of the K&A Gang by these two proud Kensington natives gradually won me over. The gang's wide-ranging exploits, the Runyonesque characters who made up the old Irish Mob, accounts of big scores, and their many prison misadventures were too compelling to be left to die in dingy, smoke-filled shot-and-beer joints. Those many stories had to be collected, bound, and offered to the public.

Once I embarked on what turned out to be a five-year-long project and tracked down such accomplished second story men (and captivating raconteurs) as Jimmy Dolan, Jimmy Laverty, and John L. McManus, my instincts were confirmed. A thorough account of Philadelphia's contribution to the history of burglary was long overdue.

It goes without saying that I owe a tremendous debt of gratitude to Junior Kripplebauer, a consummate career criminal and perfect gentleman (in my dealings with him) whose life and daring deeds form the centerpiece of this saga. Early on in my research the Kripplebauer name resonated. Talked about with respect and reverence by his old colleagues, protected by his loyal attorney, and living under an assumed name somewhere in Florida, he seemed as intriguing as he was elusive. It appeared for the longest time that he would be one former gang member that I would not have access to. By all accounts he was a larger-than-life figure, but one whom I could only fantasize about tracking down and incorporating into this story. Junior's misfortune was my narrative breakthrough. A devastating stroke brought him back to the area and, soon after, to a well-deserved position as focal point of *Confessions of a Second Story Man*.

Over the course of countless interviews and several years, Louis James Kripplebauer, Jr., and I not only chronicled his birth and evolution as a K&A burglar, but also became good friends. His assistance in this project has been invaluable and is deeply appreciated.

I must also thank the many other K&A men who offered me their time and recollections. They include, in no particular order, Jimmy Dolan, Chick Goodroe, Jimmy Laverty, John L. McManus, George R. Smith, Don Johnstone, Don Abrams, Bill McClurg, Marty Bell, Johnny Boggs, Owen Gallagher, and Frank Mawhinney.

My sincere appreciation must also be extended to their archenemies, the many law enforcement officers who supplied, corroborated, and augmented the stories I was collecting. They include FBI Special Agents William Skarbek, Andy Sloan, James McAleer, Klaus Rohr, Robert McClernand, George Sherwood, Henry Handy, Robert McKenney, John Bierman, James Aardweg, and Robert Bazin; Raleigh Police Officer D. C. Williams and North Carolina Judge Rick Greeson; former federal prosecutor Louis Pichini, James Smith of the Greenwich, Conn., Police Department; Richard Richroath of the New Jersey state police; Jenkintown Police Chief Carl Butzloff and Abington Police Chief Herb Mooney.

Sincere appreciation is also extended to the many former members of the Philadelphia Police Department who assisted me, including John DelCarlino, Jack Lanzidelle, Frank Wallace, Joseph Brophy, Joe Dougherty, Frank X. O'Shea, Frank Friel, Francis Lederer, Robert Shubert, Bill Fleisher, John Wilson, and Jim Catahlo. Former ATF officers William Drum and James Kelly and former U.S. Marshal Tom O'Rourke provided valuable information as well.

A special note of thanks must be extended to the late Herbie Rhodes, a former Philly police officer and member of Clarence Ferguson's Special Investigative Squad, who championed my efforts during this long project (when he wasn't encouraging me to drop it and write the definitive account of the infamous Pottsville Heist). Herbie had an integral role in the Pottsville drama, knew the key players intimately, and was unquestionably correct when he said that Pottsville deserved both a book and a movie of its own.

During the early stages of my research, I drew upon the services of Margaret Jerrido of Temple University's Urban Archives and Frank Donahue of the *Philadelphia Inquirer.* Both institutions offered an invaluable collection of old newspaper clips that not only provided a jumping-off point for my investigation but also helped document the activities of individual members of the K&A Gang.

Martha Woodall of the *Philadelphia Inquirer* very kindly shared information collected during her days as a reporter for the *Greensboro Record*. Ms. Woodall was one of the first to recognize the unique qualities and importance of the Hallmark Gang (as they were called in North Carolina) and produced substantive magazine pieces on the gang for both papers.

Also deserving a special thank you is Stephen LaCheen, an attorney of unquestioned ability and loyalty who represented many of the K&A burglars over the decades and won their respect and friendship many times over. Steven provided me with illuminating vignettes of his clients as well as Junior Kripplebauer's lengthy legal file, which greatly assisted me in untangling the impressive and varied list of Junior's criminal cases around the country. After interviewing so many key players in the criminal justice community in the course of writing this book, there is little question in my mind that if I ever needed a criminal defense lawyer, Steve LaCheen would be the man for the job.

In any research project, particularly one of this magnitude, many individuals help the author do the heavy lifting. Although there are too many to mention, I would like to pay a dept of gratitude to Carole Heidinger, Arlene Burke, Al Zabala, Marvin Edelman, Ron Avery, Joe Daughen, Joel Moldovsky, Sal Avena, Al Ronconi, Gene Pedicord, Virginia Chiucarelli, Larry McMullin, Eddie Rief, Buddy Brennan, Edward Froggatt, Mary Kober, Andrew Guckin, Gil Slowe, and Torben Jenks.

George Holmes shared his incisive knowledge of Kensington and offered able assistance during those occasional but still nerve-wracking computer meltdowns.

Also deserving a special thank you is Laura Lister, who hung in there during some of the more trying periods of this project, as well as Peter Steinberg, my literary agent, and Micah Kleit, my editor at Temple University Press, who recognized early on that Philly's K&A Gang was truly something special and long overdue for book-length treatment. I would also like to thank Jane Barry for attending the many English classes I did not, learning the evils of dangling participles, and thereby making a good but flawed manuscript considerably better.

Notes

Books, whether for a scholarly audience or a more general readership, tend to be written about people and events that have already received a good bit of attention. Some of us, however, are not particularly interested in writing the two-hundred-twenty-fifth biography of Benjamin Franklin—or the fifth book on John Gotti, for that matter. Instead of rehashing long-known tales, such writers seek out previously unexplored stories or phenomena, even when there is little written documentation to help in the investigation.

In the field of organized crime, especially during the past half-century, telling a new story can mean going out on the street and tracking down both the players and the observers of your target population. Biker bars, shot-and-beer joints, gambling halls, and rat-infested back alleys are not conventional research venues—they certainly lack the scholarly aura and amenities of university libraries and historical societies—but they provide a wealth of information. This is particularly true when you are exploring a legendary urban phenomenon like the K&A Gang.

Mythic in certain neighborhoods throughout Philadelphia—as well as numerous cities and towns around the country—Philly's old Irish Mob had long been in the shadow of Italian organized-crime activities in the area and was overdue for serious attention, scholarly or otherwise. Operating over a vast geographic area and several decades, Kensington's well-known and respected community of burglars (and later meth dealers) went unclaimed and unexamined by both academics and journalists. With no one to chronicle their accomplishments, they had become legendary bandits whose legend was gradually fading with the passage of time. The thieves themselves, famously uncooperative, collaborated in their own anonymity by keeping investigators at arm's length. Outsiders—journalists, scholars, or members of the law enforcement establishment—were aggressively encouraged to stay out of their "business."

I was fortunate enough to have established friendly relationships with both cops and cons over the years and have been a board member of a diverse cross-section of criminal justice organizations, including the Pennsylvania Prison Society and the Pennsylvania Crime Commission. These contacts led to others, and I was passed along from one knowledgeable source to another until I was eventually among the burglars themselves and the lawmen whose job it was to hunt them down. No accurate account of the K&A Gang could be based on old police files, newspaper clips, and legal documents alone. Without my access to the burglars themselves, the true flavor of the gang, their individual characteristics, their private motivations, and the outrageous experiences that the law and the press never heard about, would have been lost. It is those deeply personal traits and adventures that give life to the story presented here and explain, in part, the gang members' endearing qualities and mythic status.

Having said that, I should add that half-century-old newspaper articles, police reports, and the burglars' own legal files greatly augmented the large array of oral histories I was collecting. I made it a point to try to document every anecdotal account or claim by a burglar with a similar recollection by a law enforcement officer or public document before I would accept it as fact. That formula appeared to work in just about every case.

Obviously, the criminal career of Louis James Kripplebauer, Jr., is the central thread running through this story. His busy career, a veritable laundry list of illegal activities, is almost too exhausting to catalogue, much less recount in a book-length treatment. Much of his life story can be confirmed by other criminals, law enforcement authorities, government documents, and news articles. However, many of his criminal endeavors escaped the notice of authorities and newspaper scribes and therefore went unrecorded—to his gratification, I may add.

CHAPTER 1. NORTH CAROLINA: THE DIXIE MAC MACHINE

Information on the Kripplebauer crew's repeated forays through North Carolina was gathered through extensive interviews with Junior Kripplebauer and numerous other K&A burglars who periodically traveled to that state. Though North Carolina was the focal point of this chapter, any of two dozen other states could have been used to introduce the burglars, since their game plan was fairly similar for all locales.

Additional facts were gleaned from a series of excellent news articles on the Hallmark Gang written by Martha Woodall and published in the *Greensboro Record* over five days beginning on April 26, 1981. Woodall's articles graphically present a community under siege and the monetary and social costs involved in the Philly burglars' annual jewel and cash harvest in the Tar Heel State. Many other North Carolina newspapers provided less extensive coverage of the Hallmark Gang.

Repeated interviews with former Raleigh police officer D. C. Williams and Judge Rick Greeson also supplied important background for this chapter.

CHAPTER 2. "JUNIOR"

The description of Centralia, Pennsylvania, was based on a series of newspaper and magazine articles that tracked the gradual decline of this mining community, as well as the vivid recollections of Junior Kripplebauer.

Junior's shootout with Florida authorities and subsequent imprisonment were covered in news articles that appeared in the *Philadelphia Bulletin, Philadelphia Inquirer,* and *Philadelphia Daily News*. Those same papers also provided useful articles on Kripplebauer's first partner in crime, Tommy Lyons, a promising young jockey whose successful career was derailed by a severe drug addiction.

Details about Kripplebauer's introduction to the K&A Gang at North Philadelphia bars such as Marty's and the Shamrock were provided by bar owners and a number of former bar patrons and burglars, including Bill McClurg.

CHAPTER 3. KENSINGTON

My account of Kensington's social and political history, including its gradual transformation from fishing village to industrial powerhouse, is based on numerous published sources. Some of the most helpful were: Peter Binzen, *Whitetown U.S.A.* (New York: Random House, 1970); Elizabeth M. Geffen, "Industrial Development and Social Crisis 1841–1854," in Russell F. Weigley, *Philadelphia: A 300 Hundred Year History* (New York: W. W. Norton, 1982); Dennis Clark, *The Irish in Philadelphia* (Philadelphia: Temple University Press, 1981); "Kensington: From Fishing Village to Industrial Center," in Jamie Catrambone and Harry Silcox, *Kensington History: Stories and Memories* (Philadelphia: Brighton Press/Institute for Service Learning, 1996); *Kensington: A City Within a City* (Philadelphia: Keighton, 1891); and an array of nineteenth- and twentieth-century articles from the *Public Ledger.*

Long-time Kensington residents Jimmy Moran, George Holmes, Andrew Guckin, Torben Jenks, Paul Melione, and Brother Hugh McGuire also contributed to this chapter through interviews.

Quotations come from the following printed sources:

"home to a hundred thousand": Binzen, *Whitetown U.S.A.*, p. 81.
"alien, papist, anti-democratic": Weigley, *Philadelphia: A 300 Year History.*
"pledged themselves to an unremitting": ibid.
"No theme in these textbooks": ibid.
"bloody Irish transports": Binzen, *Whitetown U.S.A.*, p. 88.
"This is the fatal evil of Philadelphia": Geffen, "Industrial Development."
"thoroughly stigmatized white men": ibid.
"a labyrinth of social and class": ibid.
"enterprise dotted with factories so numerous": A City Within a City.
"two-thirds of the insane in the state": Clark, *Irish in Philadelphia.*
"reputation for alcoholic intake": ibid.
"an oasis of camaraderie for the worker": ibid.
"Drink, accursed drink is the cause": ibid.

CHAPTER 4. PRODUCTION WORK

Numerous interviews helped illuminate the early years of the K&A Gang. Especially helpful in explaining the rudiments of production work, and recounting the lives of Willie Sears and Effie Burke, were Jimmy Laverty, Don Abrams, Bill McClurg, Jimmy Dolan, and Jackie Johnson. Arlene Burke and Carole Heidinger, Burke's wife and sister-in-law, also contributed valuable information to this chapter.

Police officials who told of their run-ins with members of the K&A Gang in the 1950s included Clark Cutting and Herb Mooney from the Abington Police Department, Carl Butzloff from the Jenkintown Police Department; and John DelCarlino, Joseph Brophy, and Herbie Rhodes of the Philadelphia Police Department.

Once again, numerous articles in the *Philadelphia Bulletin, Philadelphia Inquirer*, and *Philadelphia Daily News* proved helpful for this early period in the gang's development.

Some of the more useful articles included: "City's No. 1 Thief Slain in Gangland Style," *Philadelphia Daily News*, February 21, 1964; "Bad Man Willie Sears Has Some Bad Luck," *Philadelphia Sunday Bulletin*, June 22, 1958; "Anatomy of a Burglar," *Philadelphia Inquirer*, February 2, 1964; "Parolee Is Caught in Stolen Auto," *Philadelphia Evening Bulletin*, October 13, 1942; "Autoist, 16, Seized After Wild Ride," *Philadelphia Inquirer*, October 14, 1942.

CHAPTER 5. ROAD COMPANIES, BRUTES, AND SAFE CRACKERS

The account of the "Houston Airlift" is largely based on articles that appeared in the *Houston Chronicle*, official FBI and local Houston police reports, and Kripplebauer's legal file.

On the far-flung travels of the K&A Gang, their strategies, and their various burglary tools and safecracking techniques, Jimmy Laverty, Jimmy Dolan, Chick Goodroe, Don Johnstone, Johnnie Boggs, and John L. McManus proved particularly helpful.

Many individuals, including Jimmy Moran, Jackie Johnson, and Jay Tipton, shared information on the #9714 screwdriver or "brute."

Newspaper articles contributing to this chapter include: "Suspects Trailed for Three Weeks," *Philadelphia Inquirer*, July 7, 1959; "Philadelphia Quartet Held in Upstate Burglaries," *Philadelphia Daily News*, July 7, 1959.

CHAPTER 6. THE POTTSVILLE HEIST

The 1959 Pottsville Heist is one of the most written-about criminal events in Philadelphia history. There are literally scores of articles on the burglary itself, the fascinating cast of characters (from Lillian Reis to Captain Clarence Ferguson), the murders of the Blaney brothers, and the subsequent criminal trials in Pottsville. Some of the more helpful newspaper and magazine pieces were: Alfred G. Aronowitz, "They Call Me Tiger Lil," *Saturday Evening Post*, October 23, 1963; "Star Witness in Pottsville Theft Is Shot," *Philadelphia Evening Bulletin*, August 14, 1960; "$478,000 Loot Fantastic, Pottsville Victim Insists," *Philadelphia Evening Bulletin*, April 5, 1960; "Theft Story Is Given by Informer," *Philadelphia Evening Bulletin*, March 16, 1961; "Big Heist Crimetable," *Philadelphia Daily News*, October 19, 1961; "Lillian Reis and Staino Fight Police After Chase," *Philadelphia Evening Bulletin*, February 25, 1963; "$30,000 in Box Is Linked to Pottsville Theft," *Sunday Bulletin*, April 24, 1960; and Ron Avery, *The City of Brotherly Mayhem* (Philadelphia: Otis Books, 1997).

Recollections of the Pottsville caper stood out in the minds of just about everyone I talked to, but particular mention should be made of the contributions of Herbie Rhodes, Joe Daughen, Al Ronconi, Sal Avena, and Virginia Chiucarelli, each of whom actually played a role in the decade-long drama.

Specific quotations come from the following printed sources:

"Rollicking as a roller coaster": Leonard J. McAdams, "Pottsville Burglary: An Incredible Caper That Had Everything," *Philadelphia Inquirer*, October 30, 1966.
"In my 45 years as a policeman": quoted in Aronowitz, "They Call Me Tiger Lil."

"It was the most incredible": McAdams, "Pottsville Burglary."

"She really made an impression on me": Aronowitz, "They Call Me Tiger Lil."

"almost fainted": "6th Suspect Gives Up, Denies Pottsville Theft," *Evening Bulletin*, April 7, 1960.

"money stacked in bundles": ibid.

"It's a very puzzling case": Roland T. Moriarty, "Probe of Theft," *Evening Bulletin*, April 6, 1960.

"were at his side when he drank": "Blaney Took Gamble, Didn't Inspect His Car," *Evening Bulletin*, July 28, 1961.

"drove him back to Philadelphia": ibid.

"was blown into eternity": *Philadelphia Daily News*, July 28, 1961 (other quotations on the car bombing come from this source unless otherwise attributed).

"standing mute when being questioned": Avery, *City of Brotherly Mayhem*, p. 104.

CHAPTER 7. NATURAL SELECTION

This overview of the lives and criminal pursuits of Jimmy Dolan and Chick Goodroe was based on numerous interviews with both subjects, augmented by news articles, police files, and the recollections of many of their associates.

CHAPTER 8. BLUE COLLAR ROBIN HOODS

Kensingtonians' perspective on their homegrown criminal element was elicited through interviews with scores of long-time community residents, a cross-section of businessmen, clergy, and average homeowners. Particularly helpful in understanding the neighborhood's opinion of their local second story men were Gil and Ronnie Slowe, Carole Heidinger, Mary Kober, George Holmes, Jack Dempsey, Joseph Edelman, Bob McClernand, Brother Hugh McGuire, Paul Melione, Joseph DiLeo, Ed Froggatt, and Andrew Guckin.

Former Assistant District Attorney Joel Moldovsky also contributed information to this chapter, as did Jimmy Moran and Jimmy Laverty.

CHAPTER 9. PUGILISTS, DRUNKS, AND MISFITS

Recollections of Kensington's screwball characters were garnered through interviews with dozens of past and present neighborhood residents. Particularly helpful in their contributions were Herbie Rhodes, Don Abrams, Al Zabala, Jimmy Laverty, Jimmy Moran, Gene Pedicord, Marty Rubin, Tommy O'Rourke, John Kellis, John L. McManus, Jimmy Dolan, George Holmes, Jackie Johnson, Marvin Edelman, and Marty Bell.

Articles from the *Philadelphia Bulletin, Philadelphia Inquirer*, and *Philadelphia Daily News* drawn on for this chapter include: "Dismissed Patrolman Is Held Without Bail As Theft Gang Lookout," *Philadelphia Inquirer*, December 10, 1954; "Police Eye Reports of Mob Killing," *Philadelphia Inquirer*, February 19, 1959; "Fugitive from Chain Gang Caught," *Philadelphia Evening Bulletin*, January 19, 1935.

CHAPTER 10. KEYS TO THE KINGDOM

This chapter is based on the criminal career of Junior Kripplebauer and focuses on the period from the early 1960s through the mid-1970s. Much of the story was acquired during scores of interviews with Mr. Kripplebauer, his friends and associates, and various law enforcement officials over the course of several years.

Augmenting the Kripplebauer interviews were dozens of newspaper articles covering a wide range of criminal activities and Kripplebauer's extensive legal file, which provides extensive background material on such events as the Food Fair burglary and the Shore Brothers Pontiac caper. Interviews with such close observers of events as his attorney also proved quite helpful.

Official court documents from the Magistrates Court and Commonwealth Court of Pennsylvania, plus various pieces of legal correspondence, helped to illuminate this period of Mr. Kripplebauer's criminal career.

CHAPTER 11. THE COPS STRIKE BACK

A wide array of local, state, and federal officers recounted and analyzed the law enforcement response to the activities of the K&A Gang. Retired FBI Special Agent William Skarbek and retired Philadelphia police officer John DelCarlino were particularly helpful in laying out national and local operations in pursuit of the thieves.

Other law enforcement officers contributing to this chapter included a cross-section of local and national crime fighters: James Smith, William Drum, Robert Bazin, Joseph Brophy, Richard Richroath, D. C. Williams, and John Lanzidelle.

Letters from Robert Tunny of the Maryland state police and memos from George Bassett of the Greenwich, Connecticut, Police Department revealed how different communities responded to the K&A threat.

Others contributing to this chapter were Al Zabala, Chick Goodroe, Jimmy Dolan, and Donnie Johnstone.

I consulted official Philadelphia Police blue books, as well as facsimiles from states along the eastern seaboard. Other published aids included Joel Moldovsky and Rose DeWolf, *The Best Defense* (New York: Macmillan, 1975).

CHAPTER 12. PHILLY'S BONNIE AND CLYDE

A series of lengthy interviews with Mr. Kripplebauer were the main source of information for this chapter. His reflections were augmented by a vast array of documents: Martha Woodall, "The Hallmark Story," *Greensboro Record*; articles from the *Raleigh News and Observer* and other North Carolina newspapers; letters from the law offices of Locke Clifford, Kripplebauer's North Carolina attorney; and documents belonging to several North Carolina police departments, as well as FBI documents on everything from reports of stolen property to official investigation reports and individual arrest records.

Jackie Johnson, Bill McClurg, Jimmy Dolan, Donnie Johnstone, Steve LaCheen, and William Skarbek also provided important information.

CHAPTER 13. ON THE RUN

The bulk of this chapter is based on Mr. Kripplebauer's recollections of, augmented by numerous interviews with several Kripplebauer associates and law enforcement officers. Articles on the Trading Post jewelry store heist and Richard Henkel appeared in several Pittsburgh newspapers.

CHAPTER 14. COURTROOMS AND PRISONS

This chapter is primarily based on Mr. Kripplebauer's recollections. Interviews with D. C. Williams, Rick Greeson, and Jimmy Dolan also contributed to it.

I also relied upon the many articles about the Hallmark Gang that appeared in various North Carolina newspapers; court documents of the Eighteenth Judicial District in Greensboro, North Carolina; records of the Raleigh Police Department; documents of the Supreme Court of Pennsylvania and the United States District Courts for the Eastern and Middle Districts of Pennsylvania; the Court of Common Pleas of Bucks County, Pennsylvania; and FBI documents, including individual arrest records of members of the K&A Gang and criminal investigation reports.

Also helpful were letters to and from the North Carolina Parole Commission about Mr. Kripplebauer's status and documents from Piedmont Community College, Roxboro, North Carolina.

Other useful material come from the legal correspondence between Mr. Kripplebauer and his various lawyers, including Michael Healey, his attorney in Pittsburgh; Locke Clifford and David Rudolf, his North Carolina attorneys; and the notes, memoirs, and correspondence of his Philadelphia attorney, Stephen LaCheen.

CHAPTER 15. FROM BURGLARY TO DRUGS

Information in this chapter was procured from numerous interviews with Mr. Kripplebauer. The story of the K&A Gang's switch from burglary to drugs came from interviews with the burglars as well as the police, FBI agents, and others. They included Frank Wallace, James McAleer, John Wilson, Jim Catahlo, Jimmy Dolan, Jackie Johnson, Chick Goodroe, Steve LaCheen, and Donnie Johnstone.

Among the published documents contributing to this chapter were numerous newspaper articles, portions of the Pennsylvania Crime Commission reports for 1980 and 1990, and Ed Moran, "The Double Life of Ronald Raiton," *Philadelphia Inquirer Sunday Magazine.*

EPILOGUE

Numerous interviews with Mr. Kripplebauer, many of his past criminal associates, his attorney, and several local police and FBI officials were the basis for this chapter.

Index